JUDAISM
Development and Life
Third Edition

Of related interest . . .

THE WADSWORTH SERIES IN RELIGIOUS STUDIES

America: Religions and Religion, Catherine L. Albanese

Ways to the Center: An Introduction to World Religions, Denise L. and
    John T. Carmody

Between Time and Eternity: Essentials of Judaism, Jacob Neusner

American Buddhism, Charles Prebish

Exploring Religion, Roger Schmidt

THE RELIGIOUS LIFE OF MAN SERIES   Frederick Streng, editor

Understanding Religious Life, second edition, Frederick Streng

The House of Islam, second edition, Kenneth Cragg

The Way of Torah, third edition, Jacob Neusner

The Hindu Religious Tradition, Thomas J. Hopkins

The Christian Religious Tradition, Stephen Reynolds

Chinese Religion, third edition, Laurence G. Thompson

Japanese Religion, second edition, H. Byron Earhart

The Buddhist Religion, second edition, Richard H. Robinson and Willard L.
    Johnson

Islam From Within, Kenneth Cragg and R. Marston Speight

Life of Torah, Jacob Neusner

Chinese Way in Religion, Laurence G. Thompson

Religion in the Japanese Experience, H. Byron Earhart

The Buddhist Experience, Stephan Beyer

OTHER BOOKS BY LEO TREPP

A History of the Jewish Experience: Eternal Faith, Eternal People. New York:
    Behrman House, 1973

The Complete Book of Jewish Observance. New York: Behrman House—
    Summit Books, 1980.

JUDAISM
Development and Life
Third Edition

LEO TREPP
Napa College

Wadsworth Publishing Company
Belmont, California
A Division of Wadsworth, Inc.

ISBN 0-534-00999-9

Note: The Hebrew letters in the dedication are an abbreviation, standing for *Zikhronom le-Berakhah:* "May their memory endure as a blessing."

Religious Studies Editor: Sheryl Fullerton
Production Editor: Carolyn Tanner
Designer: Adriane Bosworth
Copy Editor: Susan Weisberg
Technical Illustrator: Pat Rogondino

Printed in the United States of America

4 5 6 7 8 9 10—86 85

Library of Congress Cataloging in Publication Data

Trepp, Leo.
  Judaism, development and life.

  Bibliography: p.
  Includes index.
  1. Judaism. I. Title.
BM561.T7 1982   296   81–10314
ISBN 0–534–00999–9   AACR2

In memory of my parents,
Maier and Selma Trepp ז״ל
foremost of my teachers,
who sealed their faith by their lives.

CONTENTS

PREFACE

This book is intended as an introduction and does not presuppose previous knowledge of Judaism. It is written, for both Jews and Christians, to contribute to mutual understanding and love, based on open dialogue.

As an introduction, the work is necessarily of limited length and general character, and may fail to do justice to the nuances of some concepts. The presentation is self-contained; additional material should not be required for its understanding. The Bible should be consulted, however. The bibliography is intended to lead the reader further into subject matter of particular interest.

It is my hope that this work may convey an understanding of Judaism as a living faith, a feeling for its scope and sway, and an awareness of its abiding contribution to humanity. I regard Judaism as an organism in evolution, and have myself experienced the life-sustaining strength stemming from its traditions. My approach has generally been conservative-traditional, without overlooking scholarly and scientific research. This approach, I hope, may show how Jews, throughout the centuries, have seen themselves and how they presently see their heritage in light of the insights revealed by scholarly investigations. I regard all denominations in contemporary Judaism as legitimate expressions of the Jewish mind and have taken no position favoring any of them. The presentation and interpretation is my responsibility; Judaism has no official body granting imprimaturs.

The book opens with a definition of the Jew and the fabric from which Judaism is woven. Chapters 2 through 6 sketch the essential external developments of Jewish history, including the impact of Christianity (Chapter 3). Current interest in mysticism prompted inclusion of a separate chapter (5). The student who is interested in a survey of Jewish history should turn to these chapters and, for a fuller understanding, should also consult the chapters on Tenakh and Oral Torah.

New emphasis has been placed on Zionism and the State of Israel (Chapter 8) and on the Holocaust (Chapter 10). The Holocaust constitutes the greatest tragedy in the history of the Jewish people since the fall of the Second Temple. Zionism and the rebirth of the sovereign State of Israel mark the reentry of the Jewish people into active history. These events have deeply affected Jews, individually and collectively, in self-perception, spirit, and action.

Historical knowledge is essential for an understanding of an evolving historical religion such as Judaism. After a great deal of soul-searching, I decided to combine historical and intellectual strands in order to avoid repetition. Chapter 11 is devoted to the relationship between Christianity and Judaism, especially in contemporary life. Chapters 12 and 13 offer a brief analysis of the wellsprings of the Jewish spirit, especially Torah, Talmud, and Codes; Chapters 14 and 15 briefly describe the concepts, beliefs, practices, symbols, and theology that have sprung from these sources. Chapters 16 through 21 discuss contemporary expressions of Judaism in worship and life, Chapter 16 dealing particularly with the attempts to come to grips theologically with the Holocaust. A balance sheet is drawn in Chapter 22. The Glossary explains important terms that appear in the text.

In the endeavor to emphasize the equality of the sexes, the generic use of the word "man" has been changed to the plural "we," as this term encompasses both men and women, and, at the same time, does not impede the flow of the presentation. "We" therefore stands for "men and women"; it does not necessarily include the author or the reader, nor does it intend to direct the reader's behavior in any way. For example: "Structured prayer expresses *man's* feelings better than *he* could in *his* own words" (p. 269), was changed to "Structured prayer expresses *our* feelings better than *we* could in *our* own words."

I would like to express my appreciation to the Board of Trustees and Administration of Napa College for their encouragement and for adjustment of my teaching schedule to allow me to carry on this work. The Vatican; Bishop Mark J. Hurley, head of the Catholic Diocese of Santa Rosa; and Dr. Eugene J. Fisher, Director of the Secretariat for Catholic-Jewish Relations in the United States have been warmly and encouragingly helpful in providing me with continuing information on the ecumenical movement, for which I am grateful. The American Jewish Committee has also provided material.

I owe a special debt of gratitude to Professor Hans Jochen Margull, director of the "Ecumenical Seminar" of the Protestant Theology Department, University of Hamburg, Germany. As a friend and team-teaching colleague of mine at the university, he has given me valuable guidance, both personal and scholarly. Mr. Rolf Schafer, one of my students at Hamburg, has kept me abreast of developments in Germany regarding Protestant-Jewish relations.

Permission to quote is gratefully acknowledged. *The Holy Scriptures* (Philadelphia: Jewish Publication Society, 1917) was generally used for biblical translations, unless I chose my own. Judah Halevi's "Ode to Zion" was quoted in the Nina Salaman translation from *A Book of Jewish Thoughts* (New York: Block Publishing Company, 1943). Reinhold Niebuhr was quoted from his work: *Pious and Secular America* (New York: Charles Scribner's Sons, 1948, pp. 107f. and 111ff.).

Appreciation is expressed to the following publishers and authors for permission to quote from copyrighted material: N. N. Glatzer, *The Dynamics of Emancipation* (Boston: Beacon Press, 1965), © 1965 by Nahum N. Glatzer; D. R. Cutler (ed.), *The Religious Situation 1968* (Boston: Beacon Press, 1968), essay by E. Fackenheim; Richard Rubenstein, *After Auschwitz. Radical Theology and Contemporary Judaism* (Indianapolis: The Bobbs-Merrill Company, Inc., 1966), © 1966 by Richard L. Rubenstein; Anne Frank, *Diary of a Young Girl* (Garden City, New York: Doubleday & Company, Inc., 1952); Friedrich Wilhelm Marquardt, *Erwählung und Normalität* (Emuna Köln/Frankfurt, Germany: Geschaftsführender Vorstand des deutschen Coordinierungsrats, February 1969); Martin Buber, *Eclipse of God* (New York: Harper & Row, Inc., 1952); Paul Tillich, *Dynamics of Faith* (New York: Harper & Row, Inc., 1957); Wm. G. McLoughlin & Robert N. Bellah (eds.), *Religion in America* (Boston: Houghton Mifflin Company, Inc., 1968), essay by R. Rubenstein and responses, © 1966, 1968 by the American Academy of Arts and Sciences.

Permission to quote from the following copyrighted material is also gratefully acknowledged: Msgr. Antonius C. Remselaar, *Land Israel, Diaspora und die Christen* (München, Germany: Chr. Kaiser Verlag, 1970); J. R. Marcus, *The Jews in the Medieval World* (New York and Philadelphia: Meridian Books, Inc. and Jewish Publication Society of America, 1960), © 1938 by Union of American Hebrew Congregations; *Three Jewish Philosophers* (New York and Philadelphia: Meridian Books, Inc., and Jewish Publication Society of America, September 1960, first printing August 1960, all rights reserved, reprinted by arrangement with The East & West Library, London); Arthur Hertzberg, *The Zionist Idea* (New York and Philadelphia: Meridian Books, Inc., and Jewish Publication Society of America, 1960), © 1959 by Arthur Hertzberg; *The Oxford Annotated Bible, Revised Standard Version* (New York: Oxford University Press, Inc., 1962); Leo Baeck, *The Essence of Judaism* (New York and Berlin: Schocken Books, Inc., 1948, fourth printing 1967, German edition 1932); Franz Rosenzweig, *Der Stern der Erlösung* (New York and Berlin, Schocken Books, Inc., 1930); Alexander Altmann, *More Newuchim* (New York and Berlin: Schocken Books, Inc., 1935); Benno Jacob, *Das Erste Buch der Torah, Genesis* (New York and Berlin: Schocken Books, Inc., 1934); Martin Buber, *Königtum Gottes* (New York and Berlin: Schocken Books, Inc., 1934); G. Plaut, *The Rise of Reform Judaism* (New York: World Union for Progressive Judaism, 1963); Hans Küng, *The Church* (London: Search Press Ltd., successor to Burns and Oates, © Search Press, 1967); A. Roy Eckardt, *Elder and Younger Brothers* (New York: Schocken Books, 1973; © A. Roy Eckardt); *Informationen Zur Politischen Bildung*, Nrs. 140, 149, Bundeszentrale für politische Bildung, Bonn, Germany, Tables on Jewish population development, CCAR Yearbooks for excerpts of the "platforms" with permission by Rabbi Joseph B. Glaser, Executive Vice-President. *American Jewish Yearbook*, The American Jewish Committee and J. P. S. 1972, has been used for population statistics.

My special gratitude is expressed to the institutions that permitted me to photograph, or granted me the use of photographs of, sacred objects in their possession. The reproductions were deliberately chosen from items in public institutions within metropolitan areas to encourage the reader of this book to continue Jewish studies by visiting these institutions and their outstanding collections.

I am grateful to the Skirball Museum of the Hebrew Union College–Jewish Institute of Religion, Los Angeles campus, and Ms. Nancy Berman, curator, for permission to reproduce the Chair of Elijah.

I wish to express my appreciation to the Judah L. Magnes Museum (Jewish Museum of the West) and Mr. Seymour Fromer, curator, for permission to reproduce the Sukkah Plate, the painting of Mendelssohn and friends, the Mezuzah, Hanukkah Menorahs, Seder plate, Habdalah set, German breastplate, Torah curtain, and Torah ornaments. I am grateful to Kathie Minami, professional photographer, who took most of these pictures.

To the government of the State of Israel I express sincere thanks for providing me with pictures of Dead Sea manuscripts and the Shrine of the Book in Jerusalem.

I am grateful to Congregation Emanu-El and Rabbi Joseph Asher of San Francisco, who permitted me to reproduce their sanctuary, Ark, and Torah scrolls.

I wish to thank Phyllis Friedman, professional photographer, who took the picture of the crowd on the way to the synagogue for festival prayer service.

My special gratitude is expressed to Mr. Robert McKenzie, professional photographer at Napa, California, who took and permitted me to use the picture of the sounding of the Shofar.

The other pictures are my own.

I gratefully acknowledge the suggestions and comments by my colleagues who saw all or part of the manuscript: Rabbi Theodore S. Levy, Temple Society of Concord; Franklyn D. Josselyn, formerly of Occidental College; Francis J. Buckley, S.J., University of San Francisco; C. Allyn Russell, Boston University; and Joel Reizburg, LaSalle College.

My most heartfelt thanks go to my publisher, Wadsworth Publishing Company. Ms. Sheryl Fullerton, Religious Studies Editor, conceived the project of a third, revised edition. Her support, friendship, and encouragement have been invaluable. I am most grateful to her, to my production editor, Carolyn Tanner; my designer, Adriane Bosworth; and my copy editor, Susan Weisberg.

This work is dedicated to the memory of my parents. My mother perished in a Nazi extermination camp. I was also confined in a concentration camp for some time before I came to this country. I feel a deep emotional attachment to the heritage of Judaism, though I have earnestly tried to retain the scholarly detachment a work of this type demands. If at times my own feelings inadvertently break through, I wish to be forgiven.

Leo Trepp

Jewish Population and Population Trends (Rounded Figures)

Year (C.E.)	Total	Total Europe	Eastern Europe	Western Europe	Asia, Incl. Israel	Palestine-Israel	Africa	Australia	U.S.A. and Canada [Rest of America, North & South]	Preceding Events
70	4,500,000[1]					1,300,000[2]				
1200	1,500,000					*				Migrations, Restrictions, Crusades
1300	2,000,000	300,000								
1500	1,500,000	500,000			1,000,000[4]	Several thousand				Expulsion from Spain
1650	1,750,000	700,000			1,250,000[4]				1654: 23	
1700	2,000,000	1,000,000			1,000,000[4]					
1800	2,500,000[3]	1,500,000			1,000,000[4]	10,000			1776: 2,500	
1825	3,300,000	2,800,000	2,300,000	500,000	300,000	10,000+	240,000	1,000	11,000	
1850	4,750,000	4,130,000	3,430,000	700,000	320,000	10,000+	250,000	2,000	65,000	
1880	7,700,000	6,700,000	5,700,000	1,000,000	350,000	24,000	280,000	12,000	250,000	
1900	11,100,000	9,000,000	7,300,000	1,700,000	500,000	50,000	375,000	17,000	1,200,000 [26,000]	Balfour Declaration (1917)
1925	14,800,000	9,300,000	7,600,000	1,700,000	670,000	125,000	450,000	25,000	4,400,000	
1930-40	16,800,000	9,600,000	8,300,000	1,300,000	1,000,000	500,000	600,000	33,000	5,600,000	Hitler and extermination of Jews
1945	11,000,000	2,900,000	2,200,000	700,000	1,500,000	600,000	675,000	38,000	6,000,000	
1953-55	12,000,000	4,100,000	3,300,000	700,000	1,700,000	1,500,000	700,000	60,000	6,100,000	Forced migration from Islamic countries in Asia & Africa
1980	14,300,000	4,000,000	2,700,000	1,400,000	3,300,000	3,200,000	180,000	80,000	6,100,000 [700,000]	

[1]1.5% of total world population. [2]After Bar Kokhba defeat: 800,000. [3]0.25% of world population. [4]Based on number of Sefardim in North Africa and Asia, including Palestine. *300 rabbis from Europe immigrate. [Individual population figures, rounded off, do not necessarily add up to 100%.]

JUDAISM
Development and Life
Third Edition

1

INTRODUCTION: THE JEWS AND THE FABRIC OF JUDAISM

The singular character of the Jews is revealed in the very problem of definition. At best they may be defined as individuals who consider themselves Jews, having cast their lot with that of the Jewish people. But how shall we define the Jewish people? They are not a race. Innumerable racial components are found among Jews—there are Caucasian Jews, black Jews, and Japanese Jews. From the very beginning of Jewish history there has been a constant influx of the most variegated racial groups. Some of the leading Jewish personalities—as far back as the most ancient past and including even Israel's greatest king, David—have traced their ancestry back to non-Jews. This mixture of races has continued to our own day and goes on still.

Are they a nation? In Israel, they proudly call themselves a nation. In Russia, they are so regarded and—as a nation with "foreign ideology"—are condemned to second-class citizenship. Harassed in their desire to maintain their faith and their traditions, they are being wiped out by attrition.

American Jewry, in contrast, considers itself primarily a religious group, and certainly not a national group. But religion also must fail as a clear-cut definition. It fails to take into account the deep sense of responsibility Jews feel for their brethren all over the world and overlooks their pride in the State of Israel. What then are the Jews?

The Scripture speaks of the Jewish people as a "household"—*Bet Yisrael,* the House of Israel. We may well accept this definition. A household creates a specific atmosphere through the love its members hold for one another, the common tradition that has molded them, and the experiences they have shared and continue to share. This spirit encompasses those who dwell within the family home and those who are spread abroad, those born into it as well as those who have joined it. A family has certain common ways of expressing this spirit in custom and practice; but even those who may not share the forms of expression partake of the spirit, the love, even the conflicts and "family" quarrels, and are tied to each other by a sense of kinship, which is not the same as a political union.

In good times and in hard times, throughout their history, the Jews have felt upheld by a divine Covenant. In daily morning prayer the Jew affirmed, "But we are Your people, children of Your Covenant, children of Abraham . . . descendants of Isaac . . . the congregation of Jacob, whom You called Israel. . . . Therefore it is our duty to praise You . . . and to sanctify Your Name. . . . How good our lot . . . how beautiful our heritage . . . twice daily we affirm, 'Hear, O Israel, the Lord our God, the Lord is One!'"

The **Covenant** bound its children to their God and to one another. Under God and the Covenant they were brothers and sisters. The Covenant called for a response to God; it was a duty and was expressed in Mitzvot. But duty was no burden, it was grace: Sanctification of God's Name bestowed joy on the performance of every commandment, on life under Mitzvah as a whole. The Jews saw their lot and heritage as beautiful and pleasant, in a beauty that transcended all sufferings. The Covenant gave meaning to life and survival in the face of denial of meaning by the outside world. Under it, Torah became "constitution," Mitzvot were response, Land was a laboratory, dispersion a testing ground. The convert who accepted the Covenant became a full-fledged member of the people.

In our time, among average Jews, the Covenant awareness may be vague, even unconscious. And yet it may well be a source of the spirit of mutual responsibility among Jews. A number of distinguished modern theologians have once again come to regard the Covenant as the existential root and core of Jewish being, destiny, and function.

THE TORAH

Torah is the instrument and living record of the Covenant. The character of the Jewish people has been fashioned by its tradition. "Moses charged us with Torah; it is the heritage of the congregation of Jacob" (Deuteronomy 33:4). These words are learned by the Jew in earliest childhood, to be recited daily. They reveal to us the meaning of Torah. The word itself means instruction, for the Torah is more than law; it is the compendium of instruction, the guide for life. In the narrowest sense, Torah applies to the Scroll of the Five Books of Moses, found in every synagogue. In a wider sense, Torah refers to the teachings contained in the Five Books of Moses and in the remaining books that comprise the Hebrew Scriptures. But from the very beginning, explanation accompanied the written word. Some of it was later laid down in the Talmud, but much of it continued to evolve right down to the present. Torah therefore stands for the evolving body of teachings; it is the "heritage."

Torah addresses itself to the needs of every generation of the congregation of Jacob, and each generation adds to it out of its own experiences. Thus Torah mirrors the whole Jewish destiny; it has guided it, and with every Jewish child is being enlarged. "Moses charged us" with it—Moses, who is considered the greatest of teachers but is a human being. Thus it is both divine and human: Out of human experience, in humanity's confrontation with God, Torah evolved. Out of Jewish history, God is made manifest.

At the same time, the actual text of Torah—the Five Books of Moses (Genesis, Exodus, Leviticus, Numbers, and Deuteronomy) and the entire **Tenakh** (Hebrew Scriptures)—is of fundamental significance. The masters and rabbis considered every word, and even every letter, to be of the greatest importance. The explanation of the written Torah, once transmitted orally and therefore called Oral Torah, and later laid down in the Talmud, is based on a minute study of every detail of the text, every intended meaning. To the modern Jew, knowingly and unknowingly, the text of the Torah is understood in the light of Oral Torah, which may lead, quite unconsciously, to an interpretation or understanding different from those a simple reading of the text may suggest. We may find that interpretation in this book. Thus we have indeed a living Torah. A creative tension has been fashioned between God as the Giver and the people as the respondents, who, in responding, fashion it. The Torah, in Jewish tradition, is traced back to the desert, Mount Sinai, which was no-man's-land. Thus it is tied to no specific territory. It is eternal and universal, applying to all lands and conditions. It is the heritage of the "congregation," wherever it may be found. It has fashioned the congregation.

GOD

The Torah speaks of God. He made the Covenant and sustains it. God is the Creator of the Universe, who placed the world in our hands (Genesis 2:15). Humanity, under the Covenant, stands above nature as its master but must submit to God. God is also the Master of history. We are the servants of His will. This applies to all humanity, for God is One, and there is but One God.

Ultimately, God remains hidden from the human mind, which cannot encompass Him, yet He becomes manifest in nature as in the events of life. Moses, who wishes to "see His face," is given the answer, "you cannot see My face, for man may not see Me and live" (Exodus 33:20). "You will see My back [that which God has wrought], but My face must not be seen" (Exodus 33:23). Then God recites His divine attributes to Moses: that He is "God, compassionate and gracious, slow to anger, rich in steadfast kindness, extending kindness to the thousandth generation, forgiving iniquity, transgression, and sin; but clearing the guilty, *He will not do*" (Exodus 34:6–7). The rabbis chose to interpret the passage in such fashion that the words in italics here were not included; thus God is acquitting even the guilty. More is revealed in this change than merely an example of an evolving Torah. The rabbis mean to say that God is understood and found in "imitation." This includes acquitting those who have wronged us. What God truly is, people do not know. That He *is,* they come to know as they survey history, and they cannot fail to recognize His presence in seeing His "back." In their lives, they become aware of Him as they imitate His attributes in the spirit of covenantal reciprocity.

This does not mean that the Jews did not ponder the character and attributes of God. His Oneness is reaffirmed daily by every Jew: "Hear, O Israel, the Lord our God, the Lord is One" (Deuteronomy 6:4), a statement that is theological in character. But even this Oneness, as the great Spanish rabbi and philosopher Maimonides explains, is so absolute that nothing in our experience compares to it.

In their search, other theologians have come to various interpretations, all of them facets, perhaps, of the unfathomable totality of God. To the average Jew, His presence is both the source of being and the rationale of survival.

Some modern Jews, including segments of Israeli Jewry, have come to consider the Jewish people as just another national or ethnic group. Many of these Jews have affirmed their deep allegiance to the Jewish people in commitments and heroism that may serve as examples of dedication to all of Jewry. Some of the founders and builders of the State of Israel have had this outlook, seeing in Jewish civilization the result of the creative genius of the people and the desire for a normal life as a nation. This modern trend among truly dedicated Jews nevertheless stands in contrast to the historical self-perception of the Jewish people up to modern times. Torah—that is, both Hebrew Scriptures and tradition—has regarded God as central in Jewish life and destiny. God has given the Jewish people the will to survive, and in God's will rests the ultimate meaning for Jewish survival. Almost all Jews, even in our day, have tried—perhaps inadequately sometimes—to imitate God's attributes in the life of society. But many have been unaware that their dedication to social justice has its roots in the God-centered message of the prophets.

The Jews saw God in anthropomorphic terms. This is natural: Since the average person is not a philosopher, the Torah "speaks the language of average men" (Yeb.71a; Baba Metzia 31b; etc.). "God is thus given characteristics that relate to bodily character, in order to point out that He . . . possesses Being. After all, the large mass, still being at the beginner's level of thought, can conceive of Being only if it can be thought of as bodily being . . ." (Maimonides; Guide I; 26).

Thus God became to the Jews the loving Father in Heaven, their King, their Judge. In His *hands* they have placed their body and their spirit (Psalm 95:4; II Samuel 24:14; etc.). This is an expression of Jewish awareness of God's personal concern and love. He is their shield and buckler, so love could be asked and given. Only a truly loving God could say, "You shall love the Lord your God" (Deuteronomy 6:5). He has always been their Sustainer and is recognized as their Redeemer. A truly personal relationship may then exist between every individual Jew and God. But the Jew also knows that God, being all of these, is infinitely more and thus is beyond human understanding and comprehension.

Being more, He could never be less; hence He can never assume any form, nor can He be portrayed in any form. The form is static, and God is dynamic. The form—any form—is temporal; God is eternal. The form destroys the divine unity, for form is composed of many parts. The Jewish God concept thus disagrees with the Christian concept of having God assume human form.

It is possible for a Jew to develop various theological concepts of God. We shall consider some of them in discussing Jewish theology.

All these are human efforts to pierce into the unfathomable otherness of the immutable God and—rather than diminishing Him—throw light upon some of the effects of His being.

THE LAND

The Land may be regarded as the laboratory of the Covenant. From the very beginning of history, Jewish destiny has remained inextricably linked to that of the Land of Israel. To the Jews, their history starts as Abraham is bidden to migrate to the Promised Land, for only there can be fulfill himself as the servant and herald of God. The Land is promised to his children, who never left it entirely at any time in history, neither during the centuries of the children of Israel's sojourn in Egypt nor after the destruction of the Second Temple by the Romans. The Land of Israel always remained the Promised Land, where Torah could be translated into the life of an independent nation.

Homeless people pleading for universality of ethical conduct and principles may not be sincere, nor are they so recognized; being dependent on others, they may be pleading for understanding and compassion. Not so a free people on their own soil, who may be chauvinistic. In sharing their insights with humanity, however, and in including humanity among the beloved of God, they show true magnanimity and fellowhip. *Rooted in the soil of their land,* the prophets encompassed all of humanity equally in their rebuke, and in the comfort and hope they offered in the divine Covenant.

When the Land was taken away, it forced the people to find new justification for their continued existence. People on their soil need only live; people away from it must find a rationale for survival. One rationale was that they would return to the Land when it was God's will; hence they must deepen their religious life in order to survive and to be worthy of a return. The evolution of normative Judaism, including synagogue and liturgy, stands under this impact. This hope of freely living on their land, shaping their destiny under God, gave impetus to the messianic ideal, ultimate realization of the Covenant. Out of the certainty of return, enshrined and expressed in every prayer, they found the strength to endure humiliation and persecution for centuries. Through the Land, unity was forged among the widespread community of the House of Israel throughout the world. The polarity of land and the **Diaspora** (the Jewish community dispersed throughout the rest of the world) stimulated creative thought in philosophy and poetry, for ever again the meaning both of dispersion and of their land, which they did not at the moment own, had to be made clear.

In the nineteenth and twentieth centuries, religious yearning for the coming of messianic times was translated into concrete and political terms. History has revealed that only a minority of the persecuted Jews were given the opportunity to find shelter in the Land. Still, millions were saved, who would have died otherwise. For the rest of Jewry, the Land is envisioned as a center of Jewish spirit.

Some Israelis today want all Jews to return, which is a physical impossibility. Nor does this desire meet with the feeling of Jews in free countries, especially the United States. American Jews feel proudly American; here is their home. But they look in kinship to the reborn state of Israel as a source of pride and to its spiritual, intellectual, and social achievements as a source of inspiration, perhaps even as a manifestation of the Covenant.

MITZVAH

Mitzvah is the response to God under the Covenant; it is an action response. **Mitzvah** means commandment; it implies action. Through Mitzvah, the Jew responds to God. At Mount Sinai, at the moment when the Covenant was established, the people promised, "All that the Lord has spoken we will do and hear [understand] it" (Exodus 24:7). The understanding comes in the act, provided it is performed as a service to God and undergirded by the true intent of the heart (**Kavanah**); empty performance carries little value, and neither, by itself, does the affirmation of "faith." Only faith and action together constitute service, as Kavanah enters every thought, prayer, and act. In living, we become God's co-workers.

There are two kinds of Mitzvot (plural of Mitzvah) in Torah: those of religious observance (betwen humanity and God), and those between person and person. Those relating human beings are possibly more important than religious observances; through them, God enters all human relationships. "Love your neighbor as yourself" (Leviticus 19:18) is thus the basic Mitzvah and was rightfully proclaimed by the sages as the cornerstone of Judaism.

Social justice is Mitzvah; it dignifies the doer and the recipient as children of God. Hence Judaism has placed paramount importance on social justice. Through it, God is established. Through Mitzvah, Jews attain self-identification. But they must know the source and intent of the Mitzvah; hence the study of Torah (instrument of the Covenant) in itself becomes a Mitzvah. Here lies the foundation of the Jew's concern with education: Study is Mitzvah, and in all study God is somehow made evident; it is His creation to be contemplated and penetrated.

Of the 613 Mitzvot traditionally seen as handed down to the Jews, 365 are prohibitions and 248 are calls to action. The number of prohibitions supposedly corresponds to the days of the year; every day's activity must be limited and must be confined within God's domain. The number of positive actions was said to correspond to the parts of the human body, every one of which must be ready for duty in promoting His Kingdom.

Many Mitzvot were related to the Land, to sanctify it and the people who dwelt on it. When the Land was taken away, new rules and the conscientious, detailed performance of the other Mitzvot were substituted to unify the people. This has led even to proliferation of injunctions, a psychological defense against spiritual and physical erosion. In the sixteenth century, Rabbi Joseph Karo, searching for a unifying bond which would forever keep the people together, decided on a Code of Mitzvot, the **Shulhan Arukh**, which became the authoritative work and did keep Jewry together.

Time and circumstances may prevent the people from full performance of Mitzvot, but it has been hoped that the day would come when both Israel and all humanity might no longer be impeded from freely fulfilling the Mitzvot in freedom, love, and justice toward each other, redeemed from war and persecution. This is the time of the Messiah. Many a modern Jew has abandoned religious practices, but the Mitzvah of social justice is practiced by almost all, though they may not know that it is their tradition that compels them. And Jews yearn for the messianic times at least in the sense that they hope for the day when "they will beat their swords into plowshares" (Micah 4:3). They are prepared to toil for this day.

THE COVENANT: INTERACTION OF ELEMENTS

These major forces of God, Torah, Land, and Mitzvot interact, each of them evolving from the other, each of them leading to the other. We cannot separate them. On this basis, the Jews understand their relationship with God: It is a Covenant. To be in the world as fighter for Him or as His suffering servant is the mission of the Jew. In Exodus 19:5–6, we hear of this Covenant:

> Now if you listen and listen again to My voice [in study of Torah], and keep My Covenant [in action], you shall be My treasured possession among all the peoples. Indeed, all the earth is Mine [as the universal God], but you shall be to Me a kingdom of priests [in fulfillment of His commandments testifying to God] and a holy people [in setting an example among all the peoples, that they may follow Him as well].

The Covenant idea is, of course, theological and not historically demonstrable. We may, however, state that the people saw themselves as standing under a Covenant with God and that they derived strength from it. We find that many modern Jews doubt or reinterpret the idea. There is one trend among contemporary theologians to reemphasize the Covenant. Martin Buber has emphasized it in his work *Kingship of God;* existentialist Jewish thinkers have followed him. It has served many as a strongly needed affirmation to restore Jewish confidence in Jewish survival after the terrible ordeal of the Nazi Holocaust. Leo Baeck sees it as *the* force of Jewish survival.

Explaining history in terms of the Covenant, Buber gives the following explanation of Jewish existence: God was and was to be Israel's one and only King. This Kingship was proclaimed at Sinai, a no-man's-land, in order to show that God never was and never will be linked to any locality. He will be with Israel wherever they may be in dispersion. God planted the people in the Land in order that they might establish in it an ideal society placed by Covenant under God's exclusive Kingship. Israel was therefore to be ruled by judges, temporary "vicars"—never by kings holding power in their own right, and, above all, bequeathing it by founding dynasties. Only God was King. The divine experiment failed. In choosing Saul as hereditary monarch to lead them, the people "have repudiated Me from being their king" (Samuel I, 8:7). Another source of failure was the people's worship of alien gods, a rejection of the Covenant with God. Prophets arose, rebuked the kings of Israel, and called upon the people to reject royal ordinances when these violated the spirit of social justice, of the Covenant. The prophets, too, failed, and the hope for realization of the Covenant diminished. Hope for its realization through the normal processes of political evolution faded altogether. The fulfillment of the Kingship of God was therefore projected into the future, at the end of days, when God would send His anointed, the Messiah, to establish His Kingship under the Covenant, for all times.

For the sake of the Covenant and its fulfillment, the Jews had the duty to preserve themselves, to try to live by its spirit and to become, by example, a light unto the nations: to survive, for themselves and for humanity. They came to see every act of destiny as divinely ordained and meaningful.

Christianity holds the Covenant idea and maintains that God made a new Covenant through Christ. Both Christianity and Judaism see themselves as standing under a divine Covenant and are therefore linked in calling and destiny. The sustaining power of the Covenant can be recognized in the Hebrew word for faith: It is **emunah**, meaning faithfulness, trust. *Emunah* has the same root as *Amen,* so be it. Jewish tradition has seen Amen as an acrostic, its letters spelling *El Melekh Neeman,* God is King, granting and deserving trust. Jewish faith is therefore affirmation of God's Kingship and God's presence, wherever His people may be. It is the bridge from Abraham to the Messiah. God's emunah is enduring and elicits trust as response. Every act must therefore be Mitzvah, and affirmation of the living Covenant. In the context of duty, sacred and profane lose their distinction; ethics becomes guide, emunah the watchword.

Undergirded by the Covenant concept, religion becomes a way of life. This concept has been variously expressed; a few examples may suffice:

In the nineteenth century, *Samson Raphael Hirsch* (1808–1888), developing a new theology for German Jews then on the way to becoming citizens, wrote: "Every son of Israel a priest, setting the example of justice and love . . . spreading true humanity among the nations" (*Nineteen Letters,* Sixteenth Letter). Here the function of the Jew under the Covenant is recognized in its universal setting.

Abraham Isaac Hakohen Kook (1861–1935), revered chief rabbi of then Palestine, now Israel, underscored the transformation in the life of the truly religious person who lives under the Covenant. Rav Kook defined the spirit of religion not by the object to which the religious person turns but by the quality of spiritual insight. The religious person is able to see the complete harmony of the universe, a harmony in which nothing is excluded from the realm of the spiritual, "for all the earth is Mine" (Exodus 19:5).

Martin Buber (1878–1965), in his basic work *I and Thou,* links God, man, and fellowman. God, the eternal Thou, reveals Himself to me, man, by telling me how I am to relate to my fellowman, my human Thou. The three-fold dialogue is eternal and fills the totality of every person's being. In it, God, self, and neighbor are unfoldingly revealing themselves. This is covenantal living.

Jews have not been permitted to see themselves as "the favored son." On the contrary, they have been told that their distinction consists in higher responsibility. "You only have I known of all the families of the earth; therefore will I punish you for all your iniquities," says Amos (Amos 3:2). The uniqueness of the forces that have fashioned the Jewish people must lead to a uniqueness of obligations. God-Torah-Land-Mitzvot impose responsibilities which must be met for the sake of all humanity under God.

Can we speak of the Covenant as election in a *spiritual* sense? Some modern rabbis affirm it, pointing to the miraculous survival of the Jews and their impact on modern society, including the fact that Christian church groups today are reassessing the need for a return to Jewish patterns of religion, specifically in the field of social action. Among Christians, Markus Barth sees in the survival of the Jews an intimation of God's existence, for this survival is one of the elements of history that cannot be explained, except by rec-ognizing it as God's dispensation (*New Essays in Philosophical Theology,* pp. 220–223). While none of the rabbis regard the election of the Jews as imposing anything but responsibilities—and who could speak of any divine favoritism, witnessing their history—some modern Jews, with Mordecai Kaplan as their leading spokesman, do away with the concept of Israel's chosenness. They may well lean on the prophet Amos, who addresses himself to all the nations of his world and sees for Israel only the distinction of special punishment. This does not mean, however, that with the denial of chosenness the forming forces are denied; on the contrary, they are affirmed. It does mean that Jews must con-ceive of every people as being singularly chosen by their endowment, gifts, history, land, and culture. And being chosen, they have the responsibility to utilize their endowment in Mitzvah. The chosenness of Israel through the forces that have fashioned it thus serves as an example of humanity to consider itself chosen for duty and held divinely responsible for its performance.

It cannot be said that Jews have always fully lived up to the Covenant.

At different times, some of its elements may have been given emphasis while others moved into the background of Jewish consciousness. Yet all elements are operative always. The Covenant has become internalized: God-Israel-Land are one. It has remained the force making for Jewish survival, Jewish action, the Jewish character—even in those who may be unaware of it. From it, the Jews have taken the will to survive; for it, they have been willing to die.

A perceptive insight into Judaism and the Jewish people has recently been given by a Christian theologian in Germany, Friedrich-Wilhelm Marquardt, in explaining Judaism out of its elements of God, Torah, Mitzvot, and Land, and the Jewish people as the people of the Covenant (*Erwählung und Normalität;* Emuna IV:1, February 1969). Marquardt points out that the dialogues between Christians and Jews, important as they are, have so far frequently fallen short of equipping Christians with a full understanding of the hidden forces in the Jewish heart. Christians can comprehend Jewish *religion* and can compare themselves with it, Marquardt states. But behind Judaism as religion, Christians must perceive the Jewish people in all its worldliness. The people is the bearer of religion; this includes even secularized Jews.

> Jewish worldliness *is* Jewish theology. This means, it does not contradict but rather expresses the Jewish experience of God. . . . *God* as the Other is not a philosophical concept, but experienced reality. It is a concept that does not result from an act of thought but emerges out of the act of living. . . . The One God, as understood by Jews, has this attribute of oneness not from the logic of numbers, but from his acts: He creates oneness in the world. . . . This brings God into an incomparable nearness; He can always be addressed as Thou.

> *Torah,* as understood by Jews, is . . . equated with Covenant. Torah is . . . the world map of unification, unification within human history is subject matter of the historical books, unification of the individual is the purpose of the Law, unification of present and future, the hope for unity of mankind, are expressed by the prophets; and in the Talmud the generations establish their unity with the written word.

> This unification is to be understood historically, not philosophically. . . . Therefore Judaism is not religion but people. In a people, unification is concretely achieved.

> But a *people,* seen in Jewish view, is a vehicle in the service of God.

> Here we have to speak of *election.* The election of Israel is, first of all, the election to be a people, nothing else. The Covenant formula states: You shall be unto Me a people. Israel is a people in the process of growth, eternally confronted by the "ought." That is the reaon that Torah is *law.*

> Israel is to become a great people, meant quite simply biologically. . . . But at the same time, it is to become a "blessed people" and is "to be a blessing." . . . All nations stand in need of mutual recognition in order to exist . . . but Israel, in order to exist, stands in need, not only of recognition but of achievement, namely the sharing of its existence with others. Chosenness is election to service, not favored existence . . . the historical, functional, special existence of a most normal people. Israel's life depends on its achievements, in order to be a chosen and blessed life. This is the reason why the election of

Israel has been so frequently an election to suffering. The nations of the world do not want an advocate of good, for they do not wish to have God in their midst. They strike back . . . and keep the doors closed that the King of Glory may not enter.

Israel does not find itself in a triumphant position. . . . Even in the *Land* it has not been discharged out of the ghetto, but has simply been placed in a different form of ghetto. Even there it lives suspended between being and not being, and, faced by this reality, it has to follow its vocation, namely of being good.

. . . The Promised Land is the cross to which it will hold on. Israel in the Land lives in a theologia crucis. It leads a normal life by normal means . . . but, at the same time, has to create within its life that strength that leads from not-being to being. This is called Resurrection, if I know the Bible correctly. Normal service to God is "serving God in just institutions," said Moses Hess, one of the fathers of Zionism. In the State of Israel this has not been forgotten, surely less so than among ourselves, the rest of the world.

Marquardt's analysis of reality and ideal is penetrating. Under the Covenant, the society in Israel should be "good," a light to the nations. The realities have ordained it otherwise. Israel has remained a "ghetto." War has upturned minds, thoughts, and actions. But Israel has not forgotten. Behind and beneath the surface of the abnormal actions of a state surrounded by hostility there has remained in the souls of the people the determination to implement the Covenant even now, in ways visible only to the careful observer, as conditions permit. The hope of making it real when peace is established, sometimes eclipsed by expediency, has remained alive. The unity of the people with God, Torah and Mitzvot, and Land as workshops of ethical nationhood remains the goal under the Covenant.

The Covenant offers security of spirit, a strength that permits Jews to reach out toward other religions in dialogue. Feeling sheltered themselves, they appreciate and respect the sense of shelteredness among those of other faiths who perceive themselves in similar covenantal relationship to God. Out of respect for difference thus can grow communality of actions in behalf of a better world under God. In the case of Judaism, Christianity, and Islam, history has wrought a symbolic expression of this fact. Isaiah proclaimed: "Open the gates and let a[ny] righteous nation enter, [any nation] that keeps faith" (Isaiah 26:2). Revocalizing the word *emunim* (faith, trust), the rabbis read interpretively *amenim,* those who confirm God's rule by speaking—and acting—*Amen* (Yalkut 429). The Christian *Amen* and the Islamic *Amin,* both derived from the Hebrew word—God is King, granting and deserving trust—reveal a family relationship among the three religions divinely confirmed, a distinction divinely affirmed, and a common task divinely ordained.

I

THE LOOM OF HISTORY

2

THE BIBLICAL, HELLENISTIC, AND TALMUDIC PERIODS

To many theologians, Jewish history reflects the effort of the Jewish people to fulfill the Covenant under ever-changing conditions. During the greater part of their historical existence, the Jews had to demonstrate their trust in the Covenant—their faith—by their will to survive for the sake of the ultimate future, the Messianic Age. Adjusting to physical as well as cultural and religious pressures, they became God's "suffering servants." Jewish history resulted in the evolution of Judaism. The two are inseparable.

To write even an outline of Jewish history would go beyond the framework of this book. In the following pages, we shall endeavor to trace the evolution of Jewish history as a guide and framework for those entirely unacquainted with it. It may enable them to put people and ideas into their historical setting and to follow the evolving tapestry of Judaism as the elements of God-Torah-Mitzvot-Land are woven into ever-new patterns by the Jewish people.

BIBLICAL HISTORY

Israelite history, from its beginnings to the time of Ezra (about 444 or possibly 397 B.C.E.*), is recorded in Holy Scriptures. In the *Tenakh*, we are given a picture of the interaction of political events and spiritual evolution during the formative years of the Jewish people. To the authors of the Tenakh, the spiritual element is of paramount importance, and historical facts are at times adjusted to reflect the spiritual. The Tenakh is one of the "wellsprings of the Jewish spirit." It will be useful therefore to read Chapter 12 on the Tenakh in conjunction with this historical survey. For the sake of simplicity and unity, the historical elements of Israelite history will be summarized on the following pages. A rapid survey based generally on biblical accounts, it condenses events

---

*B.C.E.—Before the common era; used to designate dates preceding the Christian era. **C.E.** designates dates of the Christian era.

14

into a whole that may give them a more unified character than this history actually possessed.

Contemporary archaeology has found that much of the historical record of the Tenakh is accurate; some parts of this record may not be exactly verifiable, but their veracity is probable in view of the accurate picture they give of the general conditions of the period with which they deal. Other parts have been slanted in line with the theological position of the writers and the message they wished to convey. There are portions that may have to be regarded as myths and demythologized in order that they may reveal their spiritual message for us today.

Early History

Toward the first quarter of the second millennium, Abraham migrated from "Ur of the Chaldees" (Genesis 11:31) to Canaan. This event may be called the beginning of Hebrew history.* Abraham made a Covenant with the One God, which does not necessarily mean that he rejected the existence of other gods, but *for him* there was only One God, "the God of Abraham" to whom he gave allegiance and in whom he put his trust. The description of conditions in the period of Abraham and the sharp contours of his personality, as drawn in the Scripture, permit us to assume that Abraham may have been a real person, not merely a hero-figure. In obedience to God, Abraham moved to Canaan and, in turn, was promised the Land as the perennial possession of his descendants. The Jewish claim to the Land is based on this promise.

It was customary among the ancient peoples of the region to sacrifice a child, usually the oldest son, to the gods, to show their submission to the deities and to propitiate them. In earnest desire to respond to his God through Mitzvah, Abraham was willing to sacrifice his son Isaac (Genesis 22:1–18). The sacrifice was rejected. Abraham's intention was sufficient to witness his love of God. At the same time, he was to learn that the *preservation* of a human life is highest service of God. "The dead cannot praise the Lord" (Psalm 115:17). We may therefore see in the event, as told us, a giant step in ethical progess: The human being, image and servant of God, can never be a *means*; human life is inviolate.

Abraham had a second son, Ishmael, whom he loved but excluded from the succession. The Arabs consider Ishmael their ancestor. In this sense, Arabs and Jews are "cousins." Since Christians consider Abraham their spiritual father (see Romans 4:11ff.), the three great religions converge in his person.

---

*The term *Hebrew* is explained by William F. Albright as meaning donkey driver, in reference to the nomadic life of those to whom it was applied. According to Albright, the term is derived from *dusty*, since these people with their donkeys raised a great deal of dust in passing over the roads. (*The Biblical Period from Abraham to Ezra*, New York: Harper & Row Publishers, Inc. [Harper Torch Book], 1963, pp. 5–6).

Isaac's son Jacob, who came to be called Israel, was the recognized bearer of the family heritage. He had twelve sons. During his time, a severe famine forced the major part of Jacob's family to migrate to Egypt; the rest remained in Israel. Those in Egypt were soon enslaved as enemy aliens and forced to build garrison cities for the pharaoh. In spite of oppression, they multiplied into a people. Each of the twelve sons' families developed into a tribe, according to the Scripture.

After many years of servitude, the Hebrews were freed, and, under the leadership of Moses, they departed from Egypt (around 1280 B.C.E.). Moses became their teacher; he gave them Torah; he founded their faith; he kept them in the desert for forty years to transform them from a group of slaves into a free people; he led them to the borders of their Promised Land. And there he died.

The Land had to be conquered and settled. The people's leader was Joshua. He achieved some victories over the native population; otherwise, the settlement had the character of slow infiltration. Joshua and his successors had the task of building a confederacy of the twelve tribes that constituted the people at the time. These tribes were fiercely individualistic, and fusion was difficult. The confederation was to be developed by centering all the tribes spiritually and politically in the Covenant with God at Sinai and in ancient traditions, and physically in a national sanctuary. Each tribe was in charge of the sanctuary for one month a year.

The spirit was to unite the people. But the culture of the Canaanites, among whom the people dwelt, was more highly developed than that of the Hebrews and exerted a great attraction. The Canaanites followed a heathen cult. As the Hebrews embraced the cult, their unity dissolved, they became politically weak, and they were repeatedly attacked and subjugated by stronger neighbors. In moments of severe distress, they united, selected an outstanding leader, and jointly took up arms against their enemies and overcame them. The leader then remained the people's guide for the rest of his life; he became a judge, deepening the spirit of unity among the people. His influence vanished with his death, and the whole chain of events was repeated with tragic monotony. Only the work of "minor judges" held the confederation together at all (see Judges 10:1–5; 12:7–15).

The people failed to realize that their strength lay in their spirit, and that in recognizing God as their ruler they would find unity and strength. Instead, they chose another expedient—a hereditary monarchy, which they hoped would guarantee perpetual leadership.

Around 1020 B.C.E. they chose *Saul* as their king. Saul was a striking man and a brilliant military leader. His son Jonathan was equally gifted. The king, at times with the aid of his son, was able to rid the people of their enemies. Soon, however, a young man—*David*—began to gain popular favor by his charismatic personality and his military abilities. At first, Saul tried to take David under his wing, even giving him his daughter Michal as wife, but very soon he found that David was rapidly replacing him in popular favor.

Even Jonathan became David's close friend. Saul, who had shown signs of moodiness and depression, now began to fear for the future of his dynasty, and henceforth he devoted his energies to capturing and destroying his rival, David. In the end, he paid a bitter price for this waste of time and resources. In battle with the Philistines, he lost his life and carried his people to destruction.

The Philistines were a warrior nation who probably originated on Crete. They were great navigators who had settled on the coastal strip of Canaan. Eventually, they were to give their name to the land: Palestine. Since they had iron weapons while the Israelites had only bronze, they were able to subdue the people. Furthermore, the Philistines were united in purpose; the Israelites were disunited.

With Saul's death around 1000 B.C.E., David became king. He reversed the tide. David was both a general and a poet, a shrewd administrator and a tender-hearted lyricist. He had every human shortcoming but also the greatness to admit error, accept its consequences, and remedy his faults. He became Israel's ideal king; he conquered Jerusalem and made it his capital and led the nation to strength. He enlarged the Land and responded in psalm and in action to the command and rebuke of God. Thus he set the image of the anointed, the Messiah, a man of his seed and of his wisdom, who would bring Israel and humanity to the age of abiding peace.

David effected a thorough reorganization of Israel. In order to expand his kingdom, David had to maintain a standing army; in order to weaken tribal allegiances, he reorganized the land in administrative districts that deliberately cut across tribal frontiers; in order to centralize his power, he established his residence in Jerusalem, a city that belonged to none of the tribes, having been taken recently from the Jebusites. There David established a sanctuary and an elaborate pattern of worship; there, too, adjacent to the sanctuary, was the king's palace, focal point of royal power.

David was unable to complete his projects. When he died, his son *Solomon* carried them through: He built the Temple, one of the wonders of the ancient world. He expanded trade and commerce, but to do so, he had to conscript forced labor and extract heavy taxes. Married to an Egyptian princess, he was inclined to see himself as an Oriental monarch. He was considered the wisest of men—probably because he surrounded himself with wise counselors, for it seems he lacked the psychological insight needed to unite the people in allegiance to the king over their tribal allegiances. Only a satisfied population could be expected to abide with the royal house. But the people were dissatisfied and restless. When Solomon died, they approached his successor, *Rehoboam*, for a redress of grievances and were scornfully rebuked. As a result, ten of the twelve tribes of Israel seceded to form the kingdom of Israel in the north; only the tribe of the royal house, Judah, and the tribe of Benjamin remained with the family of David in the kingdom of Judah.

Both kingdoms had a checkered history. In the kingdom of Israel, royal dynasties underwent frequent changes. The kingdom of Judah was ruled by the House of David. In both, the character of the reigning king determined the nature and complexion of internal and external affairs. The kingdom of Judah possessed the national sanctuary of Jerusalem and, in general, a greater awareness of its purpose under God. The northern kingdom was willing to exchange integrity for expediency. This period—beginning in the eighth century B.C.E. and stretching into the fifth century B.C.E.—marks the ministry of the great literary *prophets*. The portions of their works that we still possess belong to the greatest documents of the human spirit. The prophets preached, rebuked, and called to task, but also comforted. Their message constitutes one of the fountainheads of the Jewish spirit.

The Israelite kingdom owed its strength under David and Solomon to a lull in the power struggle between the great forces that resided at its borders, the kingdoms of the Tigris and Euphrates valleys in the east, and Egypt in the west. Now the struggle for power was resumed between the giants, and the now-divided Israelite state lay between them, a traffic artery for commerce and for armies. Israel became enmeshed and was defeated.

In 722 B.C.E., the kingdom of Israel was destroyed by the Assyrians and its ten tribes "lost." The kingdom of Judah, submitting to Assyrian overlordship, survived. From then on, there remained only the descendants of Judah—the *Jews*.

Chastened by the fate of their brothers in the north and the ever-present threat of their own destruction, some of Judah's kings were ready for religious reforms. King *Hezekiah* (715–687 B.C.E.), miraculously saved from the Assyrian armies that had destroyed the northern kingdom, saw in the restoration of a full allegiance to God a way of preservation. The pagan shrines were destroyed, pagan worship wiped out, and the observance of religious holy days which had fallen into neglect, such as Passover, was restored. But Hezekiah's son and successor *Manàsseh*, who ruled for fifty-five years, reverted to pagan worship. His son, King *Josiah* (c. 640–609 B.C.E.), once again reversed the trend: He purified the Temple of idols, restored its worship, and had the idolatrous priests put to death.

This latter religious revival had its source in the discovery of a book in the recesses of the Temple. Found in 622 B.C.E., it contained major parts of the Book of Deuteronomy. The work may have been written at that time, or it may have been written at the time of Hezekiah and hidden during Manasseh's rule; some of its material may have been of even earlier origin. Spiritual strength was restored. It was badly needed, for the end of the state of Judah was near, and only spiritual cohesion, an awareness of the Covenant, could hold the people together.

Individualism versus Unity

A further examination of the centuries just reviewed reveals the period from the leadership of Moses to the end of the two kingdoms as a time of grave inner struggle between competing forces in Israel. Conditions called for a strong national leadership, for the sake of both internal unity and a concerted defense of the nation against its enemies, but tribal allegiances and strong individualism created powerful counterforces. Only in periods of dire need were the people prepared to accept a leader willingly. The leader had to be a person of proven capability for the task and had to have charisma—a discernible divine endowment for the function. When the necessary work was accomplished, the people would dispense with the leader: At best, he might retain his power and influence during his lifetime; sometimes he would lose it sooner. In any event, he could not bequeath his power to his descendants.

This development is evident in the period of the judges and during the reign of the kings. Though we must recognize that the report given us in the Bible contains a great deal of legendary material, and, moreover, shows the bias of the writer, the basic trend is unmistakable. Moses himself, a proven charismatic leader, had to meet frequent opposition and even outright rebellion by Korah and his associates, who wished to depose him by force (Numbers 16). Moses's sons did not succeed him. Joshua, installed by Moses under divine behest, was a charismatic leader who had proven himself in battle and as explorer of the land. With Joshua's death, individual rivalries broke out again.

The Book of Judges endeavors to bridge the period up to the establishment of the monarchy. It tells us, in greatly embroidered form and with inclusion of folk stories, of five charismatic figures: Ehud, Deborah, Gideon, Jephtah, and Samson. At times, these leaders may have served only part of the people, the tribes among whom they had their roots. Though they differed greatly in character and background—even including a woman—all of them found acceptance on the basis of their charisma. Under these circumstances, it is not surprising to find an individual making the attempt to usurp power by stealth, treachery, and murder, and have himself proclaimed king. His name was Abimelekh. After three years, the people rose against him. While attempting to quell the rebellion, Abimelekh was killed. Thus ended the attempt to establish an absolute kingship (Judges 9).

Because these personalities were heroes, the people accepted their judgment. The real task of unification, however, seems to have been performed by men of whom it was merely mentioned that they judged Israel. Among them were Othniel, Tola, Jair, Ibzan, Elon, and Abdon—distinguished citizens of proven stature, who were judges in the precise sense of the word.* They adjudicated conflicts between tribes, between individual members of different tribes, or between commoners and tribal leaders. They built the unity of the people through *law* transcending tribal boundaries. The success of their work may have inspired future leaders in Jewish history: Union lies in law.

---

*(The term *shoftim*, judges, corresponds to *suffetes*, the judges at Carthage, also a semitic nation.)

The conflict between the people's individualism and the need for unification continued, as we see in the Books of Samuel and Kings. Samuel, a leader of great personal attractiveness, lost his appeal and power during the latter years of his life. The people needed and wanted a king, so Saul, a man of great charisma, was anointed and installed. As we saw, by his very desire to establish a dynasty, he failed even in his lifetime, overshadowed by the charismatic David. David did in fact succeed in establishing a dynasty. A most likely reason was his conquest of Jerusalem: He established it as a focal point of national unity. Jerusalem became both the capital and the religious center of the nation. Royal authority came to be undergirded by the authority of worship and of law.

Solomon was David's choice as his successor, not the people's, and eventually restlessness reemerged among the tribes. At Solomon's death, tribal allegiance overwhelmed the spirit of unity, and ten of the twelve tribes fell away, forming the kingdom of Israel. The tribes of Judah and Benjamin remained faithful to the House of David, for David belonged to the tribe of Judah. The davidic dynasty thus rested on three pillars: tribal identity, unity of worship centered in the Temple, and unity of law.

The history of the kingdom of Israel reveals the continued power of tribal allegiance. Its kings came from various tribes in succession and established their own national shrines and patterns of worship to undermine the impact of the Temple at Jerusalem upon the population of the northern kingdom. This worship was influenced by the religious practices of the surrounding nations and therefore was regarded as sinful by the leadership at Jerusalem and by the prophets who called for a return to true worship. Though politically split, the people retained a sense of kinship. The prophets addressed their kinfolk in both kingdoms.

As we pause here for a tentative stocktaking, we may perhaps advance some basic conclusions. Two opposing forces seem to be rooted in the Jewish character, one for unity, the other for disruption. Recognizable in the early history is the existence of a deeply rooted sense of kinship among the Jewish people. Opposing it is a pronounced individualism. There is therefore little room for any "personality cult" among Jews. Only one person, King David, so captured the imagination of the Jews that he became a symbol of Jewish unity, the ancestor of the Messiah who would redeem Israel and mankind. David was able to establish a long-lasting dynasty; the kings of the kingdom of Israel failed in this endeavor. The following chart (pp. 22–24) illustrates the changes in the period we have been discussing.

Later on, during the time of the Second Temple, the Pharisees recognized the power of law to create unity. Originally, the pharisaic group attempted to gain power by political means. Failing in this endeavor, they eventually chose the road of becoming *shoftim*, interpreters and legislators in Torah. In this they succeeded, and all major religious segments of Jewry even today regard themselves as spiritual descendants of the Pharisees.

Moses, himself plagued by much opposition, is the major figure in Judaism, not as king-prophet, but as teacher-prophet, our Master, who proclaimed the Torah.

Torah is the cement that binds Jewry together, Torah in its *widest* sense. Included in it is the Land. The Land of Israel has united the Jewish people beyond all "tribal" conflicts.

The conflicts are not always detrimental; the dialogues created by controversies have been creative.

Babylonian Exile

During the years 598–586 B.C.E., the Babylonians (having supplanted the Assyrians as the great power of the East) conquered Judah and destroyed the Temple. Only a remnant of the Jewish people remained in the Land. One part of the community fled to Egypt, but the majority were taken to Babylonia into exile. Neither of the exiled groups was lost. Having lost physical possession of the Land, they refined their faith in the crucible of exile.

Apart from feeling themselves exiles, the Jews found their lives pleasant: Subject to the state, they were given their own jurisdiction in internal affairs, and some of their members rose to high positions at the royal court. Babylonia became a spiritual workshop. The Land and its redemption were transformed into a hope and aspiration. Torah was the center of life; its interpreter, the rabbi, came to occupy a key position. Worship took the place of sacrifices; Mitzvot were both a response to God and the link which bound the House of Israel together. Synagogue and liturgy as we know them had their start.

The Effects and Meaning of Exile   In spite of the Jews' adaptation to life in Babylonia, the expulsion from their homeland to exile was a profoundly traumatic experience. Psalm 137 reflects their shock and a rather unworthy feeling of vengefulness born out of hopelessness and impotence. As they emerged from the numbness of despair, two questions came to their minds: Why did it happen, and how long is it going to last? The immediate answer was: It happened because we have sinned by breaking the Covenant. Was it going to be a short sojourn? The prophet Jeremiah made it clear to them that their sojourn among the nations might well be of long duration. He advised them to settle down and "multiply . . . and do not decrease." Dwelling among the nations, they must do more than simply come to terms with their fate: "seek the welfare of the city . . . and pray to the Lord for it; for in its prosperity you shall prosper" (Jeremiah 29:4–7). Good citizenship thus becomes a religious duty. Jews are to look at the country of their homes and birth as a permanent dwelling place. The distrust of others, preached up to now to the unique people dwelling within a heathen world, was replaced by heartfelt concern for the welfare of the nation and its citizens, its inner and outward peace, expressed in prayer and in active participation. From this time on, we

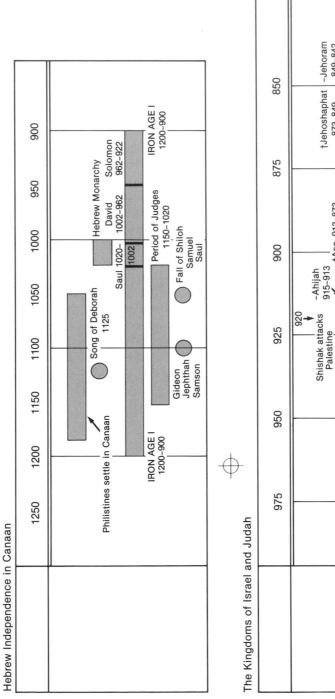

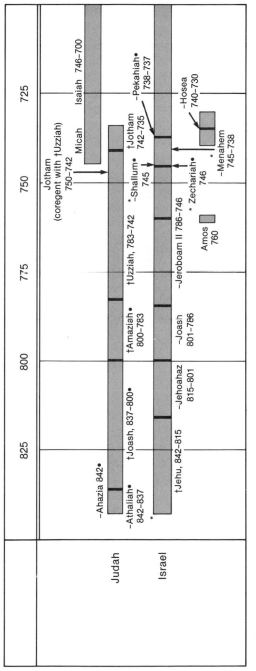

Dates given designate as closely as possible the period of each monarch's reign.

● Time of flowering

* Old dynasty overthrown, new dynasty established

† Kings approved of by author of *Kings*

– Kings disapproved of by author of *Kings*

● Assassinated

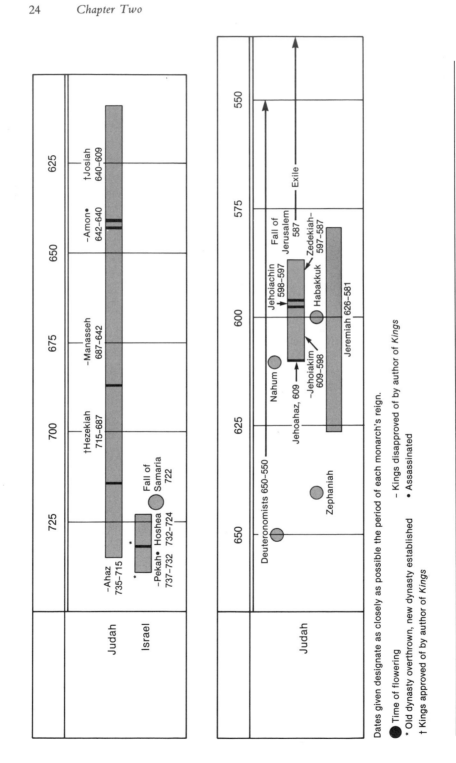

725   700   675   650   625

Judah

†Hezekiah
715–687

-Manasseh
687–642

-Amon•
642–640

†Josiah
640–609

-Ahaz
735–715

Israel

Fall of
Samaria
722

-Pekah• Hoshea
737–732 732–724

*

*

650   625   600   575   550

Judah

Deuteronomists 650–550

Nahum

Jehoahaz, 609

-Jehoiakim
609–598

Jehoiachin
598–597

Fall of
Jerusalem
587

Zedekiah–
597–587

Habakkuk

Jeremiah 626–581

Zephaniah

Exile

Dates given designate as closely as possible the period of each monarch's reign.

● Time of flowering

* Old dynasty overthrown, new dynasty established

† Kings approved of by author of *Kings*

- Kings disapproved of by author of *Kings*

• Assassinated

Source: Adapted from *The Old Testament* by H. Keith Beebe. Copyright © 1970 by Dickenson Publishing Company, Inc. Reprinted by permission of Wadsworth Publishing Company, Belmont, California 94002.

shall find Jews filled with earnest desire to promote the welfare of the countries of their dispersion.

Under these circumstances, the first question had to be taken up again: Was their life in dispersion exile and punishment, or perhaps a task? A long exile as a result of sin would actually punish the children for the faults of their fathers. Both the prophets Jeremiah and Ezekiel addressed themselves to the problem:

> Fathers have eaten sour grapes and the children's teeth are blunted. This proverb shall no longer be current in Israel. . . . If a man be just, he shall surely live. . . . If he begets a son that is a robber . . . he shall not live, having done all these abominations. . . . If he begets a son that sees all his father's sins . . . but has taken heed and has not imitated them . . . he shall not die for the iniquity of his father; he shall surely live. (Jeremiah 31:29–30; Ezekiel 18:3–17)

The impact and implication of this statement are fundamental and far-reaching.

The Babylonian Jewish community and all of their descendants were advised that they dwelt among people of other religious convictions because God had willed that they creatively participate in the upbuilding of a good society. Not sinfulness but a divine challenge had caused their dispersion.

If Jews are persecuted in some lands, again it is not the result of their sins but a divine test. The Jews, as a minority, are tested to show the strength of their faith. The majority is equally tested to show the spirit of godliness. It has an opportunity of graciously dealing with a minority; if the majority fails, then this failure points to *its own* shortcoming in thwarting the divine will. The contribution of the Jews under adverse circumstances consists in illuminating the world's failure in spiritual attainment and in calling it to account before God.

The search for the meaning of their exile led to general discussion of suffering and sin in post-Exilic Jewish literature. The second Isaiah, in his parable of the Suffering Servant (Chapter 53), demonstrates that the steadfast faith of the sufferer sets an example from which future generations may learn and profit. The legend of Job (also an inhabitant of a non-Jewish environment) dwells in great detail on the suffering the just will endure. People must accept sufferings as a test of faith, and, in accepting, they will find insight and strength. God Himself justifies Job. According to a rabbinic view (Makkot 24a), Ezekiel's statement boldly overrides a principle enshrined in the Ten Commandments—namely, that God visits the iniquities of the fathers upon the children (Exodus 20:5). This reveals the deeper insight acquired by the Jews in the course of the generations: There is no inherited guilt, there is but personal responsibility of every individual for himself and for those he may influence. This has remained the Jew's staunch conviction.

Having understood the permanence of their position among other peoples, the Jews now had to put their religious life on new foundations. The Land could now serve as spiritual inspiration. The Temple was no more; no sacrifices could henceforth be offered; the priestly caste (the family of Aaron) had lost its function. The adjustment, started in Babylonia, continued even after the return of part of the people to their homeland. It was so ingenious that it has served all of Western religion as pattern and example.

Torah and Mitzvot were strengthened to compensate for the physical loss of the Land. The word of Torah was to be read regularly to the people and explained, interpreted, and studied. This called for teachers, not priests; thus there emerged the forerunner of the rabbi. He could be a priest or a layman, rich or poor, of noble ancestry or a recent convert, but he had to be a teacher, upright in character, searching for knowledge, and dedicated to his task. His work could be carried out anywhere and at any time; all he needed was a group of students and a shelter against the elements. Thus came into existence with the rabbi the house of meeting, which also became the house of prayer. The national sanctuary at Jerusalem (like all the temples of antiquity) was not so much a place of popular assembly as a dwelling place of God. The people were primarily spectators at a set ritual. Now we find the meeting house, and the people are participants. Here lies the origin of the form of the *House of God* in Western religions. Torah, rather than sacrifices, would now be the center of worship. The recital of Torah was surrounded by prayer and psalm and made meaningful by the rabbi's explanation. A *pattern of worship* was created which was again followed by many Western religions: Scripture reading, sermon, prayer, and hymn.

Return from Exile: Home-Born and Convert

In 538 B.C.E., Cyrus, conqueror of Babylonia, permitted the Jews to return to their homeland. He was sure that in gratitude for this favor they would become a stable element in this outpost of his realm. Nehemiah and Ezra, who had been leading members of the remaining strong community of Babylonia and held high offices with the king, returned to Jerusalem ninety or one hundred years later. Insisting on the strictest family purity, they even compelled the settlers to divorce their non-Jewish wives. Their rationale was that the Jewish kinship had to be deepened among all those who were committed to unyielding obedience to God and Torah. It was felt that only a family uncompromisingly committed to Torah and Mitzvot and brought up in them for generations could assure Jewish survival. The Samaritans, a people of Jewish and non-Jewish ancestry with a religion synthesized from many practices, were rejected.

The attitude of Judaism toward converts thereby underwent a change under the impact of external forces. During their early settlement, Jews had been hospitable to converts. They were the first and only people in antiquity to receive the stranger willing to join them, while all the other nations excluded the "barbarian." The Book of Ruth, discussed in Chapter 12, is a charming testimony to this hospitality: The convert, lovingly accepted, became the ancestor of King David. Now, in the face of the dangers of erosion, a barrier was put up. Since those days, the Jewish attitude toward conversion has remained ambivalent. At times (for instance, during the period of the Roman principate), conversion activity was widespread. At the height of Jewish conversion activity, which includes the period of the emergence of Christianity, a very broad outlook prevailed. "God fearers" who were not prepared to accept all of the Jewish laws—above all, circumcision—would be accepted as "associate members." The convert became a *ger toshav*, a resident alien, entitled to enjoy the full measure of sustaining brotherhood of the Jewish people, though restricted in religious privileges. Converts could, of course, become full-fledged Jews, if they desired. The feeling was: If men or women are looking for spiritual guidance and Judaism can give it, then it must be offered. Later, efforts at conversion became minimal, partly, of course, as a result of the prohibition of Christianity against it. At present, a more liberal outlook seems to exist, at least among non-Orthodox Jews. The convert becomes a full-fledged and beloved member of the Jewish people: *ger tzedek*.

RESTORATION AND THE BEGINNING OF POSTBIBLICAL HISTORY

Restoration

After the return, the Torah was solemnly proclaimed to the people once again established in the Land, and a Covenant of obedience to it was entered by all (444 B.C.E.). Ezra may be credited with the editorship of, substantially, the Pentateuch. He reorganized the people's life by the norms of Torah (Albright, *The Biblical Period*, p. 95). A second Temple was built, to become once again the center of the nation's religious life. The priestly cult and, with it, priestly power were restored.

The arrival of Alexander the Great of Macedonia on the stage of history opened wide the gates to the influence of Greek culture (Hellenism). Conquering the known world (336–323 B.C.E.), Alexander entered Jerusalem and was so gracious to the Jews that many named their sons after him. Upon Alexander's early death, Judah fell under the rule of the Ptolemies of Egypt (the first Ptolemy was one of the generals who had divided up Alexander's empire). So strong was the influence of Hellenism that many of the pious Jews of Egypt no longer understood Hebrew. Consequently, Torah was translated into Greek to remain the guide for those Jews. Supposedly the work of seventy scholars, this early translation is known to us as the *Septuagint*, from the Latin word for seventy.

Soon, however, Judah became attached to the kingdom of Syria, the House of the Seleucids. One of their kings, Antiochus IV Epiphanes, desirous of unifying his empire by means of Greek worship and thought, but also inspired by Jewish Hellenists, endeavored to suppress Jewish religion. In 167 B.C.E., this brought on a rebellion, led by Judah Maccabee (Judas Maccabaeus, the Hammerer) of the House of **Hasmon**, not for independence but for freedom of religion. It resulted in complete independence. The victory is celebrated in the festival of Hanukkah (see p.1303). The Hasmoneans traced their descent to Aaron the high priest; they were, therefore, members of the priestly caste, the only group entitled to conduct the service in the Temple and to provide the high priest. The Hasmoneans now assumed the power of the royal purple as kings, adding to it the office of high priest. Their power was truly absolute and soon became corrupt. Possessed by political and dynastic ambitions, the rulers had forgotten that they were the guardians of the Covenant.

But gradually, with ever-growing momentum, a new direction was entered. The **Pharisees,** a group we shall discuss later, emerged from an unknown origin. They were ambitious to become the people's leaders, in competition with the priesthood. For a while, they employed political means to reach their goal, which brought them into conflict with the rulers. Eventually, perhaps under the leadership of Hillel, they changed their outlook and their method. True power, they realized, rested on ethical leadership, based on the teachings of Torah, as they interpreted it. They were highly successful in attaining this leadership.

Torah and Mitzvot in daily life and worship were placed in the central position, the rabbi's role increased, and the next centuries were devoted to consolidation and expansion of the knowledge and spirit of Torah. This has saved Judaism, for when the Temple was destroyed a second time, by the Romans, the center of Jewish life could be immediately shifted to the house of study.

Over the centuries, the search for meaning in Torah went deeper and deeper, in debate, discussion, rabbinic decision, and commentaries. This growing body of interpretations was transmitted for centuries by word of mouth; Oral Torah evolved, and eventually, when the subject matter became too voluminous and persecution endangered the lives of the rabbis who held the knowledge, this "Oral Torah" was written down. This has come to be known as the **Mishnah** (Review), which then became the source for additional commentary, the **Gemara** (Completion), completed in Babylonia. Both Mishnah and Gemara form the **Talmud** (Compendium of Learning), which has remained the "encyclopedia of the Jew"; it will be discussed later in detail.

Roman Domination, Apocalyptism

Locked in bitter struggle for the kingship, two brothers of the House of Hasmon, Hyrcanus and Aristobulus, called on Rome to be the arbiter of their claims. In 63 B.C.E., Pompey arrived on the scene, gave the power to the weaker of the two brothers, Hyrcanus, and assigned him an advisor—actually a supervisor—who would see to it that Rome retained the power that had fallen into its lap. The advisor was Antipater, an Idumaean, son of a people who had been forcibly annexed and converted to Judaism by the Hasmoneans without ever accepting the faith in sincere conviction. Antipater's son, for whom the father prepared the way to the throne, was Herod the Great (37–4 B.C.E.). He wiped out the Hasmonean family almost entirely, although he had married into the house, dealt cruelly with the people, and tried everything to please the Roman overlords. He left his mark by his numerous buildings, including the expansion of the Temple.

During these trying times, a new ideological force made itself increasingly felt among the people, affecting in various degrees all of the many sects. This was *apocalyptism*, which has bequeathed to us a vast literature. Like the prophets, the apocalyptics believed they had received a message of God— namely, a prediction of the future. We find such apocalyptic messages in Daniel. However, there is a difference between prophet and apocalyptic. The prophet related the message to the course of human history, the apocalyptic to cosmic events. The prophet proclaimed that disaster would come in consequence of the people's sinfulness but added that this disaster could be avoided if the people changed their way and returned to God. For the apocalyptic, the course of history was set; the end, eschaton, was at hand, and nothing could change it. A cosmic cataclysm would come and would arrive soon: Sinners would be wiped out, but the righteous would be saved, provided they separated themselves from the corrupt world and from their corrupt neighbors. The events of the time were seen as clear indications that the end was near, as corruption had become all encompassing. The fight against the forces of evil was therefore sacred duty. Roman domination and oppression was perceived in this light, and struggle against it was mandatory in view of the approaching end.

After Herod's death, the Romans no longer ruled in an indirect manner, namely as "advisors" to the Jewish rulers; they assumed power openly, governing as overlords through administrative agents called *procurators*. Many of these men were cruel and venal, having been sent to the province with the understanding that they might enrich themselves. In Judaea, one of their methods was to taunt the people by exhibiting the Roman eagle, a graven image abhorrent to the Jews. Arousing the spirit of rebellion, they would then cruelly suppress it, condemning hundreds to death by crucifixion and confiscating their belongings for their own pockets. Unrest grew, and the cry for freedom from intolerable oppression increased. The whole population in particular was seething with rebellion. Signs of the approaching end were perceived. *John the Baptist* called for repentance, as eschaton was near.

Pontius Pilate stood out as one of the worst procurators. It is not surprising, therefore, that he saw in the activities and messianic pronouncements of Jesus an act of rebellion, and had him crucified as "King of the Jews," to show what would happen to anyone who wanted independence and to be "king" or Messiah. Crucifixion, the brutal Roman way of execution, was the lot of many Jews, who despised Pontius Pilate and resisted him, ready to die rather than give up their tradition.

Eventually Pilate was too much even for Rome, and he was recalled. In 64 C.E., Florus, the last procurator, took office. He provoked the Jews to such a degree that they finally rose in armed rebellion. Florus could not quash it, and the Roman legions had to be called in under the command of the general Vespasian (later Roman emperor, 69–79 C.E.). After years of war, Titus, Vespasian's son, finally conquered Jerusalem (70 C.E.) and destroyed it.

The fall of the Temple during the conquest of Jerusalem constituted a cataclysmic event in Jewish history. The loss of Jewish life has been estimated at one million, surpassed only by the Holocaust in the twentieth century. Judaism had to reorient itself. The relationship to Christianity equally underwent a complete change. During the last decades of the Jewish Commonwealth, Christianity had emerged. It had begun as a Jewish sect, whose members were subject to the Jewish authorities. There existed no generally convincing historical evidence supporting the claim of the Christians that theirs was a new dispensation supplanting Judaism. With the fall of the Temple, however, the situation changed. Jewish authority ceased. Christians interpreted the fall of the Temple as a punishment of the Jews for rejecting Christ. The gospels, written after the destruction of the Temple, have Jesus predicting its destruction (Matthew 24:2; Mark 13:2; Luke 21:6). Nevertheless, Judaism and the Jewish people survived.

By the time of the Temple's fall, new foundations for the survival of the Jewish people had already been established. The all-encompassing study of Torah was to be the instrument of perpetuating the Jewish people in the spirit of the Covenant. Hillel, a great rabbi, had founded an academy and raised outstanding disciples who could assume leadership. One of them, Yohanan ben Zaccai, had obtained Roman permission to establish a religious center in a little city, Jabneh, in order that Torah could immediately take over as the central force, should the Temple fall. Torah was now the repository of the all-embracing Covenant and the guarantor of life. Yohanan, however, was not regarded as equal to Moses, which meant that he could interpret and evolve the Torah of Moses but could not abrogate it. The spirit of armed resistance had not been destroyed, either. It led to several rebellions in an effort to reconquer the land in full Jewish sovereignty. The rebellion of Simon bar Koseba (mockingly called Bar Kokhba, Son of the Stars, by the Romans after his fall) in 132–135 C.E. was the last one. It failed, broken by the Roman Emperor Hadrian. Hadrian realized that the Jews could not be overcome as long as they had Torah and Mitzvot; therefore, he prohibited both. The Jews became martyrs of faith. After Hadrian's death (138 C.E.), Jewish religion was again permitted. The province of Palestine, renamed from Judaea to deny the Jews the right of name and ownership, remained the center of Jewish life throughout the world. Jewish unity and cohesion were maintained by having a central religious and spiritual head, the Patriarch. He resided in Palestine and served as central authority for the Jewish Diaspora, which was widely spread into Babylonia, Egypt, and Rome and its provinces as far as Germany.

Gradually gaining adherents, Christianity became the state religion of the Roman Empire (the Council of Nicaea in 325 was already a high point). Jews were now subjected to ever greater disabilities under Christian Rome;

they had become the accursed race. In 425, the Jewish office of Patriarch was abolished, and the Christian bishop of Jerusalem took the title of Patriarch. By that time, the center of Jewish life had moved to Babylonia, a non-Christian country, but only the crusades put an end to Jewish creativity in Palestine for many centuries to come.

The Impact of Greek Thought

Judaism could not exclude foreign thought, nor did it wish to do so. Realizing the impact of non-Jewish culture, it recognized that only a synthesis of tradition and non-Jewish thinking could assure survival of the covenanted people. Dedicated to Torah, Judaism has remained hospitable to those ideas and practices it considers valuable, embodying some of them even into the faith itself. It has rejected only those which it considered detrimental.

Greek thought has had a particularly strong and lasting influence. The prophets had not been systematic thinkers. They were moved by the spirit of God and spoke with emotional fervor. Under Greek influence, systematic thinking was introduced, to become a permanent feature of Jewish study. Plato, Aristotle, and the Stoics were taken seriously. The **Sanhedrin**, the ancient Jewish supreme court, is reminiscent of Greek legislative bodies in its function as innovator in law.

A good example of Greek influence is the attitude of Judaism to universal study of Torah. Plato had called for a universal system of public education. Aristotle had shown that the pursuit of knowledge spells true and greatest happiness, admitting, however, that this happiness would be denied to those who lacked the material means to afford leisure for study. Combining these two elements with the injunction of Torah to teach diligently (Deuteronomy 6:7) and applying them to the study of Torah, the Jews concluded that education must be universal and that people must do with the absolutely barest minimum of existence, if need be, even self-deprivation, in order to find the happiness of study. "Eat bread with salt, drink water in small measure, sleep on the ground, accept a life of deprivations, but toil in Torah. If you will do thus, hail unto you, good will be yours, hail unto you in this world, good will be yours in the world to come" (Mishnah Abot 6:4). The Talmud itself tries to follow Aristotelian patterns of logic wherever possible. On the other hand, Judaism turned down the philosophy of Epicurus, who denied the existence of God or, at least, God's concern, and the future of the soul after death. The worst epithet that can be hurled against a Jew who has fallen away completely is Epicurean. Thus under the impact of worldly wisdom, Jewish philosophy emerged.

The Jewish philosopher Philo, who lived in Egypt during the first pre-Christian century, spoke and wrote Greek and conducted his own life in the spirit of the Stoics yet remained a deeply religious and observant Jew. Influenced by the Greek thinkers of his time, who interpreted Homer allegorically and as a guide to ethics, Philo undertook the same task in interpreting Torah. Viewed in this way, the events related in it point to deeper meanings of ethical significance; the Mitzvot are visible means by which God tries to make manifest eternal truths of reason. In studying Torah and performing the Mitzvot, Jews therefore rehearse and reveal eternal and universal truths.

The Sects

The period from Ezra to about the end of the second century C.E. was one of great activity. Under the influence of Hellenism, there emerged a number of sects, which remained in existence up to the destruction of the Temple. Each was concerned with the survival of Torah and people.

The Sadducees were religious conservatives who belonged to the aristocracy. The movement was led by the high priest and his family, descendants of Zadok, who had once anointed Solomon as king of Israel (I Kings 1:39)—hence their name, Zadokites or **Sadducees**. They were deeply concerned with Temple ritual, seeing the Temple as *the* safeguard of Jewish survival. As aristrocrats, they had come in contact with Greek learning. The majority held that Torah could be preserved if it was interpreted and enforced literally and with severity. The *written* Torah had been codified; it was to be the *only* guide to life. No deviations from the *written* word, no new interpretations were to be permitted. As judges, the Sadducees were severe. Since Torah did not mention the immortality of the soul, they rejected it as alien thought.

A statement in the "Sayings of the Fathers," one of the tractates of the Mishnah, relating the ethical maxims of the masters (see Chapter 13), reflects Sadducean teachings at their noblest: "Antigonus of Sokho . . . used to say: 'Be not like servants who serve the Master in order to receive a reward [in the hereafter], but be like servants who serve the Master without expecting a reward, and may the fear of Heaven [God] be upon you'" (Abot I, 3). The rabbi's name, Antigonus, was Greek and thus shows the influence of Hellenistic culture; he must have come from an acculturated family. He stressed that there was no reward to be expected in a future world, as this was not found in written Torah. He emphasized that the fear of God must be the guideline, keeping his disciples on the straight and narrow road of Torah observance.

A minority of the Sadducees came to feel, however, that they might as well enjoy their luxury as there would be no reward for self-denial in any hereafter (Abot de Rabbi Nathan, Chapter 5). They became hedonist and assimilationist. Caiaphas, the high priest appointed by Pilate, was one of the Sadducees, which may explain his actions.

Before we return to the most historically influential of the sects, the Pharisees, two others deserve brief mention, especially as the memorials they have left us have acquired new importance and significance in our time.

The Essenes, believing that the apocalyptic end of the world was near, cast off all worldly possessions. Some traveled about, calling the people to repentance. John the Baptist may have been one of them. Others formed monasteries, where they lived a completely secluded group life, dedicated only to God. They wished to have no contact with the world and its compromises. Then they would be the remnant to be saved on the final day of reckoning, the battle between "the sons of light and the sons of darkness."

One Essene group established itself at Qum-ran, near the Dead Sea. They followed a strict discipline; followed the practice of frequent ritual purification, by immersing their bodies in water; prayed; read Scripture; and assembled for a ritual meal, breaking bread, sharing wine. And they wrote. They wrote hymns, composed a Manual of Discipline for the members, and made copies of books of Scripture. These written documents, placed in clay jars and hidden in caves when the Romans came, were found in 1947. They are the oldest manuscripts of biblical books we possess. Others, like the Manual of Discipline, give new facts about the life among Jews in Palestine in the period between the Old and the New Testament. They have shown an even closer relationship than had been known before between Jewish ways of life and thought and the early Christian Church. These writings on scrolls, most of them now in a special shrine in the National Museum of Israel in Jerusalem, are called the *Dead Sea Scrolls.*

Shrine of the Book, Jerusalem, and portions of the Isaiah Scroll, one of the Dead Sea Scrolls. (Courtesy, Government of Israel.)

The Zealots, deeply religious, were prepared to do battle for the Lord against the heathen conqueror. Rome was the enemy of the "end of days." To them, the only good Roman was a dead Roman. After Jerusalem fell in the year 70 C.E., some of these Zealots barricaded themselves in the fortress Masadah at the Dead Sea, a palace built by Herod the Great for security and for pleasure. Masadah is located on a steep rock jutting out 900 feet over the plain. In the year 66 C.E., a group of Zealots had taken the fortress from the Roman garrison that held it. The Zealots, fired by national and religious pride, held it for almost three years after the fall of Jerusalem. Rome had to build special camps and assault ramps to retake Masadah in 72 C.E. But the Roman legions did not take any captives. When resistance was impossible, the 967 men, women, and children holding Masadah killed themselves rather than fall into the hands of the enemy.

The fortress was excavated in the years 1963–1965 by the government of Israel and Hebrew University. It is now a place of pilgrimage for Israeli youth, and on its plateau the officers of the armed services are sworn in and receive their commissions. Thus the past has been linked to the present.

The Pharisees have had a basic and lasting impact on the evolution of Judaism. When the Temple fell, all the other sects vanished, but the heritage of the Pharisees has endured. Our knowledge of the Pharisees rests largely on the characterization of the rabbis in power after the Temple's fall. The rabbis consciously saw themselves as heirs of the Pharisees and may have idealized them; a spirit of high ideals is revealed in their utterances.

The term *Pharisees* comes from the Hebrew *Perushim*, the separated ones. Originally, it may have been a pejorative designation given them by their opponents. However, it became a term of distinction for the small group of perhaps six thousand, who considered themselves "elect" in the sense that they were to set an example. We are reminded of the Puritan "elect," but the rabbis did not regard themselves as being especially elect to salvation. Love of God, love of humanity, Torah and Mitzvot seen as response to divine command in ethics and religious observance—that is their legacy. Throughout history, Jews have revered the Pharisees. Bold in interpretation, in order to adjust Torah to the people's need, they were meticulous in their performance of Mitzvot.

As the Pharisees were highly respected, they attracted imitators, who did not share their inwardness of soul but exhibited an exaggerated outward form of piety. The Talmud tells us in detail that the pharisaic leaders were well aware of these hypocrites and castigated them scathingly. But when asked why they did not remove them, the rabbis responded that, as humans, we cannot judge the motivations of the heart and must leave the judgment to God (Sota 20–22b). In accordance with pharisaic tradition, which is his own, Jesus equally rebukes these hypocritical Pharisees. Through the centuries Christianity interpreted the words of Jesus as including all Pharisees, and thus treated them most unjustly and branded them without exception as hypocrites or, at least, legal hairsplitters without the true spirit of faith. Only in our own time have Christians come to realize how unfairly they had hitherto treated the memory of these noble people. The Pharisees maintained that love for God and humanity must undergird all actions, for the intent—"the heart"—matters, not the empty act. Humility and modesty are the virtues God demands. "Do not do unto others what would be hateful to you were it done to you," was the motto, indeed the foundation, of Judaism, according to Hillel, a Pharisee. Judaism proudly acclaims the Pharisees its spiritual fathers.

At the same time, the Pharisees were bold innovators. Yohanan ben Zaccai, who was permitted by Vespasian to open an academy at Jabneh, was a Pharisee. His action is revealing. Seeing no hope for the rescue of the Temple and its offices, he took it upon himself to base the future of the Jews on the Covenant of Torah alone and to install the rabbis as its keepers. In changing times, this called for a radically new approach: The rabbis had to assume the power to legislate. They increased this power in subsequent centuries. As legislators, they had to be meticulous in observance of the word of Torah. However, they saw themselves not as innovators, but only as interpreters. Their legislation was read *out* of Torah by being read *into* the text. This called for painstaking analysis of every word of Scripture to show that the new interpretation was *already in it*. As every ordinance ultimately rested on the word of God as revealed at Sinai, its promulgators had to be exact in its performance.

In the Mishnah, we learn of the spirit that permeated the minds of the teachers: "The world rests on three things: on Torah, Service [worship, mitzvot], and acts of love" (Abot 1:2).

The rabbis merely spoke of building fences, similar to the fence Moses was bidden to build around Mount Sinai in order that the people might not encroach on the place of divine revelation (Exodus 19:12). Then it was meant literally; now it was to be understood figuratively. In reality, rabbinical interpretation frequently gave new meaning to the word of Scripture and changed its laws from their literal meaning. This was "liberalism." The Sadducees recognized it as such and opposed it.

This process of evolutionary interpretation took place in academies. The rabbis passed their teachings from generation to generation by word of mouth, and each generation added to the body of this Oral Torah. But in this form of transmission lay a twofold danger. The material became so voluminous that few could remember all of it, much less keep it in mind for discussion and decision making. Some rabbis, such as Rabbi Akiba and his disciple Rabbi Meir, saw themselves compelled to make lecture notes. In addition, the situation of the Jews frequently became precarious. After the abortive Bar Kokhba rebellion, for instance, the Emperor Hadrian proscribed the teaching and the practice of Jewish religion. But if Torah was to be preserved, teaching had to continue. The leading rabbis and their disciples had no choice; they defied the edict. They were hunted by the Roman government and, when caught, were executed under most cruel tortures. The story of "Ten [Rabbis], Slain by the Government," is told annually in the worship of Yom Kippur to evoke the spirit of commitment to Jewish heritage.

Among these Ten was *Rabbi Akiba* (50–132 C.E.). He had reached manhood as an ignorant shepherd, then fell in love with his rich employer's daughter, Rachel, who returned his love but made him promise to study Torah. Her father, upon learning of her secret marriage to Akiba, cut off her support. Akiba studied for twenty-four years while his wife, by the toil of her hands, supported him. Then her father relented (Ketubot 62b/63a). Eventually, Akiba became *the* master of his time. He was caught and put to death. When his flesh was torn from his body by red-hot pincers, he smiled. "Should I not be happy?" he told his terrified students. "'You shall love the Lord your God with all your soul,' even surrendering your life to him. Now I can meet this supreme test of love, should I not rejoice?" (Berakhot 21b). With him and his colleagues, a wealth of knowledge perished.

Mishnah

In view of the precarious situation of the Jews, Rabbi Judah, patriarch of the Jewish community and friend of the Emperor Antonius Pius (and perhaps also of his nephew, the emperor and philosopher Marcus Aurelius), decided that Oral Torah had to be edited and written down. The Mishnah, of which we shall say more later, was completed around the year 200 C.E.—none too soon, as conditions became more difficult. The masters who speak in it are called **Tannaim**, the Teachers.

Babylonian Jewry

When two of Rabbi Judah's disciples went to Babylonia during the early years of the third century to establish the center of Jewish learning, they did not take any great risk. Babylonian Jewry already had behind it a proud history extending over 800 years. As we saw, the prophet Jeremiah had written them at the beginning of their exile to consider their new dwelling place a permanent residence for many generations and to devote themselves faithfully to the tasks of good citizenship. As soon as Jerusalem had been resettled by their brethren, they considered it the spiritual and intellectual, as well as the physical, core of Jewry, but they did not neglect the development of their own institutions. Thus Hillel had received his early training in Babylonia and migrated to Judea for completion of his studies and eventual leadership. Now Abba Areka (Abba the Tall), a giant of a man both physically and intellectually, and his colleague Samuel set out to establish in Babylonia the center of leadership.

Babylonian Jewry was happy, wealthy, and respected. The community was large, counting several million. The Jews had all the rights of citizens and actually formed their own autonomous state within the kingdom, comparable to one of the states within the United States. At the head of it stood the *Resh Galuta,* the Exilarch, who was a descendant of the House of David and governor in the real sense of the word. The Babylonian Jews were well adjusted and deeply religious, and proud of their two leading academies in the cities of Sura and Nehardea (the academy in the latter city was later transferred to Pumbedita). The presidents of these academies were the spiritual heads and chief justices of the Jews and bore the title **Gaon,** which means Excellency. Abba Areka and Samuel became the presidents of these two schools. So great was Abba Areka's prestige that he became known simply as *Rab*, the Master. Henceforth, all the leading rabbis of Babylonia, who speak to us from the pages of the Talmud, were given the title *rab*, in contrast to those of Palestine, who were known by the title **rabbi**.

The Talmud

In an effort to evolve the Mishnah both in theory and in practice, an interesting system was evolved. Twice a year, in spring and fall, the scholars assembled for a whole month of discussion and debate; then they were given homework to study for the next assembly, or *Kallah*, while pursuing their regular ways of making a living. These debates, which closely followed the Mishnah, were recorded verbatim and formed the *Gemara*, "Completion" of Mishnah. Gemara is no dry code of laws. It breathes the living spirit of question and answer, legal analysis and homiletic exegesis, bon mot and jest; often it is rambling, following a free association of thoughts.

Eventually, the material became so voluminous that it had to be edited, and the *Talmud* was formed. Work on the Talmud went on in both Palestine and Babylonia. We therefore have *Jerushalmi*, the Jerusalem Talmud, and *Babli*, the Babylonian Talmud. In 360, when the academies of Palestine were forcibly closed by the Christian authorities, the Jerushalmi remained incomplete. Development of the Babli continued; it was finally edited around 500 C.E. under the leadership of Rab Ashee and Rabina.

The Talmud will be discussed in detail in Chapter 13.

Saadia versus Islam, the Karaites, and Aristotle

Study and research went on. Babylonia fell into the orbit of Islam (see pp. 56ff.), and the relationship between the two religions was good. However, a number of new spiritual problems arose: A new Jewish sect, the *Karaites*, or "Scripturites," had been founded in the eighth century. It denied the validity of the Talmud, basing itself entirely on Scripture and drawing new deductions from it. Had karaitic teaching prevailed and spread, it would have destroyed the organic evolution of Judaism that rested on shared tradition and would have undermined the unity of the people.

More important was the challenge presented by the ever-increasing knowledge and study of the works of Aristotle, whose conclusions, so logically developed, clashed with the teachings of Torah. The claims of Islam to be the only true religion had to be logically refuted as well.

The *Gaon Saadia* (882–942) addressed himself to all these tasks. He stands out as the first Jewish "scholastic," making an effort to synthesize Aristotle and Jewish tradition whenever possible. Whatever was good in Aristotle—measured by the yardstick of Jewish tradition—had a right to be incorporated. When synthesis was impossible, he refuted Aristotle by logic. In his *Book of Doctrines and Beliefs*, Gaon Saadia was to claim Judaism as the religion of reason. We shall discuss his philosophy later (see Chapter 15).

He likewise attacked the views of the Karaites in tract after tract. For the use of his people, he translated the Bible into Arabic, compiled a Hebrew grammar, and edited the prayer book. His life was stormy, but his intent was clear: The living Torah, growing and evolving, had to be preserved against the deadening outlook of Karaites and against any influences of alien philosophical thought. By the Karaite interpretation, Mitzvot would assume a totally changed character, different from the form the rabbis had given them. This had to be avoided at all costs, as Torah and Mitzvot were the mainstays of Diaspora Jewry.

Eventually, as disturbances and wars swept over the Near East, Babylonian Jewry lost its key position, although a Jewish community in Persia exists to this day. By around the beginning of the eleventh century C.E., however, new centers had arisen in Spain and in Germany, as we shall see in the following chapters.

3

THE IMPACT OF CHRISTIANITY

    The period whose events we have traced witnessed the emergence and rise of Christianity. As we turn to a brief discussion of Christianity's impact on Jewish history, it should be recognized by non-Jewish readers as an analysis of the manner in which Christianity has *appeared* to Jews. It may surprise and at times even disturb Christian readers to find concepts and ideas questioned which to them are self-evident, as they have been brought up on them. It is my belief, however, that they will want to know and understand in order that a fruitful dialogue may become a durable reality.

    The emergence of a genuine dialogue between the faiths may be considered one of the positive developments of our time. It holds great promise of true human fellowship and concern among the faithful of these two religions, as among all people. In spirit and in character, it is totally different from the religious "disputations" convened by the Catholic Church during the Middle Ages, whose outcome was a foregone conclusion, and whose purpose was simply to prove to the rulers, the world, and the Jews the "error" of the Synagogue and the triumphant truth of the Church. The spirit of these disputations can still be noticed in the sculptures on great cathedrals, such as that at Strasbourg: the Synagogue in collapse, her eyes bandaged, her staff broken; the Church holding her banner aloft, with crowned head and proud eyes confidently viewing both time and eternity. Seen in this manner, and treated harshly on account of their "blindness," the Jews were naturally afraid of the Church.

    The fortunate change that has come within our own time can be ascribed to a number of causes, among them the scientific temper of the twentieth century, the deepening of the democratic outlook which called for freedom of religion, and the secularization of life in general. The spread of atheism and communism actually called for a spirit of cooperation among the religious forces in the struggle against God-denying ideologies and forces. The Holocaust, claiming millions of Jews as victims of the accumulated impact of centuries of anti-Semitism, weighed heavily upon the conscience of humanity. It aroused Christianity to a profound self-examination, leading to a renewed commitment to world leadership in the spirit of Christian ethics. In this spirit of love that binds Christians and Jews, we shall try to view briefly some of the impact of Christianity upon Judaism as seen by a Jew.

JESUS AND THE JEWS

The life, the passion, and the resurrection of Jesus, the Christ, are related to us in the *Gospels.* They are a document of faith (as are the Hebrew Scriptures); they are not a detached historical account. The historical Jesus is less their object than the Risen Christ. Piety permeates the story. It became subject to embroidery and error, as is the case in any oral tradition. The Gospels were written *after* the ministry of Paul and under the impact of his teachings. Paul's theology, as we shall point out, contrasts sharply with basic Jewish principles and it subjected him to Jewish attacks during his lifetime. This antagonism is reflected in the Gospels.

Written in part by Jews and in part by non-Jews, the Gospels reflect the changing relationship between the Jewish community and the emerging Christian one. The Jewish Christians, who were convinced that Jesus was the Messiah, regarded themselves as authentic Jews. They were filled with the deep desire to win over their brethren to the "good news." They endeavored to show that Jesus had spoken primarily and specifically to Jews, as is reflected in many passages of the Gospel of Matthew that are positively and specifically addressed to the Jewish community (5:17ff.; 10:5; 15:17ff.; 15:24; 23:2). By and large, the Jews did not respond positively to this message. This must have been a deep disappointment to the new Christians, convincing them that their hope lay in the conversion of gentiles. This frustration and shift is mirrored in other passages of Matthew, which have a universalistic-anti-Jewish character (2:43; 22:7; 28:18ff.).

The non-Jewish writers were antagonistic to Jews. They maintained that Judaism had been superseded, an attitude not entirely surprising for people who had chosen one religion over another. The fall of the Temple in 70 C.E. served the Christians as evidence that God had punished the Jews for their refusal to accept Christ. Words of prophecy to that effect were ascribed to Jesus (Matthew 24:2; Mark 13:2; Luke 21:6). However, the Christian community itself was still in flux, and beliefs and doctrines clashed. The predominant faction might then characterize nonconformists pejoratively as "Jews." Such references in the Gospels need not be regarded as judgments on Jewish thought and action in general.

Finally, the writers had to whitewash the Roman government if Christianity was to be tolerated at all. Even Pilate, one of the most cruel and venal of procurators, is exonerated. As we have seen, he was so cruel that Rome had enough of him and recalled him. But he is shown washing his hands, thus performing a Jewish ceremony symbolically pleading for remission of sin in connection with the death of an innocent man. The ceremony as described in the Gospels has been misunderstood, however. (See Deuteronomy 21:1–9, dealing with an unknown murder victim found at a crossroads in the countryside: The elders of the closest city wash their hands, symbolically expressing their innocence of this crime that resulted from a lack of protection and help extended within their territory. Then they ask divine forgiveness for the crime *having been* committed by unknown hands, not one they *are about* to sanction by consciously approving it.) We cannot assume Pilate suddenly adopted a Jewish practice, considering how deeply he hated the Jews and how determined he was to antagonize them by offending their religious beliefs. (Unless, of course, he had heard about the practice and repeated it in mockery, which throws an entirely different light on his action: It then becomes a blasphemous provocation of Jewish tradition.)

In the Gospels themselves, we find contradictions regarding the year of Jesus's birth and crucifixion. Basic elements of his trial and conviction, as related in the Gospels, cannot be reconciled with Jewish life and practice. Jesus lived a simple life. The circle of those who knew him was small. His impact, and that of his teachings, was slow in emerging. Jesus himself may have passed through his lifetime without being known either personally or by his teachings to the overwhelming majority of his Jewish contemporaries in Judea or to the millions in the Diaspora. The Jewish historian Josephus, a meticulous chronicler of Jewish history during his period, does not mention Jesus. (A statement in Josephus about Jesus is generally considered a later addition by an unknown, possibly Christian, writer.) Josephus did, however, hold a strong bias in favor of Rome, which may have led to his silence. But the Jewish philosopher Philo, who lived in Egypt from about 25 B.C.E. to about 50 C.E. and was a spokesman for the Jews, does not mention Jesus either.

Jesus was true to the teachings of the Pharisees, yet it is not unlikely that he may have made enemies among them. The hypocrites within the pharisaic group may well have hated him for his rebuke. The leaders of the Pharisees were themselves well aware that their ranks had been joined by unworthy members, but they refused to expel them because they maintained that only God could judge the human heart. (The author of Acts perceived the character of the Pharisees; he has Gamaliel, the Pharisee, plead in behalf of the apostles, who, according to Acts, had been brought before the council and high priest accused of teaching in Christ's name. Gamaliel advised the court not to judge, but to let God be the judge of the truth of the apostles' message (Acts 5:34–39). According to Acts, the apostles were flogged but not killed.)

To some of the Pharisees, Jesus's actions may have been too radical. For instance, Jesus performed healing on the Sabbath (Luke 14:1–6). The Pharisees permitted rescue work on the Sabbath but only when there was actual danger to life. At one time, they had taken action on a Sabbath when they found Hillel close to death on account of exposure to the elements. In Jesus's case, they kept silent and did not express disagreement, but they may have doubted whether there was real danger for the patient's life and may have found Jesus's action too precipitous.

The Pharisees had no problems with Jesus's messianic claims. The idea of a messianic claimant, who lived as a Jew, obedient to law and tradition, and who was not a sinner, was acceptable to them. In fact, Akiba was to proclaim Bar Kokhba as the Messiah one hundred years later.

Jesus believed in resurrection, as did the Pharisees. He based his own teachings on those of John the Baptist as described in Matthew 3;4:17, and we find no opposition to John's activity among any Jews.

To the questioning Pharisee, who wanted to know the greatest commandment in Torah, Jesus reiterated succinctly the Torah's words of the twofold love—the commandment to love God (Deuteronomy 6:5) and the commandment to love one's neighbor (Leviticus 19:18). He combined these commandments in simple sentences, as the Jewish children of the time learned them in catechetical instruction (Matthew 23:37–39). Affirming pharisaic teaching and his bond to the people, Jesus implicitly rejected the teachings of the Essenes to love one's neighbor and hate the enemy, which contradicts the commandments of Torah (Matthew 5:43,44; compare Exodus 23:4,5; Leviticus 20:17f.). The disciple who asked Jesus for a special, distinguishing prayer, just as John the Baptist had given his disciples a special prayer, was led to the simple prayer spoken by the common Jewish folk: "Our Father, who art in heaven . . ." (Luke 11:1–4).

Hostility against Jesus was more pronounced on the part of the Sadducees. First of all, they did not believe in resurrection (Matthew 22:23–33). They saw the survival of the Jewish people inextricably linked to the Temple, its existence, and its ritual, yet Jesus reportedly attacked these. The Pharisees could see a Jewish future without a Temple; the Sadducees could not.

We may assume that, faced with the danger of destruction for the whole people, Caiaphas, a Sadducee high priest, became alarmed and counseled that it was better for one man to die than for the whole people to perish (John 18:13). Was he afraid that Jesus would endanger the whole people by his messianic claims? The Roman procurator did not understand the subtleties of such a claim. To him, Messiah meant the Anointed and was equivalent to King. Jewish kings had always been anointed with oil. To Rome, then, a Messiah was an insurrectionist, bent on overthrowing the Roman rule. Rome's retaliation was inevitable, as Caiaphas saw it, and would spell destruction for the Jews. It might even lead to the razing of the Temple. In fact, most likely Pilate had to hear only one word to make up his mind—the word *king*. Mocked as "King of the Jews," designated as "King of the Jews" by the inscription over his cross, Jesus was executed. "Trying to release him," Pilate led Jesus in front of a Jewish crowd, who knew of the accusation against him. Was Pilate playing with them to get their reaction, intending to arrest them, too, were they to side with Jesus? Perhaps they were afraid to respond honestly. It was better to affirm loyalty to Caesar and permit one man to die, as Caiaphas had advised. Then the people might survive (see John 19, etc.).

Who were these people, assembled at the residence of Pilate, a man bitterly hated? They may have been just rabble, or perhaps they were assigned to this task of representing "the voice of the populace" by the high priest, to prove to the procurator that the Jews wished to have no part in Jesus's insurrection. They were no more representative of the Jewish people than were the legionnaires representatives of the entire Roman people, but for centuries "the Jews" as a whole were implicated in the conduct of these few. It is hard to assume that the Jews would suddenly adopt a new religious principle—namely, accepting guilt for their children and for future generations. This would run counter to the fundamental conviction of the Jews, so firmly instilled in them by the prophets, that there is no such thing as an inherited guilt (as we saw in the discussion of Jeremiah and Ezekiel).

The trial of Jesus by a Jewish court is so difficult to explain that Samuel Sandmel writes after close study, "The entire trial business is legendary and tendentious" (*A Jewish Understanding of the New Testament;* Cincinnati: Hebrew Union College, 1957, p. 128). The proceedings ran counter to all the then-existing laws of trial procedures, evidence, and so on; in short, they flouted the entire body of legislation, which was strictly binding and permitted of no exceptions.

Solomon Zeitlin has advanced a different theory. This theory, not endorsed by scholars in general, yet has the advantage of cutting through many of the inconsistencies, especially the discrepancies between the trial of Jesus as reported and the basic provisions of Jewish criminal law. In his book *Who Crucified Jesus?* (New York: Bloch Publishing Company, 4th ed., 1964), he arrives at the conclusion, backed up by *his* researches, that there actually existed two Sanhedrins—one for religious matters, the other for political matters. The Sanhedrin for religious matters was composed of scholars, met at appointed times, and was bound by Jewish law. Therefore, it never sat at night, never handed down a conviction in criminal matters on the day of the trial, and hence never held any trial sessions on the day before the Sabbath or any holiday. The other Sanhedrin was government appointed and composed of partisans of the Romans who were willing to give the semblance of legal sanction to acts of the Roman overlord. It could be called into session at any time.

Zeitlin postulates that this political Sanhedrin was called by Caiaphas to meet in his home and hand down the death sentence Pilate had requested for the insurrectionist. Jesus was hastily convicted to please the Romans and avert trouble. The trumped up charge was blasphemy, although according to *Jewish* law, Jesus had not committed blasphemy at all. With the conviction handed down, the Romans took over again, treating Jesus as a *political* criminal, affixing notification of his "crime" on the cross and confiscating his clothes as a political offender. (The property of a religious offender was not subject to confiscation.) After Jesus had died, we find a Jew approaching Pilate: Joseph of Arimathea pleads with Pilate to release the body of Jesus, which was in Roman custody, in order that he might be given burial as Jewish tradition prescribes

(Matthew 27:58ff.). This act, most likely, mirrors the attitude of the average Jew toward Jesus: He was another martyr, put to death by a cruel Roman government. If we see in Acts a reflection of the mood of the time, then the words of Rabbi Gamaliel mentioned above (Acts 5) reflect the attitude of the Pharisees. The eventual action of the court—the flogging of the apostles for teaching in the name of Jesus—may then be regarded as a compromise between Pharisees and Sadducees: the former group prepared to let them go free, the latter, perhaps still afraid of the political repercussions of their missionary work, wanting to kill them.

It must be remembered that the new sect of Nazarenes (the term *Christians* came later), standing under the leadership of Peter, strictly obeyed and practiced Jewish law and expected converts to do the same as a condition of their admission.

PAUL AND THE PARTING OF THE WAYS

In the apostle Paul's emphasis on faith as opposed to Mitzvot, we find the beginning of the dissent between the two faiths. Nevertheless, Paul himself was full of pride in his Jewish background and full of love for his Jewish brethren.

In Paul's missionary work, the strong foundations of Christianity's growth were laid; it became widespread, powerful, eventually the official religion of the Roman Empire. Non-Jews quickly outnumbered the Jewish Christians. The new religion saw in Judaism a rival faith, engaged in widespread missionary activity. Antagonism developed. As a result of Paul's doctrines, Judaism and Christianity had to go their separate ways. For this reason, the Jewish foundations of Paul's thoughts and actions deserve to be noted.

Paul's Background, Diaspora Jewry, and Missionary Work by Jews

Paul grew up as a member of a strictly observant Jewish family in the Diaspora. Diaspora Jewry outnumbered the community in the homeland by millions. The several million Jews of the dispersion were generally accepted and had the right to practice their religion, even when this practice interfered with the duties generally imposed on citizens. As observers of the Sabbath, for instance, they had to be exempt from military service, a privilege granted them. Paul was proud of his ancestry (2 Corinthians 11:22; Romans 11:1) and of his people's place in the world, for they were conscious of being God's people (Philippians 3:5).

Being God's people entailed duties and obligations. Isaiah had urged them to be "a light unto the nations" (Isaiah 42:6), and the prophets had made it clear that the convert was precious in the eyes of God (Isaiah 56:6–7, etc.). Many of the leading Pharisees therefore favored missionary activity. Hillel declared, "Be of the disciples of Aaron, loving peace, pursuing peace, loving all of God's creatures, drawing them to Torah" (Abot 12:1). All gentiles had to be given the opportunity to accept Torah and cast their lot with the Jewish people, in order to find salvation. Then, and only then, could they be held responsible for their idolatrous way of life (Pesikta Rabba 161a). (The concern for the conversion of heathens shown by the Pharisees is reflected in Matthew 23:15).

Diaspora Jewry engaged in widespread missionary work. As we saw, there were two categories of converts: the full convert, who had undergone the full procedure as prescribed; and the "God-fearers," who had committed themselves to observe the Sabbath and other laws and to uphold Jewish ethics, but who had not undergone circumcision. The concern of the Jewish missionaries was to bring many people yearning for a spiritual faith, under the wings of God and of His salvation. Paul, as a youth, was a witness to these activities. They may have inspired him to go out himself as a missionary to save people.

Diaspora Jewry was strongly influenced by Hellenistic civilization. To the Jews in Palestine, Torah was *instruction,* the guide on their road of life; it contained the laws that were part of the Covenant binding Israel and God. To the Diaspora community, Torah was *nomos—Law*. Law was Covenant: a much narrower outlook that had resulted from the impact of many other intellectual and philosophical forces stemming from Hellenistic civilization. At the same time, Jews such as the philosopher Philo interpreted Torah allegorically and saw in the laws of Torah symbols showing the road toward the laws that God had *naturally implanted* in humanity. Philo's thinking was to affect Paul in a twofold way: Torah became for him just Law; and, if the human soul was sanctified, the divine Covenant might be found outside the Mitzvot of Torah.

Paul therefore stood under an inner compulsion that was truly Jewish: Humanity had to be saved. He came to deviate from Jewish tradition partially as a result of his Diaspora experiences. He started out as a Pharisee, and a zealous one, and called himself a Pharisee throughout life (Philippians 3:5). As a Pharisee, he became a missionary, originally an uncompromisingly strict orthodox one (Galatians 5:11 may refer to his earlier missionary attitude). Like the rest of the Pharisees, he earned his living by the toil of his hands—he was a tentmaker. But Paul was also a man of extremes: The compromise solution of two types of converts was not for him. If the Law was to be observed, then all of it had to be observed, or the Law in its entirety was irrelevant as a means of salvation.

Paul became a persecutor of those Christians who denied the validity of Law and tradition (Galatians 1:13; Philippians 3:6). He had no quarrel with the mother Church—the first church, presided over by Peter, and central in prestige and authority—in Jerusalem, which demanded obedience to the Law in addition to faith in Christ from its adherents. The mother Church took no notice of him at this stage of his career.

Paul was convinced that the Law was holy and just and good, and he was to state even later: "In my innermost self I delight in the law of God" (Romans 7:22). He became zealous for the law—until suddenly his outlook was transformed by the personal illumination that the law had been superseded by faith in Christ.

Paul's Revelation

Sent to Damascus by the authorities to punish the Jewish Christians who preached the abandonment of the law (not to bring them back to Jerusalem, for the Jews no longer had that power; they could only inflict the punishments of the congregation, which included scourging), Paul had a vision of Christ, a revelation: With the coming of Christ, the Covenant of Law had been replaced by the Covenant of Christ. The Law no longer held any compelling power. Humanity comes to God through Christ. In a sense, Paul's conclusion rested logically on the thoughts advanced by the Hellenistic Jewish philosophers. To them, the Law was the instrument of education bringing humanity to obedience to God's *natural law*. But Paul's conclusion was radical: Through Christ, a new spirit would enter the souls of the faithful; obedience to natural law was the fruit of the spirit not of Law. He came to understand the position of the Hellenistic Jews at Damascus, whom he had been sent to castigate. Paul's personal experience and his sense of spiritual renewal through this knowledge that Law had been abrogated were now to become the foundation of a fundamental and universal principle upon which he built his ministry and his missionary work.

Paul's Missionary Activity

Paul's stand caused controversy and conflict. Moved by the urgency of his task, Paul immediately set out on his missionary work. He did not feel it necessary to go to Jerusalem first in order to obtain authorization from the mother Church. He regarded himself as called by Christ and therefore of equal standing with the disciples. Although he probably had not known Jesus during his lifetime, he had received the vision of Christ, and it was Christ whom he was preaching rather than the story of the man Jesus on earth. Paul's vision placed him in the same position as the prophets of old to whom God had granted His revelation. He saw his task as more pressing than theirs had been, for the end of days, be believed, was about to come, and as many as could be reached had to be brought to Christ before then.

Paul went abroad and made many converts. His success caused rejoicing among the leaders of the mother Church at Jerusalem. But Paul taught his non-Jewish audiences that the Law, including circumcision, not only was not necessary but actually was an impediment. He had to go to Jerusalem to defend himself before the leadership of the mother Church. There he insisted that he was authorized in his own right to teach that the Law, including circumcision, had been abolished and that he would continue his preaching of this doctrine. The leadership at Jerusalem became convinced, at least to the point of making him apostle to the Gentiles. Paul equally succeeded in convincing Peter to join the new Christians at the table when Peter visited Antioch, breaking bread with them—a breach of the dietary laws, we may assume (Galatians 2).

Against the majority of the leadership of the Church, Paul maintained that he was right, and he prevailed. This was typically Jewish. Had not the Jews maintained that their God was the one and only God who had made a Covenant with them, even while they were alone in this position, even while they were opposed by an entire world? Were they not going to maintain throughout the ages that they were abiding under God's Covenant, even while being persecuted for their position by the Christian world?

Returning to his activity, Paul traveled throughout the greater part of the civilized world of his time. He frequently preached in synagogues to Jewish and non-Jewish audiences. His teachings quite often caused severe trouble, however. Many Jews regarded his teachings as destructive, for they contradicted the law of Torah and abolished the Mitzvot. Penalties were invoked against him (II Corinthians 11:24ff.).

In return, Paul attacked the Jews violently (Romans 2:21–24), and specifically the practice of circumcision (Galatians 5:12; Philippians 3:2). His utterances were frequently used against the Jews later in history. But we must understand them in context. Paul was incensed; he responded to violent argument in his own violent manner. It was an internal squabble between Jews—Paul and his opponents. His words were motivated by the excitement of the moment. An intra-Jewish argument, an aside voiced perhaps to forestall questions, was later made into principles. Paul spoke as the moment bid him to do; he spoke to concrete situations. When his words were gathered and canonized, they assumed the character of basic writings, and every word was considered of equal importance.

Essentially, Paul was loyal to the Jews. His heart went out to his Jewish brothers, people of covenants, patriarchs, Messiah (Romans 9:1–5); he regarded them as lost because they did not accept his teachings. Although he saw in the followers of Christ the new Israel, Paul loved his people.

We have followed the life of Paul at some length because it is inseparable from his teachings. His theology springs from his life. Through it, the Church was given the means of growth; without it, Christianity might have remained a sect within Judaism. Non-Jews became its leaders and its faithful. By unifying the Church, Paul led it out of Judaism. In his preaching, however, Paul followed the pattern of Jewish exegesis. His sermons were discussions in the manner of Jewish study. He drew his conclusions from the text of Scripture (see Romans 9). The Christian sermon, therefore, has followed the pattern of the Jewish sermon. At the same time, the "Old Testament" was seen as a prophecy of the coming of Christ; this has resulted in frequently divergent interpretations of the Hebrew Scriptures by Christians and Jews.

What are Paul's basic teachings?

Paul's Basic Teachings

In his Epistle to the Romans (Romans 7), Paul gives us a report of the anxieties that led him to his conversion. Taking delight in the Law of God (Romans 7:22), he found that this same Law tempted him to break it. The Law said, "You shall not covet" and thereby aroused in him all kinds of desires. The seductive power of sin entered his heart through the commandment; its effect was "killing" rather than quickening (Romans 7:7ff.). Many contemporary biblical scholars maintain that this report is not autobiographical, but rather a poetic illustration of the effects of the Law as Paul perceived them *after* his conversion. These scholars hold that Paul actually did *not* feel any distress in observing the Law during his earlier years—in spite of his own words. In looking back upon his former state, he now felt that his life under the Law must have been distressing.

Paul found himself transformed by a personal revelation. This revelation raised to absolute conviction in him several fundamental truths by which his life henceforth was shaped. These truths—related to divine dispensation, and emerging from it, his own calling—were: Jesus Christ is the Lord; through Jesus Christ, God has provided for the salvation of all believers; Christ will return to bring about the end and consummation of history. Paul's own mission, ordained by God, rested on these truths: He was to be the apostle to the Gentiles.

From these convictions, Paul drew several conclusions. God's sending salvation through Christ meant that God saw humanity's need of salvation. Christ's death revealed that the Law, hitherto regarded as the road to salvation, did not lead to salvation—Christ alone was the way. "If righteousness should come through the law, Christ died in vain" (Galatians 2:21). Obedience to the Law in the assumption that it leads to salvation is therefore sin, for humanity cannot bring about its own salvation. The Law did have a function, however: It quickened the awareness of sin (Romans 7:7ff.). From this perspective, there was a form of righteousness in obedience to the Law because of its capacity to reveal its own deficiency, open human mind and soul, and pave the way to true faith—namely, that Christ brings salvation (Philippians 3:4–12). Jewish righteousness came through the Law; hence Jews need not abandon it, but they must—through it—come to Christ. As far as the Gentiles were concerned, the Law had resulted in a separation between those who observed it and those who stood outside of it. This separation must be broken, for in Christ's Spirit all of humanity, Jews and Gentiles alike, has been freed from the powers of sin, death, and the Law (Romans 5–8). All human beings must form a union of equals with equal access to salvation; all are one body (I Corinthians 12:12ff.). Paul therefore turned sharp words against those converts who wished to observe Jewish law, as this would create divisiveness (Galatians 3). Initially, the Law had been given by God as a means of education, but the tutorship of the Law had now ended.

The community of believers formed one body, an organic whole. One could not belong to it while, at the same time, participating in another one. Paul therefore equally warned his followers against any action that harms the wholeness of a person's physical body: ". . . The body is not for fornication, but for the Lord, and the Lord for the body . . ." (I Corinthians 6:13–20). This is not "law" but the result of the simple realization of the Christian's condition (I Corinthians 6:12).

Without needing any Law, but guided by the Spirit, Christians are under the compulsion to establish and follow those ethical principles that even the Gentiles follow by natural insight (Romans 2:14f.; Galatians 5:19–26). In this manner, Paul reinstated rule, but as fruit of the Spirit. Significantly, he drew the details of these ethical requirements from Hebrew Scriptures; as Jew, he saw no need either to improve on them or to find new ones.

The difference between Paul and the Jewish outlook may appear to be merely semantic. In Judaism, the rules of conduct are *commandments,* law; in Paul, they are the fruits of the *Spirit.* But we should remember that Paul had been brought up on the methods of the Talmud and the Mishnah and had internalized them. For the Talmud, each separate term, even a nuance, found in Scripture may hold a new meaning and lead in different directions. Since Paul argued in a talmudic manner, the distinctions become basic.

Paul held that the miracles presented to the Jews and the commandments given in Torah are to be understood symbolically (I Corinthians 9:9–12; 10:6). They lead to that natural law by which the Spirit guides all humanity. The Christian should do that which is naturally and universally accepted: not give offense (I Corinthians 10:32); promote unity; and, above all, love (I Corinthians 13:1 ff.). In this symbolic interpretation of the laws, and in Paul's reliance on natural law, implanted in humanity, we recognize the ideas of the Jewish philosopher Philo—with one difference: Philo insisted on faithful observance of the Mitzvot, giving them an additional, symbolic meaning; Paul saw no purpose in the observance of *specific commandments.*

There are both fundamental agreements and disagreements between Paul's teachings and Jewish doctrine. According to Judaism, salvation is assured every Jew on the basis of belonging to the Covenant. "All of Israel, every one of them, have a share in the world to come [salvation], as it is stated: 'Your people, altogether they are righteous, they will forever inherit the earth . . .' (Isaiah 60:21)" (Sanhedrin 104b). Salvation is attained by God's grace, *not* simply by the Law; humanity does *not* bring about its own salvation. For Paul, all of the newly covenanted people have a share in salvation on the basis of the Covenant of the body of Christ. According to Judaism, salvation is equally assured every righteous person among the Gentiles. "The righteous of the nations of the world, every one of them, have a share in the world to come" (Tosefta Sanhedrin 13). What makes them "righteous" is the observance of the Noahide commandments, imposed on Noah's descendants, the entire human race.

> The sons of Noah were given seven commandments relating to [the pro-
> hibitions of] idolatry, unchastity, the shedding of blood, the profanation of
> the Name [of God], [the establishment of] justice [just laws, to be adminis-
> tered through just courts], [the prohibitions of] robbery, [the cutting of] a
> limb from a living animal. Rabbi Haninah ben Gamaliel said: also wounding
> a living being. . . . Rabbi Simon ben Johai said: also witchcraft. . . . [Gen.
> Rabba: Noah, 34:8]

(The rabbis felt that those persons willfully violating the Noahide commandments would not be granted salvation. This included many of the gentiles of
their time, who pursued practices that violated basic Noahide commandments.)

The laws are seen as basic elements of natural human morality, designed to establish a society under God with respect for human life and family,
for property, for animals as God's creatures, and for a just society. Paul equally
expected observance of the Noahide commandments; Galatians 5:19ff. corresponds to them. In addition, however, he required faith in Christ as condition
for salvation. According to Judaism, gentiles do attain salvation but do not
enter the Covenant of Israel; it is not required of them. To Paul, gentiles do not
enter the Covenant of the body of Christ, and it is necessary for them to be
under this Covenant in order to attain salvation.

Why does humanity stand in need of salvation? Paul maintained that,
with Adam's sin, death entered the world. *Because* Adam sinned, all his
descendants—the entire human race—are in the throes of sin and death. The
law kept humanity in check during a period of education. Ultimately, however, God by free grace sent into the world Christ, who, by his death, redeemed humanity from the Law, from sin arising out of the Law, and from
death. Through baptism, the old humankind is buried with Christ and reborn
in Christ (Romans 5:1–15). Adam, who sinned, was the father of humanity so
far; Christ was the beginning of a new humanity, saved through him.

Judaism, by contrast, has held that human beings sin not *because* Adam
sinned, but *as* Adam sinned. Each individual person *will* sin (Ecclesiastes 7:20)
but by the grace of God will receive forgiveness as humanity returns to Him.

In proving his point that faith in Christ is the only way to salvation,
Paul arrives at conclusions different from the teachings of Judaism but uses
methods typical of Jewish exegesis (Romans 4; Galatians 3:6).

In Genesis 15 (1–6), God promised Abraham, who was already very
old, that he would have an heir and that his descendants would be as numerous
as the stars in heaven. "And he had faith in the Lord, and He reckoned it to him
as righteousness" (v.6). Later, in chapter 17 (9ff.), God established the Covenant of circumcision with Abraham. Paul concluded, therefore, that Abraham
was regarded as righteous before God, even before Abraham performed the
Law of the Covenant, circumcision. Abraham was considered righteous because he had *faith.* The Hebrew word is *he-min,* he trusted, which has the same
root as *Amen.* In spite of all counterindications, Abraham trusted God and was
convinced that God would do whatever He promised. This same trust, or faith,

must permeate the Christian—namely, that Christ is the Redeemer from sin. Then God "will reckon it to him as righteousness," God will justify him. (Jewish interpretation, among others, holds that God rewarded Abraham for the commandments he had already fulfilled, leaving his homeland on God's command, offering sacrifices, tithing himself, etc., as found in Genesis 12-14). "[Abraham] hoped against hope . . . that is why his faith was 'reckoned to him as righteousness' " (Romans 4:18,22). This faith was met by God's grace, and the faith of the Christians in Christ as Redeemer will result in God's grace too. Those who have faith are the children of God, the new Israel under the new Covenant. Through Christ, all powers that might separate humanity from the love of God are removed (Romans 8:38–39). Through Christ, God gave proof of His love and freely granted grace that does not depend on observance of the Law—in fact, would be hampered by it. Thus the faithful are justified and reconciled with God (Philippians 3:14, etc.). Death and corruption have no power over them, for Christ lives in them (Galatians 2:20).

Why was Christ sent? Out of God's free-will grace, and not in reward of any good human deeds.

Paul and the Jews—Implications

How did Paul feel about the Jews who did not accept his message? God has not rejected His people; to Him, they are merely blind. Yet this blindness can be a blessing for the world, to stir the Christian world to live in such a fashion that the Jews will be "jealous" (Romans 11). Israel is the root that sustains the plant. But now the Christians are called upon to live in a way that the Jews will wish to emulate.

Commenting on these words, Hans Küng, the German Catholic theologian, writes regarding the Church and the Jews:

> Only one course of action is permitted to the Church on this common journey [with the Jews]—not "tolerating," not "missionizing," not "converting," but only "making Israel jealous" (Romans 11:11). The Church can make Israel jealous of the "salvation" it has received, in order to spur Israel to emulate it. But how? The church, in its whole existence, must be a token of the salvation it has received. In its whole existence, it must bear witness to the messianic fulfillment. In its whole existence it must vie with Israel in addressing itself to a world which has turned its back on God, and in demonstrating to it, with authority and love, the word that has been fulfilled, the righteousness that has been revealed, the mercy that has been accepted, the reign of God which has already begun. Its whole life, lived in a convincing way, would be a call to all men to believe the good news, to experience a change of heart and to unite themselves with its Messiah.
>
> This is how Israel and the Church must confront one another—not in theoretical debate, but in existential dialogue; not in an uncommitted battle of words, but in committed competition. By its whole life the Church must witness to the reality of redemption. Is this the case? Is this the witness of the Church? The Jews do not think so. The reality of redemption asserted by the New Testament seems to them, particularly in the light of the Old Testament,

to have been an illusion. (Hans Küng, *The Church,* London: Search Press Ltd., successor to Burns & Oates, Ltd. © 1967 p. 149.)

Seen in this light, Paul's words about the Jews reveal how deeply he loved them. Upon his Christians he placed the heavy burden of promoting love and peace in the world.

THE SPLIT WIDENS

Though Paul affirmed that a new Covenant had come into being, a new Israel had emerged, he also affirmed that the old Covenant was still in existence, and the promises made by God to the Jews had never been abrogated. The Jews denied the existence of a new Covenant, yet the early church dwelt and grew within the precincts of the Synagogue. In the Roman empire, adherence to the state religion was required by law, and severe penalties were meted out to "atheists." Exempt from this obligation were only the specially recognized, licit religions. Judaism was a licit religion; Christianity, being new, was not, but it could exist within the Synagogue.

Nevertheless, Paul's teachings created tensions. The Jewish leaders could see a danger in it: Jews might break away from Mitzvot, Jewish peoplehood might be weakened. This tension grew with the fall of the Temple in the year 70 C.E. because of the danger to survival in which the Jews found themselves. Barriers had to be established. After the defeat of the Bar Kokhba rebellion, Hadrian proscribed the Jewish religion. Now the Christians, specifically the Gentiles among them, saw the need to distinguish themselves from the Jews: Their religion had nothing to do with Judaism. This may account for anti-Jewish expressions found in the New Testament. The Jews, on their part, discouraged the admission of converts, especially when they found informers among the newcomers. Animosity grew on both sides.

Soon Christianity greatly surpassed Judaism in numbers and political power. To those in search of a spiritual religion, both faiths opened a road of salvation. They were competitors. In search of a faith that would unify the populace, Constantine elevated Christianity to the religion of the state. The now-Christian state repressed Judaism, and the theologians provided the reasons and justifications for this action. The split was complete.

Out of their own experience of increasing oppression, the Jews came to cling with ever greater tenacity to their ancient conviction that the Messiah had not yet come. Had he come, there would be no more oppression and persecution. In affirmation of their will to survive, for their own sake and for the sake of the world and the coming of the Messiah, they held on to the laws of Torah with ever greater fervor and in *joy* of obedience. As Leo Baeck, rabbi and leader of German Jewry in the time of Hitler, pointed out, the Jews did not see in the Law a burden; they saw in Judaism "the religion of . . . divine law . . . that tells man what God demands of him, granting him the right of

determination and decision, demanding of him that he fulfill the will of God
. . ." (Leo Baeck, *The Essence of Judaism,* New York: Schocken, 1961; German
edition, *Das Wesen des Judentrems,* Frankfurt; Kaufmann, 1932, p. 296). This
law was received by an act of divine *grace.* There existed no contradiction
between law and grace; both were interwoven.

In Judaism, as we can see from the debates between Hillel and Shammai, two opinions can be equally regarded as "the word of the living God."
Christianity, however, was influenced to a greater degree by Hellenistic thinking. The Greeks asked for definitions, and nothing could both be and not be
at the same time. In this light, the Covenant of faith and the Covenant of Law
could not coexist as equals. Paul had to explain to his gentile listeners that the
new Covenant, the Covenant of faith, had superseded the other, the Covenant
of Law. From this viewpoint, if living under faith was freedom, then living
under the Law was being under a yoke. If Christianity was true, then Judaism
was no longer true; if Christianity was accepted by God, then Judaism was
outdated. This either-or theology caused and sustained the split to the present;
only now is it beginning to heal. Judaism, in contrast, is not bound by the
either-or. Christianity as a world religion has not been a theological problem
for it.

Modern Jewish theologians have placed Jesus within Judaism and the
pharisaic tradition; Martin Buber calls him his brother. The Jews in Jesus's
time, except for his close disciples, who must have interpreted Scripture differently, did not see in him the Messiah. This was natural and logical, for Jesus
did not bring about the predictions of the Jewish Scriptures regarding the time
of the Messiah (e.g., Isaiah 11). These have not yet come to pass, for the spirit
of universal love is not yet found in man and beast. The time of the Messiah
is for the Jew the time when God alone will rule in history. Faithful to Torah
and its qualifications of the Messiah, Jews cannot acknowledge Jesus as Messiah. But it was no crime for any individual to claim messiahship as a human
person. In the Jewish view, the Messiah is human.

With Paul, the Church moved out of the confines of Judaism. The
acceptance of Paul's message would have meant the end of the Covenant of
Torah and Mitzvot and the end of the Jewish people, with whom God had
made an eternal Covenant. With Paul, faith, as Jesus who lived in the spirit of
Torah held it, would have been transformed into faith *in* Jesus, as the Christ.
The concept of God becoming human was and is contrary to the Jewish
concept of God's absolute oneness and absolute transcendence.

This has led to two widely divergent forms of monotheism. Jewish
monotheism is categorically unitarian; Christian monotheism is trinitarian.
Jews did not then, and do not now, consider themselves forerunners of a new,
Christian dispensation. Jewish Scriptures held no hint of such an event; Christianity later read into them predictions of Christ. In consequence, Jews and
Christians may at times read the same words of the Old Testament and understand them differently. Jews have felt that they have an abiding function in the

world under God's plan. Jews have held that the world is not redeemed but, in line with their messianic hope, it is redeemable, and humanity is God's co-worker in this task.

Yet Jews regard Christianity as vital under God's will. This permits the possibility of a dialogue—if each partner sees the worth of the other.

By its religious and ethical teachings, Christianity is of paramount importance in God's scheme for humanity's salvation. Maimonides, in the twelfth century, pointed this out. In the twentieth century, Franz Rosenzweig regards Christianity and Judaism as actually dependent on each other. Martin Buber has pointed to the fact that Christian faith—*pistis*—is weighted toward renewal through the rebirth of the individual, whereas Jewish faith—*emunah*— is weighted toward renewal through the rebirth of nations. We may have reservations in regard to this sharp distinction, but we can accept Buber's conclusion that the two religions may have things to say to each other as yet unsaid, and a help to give to one another whose blessed results cannot even be fully conceived at the present time (Buber, *Two Types of Faith,* New York: Harper & Row, Harper Torch Books, 1961).

Common Values

Our time has witnessed the resumption of the dialogue. The fruit-fulness of the dialogue will be enhanced by the ideals which Christians and Jews share—above all, the idea of One God, who is the God of love and mercy. "Have we not all one Father? Has not one God created us? Why then are we faithless to one another, profaning the covenant of our fathers?" the prophet Malachi cries out (Malachi 2:10). From the oneness of God as the Universal Father emerges the Covenant of human fellowhip. We may well regard it as significant that the two basic commandments of Torah regulating our re-lationship to God and humanity are literally repeated in the New Testament, thus strengthening the bond of common obligation. These commandments are: "You shalt love the Lord your God with all your heart and all your soul and all your might" (Deuteronomy 6:5; Matthew 23:37), and "You shalt love your neighbor as yourself" (Leviticus 19:18; Matthew 23:39).

Out of these and others which will be discussed, there springs the common challenge to establish God in this world, to do battle against injustice, to fight for human equality, as all people are created in the image of God and therefore are fellows. It should not be forgotten that Jews and Christians equally draw their spiritual sustenance from the books of the Bible, the so-called Old Testament.

Both religions have experienced persecution and have produced saints and martyrs by whose example humanity can learn steadfastness in faith. Judaism does not have saints in the manner of the Catholic Church, but it accords this title to those who laid down their lives "for the sanctification of God's Name."

Finding themselves ostracized and defamed for so many centuries, the Jews may also serve as witnesses to the world, proving that faith in God has the power to sustain human strength under the most adverse circumstances, that it can purify human hearts to overcome hate even against persecutors, and that it can safeguard emotional balance and equilibrium. Jews have stood the test of unrelieved adversity for longer periods than any other faith. By this experience, they can support the faithful of all religions in times of testing, whenever they may come.

4

THE WORLD OF "JEWISH MIDDLE AGES"

FROM THE AGE OF ROME TO THE AGE OF REASON

The medieval world was divided into two religiously oriented spheres of influence. As we have seen, the Roman Empire, extending through Western Europe as far as Britain, became Christianized in the fourth century. In the seventh century, Islamic influence spread from Arabia eastward to Babylonia, and westward across North Africa and into Spain. Migrating and settling within these two spheres, the Jews developed a number of varieties in customs and practices, including different pronunciations of Hebrew. These differences still exist, though they have not destroyed Jewish unity.

One group, following the road of the Roman Legions, settled in Italy, France, Germany, Britain, and eventually Eastern Europe. They established great centers of learning, particularly in Germany, and later in Poland and Russia. They are called **Ashkenasim** because it was assumed that the term *Ashkenas* in the Bible meant Germany. Their descendants constitute the majority of present-day Jewry.

The other group followed the advance of Islam and established settlements in North Africa and in Spain, making the latter a center of Jewish learning and of flourishing Jewish culture. This group is called **Sefardim**, the word *Sefarad* in the Bible being interpreted as meaning Spain. Their pronunciation of Hebrew has been adopted as the official one in the State of Israel and, as a result, will probably become universal among Jewry.

We shall return to these two groups after a consideration of the relation between Judaism and Islam.

The Impact of Islam

Islam, the religion of "submission" to God, emerged in the seventh century of the common era. Its founder was Mohammed (c. 570–632), one of the great ethical and religious personalities of history. He pondered deeply over the lack of true religion and morality he perceived among his people and felt the need to establish a new life for them on new religious foundations.

56

Mohammed was born in Mecca, in what is now Saudi Arabia, on the crossroads of trade between East and West. He had contact with both Jews and Christians and learned from them. Mohammed was also a visionary and a mystic. While contemplating in solitude, he received a revelation. God, through the angel Gabriel, called him and appointed him His prophet. From then on, divine revelation was granted him over a long period of time, and the message he received, as dictated by Mohammed to a faithful disciple, became the *Quran*, the Book of Recitation. To this day, the Quran is recited in a form of recitative, and large portions of it are learned by heart by faithful Muslims.

Immediately after his initial revelation, Mohammed began his ministry among the people of Mecca. But they did not listen to him; they jeered and persecuted him. He therefore decided to emigrate to the city of Medina. This migration, called *Hejra*, occurred in the year 622 C.E. and marks the year 1 in the Islamic calendar. In Medina, Mohammed succeeded. He established himself as master of a large following, allowing him to create a military strike force. Persuasion was reinforced by military action. The opponents were crushed. Eventually, Mohammed returned to Mecca, establishing it as the center of the new faith he had created.

Mohammed acknowledged his debt to Judaism and Christianity, both of which he regarded as genuine revelations of God, but for their own time. Both Jews and Christians had corrupted the will of God by their interpretation. Therefore God had sent him, Mohammed, to teach the true faith and set it down in the Quran. It was the final and unchangeable revelation, never to be surpassed. The fact that the Quran was revealed in Arabic was a sign that God's favor rested on the Arabs. The faithful were instructed to spread the faith and to establish—even by means of war—an empire in which religion, political power, and society formed one indissoluble union. Moved by the divine imperative, Muslims were to create an empire within the next hundred years that extended from Spain to India. In this empire, the members of other religions could be "tolerated," but they could never be given equal rights.

As the Quran—its principles and laws—is the final and ultimate word of God, Islamic faith is not open to evolution as are Christianity and Judaism. The primary additional source of authoritative teaching outside the Quran is *Hadith*, the utterances and practices of Mohammed in his everday life, as verified by authoritative tradition.

When Mohammed appeared on the scene of history, the Jews constituted a fully integrated community on the Arabian peninsula. Their style of life was the same as that of their neighbors. For example, they may have introduced the cultivation of the date palm into Arabia. Only their faith distinguished them from the rest of the population. Known as "the people of the book," they were admired by their neighbors for their religious steadfastness. Seeing himself as a new prophet, Mohammed was convinced that the Jews would accept his teachings, especially as they were held by the Arabs as a kindred people. The belief had developed that the Arabs were the descendants of Ishmael, while the Jews were the descendants of Isaac, both sons of Abraham (Genesis 16, 21). When the Jews resisted Mohammed's teachings, the conflicts that resulted led to killings and expulsions of Jews. Many went to Palestine. Originally, Mohammed had planned to make Jerusalem the center of his new faith, symbol of the continuity-in-evolution with Judaism. As the Jews rejected Islam, however, Mohammed decided to emphasize the break between the religions and chose Mecca as the permanent center of Islam.

In contrast to trinitarian Christian monotheism, Islam was unitarian monotheism, like Judaism. Mohammed preached unity: "O men, see, We [God] created you from one man and one woman, in order that you may know each other. . . . He who is greatest in reverence of God is the most honored of Allah [God] in your midst" (Quran, Sura [chapter] 49, entitled "The Chambers," verse 13). He emphasized the link between the faiths: "Speak you: We believe in Allah and His message to us, as He sent it to Abraham and Ishmael and Isaac and Jacob and the tribes, and as it was given to Moses and Jesus, and as it was given to the prophets from their Lord: We make no distinction among them" (2:136). He proclaimed that Jews and Christians need not be afraid on the Day of Judgment. "The possessors of Scripture shall have nothing to fear on the Day of Judgment" (2:59). He declared the food of Jews to be lawful to Muslims, as both observed dietary laws. And he permitted Muslim men to marry Jewish or Christian women (5). (A non-Muslim was not to marry a Muslim woman, however, for he would thereby attain dominance over her.) Converts were not to be won by force (2:257). In a Hadith, we find Mohammed stating that he himself will speak up against those that unduly wrong them and burden them (Balduri 162; Abbu Yussuf 71). One great chapter deals with the conception and birth of Jesus (Mary, Sura 19). In Sura 3, entitled "The House of Imran," we read: "the Messiah Jesus, son of Mary, is Allah's messenger and His word which he put in Mary and spirit of His spirit" (3:171).

Mohammed's hopes of winning the Jews to his new faith were not to be realized. To his chagrin, the Jews steadfastly refused to give up their religion, in spite of the fact that Mohammed had incorporated many Jewish ideas and laws in the Quran. Consequently, he turned against them with great vigor. Now he proclaimed that both Jews and Christians would be severely judged and condemned on the Day of Judgment (3:79). He regarded it as essential that Arabia and the Arabian people be united under one faith. Therefore, we find in the Quran an ambivalence in regard to both Jews and Christians—on the one hand, praising them for their adherence to the One God and His Scriptures, and, on the other hand, rebuking them for their unwillingness to accept Islam as the final and highest divine revelation, in which the messages of Moses and Jesus were both contained and transcended. Abraham became for Mohammed "not a Jew nor a Christian but a Muslim" (Sura 3), a man "submissive to God."

As Mohammed had found the Jews actively hostile in his direct contact with them, his judgment of Judaism became harsher than his position on Christianity. After Mohammed's death, his successors permitted the Jews

living in the ever-expanding Islamic sphere to remain and hold their possessions, but merely as "tolerated people." They were subjected to restrictions,
which varied according to the rulers. At times, these restrictions were very
severe. For instance, Jews were not permitted to ride on a horse in Yemen, lest
they look down on Muslims. The Muslims imposed distinguishing marks on
Jewish dress long before Christian Europe introduced the yellow badge and
"Jew hat." At times, zealous rulers would expel Jews from their territories.
Compared to the Jews in Christian lands, however, their fate was better.
Muslims could not accuse them of deicide (murder of God), as Christ was not
divine in Islamic tradition. Nor could they claim that the Talmud slandered
Muslims, as the Talmud had been completed by the time of Mohammed. In
addition, the rulers were frequently pragmatic; because they could benefit from
the abilities of Jews and could use their special taxes, there were some periods
of peace and prosperity for Jews in Islamic lands, especially in Spain. In the
Islamic heartland, Arabia, Jews were not permitted to live, nor are they allowed to enter today.

Islam has witnessed periods of great expansion, power, and wealth
alternating with periods of withdrawal and societal stagnation. It saw in victory
and success a sign of divine approval, in withdrawal and defeat a sign of divine
disfavor and rebuke, a mandate to redress the situation. It reached its highest
peak when political greatness led to cultural achievement. Baghdad in the ninth
and tenth centuries was not merely a city of splendor, it was also a center of
philosophy—the thought of Aristotle had become known and was synthesized
with Islamic revelation. Moorish Spain from the tenth to the thirteenth centuries left us magnificent works of art. Generally speaking, the periods when
Islamic political success was combined with intellectual and artistic achievements were good times for the Jews. They were valuable partners in an unfolding civilization, while, at the same time, Islamic orthodoxy was tempered
by a more universalistic outlook that found room for non-Muslims.

After a long period of stagnation and withdrawal, Islam has once again
moved into the center of history. The transition has been sudden and traumatic;
oil is the cause. Near Eastern oil has given it power, and its impact is deeply
felt both in Israel and throughout the world. It may well see in these gifts of
precious resources a sign of God's favor and with it a mandate to return to strict
compliance with the will of God. But the very blessing thus granted holds a
danger: Western, non-Islamic ideas and influences have penetrated the heartland of Islam, though they are held back by stern governmental measures.
Some Islamic thinkers have expressed deep apprehension that the impact of the
outside world may sweep like a wave over an unprepared society and draw it
into the sphere of materialistic ideology. Perhaps there will emerge out of the
encounter between Islamic tradition and Western values a new, Islam-centered
but universal, culture, inspiring both East and West and bringing about a true
flowering of Islam as world force making for peace. How such a goal may be
obtained by Islamic cooperation with the best Judaism and Christianity have to

offer may perhaps be demonstrated by the example of Jewry in Moorish Spain, which we will discuss in the next section. The fruits, reaped by all, were precious, the results enduring.

THE SEFARDIM

In the Islamic sphere, Jews theoretically were not considered equal to Muslims; in practice, particularly in Spain, they were free to participate in the fullness of political, social, cultural, and economic life. Many of them rose to high office at the court of the califs, the Islamic rulers, and used their position to safeguard the position of their brethren.

Living under Islamic rule, the Jews developed a flourishing Jewish culture and produced outstanding thinkers and leaders. The following brief sketches of some of these personalities may offer a glimpse of the conditions of Spanish Jewry and of Jewish reaction to non-Jewish civilization.

Jews had lived in Spain for centuries. Under Roman rule they were free, prosperous, and respected. Their peaceful life was disrupted by the invasion of Spain by Germanic peoples—first the Vandals and then the Visigoths, both of whom arrived in the fifth century. The Visigoths eventually became Christians and, with this change, the fate of the Jews turned from prosperity to persecution. But in the eighth century, the Arabs conquered the land, established a glittering civilization centering at Cordova, and granted the Jews new freedoms. The royal court became the center of art and thought, and many learned Jews flocked to it.

Hasdai Ibn Shaprut (912–961): Builder of Foundations

Hasdai was one of the Jews brought to the court, where he was royal physician and adviser. He established the foundations for the brilliant Jewish culture in Spain that was to synthesize Jewish heritage and the intellectual traditions of the Western world.

A Jewish scholar in his own right, Hasdai was burdened by the fact that Spanish Jewry, so deeply immersed in general culture, had not yet developed leaders of Jewish learning.

At just this time, one of the masters of the Babylonian academies, Moses ben Enokh, appeared on the scene. The ship on which he had been sailing had been seized by pirates, and he was captured. The Jews of Cordova ransomed him and entrusted him with the development of a Jewish academy. Thus was ushered in a period in Jewish history, lasting three centuries, which led Spanish Jewry to its greatest heights. Hasdai, the Jewish courtier, became spiritual founder of an era of glory. Hasdai's work rested on the work of Enokh, through whom the center shifted from Babylonia to Spain. Enokh was the basic teacher and Hasdai, a scholar himself, the developer.

At the time, as later, the Jews were frequently told mockingly that all their power and independence had forever vanished. No longer was there an independent Jewish state. Then Hasdai learned that around 740 the king and the entire nation of the Chazars, a people dwelling on the eastern shores of the Black Sea, had been converted to Judaism, and that this sovereign Jewish state was flourishing. After strenuous efforts, Hasdai received confirmation; it was indeed true. (However, the Chazars eventually intermarried with the rest of Jewry and disappeared as a distinct group.) Hasdai's discovery was to lead to a great theological work by Judah Halevi—the *Chuzari*, which will be discussed below.

Samuel the Prince: Power in Creative Service

The work so auspiciously started by Hasdai was carried forward by Samuel Hanagid. Like his predecessor, he never forgot the duty toward his fellow Jews that his high position entailed.

Samuel (993–1069), whom his people called ha-Nagid, the Prince, was born at Cordova and started his life as a dealer in spices. He rose to become the vizier of the king of Granada. He served his master well, giving the state an exceptional administration, and headed the royal troops victoriously as a general in battle. Yet he was also a Jewish scholar who wrote an introduction to the Talmud, a compendium of law, and interpretations of Scripture stressing that Torah and Mitzvot had to be established ever more firmly. Through correspondence with Jewry all over the world, the bond of kinship was maintained. Lavish gifts from Samuel went to scholars who needed them, in Spain as well as abroad, that they might carry on their work undisturbed. As Samuel showed, it was indeed possible to hold highest office in dedicated citizenship and, at the same time, be a Jew devoted to God-Torah-Mitzvot—and people. As master of his own talmudic academy, Samuel himself trained a generation of leaders to carry on his work.

Solomon Ibn Gabirol: Philosopher and Poet

Among Samuel's friends was the poet and philosopher Solomon Ibn Gabirol (1021–1069), who could both sing of wine and write majestic liturgical poems which have graced the worship of the synagogue. Gabirol was also versed in general philosophy and wrote a philosophical work, *The Fountain of Life*, in which he saw all the world emanating from God (similar to the neo-Platonic view). The work was translated into Latin—and so was the name of the author, from Gabirol to Avicebron. Up to the nineteenth century, the work was regarded as the writing of a non-Jewish scholar. Spanish Jewry had indeed effected a synthesis of general culture and Jewish tradition, of citizenship and deepest Jewish loyalty. Through the Jews, Greek thought came to Europe, translated from Greek to Arabic, to Hebrew, and to Latin.

Judah Halevi: Philosopher, Singer of Zion, Pilgrim

Judah Halevi (1080–1140) was a tender soul. Born in Toledo, he was attracted to medicine, as so many Jews have been drawn to this great profession which, in its entirety, is true Mitzvah, the healing of God's children. He was a man of great charm, a poet who sang of spring and beautiful women but found his true subject when he expressed his undying love, and the love of his people, for the Land of Israel:

> Zion, wilt thou not ask if peace's wing
> shadows the captives that ensue thy peace . . . ?
> Lo, west and east and north and south—worldwide—
> all those from far and near, without surcease
> salute thee, Peace and peace from every side.
>
> To weep thy woe my cry is waxen strong,
> but dreaming of thine own restored anew,
> I am the harp to sound for thee thy song.
> Thy God desired thee for a dwelling place
> and happy is the man whom He shall choose,
> and draw him nigh to rest within thy space.

Here is the call of the Land, with its force to form the fate of its people—if not as a reality, then as hope and aspiration.

In old age, Halevi left the comforts of his home in Cordova, where he had settled, to make his pilgrimage to the Holy Land. Legend will have it that he sank into the dust in adoration at the sight of the city of Jerusalem; a Bedouin galloping by crushed him under his horse's hoofs.

Halevi was also a philosopher. Taking the story of the Chazars as a framework for his discussion of Judaism, he related that the king of the Chazars, unhappy with his heathen religion, called in three sages, a Moslem, a Christian, and a Jew. The Jew convinced him of the value of Judaism, which offered Halevi the opportunity to expound the ideas of Judaism. The Jews are indeed God's chosen people, but chosen to serve humanity. They are the heart of humanity, beating for humanity as the heart beats within the body, according to the body's needs, suffering for it, and indispensable to it. Torah and Mitzvot are explained in this work of Halevi's—the *Chuzari*—and the kinship of the people is strongly emphasized. To this sense of kinship, Halevi—in poetry, life, and death—adds the Land of Israel as the force which, under God, has maintained the Jew as a guiding light and suffering servant of all humanity.

Moses Maimonides: Universal Genius

The most famous of all Spanish Jews was **Moses Maimonides** (1135–1204), a universal genius of whom it has been said that "from Moses (the Master of Sinai) to Moses (Maimonides) there was no man like Moses." In him we see clearly the interplay of internal and external forces that have shaped

Judaism and the Jews. At the time he was born in Cordova, Jewry found itself oppressed by a fanatic Islamic sect and was forced either to accept Islam or to emigrate. For ten years, Maimonides's family had to move from country to country, which gave the boy a chance to study under many masters. The Land of Israel drew Maimonides to spend some years there, but finally he settled in Fustat (Cairo), Egypt, where he was to become court physician and head of the Jewish community. In Cordova, city of his birth, a square bears his name, and a statue of recent date honors him; in Acre (Acco), Israel, the gate through which he entered is marked by a plaque; and at Tiberias, the grave, to which he supposedly was transferred in death, is shown. Legend has it that his body, placed on a leaderless donkey, was deposited by the animal at the place where his tomb is now found. God guided the animal's steps. Thus is marked his spiritual pilgrimage through the wisdom of Israel and the world to become the master of Judaism and one of the world's great philosophers.

Maimonides's first concern was preservation of Torah. In its behalf, he wrote a commentary to Mishnah, synthesizing Jewish thinking and Aristotelian philosophy. His "Eight Chapters" in explanation of the Sayings of the Fathers are still widely studied in popular courses; they fuse Aristotle's ethics with Jewish tradition. Being a systematic thinker, he tried to condense basic Jewish beliefs in a form of creed. Maimonides's creed came under attack immediately after his death. His critics held that Judaism cannot and should not be creedally confined. The critics held that Maimonides had followed Islamic and Christian examples, perhaps in response to the desire by contemporary Jews for a Jewish creed, which they wanted since the other religions had creeds. But his creed is still followed by traditional Jewry. It was later rendered in the form of a poem, the *Yigdal*, which is widely used as a hymn in public worship.

Maimonides's creed is expressed in thirteen basic beliefs:

1. That God alone is the Creator.
2. That He is absolutely One.
3. That He has no body or bodily shape.
4. That He is the first and the last.
5. That only to Him may we pray and to no other.
6. That the words of the Prophets are true.
7. That the prophecy of Moses is true, and that he is the father of all prophets.
8. That the Torah, now found in our hands, was given to Moses.
9. That this Torah is not subject to change, and that there will never be another Torah from the Creator.
10. That the Creator knows all the thoughts and deeds of man.
11. That He rewards and punishes according to the deed.
12. That the Messiah will come; though he tarry, I will expect him daily.
13. That the dead will be resurrected.

The power of his statement of principles is exemplified by the fact that the twentieth-century martyrs of the Warsaw ghetto went to their death with a hymn on their lips based on Maimonides's fundamentals of faith—"I believe." The eternal validity of Torah was thus impressed once again on the people.

Maimonides may have been motivated by Christian and Islamic affirmations of faith to write these Jewish principles of belief. He found it necessary to give his own people a similar creed. He maintained that even the average person, not schooled in philosophy, needs to have an awareness of God's character and providence.

Maimonides's second concern was Mitzvot. He underscored their social significance in addition to their spiritual one. Feeling that the law of the Talmud needed clarification and codification, he wrote a compendium of the entire Oral Torah, called *Mishneh Torah*, which, he felt, would enable anyone, especially a rabbi, to find authoritative answers quickly. It was a complete digest of Torah and Talmud, systematically arranged and rationally explained. There could be no doubt any more about the importance and the practice of Mitzvot.

His third work, *The Guide of the Perplexed*, shows the impact of his surroundings, and his own conviction that philosophy is necessary to reinforce the faith. It will be discussed in Chapter 15.

Open to all influences, Maimonides thus built the structure of Jewish life and learning on their synthesis. The inner forces he stressed—God-Torah-Mitzvot-Land—permit admission of external ones if they can be assimilated.

As noted, Maimonides was attacked for his ideas. The conflict, already underway at the time of his death, reached vast proportions immediately afterwards. Many of the rabbis, exclusively devoted to the study of the Talmud, saw in him too much of a rationalist, saw him as standing too much under Aristotle's influence. Others came to his defense. Communities became divided.

In scholarly circles, the debate is still going on. Was Maimonides of divided mind, traditionalist as author of Mishneh Torah, "Greek philosopher" as author of the Guide—or is his work of one cast? Whatever the answer, his influence on Jewish and Christian philosophy—including that of St. Thomas Aquinas—has been profound.

There were other great minds, exegetes, poets, world travelers, and mystics who reached out to the divine beyond. The few we have mentioned offer a picture of the greatness that was Spanish Jewry's.

Christian Conquest: the Inquisition

As the Christians pushed slowly forward, dislodging the Moors, the lot of Spanish Jewry deteriorated. At first, Jews still served as royal counselors in the newly established Christian kingdoms, but the task of protecting their brethren became harder and harder. In 1233, the Inquisition was introduced in Aragon, directed by the newly created order of Dominicans.

In 1263, the leading rabbi of the time, Moses Nahmanides, was compelled to engage in a public disputation with the Dominican friar Pablo, a converted Jew, on the question "Has the Messiah come, or has he not yet come?" Nahmanides knew he could not be permitted to win the argument, which was conducted in the presence of king and court at Barcelona; the cards were stacked against him. He even pleaded with his opponents to stop the event, from which he foresaw only evil for his people, but this was not permitted. A few years later, Nahmanides left Spain, which he had loved, and went to the Land of Israel.

Expulsion from Spain

Jews had to listen to Christian sermons even in their own synagogues. Popular opinion turned against them, and the rabble rose. In 1492, after expelling the last of the Moors and uniting the territory, King Ferdinand and Queen Isabella decreed the expulsion of the last remnant of infidels, the Jews, from Spain. (Estimates of the number expelled range from 100,000 to 800,000; the most generally accepted number is about 250,000.)

Only converts could remain, and many Jews accepted Christianity as a veneer, practicing their faith in secret. This was extremely dangerous, for to have once accepted Christianity and turned from it was apostasy. On the slightest suspicion, the Inquisition would swoop down on those suspected of being secret Jews, extract confession through torture, and have them burned at the stake. The people in general distrusted the converts, calling them *marranos*, dirty fellows. Surviving in spite of it all, some of the descendants of the marranos in Spain reemerged openly as Jews only in the twentieth century. It has been claimed that even Columbus may have been a marrano, though the proofs are inconclusive. In any case, he speaks in his diaries with great compassion of the departing Jews, whose rickety boats he passed on his way toward a new world.

This was the end of Spanish Jewry as such, but the Spanish government of today favors the return of the Sefardim, once Spanish citizens, who may wish to claim their citizenship right. Jewish congregations have been officially recognized ever since the days of the Spanish Republic, and, in the spirit of Vatican II, have even engaged in some early stages of dialogue with the Church. The edict of 1492, expelling the Jews and prohibiting them from settling in Spain, was finally revoked officially in 1969, 477 years after it had been issued.

Unity through Law: Joseph Karo

The fugitives expelled by Ferdinand and Isabella settled in Holland, Turkey, and other countries, all of which profited from their abilities. Some groups went to Palestine, others to the colonies of the new world. Seeing the distress of a dispersed and persecuted Jewish community, a leading rabbi in Palestine strove to establish a central rabbinical body there, a Sanhedrin, to unite the people around Torah and Land. He failed, but one of his disciples, *Joseph Karo* (1488–1575), succeeded in a different way. Joseph Karo, born in Spain, experienced the expulsion of Spanish Jewry as a child. He grew up in Turkey where he eventually established a great reputation as a talmudic scholar and attracted many disciples. Karo was also a mystic. The Mishnah became for him a person, speaking to him and guiding his daily actions. Mystical longing made him settle in the Holy Land. He recognized the need for a unifying bond and found it in Mitzvot. He wrote a code, the *Shulhan Arukh*, The Well-Prepared Table, outlining in every detail the minutiae of Jewish law. With additions and adjustments to Ashkenasic usage (by Moses Isserles, 1530–1572), it became and has remained *the* code of traditional Jewry.

THE ASHKENASIM

In the destiny of Ashkenasic Jewry we see reflected the struggles and conflicts of kings and popes, of nationalism against the universal Church, of Renaissance, Reformation, and Enlightenment, of social unrest and political revolution.

Medieval Society and Spirit and The Jews

The destiny of the Jews in Northern Europe, the Ashkenasim, can be fully understood only against the background of medieval society as a whole. For the Jews, it was a time of great hardship. While we may speak of the Middle Ages as beginning with the collapse of the Roman Empire and ending with the Renaissance of the sixteenth century, the Jewish condition in Western Europe remained unchanged until the eighteeenth century. As far as Jewry was concerned, the Middle Ages began to recede in the West only with the Age of Reason; in the East some conditions still bear medieval character. "Jewish Middle Ages" is therefore not identical with the Middle Ages as commonly understood.

During the first Christian centuries, the Roman Empire was able to contain the pressure of Nordic nations pushing against its borders. Strong fortifications, from England to the Black Sea, kept the barbarians out. In the fourth century, the pressure became an avalanche. Pushed by the Huns who had come from the Far East, the Germanic tribes were on the move. In the great upheaval, Rome collapsed, and with it Greek and Roman civilization fell. Up to around 800 C.E., Western Europe dwelt in a twilight zone, politically and culturally. Cities disappeared, trade and commerce ceased, nations displaced one another, and warfare was universal. Christianity made gradual inroads into the chaos—without it there would have been no culture at all.

Eventually, Europe emerged from these "dark ages." With the exception of Spain, which had been conquered and developed by the Moors, it had become Christian.

Medieval society had several distinguishing features. Molded by Christianity during its early years, it became saturated with religion: Faith and life were one. There was no action, object, or thought of an individual or of society as a whole that was not permeated by Christian faith and correlated with Christ and salvation. Medieval people were generally uneducated and their thinking simple; they needed concreteness in every concept and idea and saw all contrasts in black and white. Consequently, every person and group was neatly placed in a definite category, according to the scheme of God. Kings were divinely ordained and, under the feudal system, stood at the head of a hierarchy of Christian knights and nobles. Yet the system did not work. Central power was too weak, especially in the Holy Roman Empire; consequently, there was constant warfare and endless power struggle. Society was Christian and closed; the craft guilds rigidly controlled; the peasants poor, ignorant, and oppressed.

To spread its message throughout this society, the Church appealed to senses and emotions. Everything in life and world became a symbol. Locked in conflict, moved by emotions, unable to see nuances, medieval people lived a life of uncertainty and violence.

Up to the close of the eleventh century, while culture was still plastic, the life of Jews was comparatively undisturbed. The Church did teach, then and later, that Jews had to survive in order to give by their own dejected status evidence of the Church's victory. The Jews were accursed for having crucified Christ, the Church taught, but they would eventually accept Christ. Then, in the end, the curse would be removed from them, as it would be removed immediately from any Jew at any time as soon as he accepted Christianity. The Jews therefore had a place in the scheme of the Church. Oppression against them was dogmatically founded, and it was pragmatically desirable to motivate them toward conversion. At the same time, they demonstrated to Christians the fate of "the enemies of Christ."

The harsh principles of the Church's teaching, however, were mitigated by the practical necessities of life. Many rulers, both spiritual and temporal, needed an element in society able and dedicated to promote trade and commerce. The nobility regarded engaging in trade as beneath their dignity and had no skill for it; the peasantry was wholly uneducated. The Jews could read and write and had international contacts with their coreligionists, with whom they could also communicate in a common language, Hebrew. Because they were thus equipped to fill this function, Jews were frequently invited to settle in a kingdom or community and were even given privileges. They were outside the Christian life but related to it, and they had a definite place within society. They, in turn, adopted the language and customs of this society and often established friendly relationships with some of their Christian neighbors.

The Crusades brought a radical change for the worse. By the end of the eleventh century, the "infidel" Turks were firmly in possession of the holy places of Christianity in Palestine. The Church, regarding itself strong enough to dislodge them, called for an armed reconquest, under the sign of the cross, of the Holy Land. But crusades were conducted not only against the Moslems in Palestine; they were also organized against nonconformist Christian sects, heretics, and other enemies of the Church.

In 1096, as the First Crusade began, religious fervor and emotions rose to fever pitch. Overheated imagination endowed the "enemies of Christ" with devilish traits—they had to be exterminated. The Jews fared ill under those conditions.

Christianity came to be locked in battle against the infidels, both in Palestine and in Spain. Now it took an emotional view of the Jews, the infidels in its own midst: They were demons, the brood of Satan, the Antichrist. Fiery sermons were preached against them from the pulpits of churches and cathedrals, and it was foretold by theologians that the person of the Antichrist would emerge from their midst. They were the incarnation of evil and were compelled to show it in their dress in order that their role might be publicly and symbolically recognized. Their lives were insecure. When emotion roused the masses to violence—as, for instance, during the Black Death of 1349—they might attack whomever they thought "guilty." Scourging themselves publicly, while traveling through the land, stirring passions, calling for repentance, the "flagellants" of 1349 turned against the clergy. But, inevitably, attacks on the Jews were part of every agitation, whether large or small. The tenor of the times was violent; victims were numerous and varied, but the Jews were always among them.

During the Renaissance, ecclesiastical and temporal authorities felt that contact with Jews might further weaken the already frayed fabric of faith; they had to be sequestered.

It is remarkable that, in spite of these conditions, relationships between Christians and Jews were often friendly, and cultural ties of mutual influence existed.

The Fate of Ashkenasic Jews

The Jews may well have come to Germany with the Roman legions; first documentary proof of an established Jewish community goes back to 321 C.E. By the time of Hitler's efforts to exterminate them, the Jews had lived in Germany longer than any other ethnic group. They presented to the German people an opportunity to establish a true spirit of justice, for these Jews demanded but one thing; to be permitted to live as human beings in the full expression of their religious tradition. That Germany failed to live up to this ethical challenge is one of its greatest tragedies.

In the beginning, the Jews were treated well. When Charlemagne consolidated his empire (800–814), he treated them kindly, and we find a Jew named Isaac among the delegation the emperor sent to Harun al-Rashid, the calif of Baghdad. Isaac, the only one to return, having survived the rigors of the journey, brought back an elephant as a gift from the calif to Charlemagne; the animal, previously unknown in Germany, created a sensation.

At that time, the Jews were welcome in Germany, where they served as merchants, providing the link between the farmers and the nobility, a position they also held in other countries. Permitted to own real estate, they established stately homes when their means permitted it.

The famous Calonymus family, from which great scholars, poets, mystics, and saints were to emerge, was called by the German emperor— perhaps Otto I, the Great, Emperor of the Holy Roman Empire of the German Nation (ruled 936–973)—from Lucca (in Italy) to Mainz probably between 917 and 990. They were granted the right to exhibit the imperial eagle as a sign of the emperor's favor. The pillar on which it was shown was destroyed during an air raid in World War II, but photographs exist. It has a medallion with the emperor's portrait, beneath which a humble man, unclad, offers his homage on bended knees. Thus did the family acknowledge their debt to their imperial master, who was the source of their food, shelter, and clothing, and to whom they felt deeply obligated in love and heartfelt allegiance. These were, indeed, years of well-being for the Jews.

As the fervor and the worldly ambitions of the Church increased, the status of the Jews declined. The call for stricter enforcement of Church law and for a tightening of discipline emerged from a monastic order at Cluny, France. As the "Cluniac reforms" of 910 included a strong prohibition of money trade by Christians, the Jews were pressed into it.

The Crusades marked the turning point in the fate of the German Jews; thereafter they were oppressed. Many crusaders felt that, before going to the Holy Land to free it from the infidels, they might as well start with those who lived among them—the Jews. This also promised rich loot. The Jews in the Rhenish cities of Mainz, Speyer, and Worms, mother cities of Jewry, fought valiantly, but they were overcome by the hordes and preferred to die rather than give up their faith. Thousands perished.

Their lives became most precarious with the decrees of the Lateran Council of 1215. Pope Innocent III, who saw himself as supreme head and arbiter of all Christianity, determined to plunge the Jews into shame, degradation, and despondency. As an accursed race, they had to wear on their breasts the yellow badge of outcasts, and on their heads a cone-shaped hat, the horn of the devil, whose brood they were (see p. 68). This made them easy prey for their tormentors. Seclusion and persecution were officially ordered.

Emperors and kings considered the Jews their personal property, forcing them to engage in money lending, which was considered illegal for Christians by religious law of the time. This suited the Christian businessmen, who had by now acquired the skill to engage in all other branches of trade, and who thus insisted that Jews be pushed out of the trades. The craft guilds never accepted them, which prevented them from pursuing the crafts. As money lenders, the Jews served the rulers as "sponges to be squeezed out." They might enrich themselves for a while; then their goods were expropriated. A ruler might give the Jews of a town as a "gift" to a vassal or a community, which meant that the Jews' belongings were surrendered to the "receiver." They might even be driven out, naturally leaving everything behind. Or the debts owed them by Christians might be cancelled by order of the ruler.

Forced to borrow from the Jews, and at high rates, the population naturally developed a deep animosity against them, often attacking them in mob action. The rates were high because the risks were great. Funds had to be available for unexpected demands, and the rulers did not care how the Jews accomplished this—they merely insisted on having needed funds in full and immediately.

The Jews learned to know the precariousness of worldly possessions. Every child from earliest youth had to recite: "The Torah, and the Torah alone, is the [assured] heritage of the congregation of Jacob." Nothing else was secure. Such conditions knitted the Jews closely together. The wealthy Jews of today might be homeless fugitives tomorrow; thus they would give hospitality to any Jew who knocked at their door. When communities needed Jews again, they would invite those they had driven away only yesterday to come back and settle—for a while. It was a sad merry-go-round.

Eventually, Christian bankers in many lands began to ignore the prohibitions of the Church and set up money lending on a grand scale, taking even higher rates of interest. The Jews were pushed out, to be permitted money lending only on the lowest level, or trade in old clothes; this was all that was left to them. When they were no longer needed as money lenders, they were expelled from the country altogether.

Vicious slanders were spread about the Jews. One of the worst was the accusation that they were using the blood of Christian children for the Passover service. A similar accusation had been leveled against the early Christians by those who did not understand the character of the Mass, the transubstantiation of the wine into the blood of Christ: Christians had been accused of killing heathens to obtain their blood for communion. Now Christians used against the Jews the very slander from which they themselves had suffered so much. The popes raised their voices to proclaim the falseness of this accusation, and to prohibit it, but the mob would not listen. Jews were accused of desecrating the sacred host, thus attacking Christ. It did not matter that the Jews did not believe in transubstantiation and the sanctity of the host, and that such a desecration, which implied acknowledgment of this sanctity, would be meaningless and never occur to them. The slander persisted and claimed its victims.

England, France, and Germany

Among the places where the accusation of using Christian blood in the Passover service was used to incite the population was Lincoln, England

(1255). The relationship of king and people to the Jews became so difficult that the Jews were finally expelled from the country altogether, in 1290, only a few years after the incident.

It is not surprising that there were Jews who escaped by becoming Christians; in fact, it is remarkable that there were so few of them. Some of these converts, in order to justify their actions, now became rabid Jew-haters and ardent missionaires among Jews. Realizing that Torah was the source from which Jewish strength was renewed, they vented their hatred against it (not against the Scriptures, which were shared by the Christians, but against Oral Torah, the Talmud). The Talmud was accused of containing anti-Christian statements. One such accusation led to the public burning of carloads of precious manuscripts in France (1242). Singled out by this public condemnation of their holiest treasures and branded as bearers of a hostile outlook based on subversive teachings, the Jews came to be regarded by the people not only as anti-Christian but as enemies of the emerging nationalism.

As people in France rose against the burdens of taxation (induced, they felt, by the Jewish money lenders with their alien spirit), the king appeased them by expelling the Jews from French soil (1394). Only in the papal province of Avignon were they permitted to remain. The expelled Jews now sought homes in Germany and Poland. A few years before the events in France, a terrible fate had befallen Jews throughout Europe. In 1349, the Black Death swept over Europe, leaving death and destruction in its wake and stirring the downtrodden masses to rebellion against their fate. Again, the Jews became scapegoats. They were accused of poisoning the wells and were massacred or expelled. Many of them left Germany forever to find a new haven in hospitable Poland, which needed their skills. This was the beginning of large-scale settlement there. They did not know how short-lived their peace was to be.

A great many Jews remained in Germany, however. This was possible because the Jews were considered personal property of the Emperor, who could squeeze them out whenever he pleased. In 1356, the "Golden Bull" established the election procedures for the imperial office. Seven electors (the highest dignitaries of the Empire, both spiritual and temporal lords) had the right to elect the emperor. In this bull, the Jews residing in the territories of the electors were turned over to the electors as their "property" with full right of exploitation.

After the Black Death, many states and cities were glad to accept the Jews back, a privilege for which the Jews had to pay heavy admission fees and annual fees for the renewal of their residence privileges. But now they had to dwell within a separate district, a few small streets, entered through gates that were closed at night—the *ghetto*. Since this ghetto could not be enlarged with the growing population, story had to be built upon story in crowded quarters, until the very light of the sun was practically excluded, even as the Jews' contact with nature had long been cut off. (They could not become farmers, and could not even venture into the countryside without risk.)

Masters of the Ashkenasic Community

Like Sefardic Jewry, the Ashkenasim produced great masters. A few of them shall be discussed briefly because they are of abiding importance.

The work of these masters reflects their concern with Jewish survival under conditions of ever-increasing segregation and isolation. Great inner strength was required to withstand the indignities imposed upon them; the Jewish community had to strengthen its conviction that it was the congregation of the Covenant and had to deepen its solidarity. Deeper immersion in Torah and Mitzvot were the answer. Philosophy was not part of the endeavor, not only because Jews were isolated from the rest of the cultural world, but because

Synagogue at Worms, Germany, interior, originally built in 1034, destroyed by the Nazis in 1942 and reconstructed. Note the Bimah in the center of the room, the Ark and curtain on which the seven-branched Menorah is embroidered (of recent date), the candles of the Hanukkah candelabrum, and the eternal light over the Ark. Some of the great Ashkenasic masters mentioned in this chapter prayed here. (Photo by the author.)

they *wished* to remain isolated from its stream and its influences. Thus the outlook and works of the Ashkenasim differ from those of Spanish Jewry.

Each of the masters whom we shall mention may be regarded as a representative of the various facets in the total effort to arm Jewry against the forces of adversity and disintegration, to strengthen within it the awareness of being the Sons of the Covenant. Under the leadership of these personalities and their families, disciples, and academies, the cities of Speyer, Worms, and Mainz (abbreviated Sh-U-M to signify the unity of the three cities as teaching centers) became centers of Talmud study and authoritative decisions for Western Jewry.

The Calonymus Family: Scholars, Poets, Martyrs, and Mystics

The house of Calonymus, mentioned previously, used its wealth and prestige to develop academies of learning. Its outstanding representative, Rabbi Calonymus Ben Meshullam (eleventh century) of Mainz, is the author of one of the greatest liturgical poems of Jewish literature, expressing the holiness of the Days of Awe and acclaiming God as supreme Judge, who decrees human destiny but is ever ready to accept repentance, prayer, and deeds of love in expiation of any sin (see also p. 78 ref.). Thus the poet held out to his people the assurance of God's love in spite of "severe decrees," and His acceptance of their repentance. Calonymus's son and grandson were given the right to settle in Speyer (1090), where they established a house of learning. Judah, another member of the family who arrived later from Italy, died at the height of the Crusades (1200). He lived both in Worms and in Ratisbon and moved in a somewhat different direction from the rest of his family, immersing himself in prayer and mysticism. His response to life was escape into a world other than the one that was so unhappy. He was called Judah Ha-Hasid, Judah the Saint (mystic), and through him the mysticism of *Hasidism* (see pp. 81, 82, 86 ff.) found a foothold in Europe, to be transplanted and given new appeal by the Hasidim of later Poland.

Gershom ben Judah: Master Mind and Legislator

During the years 960–1040, Gershom ben Judah was head of the Academy of Mainz. So great was his prestige that he became known as the "Light of the Diaspora," and so great was the prestige of his school that its ordinances were accepted as binding by all of Western Jewry. He ruled that no one might read a letter not addressed to him and that no woman might be divorced against her will; he prohibited polygamy, which had long been discarded but not yet legally outlawed; and he trained many disciples.

Rashi, the Giant: The Commentator Who Unlocked Torah and Talmud

Out of Gershom's school and the academy of Worms emerged the most important of all medieval Jewish scholars, Rabbi Solomon ben Isaac, abbreviated **Rashi** (1040–1105). He opened for his people the treasure house of Torah and Talmud; without his commentary, the Talmud would be for us a closed book. Born at Troyes, France, he spent his youth studying in the cities on the Rhine. He returned home to a small vineyard and wine business, by which he made a living, and to the academy he headed without accepting any remuneration for the work. Returning to France just in time to escape the massacre of the First Crusade, he died in the town of his birth.

In the simplest words and utter clarity of style, Rashi wrote a commentary to both the Bible and the Talmud, following them sentence by sentence, clarifying obscure passages, analyzing the text, elucidating its meaning. Sometimes he would even translate difficult words into the French spoken by the Jews, a sign of their adjustment to their surroundings. Unlike modern commentators, Rashi did not have at his disposal the results of critical scholarship or of archaeology and comparative linguistics. He saw Torah as the divine word and explained it by clarifying difficult terms and sentences, often by referring to the Aramaic versions of the Scripture. Above all, he brought in the Aggadah and Midrash of the Talmud in simple, condensed form to elucidate the deeper meaning of the text as the rabbis had understood it.

Recognizing the importance of Rashi, posterity has seen in his abbreviated name the contraction of another three words: *R*abban *s*hel *Y*israel, the Teacher of Israel. His commentary was to be influential in Christian circles as well. Nicholas de Lyra (ca. 1270–1340) studied Rashi's work extensively. De Lyra, a Franciscan, was professor of theology at the Sorbonne, and his fifty-volume work *Postillae Perpetuae* was a running commentary to all the books of the Old and New Testaments. He was famous and widely read during the Middle Ages. De Lyra studied especially Rashi's Bible commentary, and his work, in turn, became Luther's guide in his translation of Scripture. Rashi's clear explanation may well have put doubt in many minds regarding the interpretation of the Roman Catholic Church, thus contributing to the spirit that led to the Reformation.

Tosafot: Rashi's Descendants and Supercommentators

During the twelfth and thirteenth centuries, the masters of the French schools wrote additional commentaries, based on Rashi, analyzing specific points in the Talmud; these are called **Tosafot**, additions. Every edition of the Talmud contains Rashi's commentary on the inside margin of every page and Tosafot on the outside margin.

Rabbi Meir of Rothenburg: Thwarted Escape to Palestine

In 1286, a great rabbi, Rabbi Meir of Rothenburg, who had cried out in bitter elegy at the burning of the Talmud, decided to migrate to Palestine; there alone could Torah be developed, for "the air of the Land makes wise," while in Germany there were only trials. Meir failed; he was recognized and captured during his journey and was imprisoned for ransom by order of the Emperor Rudolph von Hapsburg. Meir forbade his people to pay it lest a precedent be established and more rabbis be captured for ransom. He spent seven years in confinement, and then the ransom had to be paid anyway—for his body.

Rabbi Mordecai ben Hillel: The Martyr

Meir's disciple, Rabbi Mordecai ben Hillel, decided that Mitzvot must be emphasized to provide stability among the physically rootless, and he proposed a code. He died a martyr's death at Nuremberg in 1289.

Rabbi Asher ben Yehiel: The Escape Succeeds—
Code of Law as Unifying Force

Mordecai's colleague, Rabbi Asher ben Yehiel, succeeded in escaping to Spain, thus linking the Ashkenasic tradition to the Sefardic. Synthesizing the work of the German and Spanish masters, he and his son Jacob completed the proposed code, calling it *Turim*, "Rows," after the four rows of precious stones in the breastplate of the high priest; Mitzvot are the precious stones. It was a four-volume work. Joseph Karo based his *Shulhan Arukh* on both Maimonides and the Turim. Writing his work in Palestine, Karo thus symbolizes the unity of the Jewish people through Mitzvot and Land.

Rabbi Moses Isserles: Ashkenasic Religious Practices

Customs and practices (**Minhagim**) vary among Jews in various lands as they are based on the interaction of outward and inward forces of environment and tradition. Hence a supplement had to be written to the *Shulhan Arukh* for Ashkenasic Jewry. This important work was done by Rabbi Moses Isserles.

Rabbi Moses Isserles (1530–1572) lived in Cracow, Poland. At his own expense, he established and headed a talmudic academy and, in spite of his youth, became so widely recognized that rabbis from far away consulted him for authoritative answers to questions on Jewish law. He called his supplementary notes to the Shulhan Arukh "Mappah," the tablecloth, for Karo's Well-Prepared Table.

RENAISSANCE AND REFORMATION

The Renaissance did not bring much change in the conditions of the Jews.

Italian Jews, from the distance of their ghetto shared in the cultural revival of the time, and their ideas came to the attention of many influential scholars. The newly invented art of printing aided the spread of Jewish works. But the general position of Jewry on the continent did not improve. Actually, the ghetto in Italy was established at this time. The fact that Jews were sequestered in a ghetto may be explained by the fear of the Catholic Church that the spirit of the Renaissance, which had led to the Reformation, might lead the people toward new heretical concepts out of their contacts with the Jews. The Jews had to be sequestered. Pope Leo X, the humanist, did, however, order the printing of the Talmud because he felt that ancient literature ought to be preserved.

In Germany, as in Italy, the humanist movement sparked the interest of Christian scholars in Hebrew, the Hebrew Bible, and Jewish literature, including Jewish mysticism and especially the works of the Kabbalah. A courageous humanist, Johannes Reuchlin (1455–1522), at great personal risk, defended the books of postbiblical Jewish literature against an accusation by Johannes Pfefferkorn, a Jew who had converted to Christianity. Pfefferkorn agitated that these Jewish works contained attacks against Christianity and should be suppressed. Reuchlin, who had a direct acquaintance with some of the Hebrew originals, refuted him. It was a bitter struggle. Maintaining that the Jews should be converted to Christianity, Reuchlin nevertheless opposed persecution as the method for doing so, and proposed kindly persuasion instead. Reuchlin called for protection of the Jews, as they were members of the Holy Roman Empire, that is, the German empire. Reuchlin's pattern of thought is reflected in that of Martin Luther, his contemporary.

Martin Luther (1483–1546), like Reuchlin, was a man of great courage, committed to his ideas and ideals, which he drew from the study of the original texts of Holy Scripture. Regarding the Jews, he felt that persuasion would bring them into his fold, especially as he had purified and reformed Christianity. At the outset of his activity, therefore, he favored the Jews, in the hope that they would join his movement. (Here we recognize a similarity to Mohammed.) When they refused, Luther (again like Mohammed) turned viciously against "The Jews and Their Lies" (1546). By doing so, Luther added to his doctrines a spirit of hatred for the Jews: " . . . burn their synagogues, destroy their houses, seize their possessions, confiscate their writings, forbidding them by pain of death to teach or hold services, denying them safe conduct; force them to work, and treat them with all unmercifulness. . . . " He admonished the princes to "expel the hardened blasphemers." All this was to occur in Germany 400 years later.

Luther's theology and thought contained two elements that were to bring the greatest suffering to the Jews: The first were these anti-Jewish utterances of his later years, which influenced many adherents of his church. The second was his insistence that only faith and not works brings salvation, and that the Lutheran church in all temporal matters had to obey the rulers. In Nazi times, the church therefore spoke up only when its own faith was threatened by the government and the faith of its people was being attacked. It did not take a stand against the un-Christian, murderous actions of the Nazi rulers against the Jews, a stand that might have had some effect. This historical background may shed light on some facets of German anti-Semitism.

In 1934, while Nazi power was in ascent, a group of Protestant leaders met in convention at Barmen, declaring that their allegiance was to Christ alone. At this synod, the "Confessional Church" was organized in opposition to the official Protestant-Lutheran Church, which had become nazified. The Confessional Church resisted the incursion of Nazi doctrine. Karl Barth, perhaps the greatest Protestant theologian of the twentieth century, was its guiding spirit and drafted the platform. As late as 1967, Barth revealed that he had always reproached himself for not introducing "the Jewish question" as one of the planks, although he ruefully added that such a text would not have been accepted in 1934, considering the participants' outlook on the Jews. To its honor, the Lutheran church has publicly confessed this error, calling itself to repentance. It has repudiated Luther's anti-Jewish teachings; in large measure the church's contrition is due to Barth's influence.

Only in England do we find a decided change in the status of the Jews as a result of the Reformation. Oliver Cromwell became convinced by his study of Scripture that Christ would not return until Jews were spread out over all parts of the world; hence they had to come to England again. Negotiation with a Dutch Rabbi, Manasseh ben Israel, eventually led to the formal declaration (1655) that there was nothing in English law preventing their settlement on English soil. This marks the beginning of the modern Jewish community in Great Britain.

In spite of their trials, the Jews kept their faith, their mental balance, their sense of humor, and even their contact with the world. Never knowing how long a family might remain together, they deepened its spirit. Never certain if the precious manuscript they owned might be burned tomorrow, they immersed themselves in its contents, the study of Torah. Never assured that their possessions might not be taken away at a moment's notice and they themselves uprooted overnight, they gave help and hospitality to fugitives from other areas. Through Torah and Mitzvot, in the fervent hope that the Messiah might come at any time to restore them to the freedom of their land, they retained their emotional equilibrium. This in itself is proud evidence of the power stored in the Jewish heritage, environment, and tradition.

Commitment to Custom: Maharil

By the fifteenth century, the customs of German Jewry had already diverged from those of Polish Jewry. The rabbis of the period collected these customs and ruled on their performance. Rabbi Jacob Levi Moelln (also called in abbreviated form *Maharil*), who died in 1427, established these Minhagim as valid guides to practice. He was also an accomplished cantor (singer of liturgy) and ruled that the traditional tunes, which spoke of the yearnings of centuries, could not be changed—especially those of the high holy days, to which people had become accustomed. His own city of Mainz abided by this rule most faithfully, so that modern cantors who had been trained in the standard tunes, had to undergo a special training to acquire the special melodies used in the community. Transmitted by ear, these songs are unhappily going to be lost unless German Jewry, now overaged and in danger of extinction within a few generations, is replenished through immigration.

A distinct difference thus developed, in such customs as Jewish music, between Eastern European and Western European Jewry. These differences increased the difficulties Eastern European Jews encountered when they began to settle in large numbers both in Western Europe and in America and created conflicts between the two groups.

Cooperation amid Uncertainty

It would be a mistake to assume that, because Jewish life was uncertain, it was unrelieved sorrow. Although legal ordinances continued to isolate the Jews, cultural cross-currents that influenced both Jews and Christians point to an interchange on the popular level. The Jews spoke the language of their environment—for example, German, which was to develop into Yiddish, and French, as is seen in the Rashi commentary, where the author translated difficult Hebrew words into the vernacular. The Jewish mystics drew widely from Christian mystical thought. From the Church, the Jews took the Yahrzeit's light (the light kindled at the anniversary of a parent's death). From the Synagogue, the Church derived the Dies Irae of the Requiem Mass; it is based on Rabbi Calonymus's poem for Rosh Hashanah (see pp. 73 and 295). Because the Jews were excluded from the craft guilds, Christian artists fashioned the silver ornaments for Torah and the valuable candlesticks and kiddush cups for religious use.

The Jews could read and write, and this alone made them a necessary agent in a society where usually only clerics mastered these skills. In the thirteenth century, the Jews even produced a "minnesinger," who, like his most famous contemporary, Walter von der Vogelweide, traveled from court to court, entertaining great lords and ladies with his songs of love and chivalry. His name was Süsskind von Trimberg.

The conditions of Jewry varied with the principalities in which they lived and the attitude of the princes. In periods of relative ease, the Jews enjoyed wearing fine clothes, and dance houses were found in practically every Jewish community.

EASTERN EUROPEAN JEWRY

The fate of Polish and Russian Jewry appears like a condensed version of Jewish destiny throughout history, ranging from well-being to abysmal suffering.

Migration to Poland began with the Crusades, as conditions in Germany became unbearable for many Jews, and increased with subsequent peaks of persecution, such as during the Black Death, when escaping Jews in great masses streamed eastward. The rulers of Poland welcomed them, although the Catholic Church disliked them intensely.

The Polish kings saw the economic advantages that the Jews could bring to an undeveloped Poland, badly in need of a middle class of merchants. They took the Jews under their protection as their own "property," allowed them to settle throughout the land next to the Christian inhabitants, and accorded them freedom of movement and of enterprise. Subsequent centuries saw the Jews as pawns in the struggle between kings and Church: If the Church found itself powerful enough to have its will prevail, the Jews suffered; if the kings prevailed, opposing the Church in their own effort to retain absolute power, the lot of the Jews was happier.

In general, the status of the Jews deteriorated rapidly. The native population had neither a fully developed language nor a culture. The Jews, therefore, retained their German language, transforming it into **Yiddish**, and their German garb, the *caftan*. Their culture was that of Torah. Recognized as aliens and regarded, therefore, with suspicion, they formed an easy target for the preachments of the clergy against them, and, as their "error" of being Jews was constantly impressed upon the Poles, they could serve as scapegoats in times of disaster or social unrest. When a fire broke out in Cracow in 1494, they were baselessly accused of having caused it and, on restoration of the city, were placed in a ghetto.

Afraid of the brutality and ignorance of the civil magistrates, the Jewish community early in its history in Poland had pleaded for and obtained the right to self-government. The chief rabbis of the communities were recognized by the kings as Jewry's justices and chief administrators. A central council was organized—The Council of the Four Lands (of which Poland was composed), which met regularly, allocated taxes, and represented Jewish interests, especially through those of its members who had access to the court as royal financiers. District Councils carried out the ordinances of the Central Council, and each congregation (**Kahal**) formed an administrative unit, regulating every aspect of life, conduct, law, custom, and relations with the non-Jewish population. Indeed, the Jewish community formed a body within the body of the state, sternly controlled and disciplined. Thus the power of the Jew of status, the *Shtadlan*, became great; it was to be felt even in the eventual organization of American Jewry, so largely composed of immigrants from Eastern Europe. Upon settling in America, the Eastern European Jews, used to communal life, for a generation remained close together in small congregations reflecting the customs and habits of their home towns in the old country.

The separation from the rest of the world and that world's lack of a comparable culture provided an external safeguard against corrosion; immersion in the Talmud gave inner strength and conviction. Early on, printing establishments provided an abundance of books [the Bible in 1530; the Talmud (first printed in Lublin, Poland) in 1559]. The Talmud provided escape into a better world.

Pilpul, the Exacting Study of Talmud

Rabbi Shalom Shakna (1500–1559) developed a method of Talmud study that corresponded to the outlook and need of his people. It led to the most detailed analysis of every verse and word in an effort to bring about a basic "agreement" in the opinions of a variety of conflicting commentaries, written by numerous authors in a variety of countries and during different ages. This was necessary in order to preserve the link with the past. Each generation rested on the back of the preceding ones, which were regarded as more learned and closer to the source. None of these "early ones" could be assumed to have been in error, even in a single case. The chain of tradition had to be without any weak links, so the chain of conviction would be equally strong. Ways had to be found to link divergent opinions of different centuries and to bring all opinions into agreement. But this was possible only by hair-splitting logic; it became a kind of mental gymnastic which sharpened the mind but was actually meaningless. This method of **pilpul** has remained in some of the old-fashioned religious academies and has removed them from the mainstream of Jewish evolution.

Now commentaries were piled upon commentaries. Education was practically universal. At an early age, a boy was taken to **cheder** (the schoolroom), where he started to study Bible and Talmud from early morning until late at night, often under the guidance of a teacher who was far from being a pedagogue. Advanced students were sent to a **yeshivah** (academy) in the city where the people took turns providing them with their meals, having a different student every day. During this period, girls received only a basic education, which trained them to fulfill religious obligations, keep a kosher home, and influence their children through the home. In later times, some received a more thorough education.

Now study became the young man's full vocation, deep into the night; the bloom of youth would fade from his cheeks. Many never emerged from this mode of life. When they married, their inlaws might provide for them; if this was impossible, the wife would eke out a living for the rest of her days to afford undisrupted study for her husband. The prestige of the learned was high; the great rabbis were revered; brilliant students were sought by the wealthy as most suitable sons-in-law.

Chmielnicky: Persecution Erupts into Pogroms

The seventeenth century was to witness the first of the many truly frightful and large-scale persecutions of Eastern European Jews, the *Chmielnicky Massacres*, the first in a long series of mass murders of Jews, the pogroms. Chmielnicky was the head of a free-roaming band of warriors, the Cossacks. Professing the Greek Orthodox faith, they rebelled against the Roman Catholic Poles, and the Jews were in the middle in the ensuing civil war. The serfs, dissatisfied with their fate, joined the Cossacks. Jews were slaughtered by the tens of thousands, while the entire country was ravaged.

When it was all over, the search for redemption from these horrible sufferings moved in several directions: Immersion in the Talmud grew deeper and, with it, withdrawal from the world. Mitzvot became ever more embracing. Injunctions, such as the prohibition of cutting the corners of the beard (Leviticus 19:27) were taken literally, resulting in long earlocks never cut. Thus self-imposed seclusion was added to the enforced one. Mitzvah formed the wall of separation.

Sabbatai Zevi: False Messiah

Messianic hope grew stronger. God, the "trustworthy King," would surely bring redemption to His people after such cataclysmic experiences. The Chmielnicky pogroms were regarded as "birthpangs of the Messiah."

There was reawakening hope of a speedy return to Palestine, and history conspired to make it seem a reality. A young and glamorous man from Smyrna (in Turkey), Sabbatai Zevi (1626–1676), proclaimed himself the Messiah. Thousands in Germany as well as in Poland were captivated by the news, sold their belongings or packed them on wagons, and were ready to go. It turned out to be a cruel hoax; Sabbatai proved to be an impostor. Captured by the Turks, he was given the choice of becoming a Muslim or of being executed; he chose the former. For many years, his followers were unwilling to accept the blow: He would surely arise again. But their lives returned to the ancient pattern of suffering. Poverty deepened. The people's spirit was low.

Hasidism

At this point there arose Rabbi Israel Baal Shem (1700–1760), founder of Hasidism. By his teachings, he made clear to his people that they were not finished as the people of the Covenant. They were, in fact, co-workers with God in the work of redemption. Redemption could be hastened in every land, by all individuals within their own spheres. They need not even be learned.

Going about among the people with words of encouragement and inspiration, using the simple approach of parable and story, the **Baal Shem** gave them hope. He taught them that God Himself needed redemption, for He too was in exile with His people as a result of the world's sinfulness. In order that the world be restored to the unity that it had lost by human sinfulness, God needed humanity's redemptive act. In that task, the Jew has a major role to fulfill. Every human task, be it menial work or study or eating or drinking, can be a response to God if performed as Mitzvah in joyful service to Him. All people, even the most unlearned—and perhaps they more than others—carry the messianic burden of preparing the world for the future. Every limb of one's body can become a tool in this service.

The people flocked to the Baal Shem. They would rouse themselves into ecstasy, their bodies swaying in worship to express with every bone and muscle their allegiance to God, for prayer must pour forth out of the innermost soul to reach God and be expressed with the total personality of the worshipper. They would dance before Him in joyful abandon. They had found new hope.

The leaders of the movement were believed by the people to have a deeper insight into the hidden meanings of Scripture. They were Masters of the Divine Name (*Baal Shem* in Hebrew), that creative Word by which the world had once been shaped and by which it could be influenced again. Thus the people came to their leaders to get help in their individual needs and hung on their lips for mysterious words of revelation. Each leader was called *Zaddik*, the Righteous: He did not have to be learned, for he would inherit the divine gifts from his father.

Here lay the roots of Hasidism's eventual decay. The Zaddikim held court in princely fashion; rival groups sprang up, each clinging to its Zaddik. Eventually, the movement lost its spirit. Nevertheless, it shows the power of Mitzvah. It underscores the deep feeling of the Jews that they are related to all humanity and responsible for humanity's ultimate salvation.

The ideas of Hasidism have made themselves felt in our own time. The enthusiasm that fired the pioneers in Israel to undertake the most backbreaking tasks in redemption of the Land of Israel stems from it. Every act promoting this redemption was Mitzvah. Even by those Jews who did not adhere to formal religion in doctrine and practice, Hasidism, translated into secular terms, was applied to the physical redemption of Land and people. The dances of the pioneers have one of their sources in Hasidic abandon.

Hasidic groups have settled in the United States. Their cohesion is very strong. They have even established communities of their own, for instance in New Jersey, with complete internal autonomy. The Lubavitcher Rebbe, Rabbi Menachem M. Schneerson, has developed a network of congregations and day schools, and has availed himself of such modern technology as closed-circuit television to spread the spirit of Jewishness. His ruling that every Jewish girl should light Sabbath candles—not the mother alone—reveals the mixture of traditionalism and innovation that is typical of Hasidism. Tradition is to be instilled in the child at an early age, but the method is new and, for Orthodoxy, rather evolutionary.

The Gaon of Vilna: Hasidism's Antagonist, Defender of Reason

Elijah ben Solomon (1720–1779), affectionately called by his people the Gaon of Vilna, chose, in contrast to Hasidism, a way based on reason and vision. He felt that Judaism had to be pulled back onto the highway of reason and rational ways of study, in place of either hairsplitting logic or mystical interpretation; even some secular knowledge was advisable as it improved the understanding of Talmud and Codes. Worship was to be made more meaningful and more "modern" in a modest way. Yet this advice of great wisdom was not generally accepted; it had limited immediate appeal and looked too far into the future. Worshipped by thousands for his great personality, he did not succeed in weaning away the multitude from the method of pilpul. Had he succeeded, the transition to modern life, especially in America, might not have been so abrupt, and a good deal of alienation between children and parents would have been avoided among the immigrants to the new world.

Life under the Russian Czars

Russia became a Christian state around the year 900. Its Eastern Orthodox religion was more fundamentalist than Western Christianity. The Reformation did not affect it. Russia took the doctrine of the Jews as accursed people in all its literal harshness. When Byzantium, center of the faith, fell to the Turks in 1453, Moscow became the "metropolis" of the Greek Orthodox Church. Actually, it was regarded as the center of Christianity by the Russians, who believed that Rome had forfeited this distinction on account of the Roman Church's many heretic teachings. In a spirit of religious purity, Russia did not permit Jews to settle within its borders.

In the course of the centuries, Russia carried out a program of "imperialist expansionism" of unparalleled success, a policy that has been followed by the Soviet Union as well. The Russian empire grew from a small territory around Moscow into a world power. The method was absorption of weaker countries at Russia's borders, which were thereby pushed out further and further. One of the independent states at Russia's border was Poland, which had become enfeebled as a result of dissension among the various feudal lords. By the eighteenth century, it had become impossible to unite Poland under a king of Polish descent, and a power vacuum developed. Russia would have liked to absorb it, but there were two other powerful states at Poland's borders—Prussia and Austria—who were equally eager to expand their territory at the expense of their weaker neighbor. In the end, and as a result of three treaties, the big powers divided Poland among themselves and wiped it off the map. Later, Poland was to emerge again.

The partitions of Poland brought about one million Jews into the Russian empire. They were a most unwelcome addition, but it was impossible to expel so large a number of people, especially as no one was prepared to take them. It became Russian policy either to get rid of as many as possible by permitting them to emigrate or by absorbing them through baptism. The rest—the vast majority—were to be confined within a strictly circumscribed district, the **Pale**. Here they might live together and starve together. Jews from all over Russia were dumped into it (1804). Thousands lost their livelihood, contact with the world was cut off, and the Jews became desperately poor, sitting ducks for pogroms. The Kahal of each town had to see to it that the taxes came in on time and in full; eventually, the Council of the Four Lands became just a tax-gathering arm of the government. Jews were to open state-supervised schools for secular learning. The ultimate purpose of this was to draw the youth away from their tradition.

Then in 1812 came the Napoleonic invasion of Russia and, with it, a glimpse of the spirit of Enlightenment in the West. There were Jews who delighted in this opening up, but the community, fearing for its survival, strictly forbade study of non-Jewish subjects; these had to be studied in secret without guidance. Thus emerged the small Enlightenment movement, **Haskalah**, of dilettantes and amateurs, who were placed in opposition to religion. This movement, too, was to have severe consequences, as the intellectual became estranged from faith. Had the Gaon of Vilna prevailed, an orderly transition might have taken place.

With the defeat of Napoleon, reaction set in all over Europe, and the pressure on the Jews increased. Under Nicholas I (1825–1855), the Pale was narrowed and the Jews squeezed closer together. To enforce conversion, Nicholas ordered the conscription of Jews (1827). They were to serve for twenty-five years without any opportunity of promotion unless they became Christians. In "preparation" for this service, which was to start at the age of eighteen, children at the age of twelve could be (and were) conscripted, dragged away from their homes, mistreated, and tortured to make them give up their faith. Many perished in heroic "stubbornness."

The Russian system of elementary education was to be enlarged. A German rabbi, Max Lilienthal (1815–1882), was called to direct it, but when he found that, in essence, he was to create an organization for the conversion of Jewish children, he fled in terror. Eventually, he had a distinguished career as one of the early rabbis in the United States.

While the most severe restrictions were removed with the death of Nicholas I, new pressures were applied later under Alexander III and Nicholas II. The masses of Russia were dissatisfied and groaning under their yoke. To deflect their fury, pogroms against the Jews were instituted, beginning in 1881; they shook the world by their extent and brutality and were denounced by Christians throughout the West. The economic situation of the Jews was equally hopeless. Migration to the United States now became a torrent.

At the same time, Leo Pinsker (1821–1891) published his appeal for auto-Emancipation, and migration to Palestine got under way, led by young Jews who called themselves *BILU* (an abbreviation of the Hebrew sentence "O House of Jacob, come, and let us go!"). Another group, The Lovers of Zion, emerged, dedicated to the same purpose. Zionism was on the march. Theodor Herzl was to give it its name and organization.

The routine never varied: discrimination, even against Jewish soldiers in World War I, and pogroms. When the Czar fell, Jewry thought it was free, only to suffer persecution again. There were pogroms in the Ukraine; Jews, as members of the "middle class," were to be wiped out by the Bolsheviks (1917) as the war against religion hit them. Their persecution in Russia has not ended today (see pp. 147-150).

THE JEWS IN THE MIDDLE AGES: VALUES AND PROBLEMS IN THE BLENDING OF CULTURES

The history of the Jews during the Middle Ages was one of adversity. It is remarkable, therefore, to note how deeply they cast their roots in their new homelands. They learned to live in two civilizations, demonstrating to the world that humanity can live together and that cultures can preserve their individuality while sharing with each other the best that each has to offer. Yiddish, the language spoken by Ashkenasic Jews, and Ladino, the language of the Sefardim throughout the Middle Ages, are based on German and Spanish, respectively. These languages are frequently used as a second tongue by many Jews even today. Similarly, the caftan, once the dress of the medieval burgher, became the "Jewish dress" in Eastern Europe. As frequent Church edicts calling for stricter separation of Jews from Christians reveal, contacts with friends were retained. But the Jews would not give up their faith, even though the door of the Church stood always open and baptism would wipe out all disabilities.

The Jews never lost their zest for life. This may be a source of that peculiar kind of Jewish humor, whimsical and tender, skeptical and optimistic, born of faith and love, critical of both God and humanity, and yet encompassing all human foibles with amused compassion. This humor emerged from reflection on their fate—God's beloved, yet they could barely subsist; His chosen people, yet they were totally insecure on earth. This was indeed "divine comedy." But who could doubt Him? Their optimism, and their faith in God and humanity's ultimate goodness—evidenced even in Anne Frank's deeply moving diary—carried them through.

Yet scars remained. Their socioeconomic situation was completely abnormal. They were excluded from the soil they had so deeply loved. Known early in history for the kind of inventive craftsmanship which allowed for mass production, they were excluded from the guilds. Some of the scars are still visible in modern Jews, who are so recently removed from persecution that most of them have received eyewitness reports of it, if they were not its direct victims. In this manner, we must understand certain socioeconomic imbalances, still existing and perpetuated by present-day forms of job discrimination. We may also understand the "exclusiveness" born of long inbred apprehension about their acceptance by the world at large, and their ambition for success and acceptance, a truly ambivalent position. Perhaps we may find in these conditions one explanation for the temptation felt by a number of Jews to escape from the dominance of religion into a general humanitarianism—this could be the first time that such an escape is possible without abandonment of Jewishness.

Indications are, particularly in the United States, that conditions are becoming normal. Out of this change, new problems have arisen concerning the retention of Jewish identity in a civilization that is a great leveler. This new trend of events was slowly set in motion by the Emancipation, with which we shall deal in Chapter 6.

5

JEWISH MYSTICISM AND
THE HASIDIC MOVEMENT

Jewish mysticism and Hasidism have become widely known in the twentieth century. Many young people, in particular, have become fascinated by some of its aspects. This new interest is due to the work of two great masters: Gershom Scholem (born 1897), who has devoted a lifetime to the study of Jewish mysticism, and Martin Buber (1878–1965), who gave us a highly poetic interpretation of Hasidism.

Scholem, now professor emeritus of Jewish mysticism at the Hebrew University of Jerusalem, has given "respectability" to Jewish mysticism, regarded by nineteenth-century Jewish scholars as simply "superstition." He has explored it in rigorous scholarly fashion and has, in fact, opened the entire realm of Jewish mysticism to our understanding. Born into a non-observant Jewish family of wealth in Berlin, he settled in what was then called Palestine when he was in his twenties.

MYSTICISM

The mystic is a person to whom an immediate revelation of the divine is granted. The very character of this revelation makes conveying it to others difficult.

The great teachers of Judaism were essentially opposed to the idea of continuing revelation granted to individuals. Torah had been given at Sinai, and revelations in the form of visions had been granted to the prophets; from then on, reason was the means by which it could be understood and explained. The masters were equally opposed to mystical speculations on God, His essence, interaction with the universe and human beings in creation, history, revelation, redemption, the end of days, and so on. Nevertheless, mysticism has existed throughout Jewish history. The prophets had mystical experiences, as is revealed in, among other passages, Isaiah's vision (Isaiah 6) and the entire first chapter of Ezekiel.

A number of talmudic rabbis were mystics, though they were apprehensive that the subject might lead the uninitiated astray. The rabbis warned against mysticism and opened its recesses only to a few selected disciples, those worthy of "special transmission," or **Kabbalah**, which became the term for mysticism. The dangers and risks of such speculations were explained, for instance, in the following passage of the Talmud, as a message of warning.

> Four entered Pardes [the paradise of mystical speculations]: Ben Azzai, Ben Zoma, Aher, and Rabbi Akiba. Ben Azzai saw and died; Ben Zoma saw and lost his mind; Aher saw and lost his faith. Only Akiba entered and emerged in peace. (see Hagiga 13–15)

Even great rabbis were not immune to the dangers of mystical contemplation. Nevertheless, mysticism continued. During the Middle Ages, it was influenced by Christian and Muslim ideas. We find it in Germany and in Spain; even the codifier of Jewish law, Joseph Karo, author of the *Shulhan Arukh*, was a mystic.

The most influential sources of Jewish mysticism have been the **Zohar**—the "Book of Radiance"—and the teachings of Rabbi Isaac Luria. The Zohar was written toward the end of the thirteenth century by a Spanish Jewish mystic, Moses de Leon; however, for centuries it was erroneously ascribed to Rabbi Simeon ben Yohai, who lived in Palestine during the second century of the Christian era. Rabbi Isaac Luria (1534–1572), born in Jerusalem of Ashkenasic descent, established a center of mystical thought in Safed in what is now northern Israel. His disciples called him the *ARI*—meaning Lion, and at the same time an abbreviation of *A*shkenasi *R*abbi *I*saac.

The Zohar

The Zohar teaches that God in His essence is *En Sof*, the Infinite; as such, He is forever unknowable to us. He makes Himself manifest through the *Sefirot*, His emanations, attributes. Ten Sefirot, each lower than the preceding one, reveal Him to humanity and allow us to relate to Him.

God's Torah was with God from the beginning, even before the world was created. In its essence, Torah is God's hidden Name; as we possess it, the Torah is an emanation of God's Torah, of God's Name. Its text is for some mystics an arrangement and rearrangement of the Name of God. Could we decipher the "scrambled" text we possess and discover its true essence—that is, the Name of God—we would gain creative powers. God created the universe through the Name. If we possessed the Name, we could creatively affect the world.

Torah and world form an organism. Through Torah, the universe was fashioned; through Torah, it is maintained. The Torah was handed by God to Israel at Sinai; hence—according to later mystics—there exists an especially close relationship between Israel, Torah, and world. At Sinai, each of the 600,000 witnesses—the Israelites who left Egypt (see Exodus 12:37)—was given one letter of Torah, a "mantra" of his own; only in the days of the Messiah will each witness understand what it was and what it means. But there are consequences for the present as well.

To God, all of Torah was the letters of His Name. God arranges and rearranges these letters in accordance with His design for the world at every stage of its unfolding. This means that, at every stage of history, the letters of Torah have a deeper meaning related to the times. The Jew who immerses himself in Torah, even one verse of Torah, may release forces that can bring liberation to the world. Thus more than mere literal study of the text of Torah is called for; penetration into the depths of its hidden meanings is necessary. The term *Pardes* is understood as an acrostic for the methods of Torah study on ever deeper levels. *P* stands for *P'shat*, the literal meaning; *R* for *Remez*, the allegorical meaning; *D* for *Derasha*, the talmudic interpretation; and *S* for *Sod*, the mystical interpretation. Because Torah was given to Israel, Israel has a special function in the world. Actually this method of scriptural interpretation on several levels corresponds to the methods of interpretation given by Christian interpreters, from whom it was probably taken.

The literal interpretation of Scripture is thus only surface interpretation; the kabbalistic interpreter has to go ever deeper into the text and into himself. Thus the command given to Abraham—"*Lekh lekha*," "Go you forth" (Genesis 12:1)—is given a new meaning: "Go into yourself." As the student of the Zohar goes into mystical depth, he may affect the universe through "his letter." Even more startling is the idea that God, revealing Himself in the Sefirot, is Himself *Adam Kadmon*, Man of the Beginning. This is ultimate anthropomorphism and thus alien to the mainstream of Jewish thought.

The Ari

The Ari emphasizes *Tsimtsum*, *partial withdrawal*. Initially, God filled the entire universe. But if God fills the universe, how then can the world, God's creation, exist? In order to leave room for the world to exist, God withdrew into Himself, leaving room for creation. Otherwise there could have been no world, as God was All. As Adam Kadmon, God sent His rays into the world so that it would be filled with His presence. But the world could not contain His rays; the "vessels" broke under the power of the divine light. The rays were dispersed, scattered. This breaking of the vessels constitutes the tragedy of history: God's *Shekhinah*, His indwelling in the world, has been dispersed; the sparks are scattered; the Shekhinah is in exile. It is the duty of all human beings to "gather the sparks," to mend the vessels, and return the sparks to the vessels. A life in full accord with the divine will can promote this task; then the world will be restored to unity and will be filled with the divine. Humanity can thus redeem the world, redeem God Himself.

This restoration is called *Tikkun*. Had Adam not sinned, he could have accomplished Tikkun. But he did sin, and the task therefore rests on humanity as a whole and on Jews specifically. The Jewish community is the partner of God's Shekhinah, His indwelling in universe and society. God's Shekhinah dwells within the Jewish people. Since Israel too has been scattered and exiled, God is in double exile: exiled in a world of broken vessels and, again, with

Israel, among the nations. Through obedience to Torah, Jews fulfill a world-wide mission: With the end of Jewish exile, the divine exile comes to an end. Therefore the actions Jews perform must lead them to ever deeper *Devekut*, an ever deeper cleaving to God. Every act must be filled with *Kavvanah*, the mystical intention to bring about the unification of God's Name.

The act of unification, of sacred marriage between Shekhinah and Israel, was symbolically reenacted by the mystics of Safed on various occasions, especially on Friday evening. According to general Jewish tradition, as Sabbath arrives, a second, higher, soul enters every Jew, and abides throughout the entire Sabbath. A sacred "marriage" takes place, of Jew and the Sabbath soul; the Sabbath is the "bride." Equally, for mystics, the Shekhinah was the bride. On the Sabbath, the Jew is united with the Shekhinah, the "super" soul.

The rabbis of talmudic times would go out into the fields on Friday evenings to welcome the "Sabbath bride." The mystics of Safed would do the same, but now a mystical interpretation was added to the simple act of welcoming the Sabbath: the Shekhinah was welcomed. Like the talmudic rabbis, the mystics had marital intercourse during the night of the Sabbath (Ketubot 62b), but they gave this human union an added meaning: it reflected the mystical union of Shekhinah and humans, Jews. The Sabbath anticipates for a brief period the unification of God and universe. God therefore rejoices as human beings creatively unite in wedlock; He rejoices doubly as they do so on the Sabbath.

Traces of this practice have remained to the present. At twilight on Friday evening, the congregation assembled in worship sings a hymn of welcome to the Sabbath about to enter. This hymn, *"Lekha dodee"* was composed by Solomon Alkabez (1488–1575), one of the mystics of Safed and an intimate friend of Rabbi Joseph Karo. The hymn begins with the following words, which also form the refrain after each strophe:

> Come, my friend, the Bride to meet . . .

At the final verse, the congregation in Orthodox synagogues turns to the door, visualizing the entry of the Sabbath and welcoming the bride. The congregation sings:

> Come then in peace, crown of Your Spouse,
> come in joy and jubilation
> into the midst of the faithful, the chosen folk.
> Come ye, O Bride, come ye, O Bride!

By observing Torah, the Jew aids in the Tikkun, and the Sabbath is the fullest expression of cleaving to God's Torah. Every human being can and should contribute to Tikkun—the establishment of the world under the rule of God, the end of the exile, the building of a human universe that will be filled with divine radiance.

HASIDISM

We may now better understand the meaning of the name Baal Shem applied to the founder of Hasidism. The **Zaddik** who was master of the Name was capable of influencing God's actions. He guided his flock in *Devekut*, the cleaving to God in every thought and act. Restoration of the unity of the Name was to be the motivating force of every action. At times, we read in hasidic prayer books, preceding a *Berakhah* (blessing), the words "I am setting to performing this holy act [initiated by the Berakhah] to unify the Name." Through study of Torah and performance of Mitzvot, but also through performance of daily pursuits, the redemption of God, humanity, and universe could be hastened; the messianic age could be brought nearer. The condition was that each of these actions were undergirded by kavvanah, the holy intent to unify the Name.

The Zaddik peered into the future; he had "magical" powers. He interceded for his people and for the world, giving advice and counsel. He gathered his flock on special occasions, such as holy days. Every week, the "third meal" of the Sabbath, shared at the time of gathering dusk on Saturday, became a mystical gathering. The guests were permitted to partake of a morsel of the rebbe's food, while he, peering into the ever-deepening darkness, spoke in cryptic words about deepest things. The "third meal," adapted to modern changed conditions and feelings, was reintroduced in Israel by the poet Haim Nahman Byalik.* It became an hour of reunion and rededication for the members of the kibbutz, who shared in word and song their thoughts, hopes, and aspirations, renewing in the atmosphere of the waning Sabbath their dedication to each other and to the spirit and the Land of Israel, whose builders they were. As a spiritual fellowship gathering, "Seudah shelishit," the third meal has come to be observed among many diaspora groups as well, especially among youth. Under the name "Oneg Shabbat," Sabbath delight, fellowship gatherings after worship, such as on Friday night, have adapted Byalik's term for the meetings and some of its spirit to other occasions of Jewish celebration.

The modern philosopher Martin Buber, a deep student of Hasidism, has collected the stories of the Hasidic masters, shaped them according to his own poetic concepts, and made them available to all readers. His philosophy of I and Thou is fashioned on Hasidic foundations. Through Buber, Hasidism has deeply influenced the thinking not only of many Jews but of many Christians. In interpreting the Hasidim in accordance with his own philosophy,

---

*Haim Nahman Byalik (1873–1934) has come to be regarded as Israel's national poet. Born and raised in Poland, Byalik received a thorough talmudic education. At the age of seventeen, he went to Berlin and was exposed for the first time to the West and its culture. In 1923, following some time in Odessa after the Russian revolution, Byalik settled in the Holy Land. In his poetry, Byalik has given expression to the soul of the Jewish people, its fate, its subjection to outside pressures and deep inner conflicts as old and new clash. At the same time, he demonstrated the power of the Hebrew language to express every shade of feeling and emotion. He gave hope to the people. His inauguration of the Oneg Shabbat after his arrival in Palestine, which brought ancient tradition together with modern needs, is an example of his ideals.

however, Buber gives the impression that they are not greatly concerned about Mitzvot. This is inaccurate. Torah is binding for them in every aspect, and they are orthodox in the performance of Mitzvot, although they remain closed to the modern world.

The Jewish scholars of the nineteenth century generally rejected Jewish mysticism as obscurantism and alien to the rational Jewish mind. Scholem and Buber have sparked new interest in it. This interest may also reflect the current search for the mystical that is appearing in society in general. The mystics and Hasidim have remained on the periphery of Judaism. Though we may hold the masters of the Hasidim in esteem, they are not on the level of the prophets. We must not use mysticism as an escape from the world and its tasks that call for rational commitment.

6

EMANCIPATION AND THE MODERN AGE

WHAT IS EMANCIPATION?

The European Renaissance in the sixteenth century led to the Age of Reason in the seventeenth century and thence to the Enlightenment of the eighteenth century, whose motto was Reason and Progress. Enlightenment in turn led to the Emancipation.

Emancipation means the attainment of freedom by those who have been without it. In connection with the Jews, it had a twofold meaning. The Jews were to be given equal rights as citizens; their civic disabilities were to be removed. In return, the Jews were to cast off their isolation; relinquish their internal jurisdiction; immerse themselves wholeheartedly in the society and culture of the countries in which they lived; and adapt to the majority in their education, their way of life, their cultural and aesthetic values, and their political allegiance. Above all, the Jews had to identify fully with the countries of their newly granted citizenship and to find there the emotional security of belonging they had hitherto experienced in their own peoplehood. Meanwhile, the Jews were on probation. Society had to be shown, it had to be won over from its long-held views and prejudices.

To these demands, Western European Jews were wholly agreeable. They hoped the time of probation would be short if they adjusted quickly. Worship became modernized; Jewish law was reexamined and, in part, dismantled; Jewish tradition underwent reinterpretation: A new rationale for the survival of Jews as an exclusively religious body had to be found. In themselves, most of these goals were desirable for an evolving religion and its adherents; the ill lay in the fact that the motivation, to a large degree, came not from within but from the desire to please the non-Jewish world. This led many Jews to a complete negation of their heritage. They became baptized.

The adjustment was not entirely successful. The number of Christians of truly good will was limited. The majority remained antagonistic and the undercurrent of anti-Semitism remained strong. Equality in a real sense remained a mirage, and security was never attained. Eventually, even the Christian children of baptized Jews were forced back by the Nazis into the body of the Jewish "race."

As a positive force, the Emancipation stimulated the "science" of Judaism, new theological movements, new religious patterns, and Jewish contributions in the fields of culture, art, science, and scholarship.

Gaining Citizenship Rights

The French Revolution brought the Jews equality in France, and Napoleon carried its ideas to the lands he conquered. However, it was important for the Jews to be truly obedient to him, so he organized their congregations and even called a group of leading rabbis to Paris to form a Sanhedrin, which had the difficult task of adjusting Jewish laws to Napoleon's desire without harming Jewish tradition.

Pressured by the state, but also motivated by the desire for active participation in the life of the nation as recognized citizens, the Sanhedrin held that

> . . . the divine Law, the precious heritage of our ancestors, contains within itself dispositions which are political and dispositions which are religious: that the religious dispositions are, by their nature, absolute and independent of circumstances and of the age; that this does not hold true of the political dispositions . . . which were taken for the government of the people of Israel in Palestine when it possessed its own kings, pontiffs and magistrates. . . . (Quoted from N.N. Glatzer, *The Dynamics of Emancipation*; Boston: Beacon Press, 1965, p. 9)

The Sanhedrin could therefore proclaim that the Jews recognized no country but the one in which they held citizenship. Interfaith marriage, while inadmissible under *religious* law, was to be recognized by Jews because it conformed to *state* law. By way of compromise, the Sanhedrin declared that a person who had entered such a marriage in a justice court would remain a Jew, but that rabbis could not solemnize the bond.

Following Napoleon's example, the European states organized the Jewish communities as religious bodies, eliminating such rights as their internal self-government and the judicial powers of rabbis over family relations. Judaism was now religion. Given their citizenship rights, the Jews were willing to fight for their countries. In Prussia, hundreds volunteered in the war against Napoleon (1815). But when Napoleon had been beaten, the rights of the Jews were rescinded.

A new uphill struggle began. So harsh were the laws (for instance, in Bavaria, where marriages were restricted), that many Jews migrated to the United States. Efforts to unite Germany on a democratic basis led to revolutions in 1830 and 1848, both of which failed and forced many liberals and Jews to find a life of freedom in America.

Slowly the Jews obtained citizenship rights. In Germany, they were not granted full and unchallenged equality until 1918. Before then, with few exceptions, they could not be judges, civil servants, or army officers while maintaining their faith.

It had been the hope of the Jews that by exhibiting their patriotism they might show the world they were deserving of full equality. Insecurity turned many into superpatriots, staying aloof from Eastern European Jews, whom they supported but from whom they kept apart. Yet the developments of the time did give hope that equality would emerge, and German Jews saw in Germany their home. After all, they had lived in it for at least 1,500 years, had taken their place in its cultural life, and had benefited it economically by their industry. They were a good, substantial middle class with all its virtues and faults. About a half million strong, they left 12,000 of their youth on the battlefields fighting for Germany in World War I.

Moses Mendelssohn

In **Moses Mendelssohn** (1729–1786), German Jewry found its great leader. A small, hunchbacked man, his early growth stunted by hunger and deprivation, he was a brilliant intellect, immersing himself early in both Jewish and non-Jewish philosophy. Liberal of thought, progressive in his ideas, Mendelssohn was deeply religious and faithful in the performance of Mitzvot. As a young man, he won a prize for a work submitted to the Prussian Academy, his competitor being none other than Immanuel Kant. Admired by the literary world, a friend of Kant and of Gotthold Ephraim Lessing* (who patterned the personality of Nathan in his play *Nathan the Wise* after him), known to Frederick the Great, who granted him a residence permit in Berlin (though most reluctantly), Mendelssohn became a leading representative of the Enlightenment. But he was a truly faithful Jew, defending his faith courageously against Johann Caspar Lavater (1741–1801), a Swiss clergyman, who challenged him either to explain Judaism in the light of reason or to become a Christian. "My examination . . . has strengthened me in the faith of my fathers," Mendelssohn boldly affirmed. "I hereby witness before the God of truth . . . that I shall abide by these my convictions as long as my soul shall not change its nature."

Mendelssohn made it clear that, according to the Enlightenment, all of humanity must be assumed to have equal access to the truth that brings salvation. The ideals of religion could be found only through reason, which was granted to all. The Jews at Sinai were given not ideals but a law.

Judaism was revealed law; its core was Mitzvot. The mind of the Jew is not constrained by dogmas to be believed, but is free to follow reason into the fields of philosophy and science—in short, into general culture. Mendelssohn wished to educate his fellow Jews to be a group fully adjusted and fully contributing to the culture and thought of their environment. To guide them, he translated the Pentateuch into modern German, writing a Hebrew commen-

---

*Lessing (1729–1781) was the son of a Protestant pastor, a poet, playwright, theater and art critic, and outspoken advocate of religious freedom and equality in the spirit of the Enlightenment.

*Mendelssohn, Lavater, and Lessing in Discussion, by Moritz Op-
penheim. Fictional depiction of the three in friendly debate. Mendelssohn
is sitting at the left of the table; Lessing is standing. Oppenheim was a
nineteenth-century Jewish painter of family and religious life.* (Photo
by the author, courtesy of Judah L. Magnes Memorial Museum,
Jewish Museum of the West, Berkeley, California.)

tary as well. Thus Jewry could acquire the vernacular language—gateway to
communication and participation—out of its own most sacred treasure. In
modern German, they would be called to the performance of Mitzot as found
in Torah, and the Hebrew language would elucidate, so that they might remain
staunch adherents to divine commandments throughout life. Mendelssohn
expected the Christian world to grant full recognition to the Jewish citizens in
its midst and to respect their faith, even as Judaism respects all faiths. This was
a step toward Judaism as religion, pure and simple, even though Mendelssohn
was unaware of it.

RELIGION ADAPTS TO A NEW AGE

But what about the Mitzvot and the spirit of common destiny that
kept alive the sense of Jewish *peoplehood*? The leaders of the French Revolution
had an answer to that. Should the Jews have equal rights as citizens? "To Jews
as individuals we shall give everything, to Jews as a nation, nothing" was the
statement of Clermont Tonnère in the French Assembly in a debate on the
enfranchisement of the Jews. This principle was accepted, as Jews were granted
civil rights in 1791. The impact of this principle went deep. To be in accord
with modern life and able to enjoy the blessings of citizenship, Jews had to
remold their own thinking. Some of Judaism's age-old supports were thus
weakened. Others would have to be strengthened.

A first task was the scholarly and scientific investigation of Judaism—

its origin and the development of its doctrines and institutions—all to be undertaken with reason as the guide and modern scientific methods as tools. The "science of Judaism," founded by Leopold Zunz (1794–1886), came into being. The modernization of Judaism began.

Worship and practice had to be brought into line with the culture of their surroundings and with its forms, which Jews were quick to accept. This led to the emergence of leaders who became the founders of **Reform** Judaism (Abraham Geiger, 1810–1874); **Conservatism** (Zacharias Frankel, 1801–1875); and **Neo-Orthodoxy** (Samson Raphael Hirsch, 1808–1888). Rabbis had to be trained academically in universities and in modern seminaries—Reform in Berlin at the *Hochschule für die Wissenschaft des Judentums* (University for the Science of Judaism), where Geiger was a teacher; Conservatism in Breslau at the *Jüdisch Theologisches Seminar* (Jewish Theological Seminary), founded by Frankel; and Orthodoxy in Berlin at the *Rabbiner Seminar* (Rabbinical Seminary), founded by Israel Hildesheimer.

Struggles: Internal and External

The religious communities, both Christian and Jewish, stood under the supervision of the state. The ruling kings and princes hoped that the Jews would eventually accept Christianity. This was to be accomplished by various means. The king of Prussia prohibited every innovation in Jewish worship, with the idea that it would eventually be so contrary to modern taste that Jews would turn to the Church instead. Others promoted Reform Judaism, regarding it as a stepping stone to Christianity. The traditional rabbis preferred the Prussian solution though for the opposite reason: They believed it would create a wall between Judaism and Christianity and thus guard against conversion. They looked upon every form of modernization as dangerous, even if it was not contrary to Jewish law. There was strong opposition, for instance, to Mendelssohn's translation of the Bible on the grounds that it would draw readers to German literature, alienating them from Jewish learning and leading to religious decay. The new trends—even to Neo-Orthodoxy—were a break with existing forms of Judaism.

We might remember that during this period the influence of Hegel was at its height. Hegel saw history as the unfolding of the Absolute—God—through a pattern of thesis–antithesis–synthesis. It may be helpful to explain the new Jewish movements in roughly Hegelian terms, particularly as some of the innovators, especially Samson Raphael Hirsch, referred to him.

Old-time Judaism, pre-Mendelssohnian in spirit and action, denied an outward process of evolution in religion. God had revealed Himself. Torah, though open to minor interpretations, was eternal in its formulations, which had been laid down in written and oral law, Tenakh and Talmud. Jewish historical destiny, however, might be seen in Hegelian terms. *Thesis*: God gave His Torah at Sinai; He placed the people into their land, where Torah could be the foundation of a society living as a sovereign nation. *Antithesis*, working upon thesis: Expelled from the land, the Jews were charged with the task of self-preservation in adversity; they were segregated. By means of a new commitment to Torah, and growing through steadfastness in adversity, they would purify themselves of the dross of their errors, specifically a disregard of Torah that had caused their exile. *Synthesis*, emerging from thesis and antithesis: In messianic times, Israel, refined by trial, would be restored to its land forever to live on its own soil wholly true to God and guided exclusively by Torah.

Reform Judaism saw the unfolding of history from the perspective of the modern age. *Thesis*: the tradition based on Scripture and Talmud as understood in the past. *Antithesis*: biblical scholarship and the modern concept of ethics, reacting upon tradition and correcting it. *Synthesis*, emerging from both: a modern Judaism, retaining Jewish social ethics but unfolding within Western society through Jews who took seriously the newly obtained civic equality and the duties it entailed.

Conservative Judaism saw the unfolding within the stream of internal Jewish history. *Thesis*: pre-Mendelssohnian Judaism that had become alienated from the world and its progression. *Antithesis*: Reform Judaism, too enthusiastically endorsing the new at the expense of emptying Judaism of content. *Synthesis*, embodying and transcending both: the unfolding spirit of the Jewish people, synthesizing old and new, ever evolving out of its own inner resources and forces, ever attuned to both the past and the needs of changing times.

Neo-Orthodoxy rested on the principle that Jews had to be fully immersed in the state that had granted them citizenship rights without giving up any of the commandments of Torah. *Thesis*: "Torah-true" Judaism, obedient in every way to the rules of the *Shulhan Arukh*. *Antithesis*: Western culture, which was permitted to serve Judaism as handmaiden. As long as it did not touch the core of tradition, and especially as it enhanced traditional Judaism, this culture was approved. *Synthesis*: "Israel-Man"—fully Jew and, within his Judaism (in Samson Raphael Hirsch's view, *on account of* his Judaism), fully immersed in the society, the culture of the West, and above all, the state.

Although it is possible to analyze the developments in Judaism in Hegelian terms, the leaders of Judaism, with the exception of Samson Raphael Hirsch, whose works and letters reveal his influence, may not have been conscious of Hegel's influence on their thinking. Orthodoxy would have rejected such an analysis as it rejects the legitimacy of any non-Orthodox Jewish movement and therefore any possibility of having been influenced by it. According to our schematized analysis, the movements have influenced each other, forming a synthesis. Whether they know it or not, they need each other, be it only to strengthen their own commitment in controversy. Transcending the differences there is the *one* Jewish community: **K'lal Israel.** Because the break with tradition was in conscious response to the recognized needs of the time, a deliberate means to preserve the allegiance of modern Jews to their heritage, Reform Judaism was the first of the new movements to emerge.

Reform Judaism

Inevitably, the Mitzvot, which for Mendelssohn had still been untouchable, came under scrutiny. Did dogmas and principles relating to the Land and to Jewish peoplehood still have a place in the religion of the modern Jew as a citizen of a Western European country? What about the Mitzvot expressing these principles, or those setting Jews apart from the rest of the population? A number of conferences were called (notably in Braunschweig in 1844 and Frankfurt in 1845) to examine Torah and Mitzvot scientifically. Characteristically for this Jewish renaissance movement, particular individuals provided the driving force, forcefully implanting their ideas in the rest.

In these conferences, **Abraham Geiger** (1810–1874) stood out as the towering genius of Reform Judaism; he is essentially its founder. To him, a person cannot accept revelation as history, for science offers no proof of any revelation. Mendelssohn had seen Judaism as *revealed* law; Geiger rejected this idea, as he rejected any revealed doctrines. He refuted the hope for a return to the Land, for the land of citizenship is the land of the Jew. This was an attack on the validity of Torah, of Mitzvot, and of the Land. What remained, then, was the deep-seated sense of kinship with the Jewish people. The genius of the people served as rationale for its survival. As Geiger expresses it:

> "*Is not the Jewish people . . . endowed with . . . a genius, with a religious genius? . . .* an aboriginal power to understand more vividly, and feel more intensely the close relation between the spirit of man and the Supreme Spirit? . . . If this be so, we may speak of a close contact between the individual spirit and the Supreme Spirit . . . so that it could break through its confining limits: it is—let us not hesitate to pronounce the word—revelation, and this, too, as it was manifested in the whole people. . . . Nor does Judaism claim to be the work of single individuals, but that of the whole people. Judaism has grown from the people of revelation. . . . Judaism is a religion of truth, discovering, as it does the unchangeable and everlasting: This is its everlasting essence." (Quoted from Gunter Plaut, *The Rise of Reform Judaism;* New York: World Union for Progressive Judaism, 1963, pp. 126–127)

Forms, however, change and evolve as the insight of the individual Jew directs. Torah becomes a source of ethics, performance of Mitzvot becomes a matter of individual decision, but not binding, the Talmud and *Shulhan Arukh* have no power of commitment, and the messianic hope has been fulfilled in Jewish Emancipation that has allowed the Jews to be missionaries of ethics to humanity.

The genius of the Jewish people as teacher of ethics was strongly emphasized. The Hebrew language of prayer was to be retained, in part at least for its emotional appeal. Education, sermon, and worship now were to form Torah in this new interpretation, and Mitzvot were to be understood as the missionary ideal of spreading ethics throughout the world. For these the Jew must live. Geiger was both a dynamic personality and a scholar. His impact has been felt in all of modern Jewry. The effect of Geiger's Reform Judaism was strongest in the United States.

Conservative Judaism

Among the participants in the first rabbinical conference was *Zacharias Frankel* (1801–1875), but he left it, convinced that this radical approach was a negative Judaism. He, too, was a man of science, who knew Jewish history as a process of evolution. Judaism had never stood still; hence its future development could be promoted on the basis of a "positive historical Judaism." The Torah, heritage of the congregation of Jacob, belongs to the people. Between its instructions and the changing conditions of life exists a constant creative tension. The people, in their inherent wisdom, slowly and gradually adjust Torah to life, the Talmud being a prime example of such an adjustment. The Torah is thus anchored not in an unchanging word of God but in the *people*, who, as His co-workers, develop it continually by common, unspoken consensus.

> The positive forms of Judaism are organically integrated into its character and form a part of its life and, therefore, may not be coldly and heartlessly disposed of. . . . (Plaut, *The Rise of Reform Judaism*, p. 86)

This process is slow, but it retains Torah, Mitzvot (unless changed by the people), and the principles of Jewish peoplehood and of the Land and its redemption. The link with past and future is never broken. Study and education are essential, and, as in every living organism, cells will die and new ones will be fashioned. This is Conservative Judaism, particularly strong in Germany; we shall note its rise in America as well.

Neo-Orthodoxy

It is important to remember that Neo-Orthodoxy was a Reform movement. Measured by contemporary standards, it is not a liberal one, though pre-Mendelssohnian Jews would have regarded it as very liberal. The German sermon, the rabbinical robe, the decorum at worship were sternly enforced innovations and reforms.

Oldenburg, a small duchy in Germany, became a kind of laboratory of Neo-Orthodoxy. It first *Landesrabbiner* (government appointed chief rabbi of a state—in this case, chief rabbi of the Grand Duchy of Oldenburg, appointed by the Grand Duke), Nathan Adler, was appointed because he was the first German rabbi to have a Ph.D.: He was modern. (He later became chief rabbi of the British Empire bringing Neo-Orthodoxy to England.) His protege, Samson Raphael Hirsch (1808–1888), usually regarded as founder of Neo-Orthodoxy, had studied at the university of Bonn, which was in his favor, but he was soon almost dismissed as being too orthodox in his leadership. It may be no accident that his works, expounding his new philosophy, appeared shortly after his dismissal had been barely averted by the duke.* Hirsch wished to demonstrate that *Orthodox* Jews were *commanded* to immerse

---

*In all German states, the ruler, through his cabinet, exercised ultimate power over all religious bodies, including the Jewish congregations. These, in turn, received financial support from the

themselves in the state of which they were citizens, that they had to come to the assistance of their "non-Jewish brethren"—in other words, that Orthodoxy was the best assurance for and foundation of the most dedicated citizenship. Hirsch and his later congregation at Frankfurt eventually severed any contact with non-orthodox Jews, but he never wavered in his fullest allegiance to the State and his dependence on the state for his projects. This interpretation, commanding immersion in state and society and adoption of its ways, was *Reform*, particularly in spirit, though combined with orthopraxis, the practice of traditional orthodox laws. Rejecting any modification of the law, Hirsch never attended any of the rabbinical conferences at which such modifications were discussed. Nevertheless, he did not escape the impact of the Reform movement.

Hirsch's ideas, fusing tradition and reform, may be briefly summarized here. He was imbued with the ideas of Moses Mendelssohn and even influenced by Geiger, whom he saw as his great adversary. To Hirsch, Torah was literal divine revelation, both in law and in doctrines; hence it could never be changed. Yet the missionary ideal of which Geiger had spoken was also to be pursued. This could be done if Jews both studied Torah and lived by the Mitzvot in every detail. By setting an example of exemplary obedience to God in their religious conduct and in all human relationships, Jews could thus set a standard, showing the way back to God to a world that had become estranged from Him. The Jew could be Israel-Man: By being a Jew, one grew to be man in society.

Mitzvot were explained as symbols enshrining this message and fortifying it in the observant Jew, making him "priest of humanity," teacher, leader in ethics. The performance of Mitzvot would set them apart; beyond that they were to seek the friendship of their Christian neighbors and to immerse themselves fully in the culture and civilization of the Western world, the secular state.

> Practice justice and love as thy Torah teaches thee; be just in action, true in your word, bear love in thine heart toward thy non-Jewish brother, as thy Torah teaches thee; feed his hungry, clothe his naked, refresh his sick, comfort his sorrowers, advise his bewildered, hasten to his assistance with counsel and action in his need and danger, exhibit the whole, noble fullness of thine Israel-dom. . . .
>
> It is our duty to immerse ourselves fully as citizens in the State that has accepted us, and to consider our own welfare as inseparate. (Samson Raphael Hirsch, *Nineteen Letters on Judaism*, Altona, 1837, fifteenth and sixteenth letters.)

This was a duty, even as the esthetic values of the West were to be fully utilized in the construction of religious worship and life, provided they did not disagree

---

state. In Lutheran states, the ruler was titular head of the state church. (Compare this with the position of the Queen of England in the Church of England.) In principle, the ruler could dismiss a clergyman. In Hirsch's case, the cabinet recommended dismissal, but the Grand Duke refused.

with Torah. The Land, whose redemption was not denied, had to take a secondary place. It would be redeemed in God's own good time; to restore it through human action would be against His will.

This was Neo-Orthodoxy, strictly separating itself from all other religious groups, and requiring a highly educated Jewish community for its implementation. Initially small in America, its influence is being increasingly felt. A new generation of university-educated Orthodox Jews, no longer separated from the stream of Western culture, has found in Samson Raphael Hirsch and his works an articulate guide in its search for a synthesis of Orthodox Judaism and contemporary civilization. Hirsch's numerous works have been translated into English, and his impact seems to be growing.

The Influence of Samson Raphael Hirsch

Hirsch was Landesrabbiner of Oldenburg, Germany, from 1829 to 1841. In 1836, he received a letter from a young man telling him that Hirsch's works had transformed his life. Under the impact of modernity, he had been drifting out of Judaism, but now had found his way back. The young man was *Heinrich Graetz* (1817–1891), who was to write a monumental Jewish history. From 1837 to 1840, the two men engaged in concentrated study. For Graetz, Neo-Orthodoxy was the antithesis of old-time Orthodoxy, out of which a new synthesis was to emerge: Conservative Judaism. Graetz became one of its spokesmen and taught at the Breslau Jewish Theological Seminary. To Hirsch, such a synthesis was unacceptable, and eventually the two men parted. But Conservatism owes one of its most scholarly and articulate representatives to Samson Raphael Hirsch.

Years later, the young *Kaufmann Kohler* (1843–1926) was one of Hirsch's disciples at Frankfurt. His ideas were to become completely antithetical to Hirsch's, as he moved in the direction of radical Reform. Migrating to America, Kohler became president of the Hebrew Union College in 1903, serving until 1921. The "Pittsburgh Platform," the high-water mark in "classical" Reform, was mainly his work (see page 114). Hirsch's thinking had directed Kohler in the opposite direction, toward "Man-Israel." Societal ethics came first and foremost; Judaism was a tool to promote social ethics. Kohler became the author of the first work on systematic Jewish theology in America. Hirsch's example perhaps influenced him to undertake the work. The impact of Hirsch's personality and teaching was profound, though not always in the way he might have wished.

Nineteenth-Century Jewry

During the Emancipation period, the various branches of the House of Israel showed wide divergencies. We can discern roughly four major groups. They were to become united again by the tragic events of the post-Emancipation period. First there was the Western European Jewish commu-

nity, centered in Germany, where the Neo–Orthodox and Conservative outlook was typical, second, Eastern Jewry, Orthodox in its view; third, the Jews
in Palestine, soon to become the State of Israel, to whom the upbuilding of the
Land was part of their living religion; and finally, American Jewry (discussed
in Chapter 7), as yet amorphous but tending to be pragmatic in its approach.

In Western Europe, where Jews enjoyed citizenship rights in varying
degrees, Germany, as the fountainhead of ideology, formed the center. In
religious philosophy, English Jewry followed the general principles of Nathan
Adler and Samson Raphael Hirsch. French and Italian, and, to a degree, Austrian Jews were more inclined to follow the general outlook of Conservatism,
the school of Frankel. In all of these countries, Judaism was seen by its own
adherents and by the population in general as a *religion.*

Eastern European Jewry was primarily Orthodox in the pre-
Mendelssohnian sense. It lived by itself in deep piety. There were some stir-
rings of "enlightenment" among the intellectuals, but there was no understanding of the philosophies of Judaism and its practices advanced in Germany.
Emancipation in the full political sense never truly occurred.

THE IMPACT OF ANTI-SEMITISM

Anti-Semitism was far from dead. Anti-Jewish sentiment was found
among Christian teachings, and, for many, it had been so deeply instilled by
the events of history that it was second nature. It broke out violently in France
in connection with the Dreyfus case, discussed on page 130. There was an
anti-Semitic party in the German parliament.

In Germany, the state, assuming supervision of all religions, organized
the Jewish community along the pattern of the Protestant Church. Judaism
became a religion and no more. This was not basically in disagreement with the
ideas of Mendelssohn, Geiger, or Hirsch, so German Jews could see themselves
primarily as a religious group. Full civil equality, in fact, was given Jews only
during the short years of the German Republic (1918–1933). Prejudice among
Christian Germans was widespread. The German Jews felt, however, that if
"they demeaned themselves as good citizens, giving their country at all times
their effective support," the Germans would recognize them in their true
character, and prejudice would disappear. German Jews became fervently
patriotic and rejected Zionism, which would have directed their concerns to
another land (and which, according to Hirsch, was against Jewish law as well,
for only in God's own time and with the coming of the Messiah was the Land
to be redeemed; no premature action was permissible). Insecure themselves,
they set themselves apart from their Eastern European brethren assisting them
financially and educationally without associating with them socially. At the
same time, a considerable number of German Jews were well educated in
Judaism and faithful in observance of Mitzvot, although some groups became
outright assimilationists.

The years after World War I were troublesome. The German economy broke down. Ill equipped to understand democracy and live by it, Germans degraded their new government. The heavy war reparations did not help. It was a fertile period for demagogues. Hitler gained popular support by promising the Germans greatness, power, and wealth in exchange for freedom. The immediate tangible goal for Germans was the expropriation of the property of Jews. Useful as scapegoats, Jews also could be held out as a source of wealth, for supposedly they were very rich.

With the Germans, the Jews shared a belief in law and order, love of education, thrift, ambition. Through Torah, they had internalized their aversion to violence (as had Russian Jewry). The prophetic message, reinforced by the rabbis and instilled into generations of Jews, condemns violence. By the teaching of their leaders, they had come to accept the idea that society was improving (moving toward a messianic age). All of this conspired against them when Hitler came to power in 1933. They had frequently been made scapegoats in the years since the Emancipation, but they considered these incidents holdovers from a tragic past, which education and time would eventually help to overcome. It was inconceivable to them that the constitution, the basic law of the land, could be overthrown. They had become acculturated and could not fathom the possibility of a whole nation turning against them at the behest of a few maniacs. Because they abhorred violence, they did not take up arms (as their forebears had done in Germany when Jews were attacked during the Crusades, and as the heroes of the Warsaw ghetto were to do, after long hesitation, when their cup of misery was finally running over). Dwelling in all sections of the German cities, they had no emotional preparation, physical training, or even opportunity for united action.

From 1933 on, their lot deteriorated rapidly. Racial laws were promulgated in 1935, completely excluding Jews from the cultural, economic, and social life of the country. In 1938, the synagogues were burned down and Jewish property looted. The Jews were taken to concentration camps, which had been well prepared. This was the beginning of the *Holocaust*.

Why did Germany become the focal point of modern anti-Semitism? (Russian anti-Semitism was of the medieval type.) Because Jews had lived in Germany without interruption for close to two thousand years, there was a chance in Germany for the various forms of anti-Semitism to be piled on one another as history progressed. (They had been expelled from England and France for many centuries and gradually been accepted again later.) Prejudice against Jews became ingrained, and the Jews, as a prosperous but small minority, could therefore be used as scapegoats.

Medieval anti-Semitism was theological: The Jews, having rejected Christ, were accursed. Baptism would wash away the curse and make the Jew, now a Christian, equal. Modern anti-Semitism is "racial," allowing no escape for the Jew, even in theory. It may also have economic foundations. This will be explained in detail in the following section.

The History of Anti-Semitism

Let us briefly trace the various forms of anti-Semitism which culminated in Hitler's extermination of millions of Jews.

In Roman Days, Jews were looked at with antipathy. They would not accept the Roman gods, frowned at the libertinism of Roman society, would not eat in Roman homes on account of their dietary laws, were considered lazy as they observed the Sabbath, and engaged in widespread missionary activities, making converts among leading citizens who were looking for spiritual guidance which Roman religion could not give. In short, the Jews were a nuisance. Their ideas were rather subversive to the Roman way of life, and they were gaining adherents. Christianity would build on these foundations of Jewish missionary work.

Medieval Christianity held the Jews responsible for the death of Christ and thus considered them rejected by God. It explained their survival simply as a divine decree, that by their misery they might be the witnesses of the triumph of the Church. This was theological anti-Semitism, based on a doctrine which was declared false by the Ecumenical Council in 1965. Yet it was taught for centuries and built into German consciousness by Luther's anti-Jewish teachings. The hatred of the Jews as unbelievers and deicides led to their exclusion from agriculture and all trades except money lending, which was forbidden to Christians by the Church. Through it, however, the Jews earned the additional accusation of being usurers, sharp and dishonest business manipulators. Since the Church saw them as *one* condemned people, they were an international, accursed enemy of humanity.

The Enlightenment saw no reason for theological anti-Semitism, and in its spirit Jews were emancipated. The age of science weaned many from adherence to theological dogma and further weakened anti-Semitism. But the Enlightenment was followed by Romanticism, the age of emotion, of nostalgia for a past considered better than the present. With it came the strong outburst of nationalism. Looking back on the supposed glories of the past, the Germans found that the Jews had been excluded from the life of the nation when Germany was supposedly strong. Now, while the Jews were equals, Germany was weak. Contaminated by anti-Jewish teachings, the Germans became prey to demagogues: Why not make the Jews the scapegoats for all that had gone wrong? They were the enemies of the national state and, it was claimed, were actually an international conspiracy. A Russian forgery, "The Protocols of the Wise Men of Zion," supposedly the plan of Jewry's internatonal leaders to destroy the nations and assume world power, was put into circulation. It served its purpose of fanning hate all too well, right up to the present.

As science became the ultimate authority, replacing faith and dogma, a new science, or pseudo-science, was put to work by the already prejudiced to prove that the Jews were, scientifically speaking, a rotten, destructive race. There is no vestige of scientific truth to the fact that Jews are even a race, but the "science-minded" anti-Semites took up the idea, planting the seed that was to produce a harvest of terror.

A Jewish Renaissance

Before and during the Nazi regime, German Jewry had strengthened itself spiritually. Philosophers like Hermann Cohen (1842–1918), Franz Rosenzweig (1886–1929), and Martin Buber (1878–1965) were joined by great rabbis such as Leo Baeck (1873–1956). A Renaissance of Judaism took place. Jewish learning increased; books in Hebrew and German were published in increasing numbers, and adult academies of Jewish learning were organized in every community. In adversity, German Jewry had one of its moments of greatness.

As if in preparation for this hour of need, German Jewry produced Jewish thinkers, schooled in German philosophy but filled with a profound love and knowledge of their heritage. That some of them were *Baale Teshuvah* (Men of Return) from the fringes to the core of Judaism makes their work even more significant for modern Jews. They grappled with the problem of Torah-Mitzvot-Land, and each of them saw the essence of Jewish survival in a different one of these elements without eliminating the others.

Leo Baeck.   The spirit of inner resistance to oppression and extermination, created by these men out of the sources of Judaism, is exemplified by the life and work of Rabbi *Leo Baeck*, one of the great figures of our age. Baeck combined learning and love. As a young man, he wrote a systematic exposition, *The Essence of Judaism*. He was rabbi in Berlin, was elected head of the German rabbis and of B'nai B'rith, and taught at the liberal rabbinical school in addition to serving as congregational rabbi. When the Nazis came to power, the German Jews made him their leader. He had to negotiate with the Nazis and at the same time give strength to his people. Even when he was called to America, he refused the call and voluntarily shared the concentration camp with his fellows. He continued to teach, inspire, and give meaning to Jewish life and suffering to those in the camps, though this instruction had to be offered without books and in secret, as it was forbidden by the Nazis. Miraculously, he survived. During his last years, he taught at the Hebrew Union College in Cincinnati. Baeck's sacrificial idealism rested on the professed conviction that "this People Israel" stands under the Covenant with God from which springs the meaning of its life and history and its eternity.

7

THE AMERICAN DESTINY

When Frederick Jackson Turner read his epoch-making paper "The Significance of the Frontier in American History" before the American Historical Society in 1893, he did not think of the Jews, yet he could have cited their destiny as a prime proof for his hypothesis. Challenged by the frontier, immigrants from many European lands created a new society of Americans in a distinct American spirit, a "democracy born of free land, strong in selfishness and individualism . . . pressing individual liberty beyond its proper bounds." This society had its dangers as well as its great advantages.

JUDAISM IN A NEW LAND

Early Struggles

In 1654 twenty-three Jews arrived in the port of New Amsterdam; they had been preceded by a few Jewish individuals who had settled along the Atlantic seaboard. Their arrival marked the end of an odyssey for these Jews that had extended over generations. In 1492 the Jews of Spain were expelled by King Ferdinand and Queen Isabella. In the same year, actually on the very day of the enforced departure of the Jews, Columbus set sail for his voyage of discovery. It has been claimed that he chose this day because he had Jewish sailors among his crew and they had to be out of Spain on that day. Columbus wrote movingly about the plight of the departing Jews, whose rickety ships he passed on leaving port.

The Jewish refugees settled in many countries, including Holland. Some were permitted to find new homes in Portugal, but this hospitality lasted but a short time. King Manuel of Portugal, who came to the throne in 1495, had to promise his bride, daughter of the Spanish rulers Ferdinand and Isabella, that he would get rid of the Jews. In December 1496 the Jews were given ten months to depart. Actually, Manuel, who was aware of the economic benefits the Jews had brought him, did not wish them to depart. In 1497 he had large numbers of Jews, especially children, baptized by force. Many Jews became marranos.

The opening of the New World gave the Portuguese Jews an opportunity for escape. They settled in Brazil, which was under Portuguese rule. There, many of them openly returned to their Jewish faith. But soon the Inquisition, the arm of the Church that pursued heretics and delivered them to death, was established in Brazil.

Now Holland entered the contest for colonies in the New World. In 1624 the Dutch, having defeated the Portuguese, began to establish themselves in Brazil. Numerous Jews, formerly refugeees from Spain but now Dutch citizens, went to the new colony to develop it. In 1645, however, the Portuguese began to reconquer Brazil, and by 1654 they had won it back completely. Some of the Jews returned to Holland, others scattered throughout Central and North America.

In August 1654, the first Jew, Jacob Barsimson, a Dutch citizen, arrived at New Amsterdam. One month later, he was followed by twenty-three others, also Dutch subjects and fugitives from Brazil. They were destitute. The funds they had expected from Amsterdam to pay for their passage had not arrived, and the master of the ship that had brought them obtained a judgment against all their property in payment for his services.

New Amsterdam was a Dutch colony; its governor was Peter Stuyvesant, a harsh master and religious bigot. In letter after letter, addressed to Amsterdam, he demanded the right to expel the members of this "deceitful race." The Dutch West India Company, who held the charter of the colony, overruled him. Jews were shareholders in the Company, and could not be antagonized. The Jewish settlers had to give a solemn pledge, however, that their poor would never become a burden to the Company or the community, but be supported by their own people. Jews have held to this principle ever since.

The newcomers were not satisfied with merely being tolerated. They immediately demanded the right to purchase land for a cemetery (July 1655), and in other ways kept on petitioning the Company for rights and recognition. They obtained the right to build a synagogue. In the same year, while the colony was under attack by Indians, they requested—and received—the right to bear arms in the defense of New Amsterdam. Bearing arms was a privilege of citizens, and Jews originally were to be excluded and were to pay a tax instead. These rights were but a step toward full citizenship rights. On April 21, 1657, the Jews of the colony, already Dutch citizens, were admitted to full citizenship in the colony. In 1664 the British took New Amsterdam from the Dutch and renamed it New York. The colony became British. The status of the Jews did not change.

Only five thousand in number by the time of the American Revolution, the Jews fought patriotically. Although some of them felt conscience bound (like many other colonists) to support the British crown, the majority were prepared to give their all—life and property—to the cause of the United States.

In contrast to their European fellows, they could count on the support of the Founding Fathers of America—Benjamin Franklin, first on the list of subscribers to the synagogue building in Philadelphia; Thomas Jefferson, sympathetic to endeavors to modernize religious worship; John Adams, who expressed the hope that all prejudice against Jews would vanish from the earth through the example of the United States. In Maryland, Thomas Kennedy, a Scotch Presbyterian, spoke out powerfully for their rights; though he knew no Jews, he felt justice demanded it. Their greatest support, however, came from George Washington himself, who (in a letter to the Jewish congregation of Newport, Rhode Island) made it clear that "happily the government of the United States, which gives to bigotry no sanction, to persecution no assistance, requires only that they who live under its protection shall demean themselves as good citizens in giving it at all occasions their effectual support." This was assurance and challenge.

Jews became patriots without giving up their faith.

Early Jewish settlers established patterns for American Judaism. *Judah Touro* (1775–1854), wounded in the battle of New Orleans, became a philanthropist in the spirit of interfaith cooperation and paid one-fifth of the cost of Bunker Hill Monument. *Uriah P. Levy* (1792–1862) reached the highest rank in the United States Navy, that of commodore. He had to combat anti-Semitism, but it would never have occurred to a Jew of that period in Europe even to aspire to a military career. Levy abolished flogging in the Navy. The Jewish chapel at Annapolis now bears his name. *Mordecai Manuel Noah* (1785–1851) devised the plan to establish a Jewish state in the United States, around Buffalo, New York, to gather in the persecuted Jews. When his plan failed because Jews did not come, he advocated rebuilding Palestine, if this was the place the Jews preferred. Noah also served as United States consul at Tunis.

Their schemes and lives adventurous, these men were individualists, men of the frontier, that place where the old pushes forward toward the new.

A New Society

In this new environment—a society built in the spirit of the Enlightenment—the European form of the synagogue, its worship, and its customs eventually came to appear as an anachronism. There were no ordained rabbis in the United States until the middle of the nineteenth century, so some immigrant a bit versed in Judaism would be appointed to lead the service, teach the children, and perform religious functions. The lay leader (already a power in medieval Jewish life) became all powerful in individualistic America. As a man of success in life, he assumed dictatorial powers in his congregation, which he directed as president. Frequently religiously nonobservant in their own lives, the majority of these leaders insisted on a strict (pre-

Mendelssohnian) pattern of religion in the synagogue. They were supported by the new arrivals, who found shelter from the new world in the synagogue of old-time religion.

Yet the second and third generations could not abide it; they saw no link to life in this form of faith. Those who were attracted by the lure of the West might be swallowed up by its vastness and be lost to their faith. Those who remained in the East and South, where organized Jewish life existed, found themselves confronted with "bossism"—the absolute and harsh rule of powerful community leaders—an outmoded form of worship, and a community divided between newcomers and old-timers.

Reforms were to come, but the clash of individuals, the power of leaders prominent in the world without necessarily being religious, the independence of congregations, each going its own way—these elements can still be found in American Judaism. Under the impact of the frontier, a community had emerged to which Torah and Mitzvot frequently were, at best, psychological defenses against the overpowering experiences of the new environment. At worst, they became a mechanical performance. The universal affirmation by these Jews of their belonging to the House of Israel therefore stands as a positive element. They wanted to be full-fledged Americans, but as Jews. It was an affirmation of their individualism approved by the spirit of America.

The Old Faith and the New World

The German Jews were the first to arrive in the United States in large numbers. In Germany, they had been organized in religious congregations, synagogues. Since the French Revolution, the communal organization of Western Jewry had been dismantled, partly by governmental laws, partly by the desire of the Jews themselves. Rabbinical jurisdiction over the affairs of life had ceased; only religion held the Jews together. Meanwhile, the Reform movement was developing.

The openness of the United States, in spirit as in physical dimensions, favored Reform. Many of those who had been Orthodox at home were attracted to it. They came from Germany to escape civil repression and found a ready haven in the Midwest, where Christian Germans had settled, among them many liberals who had left Germany after the failure of the revolution of 1848. The Jews who arrived were poor but brought with them their skills, the typically German talent for organization, and, in many cases, a liberal outlook schooled on the principles of the Enlightenment. They were capable of rapid acculturation and were economically successful in the frontier region where they had settled. By 1875 the American Jewish community had reached a total of 250,000, mostly of German origin. They were prosperous and happy; they had found their niche. Adjustment of religious patterns became imperative.

The first one to undertake the task was *Isaac Leeser* (1806–1868). An immigrant from Germany, he showed so profound a Jewish knowledge that, although he was not a rabbi, he was appointed, in 1829, spiritual leader of the congregation in Philadelphia. He used his position as a base from which to affect all of American Jewry. Leeser was strictly Orthodox and deeply influenced by Mendelssohn. The Mitzvot must be upheld; at the same time, people must be educated to understand Torah. Leeser translated the Bible and the prayer book into English, published a periodical, and traveled widely. His hope was to equip strictly Orthodox Jews for living in two civilizations, as Mendelssohn had done. He was not a theoretical theologian as the German rabbis were (the American leaders were not primarily concerned with philosophical considerations) but was pragmatic in his approach, for the spirit of America is pragmatic. Later religious leaders were to follow his approach. However, Leeser's hope of developing a strictly Orthodox expression in worship and life that would, at the same time, be esthetically appealing to Americanized Jews, was to bear fruit only later, as the major trend among German Jews was toward Reform.

THE EMERGENCE OF A PLURALISTIC RELIGIOUS JUDAISM

Orthodoxy

Beginning in the 1870s, millions of Jews from Russia and Poland began to arrive in the United States. They had to face problems themselves and posed problems for the established Jewish community. Eventually, they were to shape the character of American Jewry.

For the newcomers, life in the United States spelled the transition from the Old World to the New, from a homogeneous Jewish society guided by Jewish religion in all its aspects to a heterogeneous one composed of many groups, and from life as small farmers and traders in a rural environment to urban sweatshops. True to the pledge of the first settlers, the established Jewish community gave aid to the newcomers, hoping to assimilate them quickly to American ways and the American pattern of Jewish religion, which was Reform. What they failed to see was that the immigrants needed the shelter of their ethnic surroundings as a psychological defense against the overpowering influences of the new and, later on, as a transitional stage toward assimilation. The newcomers thus refused to adjust in line with the hopes of the settled Jewish community; they maintained their Orthodox congregations (each group having its own congregation), continued to speak Yiddish among themselves, and preserved their old traditions. The result was an antagonism between the German Jews and the Eastern European Jews that time has only begun to heal.

The shock of the new culture was profound for the immigrants. But equally great was the pull of American life, especially on their children. In response, **Orthodoxy** took two widely divergent directions: Some communities chose to be led by rabbis of the "old" type—men without academic training, living a pre-Mendelssohnian type of life. They were not "Orthodox," in the sense of forming a denomination, they were simply "Jewish" as they had been in the **shtetl**, the small Eastern European town that was wholly Jewish within a non-Jewish world and that developed its own ways of life and its own culture. On the other hand, there were communities whose members felt that separation from the world could not be maintained, and that academically trained rabbis were needed to bring the people into the new era and maintain them there, guiding them to face modernity without compromising Torah, Mitzvot, and traditional Jewish observances.

To produce such educated men, the **Yeshivah** (the Orthodox rabbinical seminary) was expanded into a university. These men, equally strict in their interpretation of the divine Torah and the binding force of Mitzvot, tried to adopt a philosophy akin to that of Samson Raphael Hirsch, as far as the education of their membership permitted. But, whereas Hirsch maintained that Jewish law prohibits Jews from actively engaging in the upbuilding of the Land of Israel, contemporary Orthodoxy is Zionist in all its ranks. For Hirsch, only prayer for the Messiah was permitted; the Messiah would gather the Jews. Orthodox Jews today combine action in behalf of Israel with prayer for the Messiah.

Orthodoxy has strongly and successfully reasserted its presence and viability on the contemporary Jewish scene in America. As the generations have become more Americanized and frequently less Orthodox with the passing of time, Orthodoxy has been trying to strengthen its theological foundations, which accounts for the increased use of Samson Raphael Hirsch's works. It has extended its school system. In the Young Israel Movement, it has developed a system of neo-Orthodox synagogues and institutions. And it has successfully promoted the establishment of **Kashrut** (Kosher laws) in communal affairs and kosher eating facilities at numerous universities. Orthodoxy has also gained momentum from the immigration of whole communities from Eastern Europe, especially the Hasidim, who settled as units, surrounding the rabbi who had led them here. As noted before, the community of the Lubavitcher Rebbe (Rabbi Menachem M. Schneerson) has become the center of a network of congregations, a widespread school system, literature sent throughout the land, and even of a system of closed-circuit television broadcasts that bring his followers into live contact with the rabbi and his message.

At the same time that Orthodoxy has witnessed a resurgence, inner conflicts persist.

A group of "left-wing" Orthodox rabbis has been pressing for changes within the framework of Orthodox doctrine, along the lines of Hirsch's ideas, and some have been willing to enter a dialogue with non-Orthodox Jewry. In general, and in principle, the antagonism to non-Orthodox Jewry still exists. To Orthodoxy, there is only one true Judaism, a "Torah-true" Judaism; all other forms are aberrations. Since the chain of tradition is regarded as a transmission from a greater past to an ever less distinguished present, the decisions of previous rabbinical authorities, including those of Russia and Poland, cannot be overruled by moderns, except through interpretation, which finds only hesitant acceptance. Conservatism and Reform therefore cannot be "true" in this light.

This attitude has been strengthened by the fact that the state-supported chief rabbinate in Israel is regarded by Orthodox Jewry as *the* central authority. The chief rabbinate may endeavor to find new solutions in individual cases, based strictly on the interpretation of past rabbinical opinion, within the framework of Talmud and Codes, but arriving deductively at new conclusions. It has no understanding for the underlying philosophy of non-Orthodox movements, nor does it have any sympathy with them. By this attitude, Orthodoxy has actually alienated large segments, even of Israeli Jewry, from religion altogether. The result has been a deepening split of Jewry along denominational lines, something which is contrary to the spirit of Judaism. It is equally contrary to the spirit of America, which has always recognized unity in diversity and has followed the spirit of cooperation.

In recent years, Orthodoxy has gained from the general trend in America toward religious conservatism. Many of its adherents are men and women of achievement in the intellectual and business world. And in turn, Orthodoxy has influenced the move toward greater traditionalism in all branches of religious American Jewry. It has a great function to fulfill in setting an example of life and in developing thought. This can occur as it comes to grips intellectually and practically with the problems of our time, and as it maintains contact with other branches of Jewry as equals.

Orthodox Jewry can provide thinkers to guide all of Jewry. From the rabbis of the Talmud through Maimonides, Mendelssohn, and Samson Raphael Hirsch, it produced leaders who advanced the frontiers of traditional thought because they were aware of the world around them. Yet they were uncompromisingly observant of the Law. In the vision of Rabbi Abraham Isaac Kook (1865–1935), late chief rabbi of what is now Israel, we find similar wisdom. He was a mystic who built the secular Zionist enterprise into his own, entirely religious, system of God's plan. Thus even the most secular activity in building the Land was given religious meaning and value. Faith, wisdom, love and understanding speak out of his words:

> Faith is the song of life. Woe to him who wishes to rob life of its splendid poetry. . . . Faith and love are the very essence of life. There would be nothing of value left in the travail of life if these two luminaires, faith and love, were taken from it. Contemporary civilization throughout the world is founded entirely on unbelief and hate, forces which nullify the essence of life. It is impossible to overcome this disease of human society unless we discover the good that is contained in faith and love. The Torah and the divine precepts are the channels through which faith and love flow unceasingly.

> All the troubles of the world, especially the ills of the soul such as sadness, impatience, disgust with life and despair are due only to the failure of knowing how to face the majesty of God in utter surrender. . . .

The Torah and all its precepts form a great and mighty divine poem of trust and love. Because of our reverence and affection for the people of Israel, we lovingly observe the customs of Israel, even if they are not wholly based on divine revelation. This affection of ours is sacred, derived from a high and divine source.

The basic principle of the observance of the rules and regulations introduced by our sages is the fact that all Israel has accepted them. The honor of our nation and its historical influence are embodied in them. Hence, whatever is more ancient is more beloved, since the will and the general character of the people are revealed in it. . . . A wonderful vital force is hidden in the heart of each Jew, which impels him to attach himself to his people, whose life stream flows within him. This subconscious impulse makes him share the powerful yearning for the pure and uplifting light of truth and divine equity, a yearning that is bound to be realized some day in actual life.

The Jewish precepts, practices and customs are the vessels which contain a few sparks from the great life from above. The vital force of Torah will do its work in the innermost being of him who clings to its precepts, even though that person remains unaware of its operation. The moment a man desires to have a share in the spirit of Israel, the divine spirit enters his aspirations, even in spite of himself. All possessions of Israel are suffused with the indwelling spirit of God: its land, its language, its history and its customs.

Prayer is an absolute necessity for us and for the whole world; it is also the most sacred kind of joy. . . . (Quoted from Glatzer, *The Dynamics of Emancipation*, pp. 53–54)

Rav Kook had no sympathy for non-Orthodox forms of Judaism; nevertheless, his thoughts have inspired all of them.

As the branches of religious Jewry stay in touch and recognize each other, they influence and sustain each other. Solomon Schechter, then president of the Conservative Jewish Theological Seminary, speaking at a convocation of the Reform Hebrew Union College, characterized his stand toward Reform Judaism as "loyal opposition." This can apply to all branches. Opposition and disagreements may remain, but the loyalty of the opponent to Judaism and Jewry may never be doubted. In this way, the dialogue will never cease.

American Reform

Most of the few early rabbis who arrived in the United States were Reform. Among them was the brilliant David Einhorn, so extreme in his views that he had become unacceptable to German congregations. Then came *Isaac Mayer Wise* (1819–1900), whose fervent love of liberty had made him leave Europe. Under his guidance, Reform became a movement, acquiring structure and organization.

Wise had the hope and ambition of creating a *united* and integrated American Judaism. He started out as a Conservative, choosing a middle road which he hoped would rally American Jewry. Immediately he came into conflict with Orthodox leadership. Still striving to find a common ground for all American Jews, he inspired the formation of the Union of American Hebrew Congregations by a group of distinguished lay leaders, as an umbrella organization for all types of congregations that would not interfere in their internal affairs. The Orthodox group refused to join. Wise then developed a rabbinical seminary—the first in the Western world—The Hebrew Union College in Cincinnati. It was intended to train rabbis for all religious groups, but again Wise was rebuffed by the Orthodox group. His final hope for unity was pinned on the organization of a rabbinical body in which rabbis of all persuasions could hold membership. It led him to found the Central Conference of American Rabbis. The Orthodox rabbis refused to join; they wanted none of his spirit of even moderate reform. In his middle position, Wise suited neither the radical reformers nor the Orthodox traditionalists. If he wanted any kind of organization without surrendering his hopes for some kind of unification, he had to shift to the liberal wing. Thus he turned to Reform.

Eventually, his organization was to grow into one of the powerful wings of American religious Jewry, Reform Judaism. Yet Wise's original dream was to be fulfilled in a fashion. American Jewry became organized, not in one but in three groups, and each group followed Wise's organizational plan.

During its early stages, the Reform movement became radical. Geiger's most extreme ideas were translated into reality. Beyond that, many innovations were approved—for instance, the elimination of covering one's head in worship. Torah was no longer binding except in its ethical pronouncements; Mitzvot were equated with ethical conduct. The Land of Israel was regarded as of no concern. The messianic hope was no longer considered an anticipation of the future; it had come to fulfillment in America.

These positions were promulgated in the "Pittsburgh Platform," hammered out during the conference of rabbis in that city on November 16–18, 1885. The guiding spirit was Kaufmann Kohler, a rabbi and scholar who was to become president of the Hebrew Union College. In his youth, Kohler had been a disciple of Samson Raphael Hirsch. We find in him the same extremism and the same unreserved allegiance to state and society, though the two were on opposite sides. The platform, Kohler's "declaration of independence," proclaimed, among other things:

> It will not do to offer our prayers in a tongue which only few scholars nowadays understand. We cannot afford any longer to pray for a return to Jerusalem. It is a blasphemy and lie upon the lips of every American Jew. . . . We accept as binding only its [the Scripture's] moral laws, but reject all such as are not adapted to the views and habits of modern civilization. . . . We hold that all such Mosaic and rabbinical laws as regulate diet, priestly purity and dress originated in ages and under the influences of ideas entirely foreign to our present mental and spiritual state. . . . (Quoted from Ismar Elbogen, *A Century of Jewish Life*; Philadelphia: Jewish Publication Society, 1946, pp. 344*f*.)

So great was the prestige of the fifteen rabbis who worked out the platform, that it came to be regarded as the philosophy of Reform Judaism, even though the platform was never officially adopted by the Central Conference of American Rabbis or the Union of American Hebrew Congregations.

After the platform was passed by the conference, Isaac Mayer Wise, the presiding officer, asked the question: "What are you going to do with this declaration of independence?" It was a fateful question. The term *declaration of independence* is so fraught with meaning for Americans, that, in this context, it came to mean for many Jews that Reform wanted to pursue its way independently from the rest of Jewry. Even those who looked with favor on reforms, but did not wish to sever the bond with tradition entirely, felt there was no room for them in Reform Judaism.

The Pittsburgh Platform evoked in the rest of Jewry an image of Reform Judaism that was totally assimilationist, denying Jewish peoplehood, hostile to Zionist aspirations, and scornful of tradition. Reform Judaism has had great difficulties in living down this image. Fortunately, it saw and continues to see itself not as *reformed* in one complete act, but rather as *given to reform*. Thus Reform was to move back into the mainstream of Jewish living.

The "Columbus Platform" of 1937 reveals the evolution of Reform Judaism. It constituted a return to traditional concepts and commitments, and affirmed Jewish peoplehood and the duty to support the rebuilding of the Jewish homeland.

> Judaism is the historical religious experience of the Jewish people. . . . The Torah, both written and oral, enshrines Israel's ever growing consciousness of God and of the moral law. It preserves the historical precedents, sanctions and norms of Jewish life. . . . Being products of historical processes certain of its laws have lost their binding force with the passing of conditions that called them forth. But as a depository of Israel's spiritual ideals the Torah remains the dynamic source of the life of Israel. Each age has the obligation to adapt the teachings of Torah to its basic needs in accordance with the genius of Judaism. . . . Judaism is the soul of which Israel is the body. . . . In the rehabilitation of Palestine . . . we affirm the obligation of all Jewry to aid in its upbuilding as a Jewish homeland. . . . In Judaism religion and morality blend into an indissoluble unity. . . . Religious practice: the religious life . . . the home . . . the synagog . . . education . . . prayer. . . . Judaism as *a way of life* requires in addition to its moral and spiritual demands, the preservation of the Sabbath, festivals and Holy Days, the retention and development of such customs, symbols and ceremonies as possess inspirational value, the cultivation of distinctive forms of religious art and music and the use of Hebrew, together with the vernacular, in our worship and instruction. (Central Conference of American Rabbis *Yearbook*, vol. 18, pp. 97–100; © 1937 by CCAR)

Thus the unity of Torah–Mitzvot–Land was restored. Some of the most ardent fighters for the restoration of the Land of Israel have come from the Reform rabbinate. In connection with the American Bicentennial in 1976, the Central Conference of American Rabbis, at its San Francisco Convention, issued a statement: "Reform Judaism, A Centenary Perspective," embodying the most recent thinking of the Reform rabbinate. The statement recognizes that much has changed in the last century.

The Holocaust shattered our easy optimism about humanity and its inevitable progress. The State of Israel, through its many accomplishments, raised our sense of the Jews as a people to new heights of aspiration and devotion.

Declaring that Reform Judaism not only tolerates but engenders diversity, the Conference affirmed:

> The affirmation of God has always been essential to our people's will to survive. . . . We ground our lives, personally and communally, on God's reality and remain open to new experiences and conceptions of the Divine. . . . *The Jewish people* [italics added] and Judaism defy precise definition because both are in the process of becoming. . . . Jews, by birth or conversion, constitute an uncommon union of faith and peoplehood. . . . Throughout our long history our people has been inseparable from its religion with its messianic hope that humanity will be redeemed.
>
> *The Torah*: Torah results from the relationship between God and the Jewish people. . . . Lawgivers and prophets, historians and poets gave us a heritage whose study is a religious imperative and whose practice is our chief means to holiness.

Religious practice is therefore an obligation; it is to be combined with Jewish ethical responsibilities:

> Judaism emphasizes action rather than creed as the primary expression of the religious life, the means by which we strive to achieve universal justice and peace. Reform Judaism shares this emphasis on duty and obligation. Our founders stressed that the Jew's ethical responsibilities, personal and social, are enjoined by God. The past century has taught us that the claims made upon us may begin with our ethical obligations, but they extend to many other aspects of Jewish living, including: creating a Jewish home, centered on family devotion; life-long study; private prayer and public worship; daily religious observance; keeping the Sabbath and the holy days; celebrating the major events of life; involvement with the synagogue and community; and other activities which promote the survival of the Jewish people and enhance its existence. Within each area of Jewish observance Reform Jews are called upon to confront the claims of Jewish tradition, however differently perceived, and to exercise their individual autonomy, choosing and creating on the basis of commitment and knowledge.

The State of Israel is seen as imposing obligations as well:

> We are privileged to live in an extraordinary time, one in which a third Jewish commonwealth has been established in our people's ancient homeland. We are bound to that land and to the newly reborn State of Israel by innumerable religious and ethnic ties. We have been enriched by its culture and ennobled by its indomitable spirit. We see it providing unique opportunities for Jewish self-expression. We have both a stake and a responsibility in building the State of Israel, assuring its security and defining its Jewish character. We encourage aliyah (immigration to Israel) for those who wish to find a maximum personal fulfillment in the cause of Zion. We demand that Reform Judaism be unconditionally legitimized in the State of Israel.
>
> At the same time that we consider the State of Israel vital to the welfare of Judaism everywhere, we reaffirm the mandate of our tradition to create strong Jewish communities wherever we live. . . . The State of Israel and the di-

aspora, in fruitful dialogue, can show how a people transcends nationalism, even as it affirms it, thereby setting an example for humanity which remains largely concerned with dangerously parochial goals.

The statement recognizes a change in Jewish duties to humanity. It notes that early Reform Jews saw the major duty of Jewry as serving universal goals. This outlook, based on a belief in the growing universalism in the world and held by a Jewry newly admitted to society, stands in need of correction.

> In recent years we have become freshly conscious of the virtues of pluralism and the values of particularism. . . . Until the recent past our obligations to the Jewish people and to all humanity seemed congruent. At times now these two imperatives appear to conflict. We know of no simple way to resolve such tensions. We must, however, confront them without abandoning either of our commitments. A universal concern for humanity unaccompanied by a devotion to our particular people is self-destructive; a passion for our people without involvement in humankind contradicts what the prophets have meant to us. Judaism calls us simultaneously to universal and particular obligations.

The statement concludes with a call to sober hope:

> Previous generations of Reform Jews had unbounded confidence in humanity's potential for good. We have lived through terrible tragedy and been compelled to reappropriate our tradition's realism about the human capacity for evil. The survivors of the Holocaust, on being granted life, seized it, nurtured it, and rising above catastrophe, showed humankind that the human spirit is indomitable. The State of Israel, established and maintained by the Jewish will to live, demonstrates what a united people can accomplish in history. The existence of the Jew is an argument against despair; Jewish survival is a warrant for human hope.
>
> We remain God's witness that history is not meaningless. . . . (Central Conference of American Rabbis *Yearbook*, vol. 85, San Francisco, California, 1976, pp. 174–178. © 1977 by CCAR. Used with permission.)

The Hebrew Union College was later to be merged with the Jewish Institute of Religion, a rabbinical school founded in New York by Rabbi Stephen S. Wise, a champion of Zionism and social justice. In consummating this merger, the Hebrew Union College acquired its additional campus in New York City. As its current name—Hebrew Union College–Jewish Institute of Religion—indicates, it accepted some of Stephen Wise's spirit as well. Wise (who was not related to the founder of the Reform movement) envisioned Jewry as *one people*. His rabbinical school was to prepare rabbis who would be equipped to serve all branches of Judaism. By incorporating his school, the Hebrew Union College widened its scope ideologically as well as regionally. An additional campus has been established at Los Angeles. Finally, an institute for archaeology was founded at Jerusalem; it was eventually developed into another campus, and, since 1970, every rabbinical student is required to spend one year of studies there. The link to the Land is affirmed.

The Hebrew Union College–Jewish Institute of Religion has thus been a pioneer. A pioneering step of fundamental importance for Judaism has been the school's ordination of women as rabbis and the investiture of women, educated in the cantorial school of the institution, as cantors. This step has been strongly attacked by Orthodox Jewry.

True to Reform tradition, the Union of American Hebrew Congregations, parent body of the movement, has been active on behalf of national and international social justice. The rabbis of the movement, organized in the Central Conference of American Rabbis, have been frequent spokespersons for the rights of minority groups.

At the same time, the movement has been deeply concerned with and most active in strengthening Jewish life and consciousness. Camps have been established in many parts of the country where young people and adults live a life of Torah and Mitzvot for varying lengths of time in a total Jewish environment. In the past, Jewish education for children was confined to the "Sunday school," conducted one day a week. Numerous congregations have expanded this education, however, to three-day instruction. Hebrew is stressed in all schools. A serious concern for an integrated curriculum of Torah and life is shown in an emerging trend of establishing Jewish day schools. Liturgical and educational material has been issued; affiliated brotherhoods, sisterhoods, and youth groups are expanding; and excellent theologians have emerged.

The Reform Movement, as a group, is a member of the World Zionist Organization. It has founded and maintains kibbutzim and schools in Israel.

Conservatism

In the latter part of the nineteenth century, a new generation came along, ready to move into the mainstream of American life, yet unwilling to accept Reform Judaism, which they saw as too formal and too cold. The Reform leaders were the first to provide this generation with the means (both physical and intellectual) for the establishment of a religious movement that would synthesize American ways of life and Jewish thinking based on the thought of tradition-bound Eastern European Jewry. Living up to the American ideal of unity in diversity, the Reform (lay) leaders organized the Jewish Theological Seminary, which became the fountainhead of Conservative Judaism. They provided the funds for the seminary and, as overseers, promoted its organization and expansion.

Conservative Judaism in America has been based strongly on Frankel's principles. *Solomon Schechter* (1850–1915), the guiding spirit of the Jewish Theological Seminary, maintained that the development of Torah and Mitzvot is squarely placed by God in the hands of the Jewish people, who by unspoken consent adjust and evolve it. Schechter developed institutions for Conservative Judaism similar to those Wise developed for Reform, but he reversed the order of their creation. First came the Jewish Theological Seminary, based on a philosophy of "positive historical Judaism," then came the Rabbinical Assembly, and finally the United Synagogue, the congregational organization. The

Seminary thus remains the fountainhead, and, organizationally at least, holds the key position.

According to Conservative doctrine, the decisions of Torah and Talmud must be followed, Zionism is a key principle, and Mitzvot must be practiced, except as the people change them. Due to the autonomy of individual congregations, even in the evolution of Jewish practices, the changes vary. Some congregations, for instance, use organ music in their services; others reject it. The rabbinical leaders and the Seminary generally authorize only those changes which have been universally adopted. The approach is pragmatic and, as such, typically American. It has failed, however, to provide strong support to individual rabbis and communities while changes were being debated by their own membership. Reform may have been too categorical. Conservatism, placing decisions in the hands of the people with a rabbi but a guide, followed very much the thinking of American democracy, but it proved indecisive when firmness might have helped. A more decisive attitude of the Rabbinical Assembly seems to be emerging.

In recent years, the Committee on Jewish Law and Standards of the Rabbinical Assembly has handed down some bold decisions, as, for instance, on the status of women. These decisions move *within* the framework of **Halakhah**, the guiding law of Jewish Life, but they give it new and innovative interpretations.

At its 1980 convention, the Rabbinical Assembly approved the ordination of women as rabbis. The issue, which had previously entailed extensive and heated struggle, had been submitted to a cross-section of Conservative Jews; the opinion was generally favorable.

Those favoring ordination held that, ethically, it should be granted in the spirit of equality of the sexes. It was decidedly unfair to allow women participation in the full rabbinical program and then to deny them ordination. Many women, dedicated to Judaism as their life's vocation, had from childhood on, gone through all the stages of Jewish studies, organizational life, and commitment, only to find that, at the end of their training and development, they were denied ultimate fulfillment. The only choice for Conservative women was to transfer to one of the Reform or Reconstructionist Seminaries that ordained women if they wished to fulfill their desire. As a result, Conservatism would be impoverished. Halakhically, as a paper by the chancellor of the Jewish Theological Seminary explained, the rabbi's function in modern days was different from that of earlier times. While some restrictions might be imposed on women, there was no reason for them not to function as preachers, counselors, teachers, guides, and pastors—the main functions of the contemporary rabbi.

The opposition pointed out that ordination of women was so basic a departure from tradition that it would create cleavages between Diaspora Conservatism, already fighting an uphill struggle for recognition in Israel, and the Israeli rabbinate, and would increase the chasm between Conservatism and

Orthodoxy. Against this, it was argued that Conservative congregations would adjust. Moreover, Conservative Judaism was totally unrecognized by the Israeli rabbinate, and even subjected to grave disabilities in Israel, and Orthodoxy in this country was bound to follow the directives of the Israeli rabbinate. Conservatism was a great and vital movement and should not be overly anxious about the opinion of other groups in Judaism. If ordination of women was acceptable under Conservative principles, the movement should go ahead, as it was ethical to do so.

After finally approving the ordination of women, the convention left the implementation of the resolution to the faculty of the Jewish Theological Seminary, which has the authority to grant ordination. However, as the faculty is opposed to ordaining women, it has not implemented the resolution and whether it will do so is uncertain. In the meantime, a split developed within the Conservative rabbinate: On the one hand were those who organized a determined opposition to the ordination of women; on the other hand were those who held that the faculty should merely certify completion of the course work leading to ordination, while ordination itself would be conferred by rabbis delegated by the Rabbinical Assembly.

Conservatism has developed a wide organizational network, including men's and women's groups, youth camps, and youth groups, and it issues educational material. The Jewish Theological Seminary, headquartered in New York, also has campuses in Los Angeles and Jerusalem. The movement as a group is affiliated with The World Zionist Organization.

Conservatism has grown into a very strong movement. Both its strengths and its weaknesses are still with us.

Reconstructionism

Reconstructionism is a philosophy of American Jewry that bases itself on the American experience, the unity of Judaism, the impact of science, the significance of Israel, and above all the *centrality of the people*. It sees Judaism as an evolving religious civilization—not a revealed religion but the creation of the Jewish people. The Jewish people received its God-concept and its religious forms out of its own needs.

Starting as a school of thought, Reconstructionism reached wide circles ideologically; becoming a denomination, it may provide the strength of unified action to its adherents. Its founder is **Mordecai M. Kaplan** (born 1881), a man distinguished not only by the most profound scholarship but also by his love and deepest concern for Judaism and for individuals. Reconstructionism is an American movement, influenced by the philosophies of William James and John Dewey, and it rests on the spirit of American democracy. In addition, it articulates the image many Jews in America hold of themselves without being able to formulate it.

Numerically, Reconstructionism is a small movement, but it has influenced the thinking of a great many rabbis, especially non-Orthodox ones.

It began in the 1930s and is found today primarily in the United States and Canada. In recent years, the movement has expanded its organization, has developed its own federation of congregations and fellowships, and has published its own prayer books and instructional materials. In 1968, it opened its own rabbinical school, affiliated with Temple University in Philadelphia. Its students take all but the specific Jewish programs in the department of religion at the university, thus combining general and Jewish education. Among the innovations of Reconstructionism in Halakhah is recognizing as a Jew a child whose father is Jewish though his mother is not, provided the child has been brought up within the Jewish faith and has received Jewish education. This is counter to the tradition that Jewishness is based on the mother's being Jewish. A similar break with tradition is the 1980 provision for egalitarian divorce procedures, which allowed women to divorce their husbands through the instrumentality of Jewish law. Reconstructionism also ordains women as rabbis. For a full comprehension of Reconstructionism, a basic understanding of Mordecai Kaplan's theology is required. We will look at this further in Chapter 15.

JUDAISM OUTSIDE SYNAGOGUE WALLS

When the new arrivals from Eastern Europe landed on the shores of America in great numbers during the last decades of the nineteenth century, the well-established German Jews organized a crash program to assimilate them quickly to American life. As we have seen, the program failed. Instead of embracing Reform, the immigrants held on to their traditions with even greater tenacity.

Large masses of Jewish immigrants, "yearning to be free," huddled on the Lower East Side of New York. Embarrassed by their "lack of culture," the established Jewish community did not absorb them. They had to start on their own, as street vendors, graduating to pushcarts, eventually becoming owners of small shops. Many began as workers in the sweatshops of the garment industry, toiling under the most inhuman conditions. Of those who flocked to the needle trades, some had been tailors in the old country. Many lacked the physical strength required for other manual occupations. A good many entered the trade because the owners, themselves Jews of an earlier migration from Eastern Europe, permitted them to observe the Sabbath, exploiting them in return during the rest of the week. In this environment emerged the Yiddish-speaking society of the Lower East Side, the little Eastern European town—the shtetl—transposed to America. The immigrants shared trials and poverty and became involved in conflicts, but they rose above their miseries as the Sabbath arrived. Amid controversy there was warmth, and, above all, there was hope. This was America: The parents might not "make it," but the children surely would. And, in fact, the children did make it.

These children, brought up in America and in many cases educated in college by the severe sacrifice of their parents, often became alienated from the culture and religion of their parents, which was frowned on by Americanized Jews and appeared alien on American soil. Many of them did not join any congregations. They saw in America an example of ethnic communities living side by side and retaining their identity by folkways. Identity did not have to be based on religion.

Among the immigrants was another group who were good, though not religious, Jews; to them the Jews were simply a people. Oppressed in Eastern Europe, denied a secular education both by the opposition of their parents and by the czarist state, these people were frequently self-taught. They were committed to the Jewish spirit of social justice, which they found in socialism and Marxism. Those who remained in Russia eventually organized a strong socialist labor organization, the *Bund* (1897). Faced with the hostility of non-Jewish socialist parties and repression by the czarist government, the Bund nevertheless grew among the Jewish masses. (The Communist regime eventually liquidated it.) Among these idealistic Jews were the founders of the State of Israel.

Those who came to America brought their ideals with them. In 1888, they founded the United Hebrew Trades, eventually establishing twenty-two unions in New York City, mostly in the needle trades. In 1909, twenty thousand women workers in the shirtwaist factories in New York struck, and in 1910 the workers in the cloak and suit industries went on strike. The general public sided with the strikers. Both employers and employees were Jews, and both were appealed to to avoid the then-common violence in order not to harm the reputation of the Jews. After long negotiations, the strikers won their demands. Although there were other strikes and conflicts, some progess had been achieved.

Throughout this time, there was the grave risk that the unions would become involved in ideological conflict. Their upbringing amid the struggle for human rights in Russia led some of the leaders to see in socialism and, later, in communism *the* solution for the working person's ills. The issue of whether unions should be ideologically committed raised violent controversies that weakened the movement. Samuel Gompers (1850–1925), a Jewish cigar maker of British descent, who became the founder of the American Federation of Labor, saw the unions as simply the tool for the improvement of the workers' living conditions; ideology had no place in them. Eventually the unions rejected ideological commitment. There remained many Jews, however, who believed in socialism and even communism until the persecution of the Jews under the Soviet Communist regime opened their eyes. Through all of their activities over the years, Jews have had a lasting influence on the American labor movement.

The "cultural Jews" we have been discussing did not accept religous practices and beliefs, as they were in conflict with scientific thought and American ways of expression, yet they remained Jews, feeling strongly that survival was assured by maintaining Jewish peoplehood and culture. They had an additional example in the development of the Land of Israel, where a non-religious Judaism was emerging. Religion thus was not regarded as essential. Zionism, folkways, and culture (ethical identification) were sufficient. Eliminating God, they identified Torah with education in general. Mitzvot meant working for social justice similar to the manner in which the Social Gospel movement interpreted the message of Christianity. The Land of Israel (then only a hope) added another strong force for Jewish survival.

American Jewry thus came to consider itself either a religious group, as is more and more the case, or simply an ethnic group. The traditional respect for learning has made it acceptable among Jews to be considered an "intellectual." In American society, intellectuals have come to form a subgroup, cutting across ethnic lines. Members of this group are naturally attracted to each other and feel free to follow the conclusions of their own individualistic reasoning. Many intellectuals eventually would consider themselves ethnic Jews, but free to enter into relationships with any ethnic group they wished. This included interfaith marriage. Unfettered by tradition, they make their choice in marriage across the lines of religion and ethnicity. As interfaith marriage may increase in this group, many brilliant people may be lost to Judaism. Perhaps some will be gained, especially if rabbis and communities draw them in.

A most auspicious recent development has been the flowering of Jewish scholarship at numerous universities and colleges. Chairs for Judaic studies have been established and courses on Judaism introduced. This has had happy results in ecumenical dialogue, affecting both religious and cultural Jews. In addition, young Jews of both groups have been increasingly dedicated to the cause of Israel or support for Soviet Jewry. Some have been drawn to Hasidic groups, which represent an "undiluted" Judaism and the security offered by a fundamentalist outlook.

JEWISH ORGANIZATIONS

In 1843, a number of Jews organized the Order of **B'nai B'rith**. Its name is significant: "Sons of the *Covenant*." When an incipient anti-Semitism led to the exclusion of Jews from a number of the great fraternal orders, they decided to establish their own, emphasizing the Covenant that unites. This was well in the spirit of American self-reliance and initiative. The order was to provide fellowship and to offer assistance; for instance, an insurance program gave group protection to the members against the calamities of life. These programs have been expanded, and new ones added to them. The *Anti-Defamation League* has combatted prejudice on a wide front, educational activities have been stressed, the **Hillel Foundations** at universities provide Jewish centers for students, and youth groups initiate youngsters into their obligations as Americans and Jews. Membership is not dependent on synagogue affiliation, but the member has to be a Jew. B'nai B'rith lodges have frequently been founded in small Jewish communities, too limited in numbers and means to organize congregations. When these communities grew, B'nai B'rith often became the nucleus of new congregations. Eventually, the order spread throughout the world. The pragmatic, action-directed spirit of America can be clearly recognized in B'nai B'rith.

The American Jewish Committee (founded in 1906) and the *American* and *World Jewish Congress* (1933 and 1936, respectively) serve in the causes of Jewish defense, interfaith dialogue, and social justice in general. In the 1920s, when the fraudulent pamphlet "Protocols of the Elders of Zion" was given wide publicity by Jew-haters in the United States, a great deal of defense work had to be done; in some ways, it has had to be continued.

The Jews in the armed services have been served by the *Jewish Welfare Board* (founded 1917), which is also the sponsor of Jewish community centers similar to those run by the YMCA. Finally, in 1948, as a true sign of full acculturation, Jews established a university open to students of all races and creeds—Brandeis University in Waltham, Massachusetts.

The many other organizations—such as the *Zionist Organization* with its very active women's branch, *Hadassah*, fraternal orders, and book clubs— are a sign of the diversity of interests among Jews. Perhaps they are also a mark of the power drives of individuals and the resulting lack of unity. We have seen that every congregation is fully independent.

The one element common to these organizations is philanthropy. The work of the *United Jewish Appeal* has been unexcelled in its scope and the number of people saved and rehabilitated. Here American Jewry has responded with true sacrificial nobility to the demands of the hour. It has provided funds for Israel, made possible the rescue and resettlement of thousands of Jews— both refugees from the Nazis and, more recently, emigrés from Russia—and it has supported charitable and educational institutions.

In contrast, the *Synagogue Council of America*, supposedly the spokesman of all religious organizations, has had limitations imposed on it by the rivalries of its constituent groups. Laypeople and lay organizations are the spokespeople of religious Jewry. But this is historically conditioned, and the result of a great deal of factionalism. A true dialogue between the various branches of religious Jewry has yet to come.

CONTEMPORARY CHALLENGES AND SOCIETAL ISSUES

The devastation of Jewish life throughout the world beginning with Hitler's extermination program provided American Jewry with a twofold challenge: First, it had to provide homes and a new start for the multitude of refugees not only in the United States but in other parts of the world. All were destitute, and only American Jewry had the resources to restore them. Second-ly, it had to give help on the widest scale to the impoverished Jewish commu-nities in many lands, assistance to young settlements that sprang up as a result of migration, and aid to the upbuilding of Israel. These challenges were fully accepted. Israel, the communities in Europe, and the fast-growing Jewish communities of South America owe their emergence and development to American Jewish aid. The Land of Israel could not have been redeemed, nor could its institutions have been developed in such unique fashion, without the unstinting support of American Jews. The kinship of the Jewish people was thus affirmed, the Mitzvah of providing life was exemplified, the love of the Land was abundantly reaffirmed, and Torah was planted abroad.

Yet American Jewry, having come of age so suddenly, finds itself faced with a second challenge: to provide spiritual guidance and leadership, to develop a pattern of Jewish theology and life keyed to our time, and, by living a truly Jewish life, to provide the model for others. This has not yet been achieved. American Jews, in their overwhelming majority native born, have become fully acculturated and assimilated, belonging generally to the middle class of society. Anti-Semitism, though far from extinct, is not all pervasive. Jewish "defense organizations" such as the Anti-Defamation League, have to keep vigilance against any flareup due to societal unrest, economic reverses in the country, or subversion. The religious division of Americans is regarded as permanent, legitimate, and valuable. The American Jewish community thus sees itself primarily as a religious group, an outlook which is destined to fashion its character increasingly as time goes on.

We also find a certain amount of conversion to Judaism, a result of the fluidity in religious movement among Americans. Although differences in ideology and priorities may lead to a possible conflict between American Jews and Israel, the identification of American Jews with Israel during the wars of 1967 and 1973 has revealed that in need and danger ideological barriers quickly collapse, and unity among all parts of Jewry is quickly restored. Israel hopes that a number of American Jews will settle in Israel, whereas American Jewry sees the Land as primarily a spiritual force. Nevertheless, a new sense of spiritual oneness and affection and a small **Aliyah** (migration to Israel) have developed.

The general religious outlook of American Jews resembles that of the average American. They affirm their belongingness to Judaism, and the major-ity is affiliated with a congregation (though a sizable minority is not), but there is no great religious fervor as might be expressed in regular attendance at worship, home observance of Mitzvot, and extensive study of Torah. Al-though most children are sent to religious schools and made *Bar Mitzvah*, and their parents hope they will find Jewish mates, in daily practice there is little Jewish content. Yet there exists a feeling that one must work for Judaism. Numerous beautiful synagogues have been built, though most of them are empty much of the year. The urge to *do* something (in typically American pragmatic style) has led to a proliferation of charitable, social, and service organizations that are sharply competing with each other for membership and recognition.

The tension that has developed between some militant blacks and the Jews deserves attention. In principle, militant leaderships, faced with great obstacles, have frequently blamed the Jews for their hardships, thereby offering to their followers a simplistic explanation of the ills of society. There are certain discernible causes for this situation. Jews as a group have always been liberal and conscious of human rights; they have stood in the forefront of the battle for minority rights. Having but recently escaped from oppression themselves, they have known its injustices. But having recently escaped, many have also tried to compensate by seeking "the good life." There seemed to exist a discrepancy between their affirmations and their style of life that branded them in the eyes of minorities as hypocrites. The sections of cities in which Jews settled at the time of their immigration came to be occupied by blacks, as Jews, becoming more prosperous, moved out. In many cases, however, the Jews did not sell their property; they became the blacks' landlords. Some Jews, remaining in the area, continued as the shopkeepers that provided for the black neighborhood. The contacts of the minorities with Jews was therefore confined to landlords and shopkeepers, who, at times, did exploit them. These people came to represent all the ills of society in general, distorting the image of the Jew in the minds of many. Furthermore, the discrimination in employment experienced by many Jews led them to seek civil service careers, such as teaching. The same discrimination now prompts other minorities to look for these careers, where race and religion cannot be considered, but they find their ambitions blocked by Jews who have risen to supervisory positions and do not wish to relinquish them after struggling for years to reach them. Antagonism is the result.

In their quest for a new social order, many young people from minority groups have come under the influence of Marxist ideology. According to an often oversimplified Marxist perspective, the socialist systems are good and helpful to minorities and Third World nations, and the United States is bad and "imperialistic." Israel, supported by the United States, attacked by Russia, and in conflict with Arab states that are seen as Third World, is therefore "bad." This simplistic view overlooks the earnest desire of Israel to settle its internal problems of race justly and to help emerging nations. In spite of its shortcomings, Israel has been more successful in these endeavors than many other countries. But Marxism, taken uncritically, has created in many minority members hostility to Israel and, by extension, to American Jews since they are considered "Zionist." Because Arabs belong to the Third World, as do the black countries in Africa, Jews and Zionists have been presented as enemies of blacks, as "racists." In fact, as we will see in Chapter 8, the United Nations, on November 10, 1975, declared Zionism to be racism. Although this is false, the declaration can be used against Jews. It seems incongruous for minorities to be anti-Jewish, but an anti-Israel and anti-Zionist position may become an antagonism against Jews as a whole. Dr. Martin Luther King, Jr., saw this clearly. Seymour Martin Lipset, professor of government and social relations at Stanford University has related a remark Dr. King made to black students at Harvard: "One of the young men present happened to make some remark against the Zionists. Dr. King snapped at him and said, 'Don't talk like that! When people criticize Zionists, they mean Jews. You're talking anti-Semitism'" (*The Left, the Jews and Israel,* Anti-Defamation League of B'nai B'rith, 1969). The "established" black organizations, such as the NAACP, have combatted anti-Jewish sentiment wherever it is expressed. Once Jews assisted other minorities in a *paternal* fashion; this is not called for. It would be tragic if Jews, a minority group themselves, were to be pitted against other minorities.

In their search for equality, minority groups have promoted the idea of "quotas." This means that in employment on all levels the number of the employed should reflect the racial composition of the population, be it in the country as a whole or in a given area. A small minority themselves, Jews have had to fight long and arduously against the quota system directed against them for years in universities and employment. They won their battle but now find themselves endangered again. They are disproportionately represented in some fields, such as higher education. A quota system, many feel, would penalize the innocent of whatever origin by denying them the chance in life to which their capabilities entitle them. Quotas do not necessarily favor minorities; they may result in exclusion of the competent whose quota has been filled. Jews advocate instead a system of education, combined with the recognition of social rights, which would give all minorities the opportunity of competing on equal terms, based on the competitors' ability and training. They are prepared to promote affirmative action for social justice but will exert themselves against "quotas."

The discontent of minorities, combined with the tragic increase in the use of drugs, has caused violence, particularly in the cities. Whites as well as nonwhites, political radicals as well as drug users, have prominently taken part in this violence. Jews, largely city dwellers, have suffered much from it. Especially in the poorer sections of the cities, where poor Jews live in great numbers, they have become its frequent victims and have felt insecure. These factors have caused a swing of a segment of the Jewish population toward conservatism. Traditionally, Jews have been liberals and have advocated social change even when they would not gain by it and even when they were sure to bear its burden. Recently, many have come to feel that the principles of free enterprise, strongly advanced by conservatives, offer greater security against quotas, and conservative emphasis on law and order offers greater safety. Ironically, this swing to conservatism shows the extent of Jewish acculturation.

8

ZIONISM AND THE STATE OF ISRAEL

The emergence of the State of Israel is the result of a chain of interlocking events—of ideas and ideals, theology, history, and human actions.

Throughout the Diaspora, Jewry remained linked to the Land. Return to it and independent self-government were envisioned for messianic days (see Obadiah 1:19–21; Micah 4; Zechariah 7:9–15; etc.). This hope for the coming of the Messiah was real, its fulfillment expected at any time, in accordance with God's will, and it served as a life-sustaining force during Jewry's dark ages.

It is for that reason that we find the hope for the restoration of a Jewish commonwealth enshrined in daily prayers; in grace after meals; and in the rites surrounding birth, marriage, and death. The totality of life was permeated by this expectation. During the nineteenth century, several divergent views emerged.

Orthodoxy was divided. There were those who held that Jews were not permitted to work for the return to **Zion** but had to wait for the day of divine dispensation. They were only permitted to pray for this day. Others believed that it was permitted and even imperative to promote the day of independence and to work for it politically and by actual return to the soil of Palestine. This migration to Palestine, and now Israel, has been called *Aliyah,* ascent, a term denoting its spiritual character.

Eastern European Jewry leaned toward the second point of view, while Orthodoxy in Western Europe, where Jews were reasonably secure, tended to follow the principle of waiting and praying without eliminating from its theology the concept of return and independence.

Liberal Judaism believed that the "messianic age" had arrived with the Emancipation, that the Western European countries were the final destinations for those Jews who were their citizens, and that the same process would eventually take place in the East as well. In addition, they feared that any concern with Palestine as a Jewish homeland would create suspicion of their loyalty in the eyes of state and society.

Cultural Jews were again split between those who saw in a universal socialist society the answer to all problems, including discrimination against Jews, and those who strongly believed in an independent Jewish state as the only lasting solution. Palestine was settled largely by this latter group.

ZIONISM

Russian Jewry was suffering agonies. The thought stirred (in line with the emerging nationalism of the nineteenth century) that only a return to the Land could provide freedom. *Auto-Emanzipation* (self-emancipation) was the slogan of *Leo Pinsker* (1821–1891), a Jewish physician and leader, who saw in anti-Semitism an affliction of the world that could be cured only by national independence.

The yearning for freedom from intolerable pressure and a hopeless fate in Russia expressed itself in a number of efforts to resettle on the Land. Organizations were founded, such as the *Hovave Zion* ("Lovers of Zion"), and student groups exchanged classrooms for the wilderness of Palestine and its backbreaking work. For the new immigrants, the French Baron Rothschild established colonies in Palestine as early as the 1870s. Migration was difficult, however, since the Turkish government, in whose domain Palestine lay, placed great obstacles in the way of a large scale Aliyah. The Turkish rulers had no desire to increase the numbers of non-Moslems in their empire. Since the nineteenth century they had had much trouble with them, especially the Christians. **Zionism** needed leaders.

Ahad Ha-Am (1856–1927)

Asher Ginzberg (whose pen name means "One of the People") was, like Pinsker, a product of the Enlightenment movement (Haskalah) that had taken hold within some Eastern Jewish circles. He also believed in the Jews as a people. But no people can be creative, he felt, unless it has a spiritual and cultural center in a land of its own. Let Palestine be restored as center of Jewish life, and Judaism will be reborn. Thus *cultural Zionism* was born.

In his *The Jewish State and the Jewish Problem,* Ahad Ha-Am maintained that both Jews and Judaism had come out of the ghetto and had joined the world. Previously, self-isolation had preserved the people, but these walls had fallen. With their inevitable entry into the wider society, the Jews had lost their protective shelter. Their future was endangered. By returning to their own land and forming their own society, Jews would be able to reshape their future. They would be able to live a natural life as a national body. Out of their collective experience, they could organically develop their own culture. Through it, they could make a contribution to humanity as a whole.

Ahad Ha-Am desired the right of self-government for the Jews in their land, but he did not insist on full sovereignty for the Jewish state.

Theodor Herzl (1860–1904)

Ahad Ha-Am recognized the twofold problem faced by modern Jewry in its quest for survival: internal, the search for meaning and spiritual vitality; and external, the need for escape from intolerable persecution. Ahad Ha-Am placed major emphasis on the first without neglecting the second. By contrast, **Theodor Herzl** looked for a purely political solution as means of survival. "We are a people, one people," he stated. His was the age of emerging nationalism. By becoming an independent nation, the Jews could both find freedom from persecution and develop their cultural powers and spiritual endowments to the benefit of humanity by being in their Land.

Born in Budapest, which was then Austrian, Herzl was the son of a family strongly assimilated to Western surroundings and life. Handsome, charming, and brilliant, he nevertheless had to cope with anti-Semitism in his student years. He eventually chose the career of a newspaper correspondent; he also was a successful playwright and novelist. His paper, *Die Neue Freie Presse* of Vienna, sent him to Paris to cover one of the most sensational trials of the century, the Dreyfus trial. Alfred Dreyfus, a Jewish captain and the only Jewish member of the French general staff, was accused of having submitted secret documents to the Germans. His accusers knew he was innocent, the German emperor knew the identity of the traitor who had surrendered the documents, but Dreyfus, the Jew, was made the scapegoat. Witnesses were forced by threats to perjure themselves; Dreyfus was convicted and sent to Devil's Island. He was exonerated several years later, thanks largely to the efforts of dedicated and courageous men, including the French novelist Emile Zola and the statesman Clemenceau. However, the trial led to anti-Semitic agitation and outbursts in France.

To Herzl, it was an eye opener. If this could happen in France, mother of democracy in Europe, then Jews were secure nowhere. The only answer was a free and internationally recognized homeland. In his brochure *Der Judenstaat* (The Jewish State, 1896), Herzl proposed its creation. He then organized a Jewish congress, which met in Basel, Switzerland, in 1897, and set as its goal "the creation of a Jewish, internationally recognized homeland in Palestine." The congress outlined the steps to be taken toward the achievement of its goal. This was *political Zionism*.

The burden of implementation fell upon Herzl. His job was twofold. First of all, he had to convince his fellow Jews in Western Europe that his plan was not only feasible but desirable. He met with a great deal of opposition among those who felt secure in their surroundings and had constructed their thoughts and lives on the assumption that they were to be and always remain full-fledged citizens in the countries to which they had given their full emotional and physical allegiance. At the same time, Herzl had to meet and plead with princes, potentates, and governments to get a hearing and gain support for his project. The immensity of his task can hardly be imagined. Here was an individual, backed up by no power, representing a mass of powerless, oppressed people, venturing into the arena of power politics, where might alone spoke. In the pursuit of his mission, Herzl wore himself out completely. He died prematurely at the age of forty-four, exactly forty-four years before his hope was to become a reality. His work was taken up by his disciples, including *Chaim Weizmann* (1874–1952), a brilliant chemist who placed the high reputation his scientific work had given him in the service of his people. He was to end his life as the first president of the State of Israel. Among the early champions of Zionism in America were Justice *Louis Brandeis* (1856–1941), the great advocate of human rights on the Supreme Court of the United States, and Rabbi *Stephen S. Wise,* defender of social justice in America.

FROM BLUEPRINT TO REALITY

Early Developments in Palestine

To Herzl, awakened by the Dreyfus affair, it was initially immaterial where the homeland for the Jews was to be established. He was prepared to accept Uganda, offered him by the British government. But he ran into unalterable opposition from the representatives at the congress he convened: Palestine was the land promised the Jews in Torah and inscribed in their hearts and prayers. It became clear to Herzl that no other country was acceptable to the Jews. In addition, Jews had always lived there.

The Land of Israel, renamed Palestine by the Romans in order to destroy any association between Land and Jews, has stood under many powers over the course of history. Since the fifteenth century, the Turks—Muslims but not Arabs—held possession of the entire region, including the present states of Saudi Arabia, Syria, Iraq, and Jordan. Jews and Arabs lived on the soil, with neither holding sovereignty. The land had become poor, having lost its fertility through neglect—a barren desert, forgotten except for its holy city. Both Arabs and Jews lived in poverty, the latter supported by charity from abroad. The Jewish settlers who began to arrive in the nineteenth century reclaimed it through backbreaking toil, piece by piece, as they bought parcel by parcel from Arab owners.

In World War I, the Turks were allies of the Germans. To weaken this Ottoman Empire from within, the British promised independence to all the territories if their inhabitants cast their lot with Britain. They also pledged themselves to provide for the Jews "the establishment in Palestine of a national home for the Jewish people," provided that the rights of the non-Jewish inhabitants of Palestine and the political status and rights of the Jews outside of it were in no way affected. (This is the essence of the Balfour Declaration of 1917.) Unfortunately, the conflicting territorial claims of the various groups were not clarified.

At the time of the Balfour Declaration the war was still in progess on many fronts, but on December 10, 1917, the British general Allenby was able to enter Jerusalem, which he had taken from the Turks. In order to help the British win complete victory in Palestine, a Jewish battalion was organized by the Jews. By furnishing these five thousand volunteers, who came from Palestine and the United States, the Jewish community wished to show its appreciation in action.

The formal transfer of power to the British took place at a conference of the allied powers in 1920 at San Remo; it was approved by the newly formed League of Nations in 1922. Britain was not to own Palestine; it was to govern it as a mandate of the League. Under the terms of the mandate, a "Jewish Agency" was to be formed, comprising both Zionists and non-Zionists who were willing to support the upbuilding of the homeland. The "Jewish Agency" was charged with the development of the homeland.

When the Balfour Declaration was issued, immigration immediately increased. It grew as Eastern European Jews found themselves under increasing pressure. From 1917 to 1929 the number of Jews in Palestine grew from 56,000 to 175,000. The "Jewish Agency" bought more land from its Arab owners. In April of 1925, the Hebrew University was opened in Jerusalem.

The dismantlement of the Turkish empire led simultaneously to the establishment of the Jewish homeland and to the emergence of new and sovereign Arab states such as Saudi Arabia, Jordan, and Iraq. In attaining sovereignty, these Arab states sparked a spirit of nationalism among all Arabs. Now the Jewish homeland became a thorn in their eyes. The British, concerned with strengthening their friendship with the Arabs, felt great unease with their creation of the Jewish homeland. They began to whittle down the Balfour Declaration. While Arabs were given public land, Jews had to buy it. Under various interpretations of the Balfour Declaration, Jewish immigration was more and more restricted. The Jews had hoped to develop Palestine, in the spirit of the Balfour Declaration, as a cooperative enterprise of both Arabs and Jews, and to develop a spirit of friendship between both. The favoritism shown by the British to the Arabs was a significant obstacle and helped prevent the realization of this hope.

Tensions developed. In 1929 the Jewish inhabitants of Hebron, burial place of the patriarchs, were massacred by Arabs. Most of these Jews were aged Talmud scholars, spending their lives in sacred pursuits. Jewry had only one form of redress: A day of fasting and prayer was ordained throughout the world. I remember it, for I too, as a youth, joined in the fast. Memory of the helplessness of the Jewish community in the face of attack contributed to later retributions by the State of Israel for terrorist attacks.

With the ascent of the Nazis in Germany, immigration to Palestine grew and, concurrently, restrictive measures of the British. "Illegal" immigration led to confrontations with the British armed forces. An American woman, *Henrietta Szold* (1860–1941), founded *Hadassah,* the Zionist Women's Organization in America. During the Nazi period, she organized a Youth Aliyah, to rescue the children otherwise destined for extinction.

During World War II, Arab sympathy was with the Germans, and the spiritual leader of Jerusalem, the Grand Mufti, spent his later years as a guest of Hitler. The end of the war found Arabs and Jews aligned against each other. The United Nations saw but one solution: the division of the territory into an Arab and a Jewish sector, the latter much smaller than originally envisioned. This sector became the State of Israel in 1948. President Harry S Truman was the first head of state to grant it recognition, on behalf of the United States.

A New State and Continuing Conflicts

At the very moment Israel declared its independence the Arab states, under the leadership of Egypt, launched a war against the new State of Israel. It ended in an armistice, arranged by the United Nations. The positions of the armies at that point, which were created by the ebb and flow of military action, became the temporary border lines, ostensibly to be adjusted later. Today, they are held by many Arabs to be the permanent borders. Jerusalem became divided, the sacred Jewish shrines falling into Arab hands. Because it is badly cut up, the territory cannot be defended by Israel.

During this war, many Arabs, either in fear of reprisals or in response to the request of the approaching Arab armies, fled their homes. Those who remained became Israeli citizens. Those who fled were settled by the Arabs in refugee camps, where they have lived under great hardships, supported by the United Nations. After the war, the Jews were expelled from Egypt and other Arab states. Leaving all their belongings behind, these refugees were accepted by Israel. Thus, Israel acquired a majority (about 60 percent) Oriental population, originating in North Africa, Yemen, and as far as India.

Terrorist attacks on Israel were carried out constantly by members of the neighboring countries.

In 1956, Egypt expropriated the Suez Canal, hitherto owned jointly by France and Britain. The two countries went to war against Egypt. Israel joined them, both to free itself of constant attacks and to gain use of the Suez Canal, an international waterway. Russia threatened to intervene on the side of Egypt. The United States, therefore, pressured for the withdrawal of Britain and its allies and President Eisenhower assured Israel that the canal would be opened to it, as to the rest of the world. The withdrawal came about, but the canal remained closed to Israel.

Beginning in 1948, a United Nations force, stationed at the borders between Israel and its neighbors Jordan and Egypt, shielded the antagonists from each other. The Jews had no access to their shrines in Jerusalem or their age-old cemetery on the Mount of Olives. They found out later that its stones had been used for latrines and buildings and its sacred soil transformed in part into a road, and that ancient synagogues, monuments of history, had been destroyed.

In 1967 Egypt and its Arab allies were ready for an attack, with complete destruction of Israel their aim. They demanded and obtained the withdrawal of the U.N. border guards. Deciding to take the initiative in the inevitable war, Israel, in a lightning attack, destroyed the Egyptian air force on the ground. In what came to be known as the Six Days War, it drove deeply into Sinai peninsula and the West Bank of the Jordan River, and also united Jerusalem. There was no question that the Arabs had decided on war against Israel; yet the United Nations took a formal, legalistic position, declaring Israel the aggressor. Russia, Egypt's chief supplier of arms, broke diplomatic relations with Israel.

Holding a greatly enlarged territory with an Arab population imposed burdens on Israel. The Arabs did not suffer; in fact, their economic condition actually improved. The bridge to Jordan was kept open for trade, commerce, and personal visits. Nevertheless, the Arab population remained largely antagonistic, necessitating stern Israeli actions to maintain law and order.

As restlessness and terrorism continued, Israel agreed to "withdrawal of armed forces from territories occupied in the 1967 conflict to secure, recognized and agreed boundaries to be determined in the peace agreements." This resolution, made under U.N. auspices after the 1967 war, is still operative, but it continues to be the subject of contention. Those Arab states who have recognized in principle Israel's right to exist demand a return to the boundaries of 1948. Israel demands a settlement that will give it defensible borders. Still other Arab states and groups deny even Israel's right to exist.

The Conflict Grows

Terrorism continued. In 1972, eleven athletes sent by Israel to the Olympic Games at Munich were murdered. The United Nations was ineffective in the crisis. It merely passed a resolution condemning violence on all sides.

For geopolitical reasons, Russia gave increased support to the Arabs, hoping to establish hegemony in the region. For the same reasons, but also motivated by moral concerns, the United States aided Israel. America could not afford to have this region fall under Communist domination. At the same time, the United States remained equally concerned with the welfare of the Arab lands and peoples.

In the meantime, a new power had emerged in the region in the person of Colonel Muammar al-Qaddafi, who became absolute ruler of Libya in 1970. A charismatic person, Qaddafi returned to the most extreme interpretation of Islamic scriptures and ruthlessly pursued dissenters among his own people both at home and abroad. Qaddafi devised the plan of withholding oil from those nations opposed to him and is said to have supported terrorist movements with arms in many parts of the world. Perhaps unable to accept a non-Muslim sovereign state within the heartland of Islam, he proposed a "holy war" against Israel. As Christianity had the Crusades, so does Islam accept the concept of holy war. Some Islamic theologians supported a holy war against Israel, although most did not. If religious motivations were in force, they may explain both the position of many Arabs and the apprehensions of Israel about another Holocaust.

While peace efforts were under way at the United Nations in 1973, Egypt and Syria, perhaps motivated partly by Qaddafi, jointly went to war against Israel. Although Israel had observed troop concentrations at the Suez Canal, it took no action to mobilize.

The Yom Kippur War and Subsequent Developments

On October 6, 1973—which was Yom Kippur, the holiest day of the Jewish year—the Egyptians and Syrians struck from two sides and with great force. The Arab states declared war on Israel. Russian military aid to the Arabs and an Arab oil embargo against the West led to American involvement and raised the crisis to worldwide proportions. Eventually an armistice was signed, taking effect on January 18, 1974. The United Nations issued a resolution calling upon Israel to withdraw from the territories it occupied. Israel was willing to withdraw to defensible borders, but the Arabs insisted on complete withdrawal.

In the years following the war, Arab power grew, and Israel became more isolated. The Arabs had a powerful resource: oil. They were interested in using it to raise themselves and the living standard of their people. But they also used it politically, and the threat of withholding it created tremors in the industrial world. Pressure on Israel increased.

The oil-rich Arab countries gave their support and funds to an organization dedicated to the extermination of Israel, the Palestine Liberation Organization (PLO). Russia also gave its support to the PLO. Invited to speak before the United Nations General Assembly, PLO leader Yasser Arafat offered the palm branch to the Jews in Israel if they accepted the establishment of an Arab state on the soil of Israel. The Jews would be permitted to live undisturbed in this state; otherwise, they had to face the sword. As the influence of the PLO grew, the Arabs under Israeli rule refused to negotiate with the Israeli government, declaring that only the PLO spoke for them.

Many Third World nations broke official ties with Israel, though some retained their Israeli agricultural advisors. These countries needed oil for their development and were very poor; they may have hoped for special consideration by the oil producers. In addition, they were strongly influenced by Communist power and propaganda hostile to Israel. This coalition of Arab states, Russia, and Third World nations succeeded in passing a resolution in the United Nations General Assembly on November 10, 1975, which they all knew to be false: It declared that Zionism was racism. A new propaganda tool had been created.

Among the Arab terrorist acts at this time was the hijacking of a French airliner with many Jews aboard to Uganda, which was ruled by the cruel dictator Idi Amin. In a sensational maneuver at Entebbe, Uganda's airport, the Israelis rescued the hostages. The event took place on July 4, 1976, and stirred not only the American people, celebrating the bicentennial of the United States, but many nations throughout the world.

Lebanon, the only sovereign nation in the area besides Israel not wholly Islamic, now became a battlefield. Political and ideological discords were aggravated by the religious conflicts between Christians, on the one hand, and Palestinians and their allies on the other. Israel came to the assistance of those Arabs who wanted its help and militarily aided Christian forces. Striking beyond its borders, it briefly occupied a strip of Lebanese territory, a violation of international law. Eventually a detachment of United Nations and Syrian forces were employed to maintain a very shaky peace. The South of Lebanon had long been a staging area for raids on Jewish settlements in Israel. Terrorism into Israel has continued, and Israel has retaliated by reprisal raids.

The war of 1973 did have one great and positive result. President Anwar Sadat of Egypt, feeling that the Arab victories in 1973 offered the opportunity for negotiating with Israel from strength, decided that the time for settlement had come. In November 1978, he addressed the Israeli parliament, the **Knesset**, in Jerusalem. Sadat did not compromise in his demands for the rights of the Palestinians under Israeli rule, nor in his demands for a return of the Egyptian territories taken in the wars. But the dialogue had begun.

In the spring of 1979, at a meeting at Camp David, Maryland, chaired by U.S. President Carter, Sadat and Israeli prime minister Menachem Begin hammered out a peace treaty which was ceremoniously signed at Washington, D.C. Although the treaty entailed both economic and strategic concessions by Israel, Sadat's peace initiative and the subsequent peace were widely denounced by the Arab states, and Sadat was declared a traitor to the Arab cause.

Serious problems remained, specifically the issue of autonomy for the Palestinians under Israeli rule in the Gaza Strip and on the West Bank of the Jordan. Autonomy, according to the Arabs, meant eventual independence; to Israel, it meant internal autonomy. Granting independence was seen as too dangerous for Israeli security, as the border of such a new Arab state would be within eight miles of Tel Aviv. The situation was aggravated by settlements on the West Bank by both the Israeli government and an ultra-Orthodox group, *Gush Emunim* (Bloc of the Faithful). Prime Minister Begin felt that Israel's claim to the land was based on the Scriptures. In addition, he contended that no Jew should be prevented from settling anywhere in the world; he may have overlooked the fact that world Jewry lives as citizens of the states in which its members dwell. His actions caused conflicts and resignations within his own cabinet and disagreement from large segments of world Jewry. A "Peace Now" movement emerged in Israel, pushing for compromise solutions and for concessions.

Control of the city of Jerusalem has been another point of controversy as both Muslims and Jews are concerned about access to and protection of their holiest places. In 1980, the United States voted with other nations in the United Nations that Old Jerusalem was to be considered for return to the Arabs. Subsequently, President Carter admitted this was an error and proclaimed the U.S. vote as void. This development may have prompted the Israeli parliament to pass a law in May 1980 declaring Jerusalem to be Israel's capital, as it had been since the days of King David. This step was deplored as undiplomatic by many Jews in Israel and throughout the world as negotiations were still going on, and the Camp David resolutions had postponed discussion of the issue. The law itself, however, reflects world Jewry's overwhelming sentiment about its history. This action and others may have been acts of self-assertion on the part of Israel in the face of increasing pressures by world powers for recognition of the PLO and the increasingly condemnatory attitude of the United Nations.

Turmoil in the Middle East increased in the 1980s. As a result of the revolution in Iran, and the fall of the Shah, the whole region was plunged into new conflict. Iran joined the ranks of Israel's enemies. But Egypt and Israel remained at peace. As the region was caught in the conflict of the superpowers over their influence over the region and its oil, President Sadat confirmed his belief that peace between Israel and the Arab states was in the highest interest of the Arab states themselves, their tranquility and security. It is to be hoped that such a peace with justice for all sides may emerge in the not-too-distant future, allowing all nations to dwell in safety and develop jointly the resources and opportunities with which they have been endowed.

SOCIETAL ISSUES IN ISRAEL

From the beginning, Jews in Palestine engaged in highly important social experiments, the most significant among them being the **Kibbutz**. The Kibbutz is a cooperative whose members hold everything in common and govern themselves democratically. Without this common, communal effort, the barren soil of the land could never have been developed. Admission to the Kibbutz is by membership vote; affiliation with it is completely voluntary. The knowledge and the experiences gained by these and other settlers in the development of the land have been freely shared by Israel with emerging nations of the Third World, though lately this aid has been rejected.

A great deal of the progress made in Israel, agriculturally, industrially, culturally, and socially, can be traced to the founders. They came from Europe and had a scientific outlook and Western drive. The leadership has been highly educated. Consequently, Israel has developed as a Western country, with universities, technical schools, research institutions, modern hospitals, theater, and music. The dynamics of this society may have contributed to the conflict between Israel and its Arab neighbors, who have been used to extremely gradual development. It did create conflict between Sefardic Jews in Israel—immigrants from non-Western countries—and the Ashkenasic leadership. The former have regarded themselves as victims of social and economic discrimination. Actually, the cause for the lower status of Sefardic Jews may be found primarily in their lifestyle, especially among the old, and the lack of education among the young. The government is taking steps to train the 60 percent of Israel that is "Third World" to take over the leadership of the country.

The majority of the founders of the country were socialistic and nonreligious. They were compelled, however, to grant the rabbinate a great deal of political power, especially in connection with family law. The rabbis had held this power under Turkish rule and under the British mandate. A Jewish state could give them no less. The rabbinate was and is strictly Orthodox. It has hardly been touched by the formulations of Orthodoxy in Neo-Orthodox theology. There emerged a strange contrast: an Orthodox rabbinate with official powers in a state led by nonreligious Jews. As the rabbis remained locked in tradition and were unwilling to approve any changes, many Jews who were religious but not Orthodox found themselves stranded, as non-Orthodox forms of Judaism were denied equal status. Unlike the immigrants, the young native Israelis had never known any other form of Judaism; they frequently turned from religion to a secular nationalism. The Orthodox group has a small party in the Knesset, which has consistently held the balance of power between the parties and has therefore exerted a great deal of power in favor of the religious status quo. The solution awaits the end of hostilities; at this time, it is regarded as unwise to create any points of friction. Meanwhile, the Conservative and Reform movements have established branches of their synagogues and seminaries in Israel, but, as yet, their rabbis are not recognized. The struggle is an uphill one.

Christians and Muslims have no religious restrictions in Israel, and their institutions receive government support.

Immigration of Jews from Russia has been under way for several years. Many have adjusted well and become valuable members of Israeli society, though some have not been successful in their acculturation. To the Jews from Georgia, Israel was too secular a state. For many Russian Jews, the democratic way of voicing grievances in public was puzzling. Again, others were married to non-Jewish women and had conflicts with the rabbinate. Like all other immigrants, these Russian Jews were confronted with relocation problems, and had to learn Hebrew, adjust to the cultural and societal life in Israel, and find employment, not always in line with their previous professions. On the other hand, Israel has been enriched by the immigration of many highly educated professionals.

As could be expected from the political situation in the area, the relationship between the Jewish and Arab citizens of Israel is tense. Jews hold Arabs in suspicion as Arabs have cultural, or even family, ties with their compatriots across the border. The Arabs chafe under imposed restrictions and political and social pressures. They are represented in the Knesset but may not serve in the armed forces. Israel can accommodate non-Jews—there are Christian Israelis, and a number of Vietnamese "boat people" have come to feel at home there—but Israel cannot absorb the large number of Arabs on the West Bank without losing its character as a Jewish state. In the long run, these Arabs would constitute the majority of the population. This fact should lead to the eventual return of the territory to the Arabs.

Military service is compulsory in Israel for both men and women. Heavy defense expenditures have led to skyrocketing inflation, and the economic situation is exceedingly grave, perhaps Israel's most serious problem. Serious slum problems exist. Israel's bureaucracy has been ponderous and officious, and corruption has been discovered in government and other circles. Some Israeli Jews have emigrated to other countries, perhaps temporarily. Israel's native youth (called *Sabra,* after a native cactus—prickly on the outside and sweet within) has frequently been deficient in "sweetness" or courtesy, and a sense of humor.

Israel has been criticized from within its own ranks, and from without, for every mistake it has made. That such a criticism is possible, including censure by radical socialists, shows its democratic principles.

Israel is a new state, built by men and women who had no experience in building a state. They might have chosen a form of dictatorship. But they chose democracy, placing themselves at the will of the electorate. They built a society permeated by the principles of social justice without feeling committed to the elimination of capitalism. The *Histadrut,* the national labor union, encompasses all—management, professionals, labor. The founders built in the midst of wars and pressures and yet developed highest cultural institutions. Mistakes are to be expected of any state, new or old. It is surprising that Israel has not made more serious ones. Its population is calm in the face of danger. Its youth has been called irreligious, but, like all of Israel, they are permeated by the spirit of Scripture, whose events took place in the Land, by the ideal of the prophets who called for social justice, and by a yearning for religious expression for which there is as yet insufficient non-Orthodox outlet.

The society as a whole lives in a pale, as once did Russian Jewry: over 3 million people (of whom 2.8 million are Jews) in a small space. We should not be surprised at the great pride they take in their land and their achievement under the most difficult conditions, nor at their toughness. For almost two thousand years, Jews throughout the world tried to be "good." Unwarlike, they were derided as cowards and weaklings by their non-Jewish neighbors. In the end, they were almost completely exterminated.

No nation should be measured by absolutes, as long as other nations are not so judged. Israel is not perfect, but the vision planted by the prophets has not vanished; it only awaits another day, and peace. Measured by the standards of nations, it has not done so badly.

Israel has felt that it needs an Aliyah, especially from the West. The response from western countries has not been overwhelming. Israel's critics have claimed that it is expansionist territorially. Israel would, however, much rather develop industry and become a more heavily populated industrial nation, as Holland and Belgium are.

ISRAEL AND THE WORLD

Israel is a small country in the Middle East. With no natural resources, it is insignificant. Its location constitutes its problem. Thus it has become the pawn in the political and economic power struggles of totalitarian and imperialist nations and individuals, and the victim of propaganda. At the same time, Israel is "the Jew writ large,"—scapegoat, victim of anti-Jewish prejudices, and equally barometer of humanity's conscience.

Without the war of 1948, the state would have easily accommodated both Arabs and Jews in peace. That war created the refugee issues: Arab refugees are still an issue; Jewish refugees from Arab lands were absorbed by Israel and are no longer an issue.

Religious traditions are unquestionably a factor in the relationship between the world and Israel. Religious dialogue betwen Jews and Muslims is imperative. It can bring about a cooling off of emotions, leading to eventual conciliation and cooperation. Christians and Jews have been taught by their faith that renunciation may be in accordance with God's will; they can accept compromise in power and possession. What is the Islamic position? Does it call for a redress of compromise under divine mandate? How can it join with Judaism to meet the human needs of our time? Islam is a highly ethical faith. In dialogue, Muslims and Jews will get to know each other and eliminate misconceptions; presently, most of them entertain stereotypes of each other.

The dialogue with Christianity over Israel must equally be continued. Some church leaders have felt that Israel had a right to its holy city and were satisfied to entrust the care of the holy shrines in Jerusalem to the Jews. Some even hailed the return of the Jews to the land, and specifically to Jerusalem, as the beginning of prophetic fulfillment, heralding the second coming of Christ. Others felt unease at seeing the shrines of Christianity in Jewish hands. Some people were theologically disturbed: Was Israel not said to be an eternal wanderer?

Political liberals have, at times, measured Israel by absolute standards and found it wanting. The Jew has to be "perfect" in order to exist. The radical left, including some Jewish youth, has also condemned Israel. Some leaders of minority groups have joined in this condemnation, while others, such as Dr. Martin Luther King, have spoken out for Israel.

Israel is "like a stump picked out of the fire" (Amos 4:11) of Hitler's Holocaust. Its outward posture of strength should not deceive us. It appeals to the conscience of humanity in its will to survive, to prosper, and to create a society built on social justice.

World Jewry and Israel

In times of peace, divergences emerge between Israeli and world Jewry, and they may yet again come to the fore once the current political situation has been settled. But the wars of 1967 and 1973 revealed the bonds that bind world Jewry to Israel and its people. Reform Jews by that time had come to regard Israel as essential in Judaism, especially as several leading Reform rabbis had been its spokesmen during the years of struggle for recognition. Pilgrimage to Israel has become very common for those American Jews who can afford it. Rabbinical students of the Reform Hebrew Union College–Jewish Institute of Religion have to spend one year of their rabbinical studies at the school's Jerusalem campus. Students at the Reconstructionist Rabbinical College spend their first year in Jerusalem for supervised study. The Jewish Theological Seminary has a center there.

It was agonizing for Jews during the years from 1948 to 1967 not to be permitted to visit the holy places located in the Jordanian sector. Jewry is presently in agreement with the government of Israel that Jerusalem shall remain united, and all nations and creeds shall have access to it. Rome is the center of Catholicism, and Jerusalem takes second place; Mecca is the center of Islam, and Jerusalem takes second place; the Jews have only one holy city, in which they have dwelt since David's time: Jerusalem.

In 1969, the late Richard Cardinal Cushing of Boston spoke with deep insight of the feelings that move Jews in regard to Israel:

> The State of Israel . . . is not just a refuge for a people the world has abused—it is for the Jews the fulfillment of prophecy . . . the realization of the Covenant, the answer to the prayers of generations of the Chosen People. . . . Of course, only a portion of the Jews of the world will ever settle in Israel, but some part of every Jew belongs there; some portion of his heart, if we may say it, watches and waits upon its fortunes.

If it is said that the Jewish perspective—including this chapter—lacks objectivity and emphasizes the positive elements in Israel's developments and actions, the cardinal's insight may hold an explanation.

The greatest good fortune that could come to Israel and the whole region would be for Arabs and Jews to recognize that they are kin. This consummation must be envisioned as the goal, far off though it may appear at this time.

9

JEWS OUTSIDE ISRAEL AND NORTH AMERICA

There are roughly 14.5 million Jews in the world, almost half of whom live in America. North America has approximately 6.25 million; close to 6 million of these people live in the United States, about 300,000 in Canada, and 40,000 in Mexico. South America has a Jewish population of 600,000, of whom 300,000 live in Argentina. Over 4 million Jews live in Europe, and 2.8 million in Israel. The rest are spread among various continents: Africa has about 180,000 Jews, the majority of whom live in the Republic of South Africa. Australia and New Zealand together count about 80,000 Jews among their population.

Although the leadership of world Jewry resides in the United States and Israel, in this chapter we will discuss the significant portion of the world's Jewish population outside those two countries.

EUROPE

At the risk of oversimplification, we might make several general statements about world Jewry, specifically European Jewry. The losses of World War II have not been recovered, either in numbers or in leaders. The rabbinical leadership, in its majority, has advocated and enforced an ever-stricter Orthodoxy. This may have several reasons: First, Orthodox practice may be regarded as a greater safeguard against disintegration, as it erects barriers for observant Jews. Second, the Holocaust may have forced the European leadership to conclude that Emancipation was a mistake and a failure and should be undone, at least in its spiritual side. Third, Jewry in Western Europe was transformed by immigration of Orthodox Eastern European Jews, and some of the rabbis themselves originated there.

Jews in other parts of the world have never felt the sense of security and belonging enjoyed by Jews in the United States. Governments have been ambivalent, and the people, if not outspokenly anti-Semitic, have been unreliable. Many of these Jews live on the soil that was the theatre of the Holocaust. Comparing their present condition with that of the past, they experience their weakness and see their numbers dwindle. The core of their being, from which they derive meaning and direction, is Israel. Psychologists have discovered that the impact of the Holocaust continues to affect the children—perhaps even the grandchildren—of the survivors.

Youth have therefore followed various directions. Some have simply drifted, in the desire to enjoy life "while it lasts." During the Holocaust, the fate of the grandchildren was affected by their grandparents' identification as confessing Jews. Perhaps unconsciously wishing not to inflict such a fate upon their grandchildren, others denounce Judaism. Still others may hope that they can so improve society that there will be no discrimination leading to Holocaust. They have joined the radical left, even, at times, embracing its anti–Israel stance. On the positive side, many young people, though not religious, have identified with the cause of Israel as guarantor of Jewish future and fighter for social justice. But a good number of youth have dedicated themselves to the revival of Judaism in reaffirmation that the Jewish people must live. Among them we note a return to Orthodoxy and strict Orthodox practices, a desire to learn about the Jewish heritage, of which so many know so little.

All over the world, the demand for rabbis exceeds the supply. The shortage of trained leadership has resulted in inadequate education for many young people. It is bound to weaken an already weakened Jewish community.

In several countries, liberal or conservative religious movements have made inroads and attracted young people, though their impact in Europe is still very limited. A few examples may illustrate these observations.

France

With a Jewish population of 650,000, France has the numerical leadership in Western Europe and has been aware of the spiritual obligations this leadership entails. Before the war, French Jews used to follow a rather complacent Conservatism. Mostly Ashkenasic, this Jewry was largely wiped out. Upon this depleted population a Sefardic element was grafted, consisting of Orthodox Jews who left Algeria when it fell under Muslim rule after independence from France. Resettled all over France, these immigrants brought a wider spread of Jewry throughout the country, both geographically and occupationally. As small merchants and artisans, in contrast to the former upper-middle class Jews, they were exposed to the hazards of unemployment, old age, and disease. They imposed upon French Jewry the burden of support during their resettlement, which their fellow Jews willingly shouldered. Deeply Orthodox, they also gave new life to moribund congregations.

In recognition of its new leadership role, French Jewry has been creative. University professors became its spokespeople. Since 1955, some French universities have maintained chairs of Judaism, thus placing it in the stream of academic thought. This gave men like André Nehèr of the University of Paris (Sorbonne) an opportunity to explain Judaism to both the world and his own people. In works such as *L'Existence Juive* (1962) and *La Conscience Juive* (with Emanuel Levitas, 1963), he expressed the conviction that Judaism had to base its development upon its *own* life forces and resources. As it accomplishes its own evolution in this spirit, it holds a vital message and function for all humanity. In 1980, Nehèr's work *The Exile of the Word*, dealing with Holocaust theology, was published in English (Jewish Publication Society of America).

During the Six Day War, the late President Charles de Gaulle took a strong anti-Israel position, which has been followed ever since by the French government. This may have stimulated a numerically small, but nevertheless significant, Aliyah of French Jews since 1967. Among the group have been a number of the intellectual and religious leaders of French Jewry, including Nehèr, which has been weakened by their departure.

As the uprisings in May 1968 proved, the student movement is significant in France. Influenced by the radical left, these students have taken a strong pro-Arab and anti-Israel stand that may have an impact upon French thought. Such ideologies may have contributed to violent anti-Semitic outbursts in 1980, leading to protest action by many Christians as well as by Jews. An anti-Semitic undercurrent seems to exist in French society—from Voltaire to the Dreyfus trial, to the collaboration of the French police with the Nazis in rounding up Jews, and continuing to the present.

A small organized group of religiously liberal Jews exists in France, but its influence has been insignificant.

England

The Jewish population in England is about 410,000. The United Synagogue, hierarchically organized, is its official religious body. Its spiritual head is the chief rabbi, a position held since 1966 by Dr. Immanuel Jakobovitz. Right-wing Orthodox groups and non-Orthodox Jews have their own organizations.

The United Synagogue has been Orthodox in its character. In the past, it used to be hospitable to a fairly wide variety of ideas and practices, ranging from very Orthodox to mildly Conservative. Today, it no longer permits any deviation from absolute Orthodox *doctrine*, even when Orthodox *practices* are in no way challenged or changed. The chief rabbi has found his task extremely difficult. Confronted with an outmoded educational system, a severe shortage in the religious ministry, a declining enrollment at the theological seminary—Jews' College—and many other problems, he has to meet the difficult task of reorganization.

In consequence, the Conservative and Reform synagogues have attracted members in increasing numbers, although they are still small. Organizing a rabbinical council, the liberal movement has operated a rabbinical school for a number of years, the *Leo Baeck College*. It has attained a high standard.

Jews in Britain have been active in communal affairs, in Parliament, in government, and in the life of the country. Of specific concern to them have been the plight of Russian Jewry and the situation in Israel. They have found Labor governments to be more pro-Arab, the Conservative governments more pro-Israel.

Every year, a number of Jews have received honors from the Queen, among them the late chief rabbi, who was knighted.

Scandinavia

Scandinavia's Jewish communities, who adhere to an Orthodox or Conservative form of Judaism, are too small to exert a great deal of influence upon Jewish life in general. Sweden has 16,000 Jews, Denmark 7,500, and Norway only 950. The heroic rescue efforts of the Danish people, who saved their Jews during the time of Hitler, will always be remembered. The Swedish diplomat Raoul Wallenberg, a Christian, saved thousands of Hungarian Jews. He was arrested by the Russians and has never been heard from. He may still be imprisoned, although the Russians claim that he died.

Conversion to Judaism has been common, particularly in Denmark. This gives these Jews a "native" characteristic. The Danish Jewish community has been headed by one rabbinical family for generations, the family Melchior, all of whose members have been men of distinction. Sweden has been guided by an American rabbi for a number of years. Its chief cantor, Leo Rosenblüth, a distinguished composer, has made valuable contributions to contemporary liturgical music.

Germany

German Jewry, about 30,000 in number, is largely elderly. It is composed mostly of Jews who immigrated after World War II and their children. There are not enough rabbis to staff the congregational pulpits. In many cities, beautiful synagogues have been built, largely with the aid of the government and funds that had been expropriated from Jews whose heirs could not be found. It is symptomatic that old-age homes are attached to many of these synagogues. There appears to be little hope for a viable Jewish future in Germany, except, perhaps, in a few of the big cities. If German Jewry will be replenished by the immigration of Russian Jews, as many hope, the future will be brighter.

A renewed will to survive found its expression in 1979, when the *Hochschule für jüdische Studien* (Institute of Higher Learning for Jewish Studies) was opened as a department of the University of Heidelberg. Its purpose is to train teachers and social workers for Jewish communities; to offer the first two years of rabbinical training, allowing the students to complete this training at a seminary abroad; and to serve as the first fully integrated department of Judaism at a German university, a hope long held but not fulfilled in pre-Nazi times.

Anti-Semitic ideology is still found, mostly but not entirely covert. In 1980, some neo-Nazi terror acts occurred. But there is also an enormous amount of good will that has expressed itself in the care accorded to Jewish cemeteries and antiquities, in a small but dedicated interfaith movement, in concentrated studies of Judaism by Christian scholars at universities, and by the desire of many to become acquainted with the ideas and practices of Judaism. The situation is in flux, however. Those who have felt that they might have been more courageous defenders of the Jews in the Hitler years have looked for ways to make amends, and a second generation shows concern. But, in general, the current generation disclaims any responsibility for what happened under Hitler and has been influenced by the growing left-wing orientation of German youth. The left wing, especially those with radical leanings, are anti-Israel, an attitude that affects their relationship to Jews in general. The inroads made by Marxist ideology in Germany are a source of concern for many thinking Germans.

Holland

Holland has continued its kindly concern for its Jewish citizens. The number of Dutch people who gave shelter to Jews during the Nazi years is proportionately very high, though many of the Dutch feel too modest to talk about it. Holland's 30,000 Jews take part in the life of the country. The main trend in religious life is Orthodox, but a liberal movement has sprung up and is growing. Anne Frank's house has remained a shrine.

Smaller Communities

Spain accords its 10,000 Jews full equality but, so far, the community is concerned mainly with itself. Following the revocation in 1969 of the expulsion decree of 1492, a beautiful synagogue was built in Madrid. Other large cities also have synagogues. Jewish antiquities are reverently preserved, and streets are named after great Spanish Jews, such as Judah Halevi and Maimonides, to whom a statue was erected in his birthplace, Cordova. Regardless of the opinion one may hold of the politics of the late Generalissimo Francisco Franco, he must be given credit for saving the lives of thousands of Jews in Hitler days, refusing to join Hitler in the war or to consider surrender of those Jews who had found refuge in Spain.

Portugal has only 600 Jews and a synagogue in Lisbon. The small Jewish communities in *Switzerland* (21,000) and *Belgium* (41,000) seem to be integrated; their internal problems (Orthodoxy versus liberalism) reflect those of the other countries. *Austrian* Jewry (13,000) seems to have little hope of group survival.

Italy's Jewry gained from the influx of Libyan Jews who left after Qaddafi overthrew the king and established his rule in September 1969. Forty thousand strong, it has a rabbinical seminary and all institutions. Even before Vatican II, the friendship between the rabbi of Venice, Leone Leoni, and the then-archbishop of the city, later Pope John XXIII, is said to have been strong. Since then, Italian Jewry has gained by the spirit of ecumenicity.

RUSSIA AND THE COMMUNIST WORLD

Historical Developments

Russian Jewry has been in ferment. The Russian government seems to be unable to understand its Jews. The Bolshevik revolution gave them hope, for it outlawed anti-Semitism. But it also outlawed religious distinctions, so the Jews could not be regarded as a religious group. Nor could they be regarded as a national group within the orbit of nationalities, because they had no land of their own. After some deliberation, it was decided to give them a piece of land, in Biro Bidjan, an outlying province, and to recognize Yiddish as their language. Henceforth, their identification cards, which every Russian has to carry, were stamped with a "J," signifying Jewish.

The Russian Jews did not take to Biro Bidjan, and many of them would have preferred to get rid of the "J" and be simply Russians. But this was not possible. The Jews remained members of a "nation" without being a nation. They could not escape their Jewishness, nor could they find strength and solace in their own religious and cultural heritage, which was dismantled. Even Yiddish newspapers were eliminated by the government, especially under Stalin, who wished to tone down the ethnic distinctions among the people of Russia in order to unite them in the effort of rebuilding the country. Russia had a heritage of anti-Semitism, and Stalin himself was a hater of Jews. Possession of an identification card with a "J" on it spelled grave disadvantages in employment and society. The Jews were trapped.

Denied a Jewish education, many Jews had no knowledge of Judaism at all, and a large number had intermarried. But their status in society forced them to concern themselves with their Jewish identity.

During the war, Hitler conquered vast portions of Russia, and his armies came to the gates of Leningrad and Moscow. His anti-Semitism awakened in many Russians the ancient prejudices that had been repressed but never laid to rest. The Jews were reminded of their precarious status in Russian society.

When, in 1948, Israel became a sovereign nation, Russia was one of its sponsors in the United Nations. Golda Meir was Israel's first ambassador to the U.S.S.R., and an outpouring of Jews welcomed her. The existence of the Jewish State gave them new pride. But Stalin exhibited an ever increasing anti-Semitism. Jewish doctors were accused of having poisoned Soviet leaders and were executed. After Stalin's death, they were posthumously exonerated.

Meanwhile, Russia granted support to the Arabs, in order to extend Russian influence in the Middle East. The Jews felt more and more insecure. They were, in the words of Eli Wiesel's moving account, *The Jews of Silence*.

Synagogues were closed; prayer books had not been printed since 1917, and the offer of the American rabbinate to provide them was rejected by the Russian government. Jewish calendars, giving the dates of the holy days, had to be copied by hand from a few smuggled in.

One year, the baking of Passover matzah was prohibited. When Jews around the world learned about it, they sent matzot the following year, with permission of the Russian government. However, the parcels were held up by the Russian customs office until after Passover. The Russian Jews were kept aware that the government wished to harass them in order to undermine their inner strength. In contrast to other religious groups, who were permitted to be in touch with their religious bodies abroad, the Jews were not granted this right.

Had Russia desired to absorb the Jews, it could have found an easy way: elimination of the "J" from Jewish identity cards. Large numbers of Jews would have welcomed the opportunity for complete assimilation. But Russia did not even consider such a step—perhaps due to the spirit of long established anti-Semitism, perhaps in order to keep the Jews "on ice" should a scapegoat be needed at any time, perhaps in order to show the Arab world how the Russian masters felt about Jews.

The following account, by an Amerian Jew who had visited Russian relatives, offers a striking example. One relative was a member of the Russian Communist Party, which is reserved to only a small number of people. As a party member, he could not participate in any religious activity. One year, on Yom Kippur, he felt such a yearning for some expression of his Jewishness that he decided to change his usual route from his home to his office in order to pass by the synagogue. He did not enter it; he did not stop. The following day, he was summoned by the state police and suspended from his party membership for several months. He was sternly warned of more severe consequences were he to be found delinquent again.

When war broke out in the Middle East in 1967, Israel was viciously slandered in the Russian press, and the slander tainted the Russian Jews. When they learned of Israel's victory, they rejoiced. They knew, however, that they had become even more suspect in the eyes of the government and the Russian people. They knew that they were henceforth regarded as sympathizers with an "imperialistic aggressor." Russia broke diplomatic relations with Israel, and Russian Jews found themselves under stricter surveillance. In 1970, show trials—with predetermined outcomes, held for propaganda purposes—took place in Leningrad, accusing some Jews of dishonest financial transactions to the detriment of the state. The Jewish-sounding names of the accused were prominently featured in the press.

By heaping indignities upon Jews and threatening penalties, the government counted on silence, submission, and surrender. The aim was spiritual genocide. But the pressure had the opposite effect—it strengthened the spirit of resistance, which found a symbolic expression annually at the festival of

Simhat Torah. Defying danger, thousands gathered in the street before the Moscow Synagogue to affirm their Jewishness in dance. The Jews had found a new determination.

The Question of Emigration

Jewish emigration from Russia was surrounded by obstacles as it would bring an influx to Israel and thereby antagonize the Arabs. But Jews became daring. At first, a few applied for exit permits, declaring that Israel was their homeland and they no longer felt any affinity with Russia. The number of applicants grew. It was a fateful decision in each case. The application amounted to an irrevocable renunciation of citizenship. Applicants immediately lost their jobs, their apartments, and their rights. They had to have friends to support them during the long period of waiting for the government's reply. It might be denied, it might even lead to trial and conviction of the applicant for having slandered the Russian state by reflecting negatively on Russian conditions.

At an international conference at Helsinki, Finland, in 1975, a charter of human rights was agreed on by the nations of the world, including the U.S.S.R. However, in practice Russia gave only lip service to this resolution. A group of courageous Russians openly began to resist the denial to Jews and political dissidents of basic human rights agreed upon by the government itself. A Committee on Human Rights was organized. Its guiding spirit was a sensitive Christian, the Nobel Prize winner Andrei Sakharov. Many Jews belonged to the group; other Jews merely wished to emigrate. The reprisals of the government were swift and harsh. Long terms of hard labor and internal exile were imposed; opponents were put into insane asylums. The fate of Anatoli Shcharansky became known throughout the world due to the efforts of his wife, who had been permitted to emigrate. He may stand as one example among thousands; in 1980, he was still held in prison. Sakharov himself was exiled from Moscow to a small town in the interior.

The world came to learn of the plight of the Russian Jews, which could not be compared to the disabilities other religious groups suffered. Jews and Christians throughout the world staged rallies and voiced protests. Reports from Christians, including clergy, visiting Russia bore out the facts. Under the pressure of world opinion, Russia permitted a limited emigration. A trickle first in 1965, it reached about 30,000 in 1967; its total, by the end of 1979, came to about 100,000. Since then it has fluctuated, depending on the whim of the government. For a while, an emigration tax was imposed on emigrants. Amounting to as much as eight years' wages, it was simply ransom.

Appalled by the ruthlessness of the Russian government, the U.S. Congress passed a bill denying "most favored nation" status to "any nation restricting emigration of its citizens or imposing an exit tax amounting to ransom." Most favored nation status means that the country is granted the lowest rates of import duty; it is accorded to many nations. The Russians needed that status, and "suspended" the ransom, but not the restrictive emigration policy. The U.S. law remains in force.

Russia today has about 2,500,000 Jews. Even at a liberalized emigration rate, the Jewish population in Russia is not likely to decrease at a very fast rate. The natural increase through births will compensate for the migration. Efforts should therefore be directed toward a twofold goal: free emigration for those who want to leave, and freedom of religious and cultural expression for those Jews who wish to remain, combined with the removal of all disabilities in order that they may enjoy full and equal citizenship.

Communist Countries Outside Russia

The Jews in the Communist world have been deeply affected by political events within the various countries. Their situation in *Romania* has been good, since Romania has maintained a great deal of independence within the Communist bloc and has not broken diplomatic relations with Israel. But the future is uncertain, and many among the younger element of the 60,000 Jews in Romania are contemplating emigration to Israel.

In *Poland*, the remnant of a once-flourishing community, wiped out by Hitler, has again been the victim of vicious anti–Semitic action. Jews were made scapegoats when, in 1968, students and intellectuals rose up throughout the country in protest against repression. An anti-Jewish hysteria was created that shocked the world. The 25,000 Jews then living in Poland began to emigrate in a hurry; by 1978 about 8,000 remained. The old people will die out, and Poland will be "judenrein," a Nazi term meaning completely cleansed of all Jews. In 1981 the leadership of the then–emerging union movement "Solidarity" condemned the Communist leaders of 1968 for their inhumanity in persecuting the remnant of Polish Jews. Irreversible in its consequences, the action was to be firmly censured for the sake of the historical record.

A similar fate befell the Jews in *Czechoslovakia* after the country was overrun by the Russians in 1968. "Anti-Zionist trials" were held against some of the leading intellectuals. As many as could do so, left. In 1970, the 700th anniversary of the Old New Synagogue at Prague was observed, but no delegates from the Jewish community abroad could be invited, and no government official attended. Once a bastion of democracy and human equality, Czechoslovakia, its people, and its Jews have become tragic victims of Communist imperialism.

Hungarian Jewry has lived an insecure, but rather normal, life. With a Jewish population of 80,000, Hungary has the only rabbinical seminary within the Communist sphere of influence. The small Jewish community in *Yugoslavia* (7,000) was treated well under the late Marshall Josip Tito, but its hopes for the future are dim.

In all of these countries, emigration to Israel provides the hope for the future.

SOUTH AMERICA

The potential of South American Jewry is as yet unrealized, due partly to a dearth of rabbis and partly to internal conflicts. Argentina has a Jewish population of 300,000; Brazil, 150,000; Uruguay, 50,000; Chile, 27,000. Smaller numbers reside in the other countries. These communities gained by the influx of Jewish refugees from Hitler, including rabbis. Argentina now has two rabbinical seminaries: One is Orthodox; the other—the Conservative *Seminario Rabinico Latinoamericano*—is affiliated with the Jewish Theological Seminary of America. The concerns of South American Jewry include Israel, Russian Jewry, and the internal problem of strengthening Judaism through education. Many Jewish students have been attracted by the radical left and have expressed animosity toward Israel.

Two factors distinguish South American Jewry and its destiny. One is the volatile political situation in these countries that has, for instance, raised apprehension about the future of Jewry in Chile and Argentina, due to changing power structures. Often caught as scapegoats between the forces engaged in revolutionary warfare, Jews have emigrated to Israel and other countries. The other factor is the anti-Semitism that once made some of these countries places of refuge for Nazi leaders after the war and that still remains. Based on theological indoctrination in the past, anti-Semitism is now being attacked by the Church, guided by the spirit and principles of Vatican II.

OTHER COUNTRIES

In the Republic of South Africa a flourishing Jewish life exists. The country has about 110,000 Jews, well organized, strongly Zionist, but antagonistically divided on religious lines: Orthodox versus Reform. The racist government's policy of apartheid has not resulted in any anti-Jewish orientation. South African Jewry has confined itself to maintaining its own house—that of Jewry. South African Jews have taken a leadership role in world Jewish affairs. Bonds with Israel exist.

Australia and New Zealand together have a Jewish population of about 80,000. The communities are well organized along Orthodox and liberal lines, well integrated and secure. In *Iran*, the age-old Jewish community found itself in dire straits when the Shah was overthrown and an Islamic theocracy established in 1979. Over half of its 80,000 members took flight, most finding shelter in Israel. The future of the remaining Jews is insecure. Emigration is no longer permitted. Iran has become an outspoken enemy of Israel and has prosecuted, even executed, prominent Jews as Zionists and therefore enemies of the state. Under Islamic law, "nonbelievers" are not granted full citizenship rights. The small Jewish community in *Afghanistan* was treated similarly. They had to pay a special tax. By the time of the Russian invasion of the country in 1980, most of them had emigrated.

India's 8,000 Jews have seen their community dwindle, in spite of being well treated; many have gone to Israel. The remnant of Jews in most of the Muslim countries has felt very insecure. In Egypt there are 400; their lot has improved since peace was made with Israel. In some states, such as *Libya* (20 are left), *Syria* (4,000), and *Iraq* (350), they have been persecuted. In 1969, nine Jews and five Muslims and Christians were accused by the Iraqi government of espionage for Israel and were publicly hanged. Emigrants from these countries are generally forced to leave most of their belongings behind. Some countries, such as Syria, for many years prohibited the emigration of Jews; the members of the Jewish community served as a kind of hostage.

Japan has only 800 Jews, among them several distinguished converts, such as the late Professor Kosuji, once teacher to the crown prince, and Rabbi Okamoto, who was ordained by the Hebrew Union College in the United States. Similarities in ritual forms suggest some as yet unclear contact between Jews and Japanese in the dim past. The relationship between Japan and Israel has been good; both cultural and economic exchanges and cooperative enterprises have linked the two peoples closer together. Japanese tolerance of all religions has served to bar anti-Semitism, especially as there has been no historical foundation for it, either theologically or economically.

Reaction of many nations to pressure by Arab oil producers in the face of the rapidly growing need for oil may influence the relationship of governments, interest groups, and majorities toward the minority of Jewish citizens in their midst. It could reawaken old prejudices cloaked in new rationalizations.

10

THE HOLOCAUST

Holocaust denotes a sacrifice, a total consumption by fire. The term has come to refer to the total extermination of six million Jews under the direction of Adolf Hitler and his cohorts. It evolved in stages from repressive measures designed to force Jews to emigrate from Germany, enacted immediately upon Hitler's assumption of power in 1933, to total annihilation, ending only with the defeat of Germany in 1945 and Hitler's suicide.

The Holocaust was the apocalyptic climax of centuries of anti-Semitism—theological, economical, pseudoscientific, and racial. But only in the twentieth century did it reach the proportions of genocide. There was no escape for a Jew caught in Hitler's sphere of power, even for a mere "racial" Jew. By contrast, in all earlier persecutions, Jews were given an "escape hatch"—namely, conversion. It also constitutes a total reversal of the recognition hitherto given to human beings as inviolate by virtue of their humanity.

A LONG SILENCE ENDING

For about thirty years following World War II, there was virtual silence about the Holocaust, although its impact was strong. Recent years have seen the publication of a host of books—documents of governments, memoirs of survivors, diaries of victims. Courses have been instituted at universities, lectures have been offered, and a TV series brought the Holocaust fictionally to life for millions of people all over the world.

There may be explanations for this silence. I hope I may be forgiven for including my personal viewpoint, as I experienced part of the events. I was arrested in the *Kristallnacht*, November 9, 1938, in Oldenburg, Germany, when the synagogues were burned, and was subsequently taken to Sachsenhausen concentration camp, where I remained for approximately three weeks. At this time, Jews were released from the concentration camps if they could prove they were able to emigrate immediately. Thus compared to what happened later, conditions were "good." But even then I witnessed events that make me realize the portrayal in the TV series, "Holocaust," was toned down. I subsequently lost my mother and many relatives, who were exterminated in the camps.

The sudden transition from freedom to absolute captivity is such a shock that it affects the total life of the innocent victim both externally and, more significantly, internally. So deep are the effects that the victim cannot speak about them. Grateful to have been spared, he feels "guilty" that *he* was saved while so many others perished. He represses the experience.

As he gets older, however, he feels that he must talk. Psychologists have found that not only the rescued victims themselves but also their children may be scarred by the events; perhaps talking will help by leading to a catharsis. Furthermore, after the eyewitnesses have gone, the Holocaust may well become a mere paragraph in the history books. This must not be, for it has changed humanity as a whole. Next, theological questions arise, calling for attempts at answers. Time has given us perspective. Ultimately, there is the question, asked by the poet of the Holocaust, Nellie Sachs: If the prophets came with their message of social justice, would humanity listen?

THE ROAD TOWARD THE HOLOCAUST

Hitler's designs had been made clear in his book *Mein Kampf,* written as early as 1923. Initially, he planned no extermination, but the expulsion of the "demonic Jews." His acts were directed toward this aim. When he assumed power in Germany in 1933, one of his first acts was the boycott of Jewish businesses on April 1 of that year. By the time of the boycott, however, violent actions against Jews had already occurred. Jewish civil servants were dismissed. "Aryan" legislation made careful distinctions among Jews with four Jewish grandparents, three Jewish grandparents, and down the line. Elimination from society, business, and government service, the application of the laws of 1935 (the Nuremberg laws) sketched below, eventual sequestration, loss of property, the forced imposition of Jewish names, and eventual deportation and extermination, were penalties that all depended on the degree of racial "impurity," as spelled out in detailed ordinances. In 1935, Jews were deprived of full citizenship; sexual relationships between Jews and Aryans were penalized severely; and Jews were excluded from culture, from public parks, from all contacts, both business and economic, with Aryans. In 1936, overt anti-Semitism was reduced; Germany wished to make an impression on the world as host of the Olympic Games. In 1938, however, the pressure was resumed: Congregations lost their corporate rights, and individual Jews had to report all their property, domestic and foreign. Jews were permitted to give their children only listed Jewish names, and adults had to add the name Israel or Sarah to their given names. Meanwhile, concentration camps for individual dissenters had been in operation since 1933. The extermination of "undesirables," such as the mentally retarded, had been in effect but was suspended due to the complaints of the Catholic Church.

In October 1938, Poland declared as stateless all its citizens that resided outside its borders, an act directed against Jews, many of whom resided in Germany. The Polish Jews were therefore rounded up by the Germans, put on trains, and dumped at the Polish border, homeless and helpless. Herschel Greenspan, a young man who lived in Paris but whose parents were among the deportees, thereupon shot and killed an attaché at the German Embassy. This offered a welcome pretext for the Nazis to put into effect a well-planned pogrom. On November 9, 1938, the synagogues were burned and the male population taken to concentration camps, which were ready and waiting for them. A fine of one billion marks was imposed on the already impoverished German Jews.

During this period, there were mass demonstrations by American Jews, and a boycott of German goods was proposed. The Nazis declared that they were holding the Jews in Germany as hostages against any action directed against Germany. The rest of the world either did not believe the reports of what was happening in Germany or was unconcerned or not displeased with the thought of a displacement of the Jews from society. In 1938 an international conference was held at Evian, France to effect the resettlement of the Jews under Nazi domination; none of the great powers, however, was willing to accept Jews in any substantial number. Hitler now knew he could not get rid of the Jews by forced emigration. He also saw that there would be few repercussions for his anti-Jewish actions. The German Jews, who had internalized the spirit of peace, and furthermore did not live in Jewish sections but were spread through the cities and towns, could not offer any resistance.

The "Final Solution" Is Planned

In 1938 Hitler annexed Austria, whose population received him with jubilation; in 1939 he invaded Czechoslovakia. The invasion of Poland in the fall of 1939 led to war. Germany was victorious at all fronts, overrunning Poland and the western regions of Russia, where multitudes of Jews lived, as well as Holland, Belgium, France, Denmark, and Norway in the West. In all of these countries, and in those in Eastern Europe that fell, the "Jew laws" were immediately introduced, and storm troopers were in charge. But the number of Jews was so large that it was decided to exterminate them, through forced labor in factories as long as they were capable of work, usually a few months, and in extermination facilities attached to expanded concentration camps. This "final solution" was perfected in all its technical and organizational details at a conference at Wannsee, a fashionable suburb of Berlin, on January 20, 1942. Adolf Eichmann was put in overall charge.

Herded into ghettoes or Jew houses, forced to wear the yellow star, restricted in their movements, prohibited from buying food except during a few hours, the Jews could but wait for the moment when they would be deported. In the East, where large ghettoes such as Warsaw were established, the Jews actively resisted.

Jews in Desperate Struggle to Escape

During these years, Jews made every effort to emigrate; after 1938 the scramble turned into a torrent. However, the nations of the world refused to open their gates. The United States strictly held to its immigration quotas. Great Britain, which had mandate power over Palestine, forcefully repelled Jewish immigrants. So they arrived secretly as "illegal immigrants" in rickety ships. If a ship was discovered, it was turned back by armed force, and Jews watched their brothers and sisters drown at the shores of freedom. Had the State of Israel existed at the time, millions would have been saved. In 1939 the S.S. *St. Louis* sailed for Cuba with 930 Jews aboard, many of whom had immigration visas. Batista, dictator of Cuba, refused them entry. The attempt to gain entry to the United States proved fruitless. Sailing past the Florida shores, the ship returned its passengers to Germany and to their fate.*

The "Final Solution" is Carried Out

Nazi policies were carried out by a bureaucracy "only following orders." The chemical plants improved their poison gas, Nazi doctors developed the experiments they were to carry out on living human beings, the delivery system to the extermination camps was coordinated by the railroads. It was all done scientifically, by scientists with professional detachment, knowing well what they were doing.

The Jews were squeezed into cattle cars, standing up, without food or water, for the long ride to the extermination camps. Under a Nazi law of 1941, Jews leaving Germany lost their nationality, and their remaining belongings fell to the state. As soon as the deportation trains crossed the German borders, this law took effect, for it did not matter under what circumstances the Jews had crossed. Their treatment as stateless surplus and the confiscation of their property remaining in Germany had become legal.

When the trains arrived, many had died, the rest passed in review. Major Joseph Mengele, a physician based at Auschwitz, has become infamous for his role at the extermination camps. By a flick of his hand, he ordered the arrivals one by one to the left or the right—one group destined for immediate death, the other for temporary survival as slave workers or medical guinea pigs. In the end, the slave workers also perished. Though what happened afterward in the camps has been amply documented, it defies description.

The victims were herded in front of the gas chambers, made to undress

---

*The event was called to mind in 1980, when thousands of Cuban refugees came by boat to the United States. Fortunately, a more humane spirit had emerged in official U.S. circles, and the Cubans were admitted, as were refugees from other parts of the world.

and place their clothing carefully on various piles: men's shoes, women's shoes, children's shoes, and so on, nicely separated. Then they were squeezed into the gas chambers, tightly pressed together. The cyclon gas was turned on, entering from vents at the ceiling. The victims died. The chambers were then opened by Jewish attendants, forced to perform the task, and "rewarded" by being permitted to live a short time longer. Pulling the bodies out by hooks, the attendants extracted the crowns and gold fillings from the deceaseds' teeth, and cut the women's long hair for commercial use. They stacked the bodies like cord wood, and then piled them into the ovens of the crematoria that burned day and night and blanketed the region with the acrid smell of burning human flesh.

The deportations to the camp proceeded on schedule. The number of victims arriving at the camp surpassed the capacity of the gas chambers to kill them. They had to wait for their turn, and in the meanwhile, forced to barely exist on a starvation diet, found themselves transformed into living skeletons.

"Auschwitz" has come to represent the destruction of European Jewry by the Nazis. But Auschwitz was not the only extermination camp. A memorial has been erected for the murdered Jews in Jerusalem. Its interior is utterly simple. In one corner of the dark room burns an eternal flame. On the floor are inscribed the numerous camps where Jews were put to death. In an adjacent archives building exact records of most of the six million who died "al **Kiddush HaShem,**" in the sanctification of His Name, are kept.

Jewish Community Life During the Final Years

In the meanwhile, the Jewish communities in Europe had to be administered. This task was assigned by the Nazis to Jewish administrators and counselors. In Germany, Rabbi Leo Baeck was made head of the Jewish community. As one of the most outstanding rabbis, he had received many calls to congregations and seminaries abroad; he refused all of them, preferring to go with his people and to die with them. He survived Theresienstadt, and has become recognized as one of the great witnesses of Jewish faith. He died in England in 1951.

Under Baeck and other leaders, Jewish life and cultural activities were maintained among the starving Jews in their ghettoes. Services were conducted and holy days observed at risk, for all these activities came to be forbidden. The Jewish counselors—*Judenräte*—were victims of a deep tragedy. Should they tell their people, many of whom expected merely to be resettled, the fate that awaited them, or should they allow them a bit of hope for survival? These men were given the task of determining who should go on a transport and who should remain behind. It was a power over life and death. Naturally, they favored their families and close ones, condemning others. There were unscrupulous men among them, as there were brutal Jewish policemen in the ghetto towns. Others stood up to the Nazis in a hopeless cause, but with courage, willing to sacrifice themselves. In the final analysis, the fate of the

Jews rested to a considerable degree on the decency of those in charge. When it was over, the Jews had suffered irreplaceable losses.

THE RESULT AND THE LESSON OF THE HOLOCAUST

The very magnitude of the slaughter startles the mind. The centers of Jewish life and piety were destroyed. Upon the rest of Jewry an unparalleled responsibility has fallen: in the words of Emil Fackenheim, not to give Hitler a posthumous victory. Jews have to replenish their ranks, their spirit, learning, and piety. They must return into history and dialogue. Jews have been fearful that the message of the Holocaust may be forgotten all too soon. Having faced the unspeakable in Germany, most "enlightened" of the nations of the West, they have felt deeply the insecurity of the age. Jews have closed ranks about Israel. If Israel has been uncompromising in negotiating with others, the Holocaust may be one important reason. Israel feels that it must be secure in its borders; there must be no second Holocaust. World Jewry agrees.

The Holocaust teaches that racial prejudice has to be wiped out both by law and by education that changes attitudes. It makes mandatory a constant, living dialogue between all groups on all levels, based on mutual respect. It holds a warning against "following orders" in blind obedience to authoritarian government, the grievous fault of the Germans. It calls on governments to stand up for right as against expedient verbal solutions. Humanity alone can heal itself.

11

THE RESTORED CHRISTIAN-JEWISH DIALOGUE

JUDAISM AND THE MONOTHEISTIC RELIGIONS: THE JEWISH POSITION

Judaism has had little theological conflict in recognizing the monotheistic religions, Christianity and Islam as divinely accepted roads to God for their faithful. It has held that "the righteous of all the nations of the world have a share in the world to come" (Tosefta Sanhedrin 13:21). It also acknowledged the ethical religions—those that call for love of fellow human beings and for social justice as an integral part of the duties each person and society owes God—as roads to salvation. The dogma of a divine "partner" in Christianity posed no issue, although such a belief was not held by Jews. To the degree that the majority religions acknowledged the principle of religious pluralism and religions other than their own as a way to God, and granted all of them equality in law and life, Judaism could easily recognize them.

Conflict arose when other religions exerted great pressure on the Jews, reinforced by acts of persecution, to be converted. The Christian position was grounded in the idea that Judaism no longer stood under the covenant with God; that the Jews had killed God-in-Christ; that they were to be homeless, destitute, and by their misery witnesses to the triumph of the Church. By their ruthlessness, the majority religions confirmed the Jewish conviction that the Messiah, bringer of peace, had not come. Beyond that, persecution in the name of Christ struck such terror in the hearts and souls of Jews that they could not calmly mention the name of Jesus, who was held to be the cause of all the cruelty meted out to them.

It may be useful to quote some of the masters of Judaism to clarify the traditional Jewish position. In a lengthy statement, Maimonides deals with both Christianity and Islam. He begins by pointing out that the claim of being the Messiah—such as Jesus's and, after him, Bar Kokhba's—does not place the claimant outside the confines of Judaism. If such a messianic claimant fails in bringing peace to the world, he will go to his heavenly reward among the pious kings of Israel.

But Jesus, seen in the mirror of Jewish suffering, created a "stumbling block."

> . . . Has there ever been a greater stumbling block than this? All the prophets affirmed that the Messiah would redeem Israel, save them, gather their dispersed and confirm the commandments. But he caused Israel to be destroyed by the sword, their remnant to be dispersed and humiliated. He was instrumental in changing the Torah, causing the world to fall into error and serve another besides God.

Nevertheless, Christianity and Islam are divine dispensations—that is, they came into being by the will of God—and will lead humanity to the messianic age.

> But it is beyond the human mind to fathom the designs of the Creator, for our ways are not His ways, nor our thoughts His thoughts. All these matters, relating to Jesus of Nazareth and the Ishmaelite, who came after him [Mohammed], only served to clear the way for the King Messiah, to prepare the world for the worship of God with one voice [Zephaniah 3:9]. Thus the messianic hope, the Torah and the commandments have become familiar topics, topics of conversation even [among peoples] of the far away islands, and among many people uncircumcised in heart and flesh. These discussions, though filled with error, will prepare the people for the time when the Messiah will come and correct their errors (Mishneh Torah: Judges-Kings, Ch. 11.)
>
> There is no doubt that there are things common to all of us, I mean the Jews, the Christians and the Muslims. . . . (Maimonides, *Guide for the Perplexed*, I, Ch. 71)

Rabbi Jacob ben Meir, greatest master of the French-German school, called by the people *Rabbenu Tam*, our flawless Master, himself a victim of the persecutions in France in 1147, rose above his own suffering to declare that "in our time" the mind of Christians was indeed directed toward the Creator of Heaven, though they used the Name of Heaven in conjunction, or partnership, with another, a matter not prohibited under Noahide commandments (Talmud Sanhedrin; Tossafor: Assur, Sanhedrin 63).

Teaching at the beginning of the modern era, Rabbi Jacob Emden (1697–1776) declared:

> The founder of Christianity has given the world a twofold blessing: He strengthened the Torah of Moses by emphasizing its eternally binding power; in addition, he brought blessings to the heathens, as he removed idolatry from their midst and imposed upon them the higher moral obligations that are contained in the Torah of Moses. There are many Christians of highest qualities and outstanding morality. Would that all Christians lived by their own commandments. They are not obligated, as are the Jews, to fulfill the law of Moses, nor do they commit a sin, if they associate other beings to God as His partner, in worshipping the triune God. They will receive their reward from God for spreading the faith in Him among peoples that never before had even heard of His Name—for He looks into the heart.

For centuries, Orthodox Jews have recited the philosophical poem "The Royal Crown" on Yom Kippur eve. Written in the eleventh century by

Solomon ben Judah Ibn Gabirol, it contains the words:

> You are God! All creatures are Your servants, serving You in worship. Your honor is not diminished through those serving another next to You, for all seek to attain to You.

THE NEW DIALOGUE

Speaking to his own people, the saintly chief rabbi of Israel Abraham Isaac Kook (1865–1935) declared that the mature human mind will recognize all expressions of the spiritual life as one organic whole. Maturity in spirit will overcome the conflict between the different religions and create out of their multitude one "ensemble of faiths." Speaking to the world, Martin Buber proclaimed that, out of their respective patterns of faith, Christianity and Judaism "would have something unsaid to say to each other and a help to give one another—hardly to be conceived at the present time" (*Two Types of Faith*; New York: Harper, 1951, p. 174).

In our time, Christianity has begun to respond. We have witnessed the restoration of meaningful Christian-Jewish dialogue. Actually, it is a new form of dialogue. The dialogue during the early centuries of the Christian era, such as it was, rested on an undercurrent of turbulence and tension. The so-called disputations during the Middle Ages had to arrive at the foregone conclusion that God had chosen Christianity and rejected the Jews. The new dialogue has been conceived on the basis of mutual respect, love, and recognition. We may see in it one of the true achievements of our age. This communication was initiated by the Catholic Church.

World War II, from Auschwitz to Hiroshima, had demonstrated that the message of Christianity was no longer heeded by humanity and that humanism had failed as an ethical guide. The spread of communism, as ideology and political force, revealed the threat of antireligious materialism for all religions. In consequence of historical developments, the Church was divided and weak, unable to counter the forces that challenged it. The Church had to be updated in teachings and method, and its division had to be healed. This was clearly seen by Pope John XXIII. The pope acted; in 1962 he convoked a Church Council to address itself to these momentous issues.

The pope was equally troubled in conscience at the terrible ordeal the Jews had been made to endure, and the historical responsibility of the Church on account of its teachings regarding the Jews and the complete absence of a dialogue with them. John XXIII made possible both dialogue and a new relationship between Judaism and Christianity by placing his authority and the great power of his office in the service of this **ecumenical** task. When he convoked the Ecumenical Council (Vatican II), for the purpose of updating the teachings of the Church to meet present-day requirements in the spirit of the Church's evolving tradition, he specifically included in its agenda a statement on the Jews. It was designed to eradicate long-established misconceptions about them, and to eliminate opinions, beliefs, and practices which had done them harm. Pope John died while the Council was in progress, before a statement on the Jews could be promulgated. His successor, Paul VI, officially issued the decree in fall of 1965. Subsequent popes reinforced it.

In 1980 Pope John Paul II requested meetings with Jewish representatives in various countries he visited, such as France and Germany. These were held as affirmation of brotherhood between living religions.

THE ROMAN CATHOLIC STATEMENT

The statement on the Jews has many excellent points, offering and inviting dialogue between Catholics and Jews in discussion and life. However, as a result of extended debate, the statement bears the marks of the conflict of ideas within the Council itself. Liberals were aligned against conservatives; bishops from Arab lands transmitted the heavy pressure in their countries against any statement that would place Jews and Judaism in a new light and erase ancient prejudices held by the population. The concessions made to opposing views within the Council have been deplored by many progressive Catholic leaders as well as by Jews.

The decree itself, "Declaration on Relations with Non-Christians," consists of five sections, of which only the fourth deals specifically with the Jews. The first section outlines the purpose and underlying philosophy of the decree. The next two deal with the contributions of various religions, such as Hinduism, Buddhism, and Islam, stating in straightforward language the insights of these faiths which the Catholic Church considers valuable for itself and for all humanity. This is followed by an exhortation to the Catholic faithful to engage in prudent dialogue and collaboration with adherents of these religions. The final section is a call to universal love; it reproves all discrimination on account of race, color, condition in life, or religion. The fourth section, on the Jews, is the longest and most involved. The most salient points are condensed here:

> The Church acknowledges the spiritual ties binding it to the Jews through Abraham, the Patriarchs, Moses, and the prophets; it holds them to be the beginning of her own [the Church's].
>
> The exodus from Egypt foreshadows the salvation of the Church; the reconciliation of Jew and Gentile is in the cross of Christ. Recalling the words of St. Paul (Romans 9:4–5) that "theirs is the sonship and the glory and the covenants and the law and the worship and the promises, the fathers and Christ according to the flesh," recalling also that disciples and Apostles sprang from the Jewish people, the relationship is acknowledged. . . .
>
> Jerusalem did not recognize the time of its visitation; the Jews did not accept the Gospel in large numbers, many even opposing its spreading; yet God holds the Jews most dear for the sake of their fathers, for God does not repent His gifts or the calls He issues.
>
> In company with the Apostle [Paul], the Church awaits the day when all

people will address the Lord in a single voice.

On the basis of the common patrimony, the Council recommends and wishes to foster understanding and respect from Biblical and theological studies and from a fraternal dialogue.

The document points out that:

what happened in Christ's passion cannot be charged against all Jews, then alive without distinction, nor against the Jews of today.

It also states that the Jewish authorities and those who followed their lead pressed for the death of Christ. It affirms that:

Although the Church is the new people of God, the Jews should not be presented as rejected and accursed of God, as if this followed from the Holy Scriptures. All should see to it that in catechetical work or in preaching nothing be taught that does not conform to the truth of the Gospel and the spirit of Christ.

Rejecting persecution against any man, mindful of the patrimony shared with the Jews, moved, not by political reasons but by the Gospel's spiritual love, the Church decries hatred, persecution, and displays of anti-Semitism directed against Jews at any time and by anyone.

The final paragraph asserts the abiding belief of the Church that Christ underwent his passion and death freely, because of the sins of humanity and out of infinite love, in order that all might reach salvation. It is, therefore, the burden of the Church's preaching to proclaim the cross of Christ as the sign of God's all-embracing love and as the fountain from which every grace flows.

Jewish Reactions

Jewish reaction to the Vatican II decree was positive, with certain reservations.

Some Jews felt that the Catholic Church cannot *absolve* the Jews of the crime against Jesus, since they had never committed it. This constituted a Jewish misreading of the text, which, in fact, proclaims that the Jews should *never have been charged with* the crime in the first place, nor accused of it in the course of history.

Others were disappointed, finding that the document was ambiguous in many of its formulations. After the Holocaust, a clear condemnation of anti-Semitism was in order; merely "decrying" it was not enough, especially as a clear-cut condemnation was found in an earlier draft. However, the word *deplorare* in the text has a wider meaning than decry; the Latin term means to cry out and lament.

There was apprehension that the emphasis of the Church on *its* election as the new people of God might suggest both a devaluation of Judaism and a missionary intent, which would seriously impair any possible dialogue. Why was it seen necessary to place repeated emphasis on the Church's burden to proclaim the cross to the world in a document dealing specifically with

Catholic-Jewish relations? Was there an ulterior motive? Were Jews eventually to be converted, subtle pressure to be applied? All these issues were clarified in subsequent statements and guidelines, which we shall discuss.

Two facts must be kept in mind. First of all, the decree was promulgated as an internal document guiding the Catholic faithful. It had to take into account the total theology of the Catholic Church. To the Jews, the gospels are not holy; to the Catholic they are holy "gospel truth," allowing reinterpretation but not a challenge of the veracity of the text itself. The survival of Jewry does indeed pose a serious theological problem to Catholics, whereas Christianity presents no such problem to Jews. Jews can hold that the emergence of Christianity operates under God's plan, but Catholics are confronted with theological principles holding that theirs is an exclusive revelation. Therefore, they had to think through again the question of the continuation of Judaism as a living faith with a continuing function. Hitherto, the Jews were regarded by the Church as the remnant of a people holding stubbornly to an outworn faith that had long been superseded. Only their eventual conversion was reason for their survival under the divine plan.

Secondly, the decree on the Jews is meaningful in the context of other decrees, particularly the "Declaration on Religious Freedom, on the Right of the Person and of Communities to Social and Civic Freedom in Matters Religious." In it, the Council declared that the right to religious freedom has its foundation in the very dignity of the human person, as this dignity is known through the revealed word of God and by reason itself. It is also stated that "Religious communities have the right not to be hindered in their public teaching and witness to their faith, whether by the spoken or by the written word." The significance of this proclamation in connection with the declaration on the Jews is great, particularly in those countries where the free profession of faith in open affirmation had been hampered by problems, laws, suspicions, and misunderstandings.

In speaking of the pressure exerted by the Jews for Jesus's death, did the document cast a shadow on the masters whom Jews have revered through the centuries, especially the Pharisees? This question, too, came to be clarified in the guidelines.

The statement "Jerusalem did not recognize the time of its visitation" rests on the Christian conviction that Jesus's ministry, and particularly his crucifixion, were cosmic events of such powerful universal witness that no one of good sense could remain unaffected by them. Judaism does not hold this view. We shall see that the guidelines no longer dwell on this statement that Jerusalem failed to recognize the time of its visitation.

Would Christianity recognize the evolution of Judaism through the Talmud, codes, philosophers, and liturgists down to our day? To this, also, the guidelines gave a positive answer.

Some Jews have held that the decree is of small import. They maintain that twentieth-century anti-Semitism rests on social, political, and economic factors, and not on theological consideration. The facts have refuted this contention. In the Islamic world, religious beliefs have deeply affected political considerations and actions. In Western Christianity, too, the influence of religious teachings has been decisive in many ways. Results of a long-term study on anti-Semitism, undertaken by the Survey Research Center of the University of California and released in 1966, indicate that the majority of Christians who are anti-Jewish base their attitude on religious teachings of their churches learned in childhood. It was found that this attitude, once instilled at an early age, can never be entirely eradicated. One of the primary sources of anti-Jewish attitudes is the teaching that the Jews were guilty of the death of Christ. The declaration of the Vatican Council must therefore be considered as being of the greatest importance as a weapon against anti-Semitism.

To those most deeply concerned with a dialogue, the document offers a great deal of hope. The statement on anti-Semitism is a help. If even one soul is kept from harm by it, it is worth it. The affirmation of Jewish corporate innocence in the death of Jesus is an act of long overdue justice, proclaiming what the Jews had maintained all along. This equally applies to the rebuke of any belief that the Jews were accursed and rejected by God. The call for friendship and brotherhood is recognized as genuine, and sincerely welcomed. The implementations and guidelines were to justify this hope and trust to a large degree.

Implementations and Guidelines

Immediately after promulgation of the statement on the Jews, the Catholic Church committed itself to several highly important actions to ensure that barriers to dialogue and communal fellowship would be eliminated. Recognizing the apprehensions of Jews, due to a lack of clear articulation in some statements of the decree, the Church authorities began the process of interpretation.

On the practical level, changes had to be made in preaching and catechetical instruction. Derogative statements on the Jews in textbooks had to be eliminated, and, most important, New Testament references hostile to Jews had to be given new interpretation. Directions had to be issued to clergy, laity and Catholic school authorities. This was done in guidelines. The Archdiocese of New York was the first to issue such guidelines, in 1969, followed by a committee of French bishops in 1973. Worldwide guidelines were handed down by the Vatican itself in December 1974. A working paper, "Basic Theological Issues of the Jewish-Christian Dialogue," issued in Germany, followed in 1979. We will consider all of these statements in detail below.

The 1967 Six Day War between the Arab states and Israel made it clear to the Jews that the decree of 1965 had totally ignored the religious dimension of the Land of Israel for Jewry. The Vatican guidelines do not mention Israel. The silence of the Church at a time when Israel was in mortal danger, as well as the omission of any mention of the State of Israel by name in papal speeches, have created persistant apprehension in Jewish minds. However, this fear has been mitigated somewhat by efforts in episcopal pronouncements to at least acknowledge a basic element in Jewish faith—the restoration of Israel on its soil, the Jews' eternal hope. Clarification and recognition on the Church's highest level is hoped for by all Jews.

The *"Guidelines for the Advancement of Catholic-Jewish Relations,"* issued by the archbishop of New York and the bishops of Brooklyn and Rockville Center in 1969, framed with the cooperation of rabbis and Jewish community leaders, includes practical issues. It opens the doors for mutual action wider than ever before, reaffirms the bishops' statement that "proselytizing is to be carefully avoided in the dialogue," calls for examination of textbooks for anti-Semitic statements, strongly repudiates anti-Semitism, invites scholarly studies, and rejects the historically inaccurate notion that Judaism of the time of Christ, especially pharisaism, was a decadent formalism and hypocrisy. The life of Jesus and the primitive church are to be studied in their Jewish setting; a full explanation of the use of the expression *the Jews* in various New Testament references is to be given; and Catholic scholars are to acknowledge the living and complex reality of Judaism and that the election of Israel under special Covenant with God was not abrogated with the election of Christianity, but was permanent. All these matters are to be incorporated into Catholic teaching. Councils of Catholics and Jews are to be formed on every level, mutual invitations are to be extended and accepted, and a spirit of reciprocity is to prevail. Participation in some forms of common worship is also approved. The guidelines are also concerned with matters of religious practice, such as the respect to be accorded rabbis, permission for rabbis to speak at church services before and after the Mass, participation of Jews and Catholics as attendants in wedding services of the other faith, and so on.

The *statement of the committee of French bishops*, although never adopted as official policy, constitutes the most advanced of all guidelines and appears to have influenced subsequent guidelines. It regards the decree of Vatican II as "more of a beginning than as an achievement" and regrets the "slow course of Christian conscience." It points out that Jewish history and survival constitute a divine mystery of significance which will help Christianity to find meaning for its own vocation under God's plan. The medieval interpretation of Jewish survival, which perceived the Jews as witnesses to the victory of the Church, is implicitly rejected.

> The present existence of the Jewish people, its frequently precarious condition in the course of its history, its hopes, the tragic trials which it has known in the past and primarily in modern times, its partial ingathering on the land of the Bible, constitute more and more for Christians a given situation which might facilitate for them a better comprehension of their faith and enlighten their lives.
>
> The permanence of this people through the ages, its survival over civilizations, its presence as a rigorous and exacting partner vis-a-vis Christianity are a fact

of first importance which we can treat neither with ignorance nor with contempt. The Church which claims to speak in the name of Jesus Christ and which through Him finds itself bound, since its origin and forever, to the Jewish people, perceives in the centuries long and uninterrupted existence of this people a sign the full truth of which it would like to understand.

This new view of the Jewish people calls for new attitudes recognizing the Jew not simply as a human being, entitled to human rights, but as a member of the Jewish people to be recognized "on the level of faith." Christians have to recognize the Church's Jewish roots. Jewish religion must therefore not be regarded as simply one of the many religions on earth. It has a special place in God's dispensation. Nor has its mission in the world come to an end.

> It is not possible to consider the Jewish "religion" simply as one of the religions now existing on earth. It is through the people of Israel that the faith in one God has been inscribed in the history of humanity. It is through it that monotheism became the common good of . . . Judaism, Christianity, Islam. According to Biblical revelation it is God Himself who constituted this people . . . sealing with it an eternal Alliance [Covenant] (Genesis 17:7). . . .

> Even if for Christianity the Covenant has been renewed in Jesus Christ, Judaism ought to be looked upon by Christians not only as a social and historical reality but primarily as a religious one; not as a relic of a venerable and completed past, but as a living reality through the ages. The principal signs of this vitality of the Jewish people are the witnessing of its collective faithfulness to the one God, its fervor in scrutinizing the Scriptures in order to discover in the light of revelation the sense of human life, its search for identity amidst other men, its constant effort to reassemble in a reunified community. The signs pose to us Christians a question which touches the heart of our faith: What is the proper mission of the Jewish people in God's plan? What expectations animate the Jewish people and in what respect are these expectations different or approach ours?

The bishops extend the call to Christians to render love to the Jews. They warn their faithful against any form of "stereotyping" Jews. Then they add a significant point not mentioned in the Vatican decree—an admission of Christian guilt in the tragic fate of Jews throughout the ages.

> The Jew merits our attention and our esteem, often our love. It is that, perhaps, that was missing most and where Christian conscience is most guilty.

From this love must spring the battle against anti-Semitism. Christians must recognize that anti-Jewish actions and feelings of the past frequently had their roots in pseudotheological arguments, which must be cast out. The bishops explain:

> Anti-Semitism is a heritage of the pagan world but is still reinforced in a Christian climate in pseudo-theological arguments. It is a theological, historical, and judicial error to keep the Jewish people indistinctly guilty of the Passion and death of Jesus Christ. . . . If it is true that historically the responsibility for the death of Jesus was shared on various grounds by certain

> Jewish and Roman authorities, the Church maintains that . . . Christ . . .
> submitted Himself to His Passion and to his death so that all receive salvation.

The bishops then turn to several misconceptions regarding Judaism
widely held by Christians.

> Contrary to what has been maintained by a very old but controversial exe-
> gesis, one cannot infer from the New Testament that the Jewish people has
> been deprived of its election. The totality of the Scriptures causes us, on the
> contrary, to recognize in the faithfulness of the Jewish people to the Law of the
> covenant a sign of fidelity of God to His people.

> It is false to oppose Judaism and Christianity as one being a religion of fear and
> the other a religion of love. The fundamental article of the Jewish faith, the
> Shema Israel, begins with "You shall love the Lord your God," and is followed
> by the commandment of loving your neighbor (Leviticus 19:18). This is the
> point of departure of the teaching of Jesus, and therefore a teaching common
> to Judaism and Christianity.

> The sense of transcendence and of the faithfulness of God, of His justice, of His
> mercifulness, of repentance and of pardon of delinquencies are fundamental
> traits of the Jewish tradition. Christians who insist on the same values would
> be wrong to believe that they have nothing more to gain, even today, from
> Jewish spirituality.

The statement also attempted to clear up misconceptions about the
character of the Pharisees and their successors, the masters of the Talmud. Did
Jesus harshly rebuke the Pharisees? The bishops see these strictures as directed
only at certain Pharisees, which is in accord with the judgment of the pharisaic
masters themselves on some unworthy members of the group. Jesus speaks in
the spirit of the rabbis.

> Contrary to established reflexes, one must affirm that the doctrine of the
> Pharisees is not the opposite of Christianity. The Pharisees were striving that
> the Law become life to each Jew and to interpret the prescriptions in a manner
> that would make them adapted to different circumstances of life. Contem-
> porary researches have provided evidence that the Pharisees were not at all
> strangers to the interior sense of the Law, no more than the Masters of the
> Talmud. It is not these dispositions that Jesus challenged when he denounced
> the attitude of certain of them in the formalism of their teaching. It seems,
> furthermore, that it is because the Pharisees and the first Christians were close
> to each other in numerous aspects that they sometimes fought each other with
> such force about the tradition received from the ancients and the interpretation
> of the Mosaic Law.

The recognition given the masters of the Talmud is of special significance
coming from the French bishops, as it was in France that the Talmud was
publicly burned during the Middle Ages. The bishops' statement thus becomes
an acknowledgment of an earlier Church's grievous wrong.

In order to acquire a "just comprehension of Judaism," Christians
must gain a true knowledge of Jewish tradition and self-perception. While
affirming that the Old Testament finds its meaning for Christians only in the
light of the New Testament—as is their duty as shepherds of their faithful—the

bishops affirm that the entire Bible has relevance and value for the Christian community. Jesus himself was faithful to Torah. The Bible in its entirety

> must be affirmed, for "it is root and source, the foundation and the promise."
>
> One should not forget that by His obedience to Torah and by His prayer, Jesus, a Jewish man by his mother, the Virgin Mary, accomplished His ministry within the people of his covenant.

Israel's vocation is spelled out in clear terms.

> We should present the particular vocation of this people as the "sanctification of the Name." This is one of the essential dimensions of synagogal prayer by which the Jewish people, invested by a sacerdotal mission (Exodus 19:6), offers all human activity to God and glorifies Him. This vocation makes the life and prayer of the Jewish people a benediction for all nations of the earth. It would be underestimating the precepts of Judaism to consider them only as restrictive practices. The rites are gestures which break the daily routine of existence and remind those who observe them of the sovereignty of God. Faithful Jews receive as a gift of God the Sabbath and the rites which have as their purpose to sanctify human action. Beyond their literalness, they are for the Jews light and joy on the path of life (Psalm 119). They are a manner of "building time," and to render grace for the entire creation. All of existence has to refer to God as Paul told his brethren (I Corinthians 10:30–31).

With this statement, the bishops recognize that Jews have considered Mitzvot not as restrictions, as a yoke, but as gifts of divine grace. In emphasizing "building of time," the bishops may have followed the ideas of Abraham Joshua Heschel, an important Jewish consultant at Vatican II. Pagan gods were attached to a certain *space*—the space of their dwelling was holy, the world outside it profane. With the destruction of enemy nations went the destruction of their gods, who resided in their territory and whose power did not extend beyond the borders of the land they ruled. Even today we are concerned with space, from skyscrapers to space satellites. We have set aside for God a small "House of God," a space within otherwise God-estranged humanity.

Because of its history, Israel, by contrast, has been led to sanctify God in *time*. As Jews had no space to call their own, God was everywhere at all times. Prayer sanctifies time; social justice sanctifies time. Study of Torah, instead of "killing time," hallows it; so does the performance of Mitzvot. The Sabbath is the symbol of the sanctification of time. Israel can be the teacher, "sanctifying the Name" in time.

The bishops are thus led to an explanation of the meaning of Jewish exile-existence. It is testimony to the world.

> If Jewish tradition considers the trials and exile of its people as a punishment for its infidelities (Jeremiah 13:17, 20:21–23), it is nonetheless true that since the letter addressed by Jeremiah to the exiles of Babylon (Jeremiah 29:1–23), the life of the Jewish people in dispersion has also had a positive sense; across the trials, the Jewish people have been called upon to "Sanctify the Name" amidst the nations of the world. . . .
>
> Christians ought constantly to combat anti-Jewishness . . . which consists in

regarding the Jewish people as accursed, under the pretext that it has been obstinately persecuted. On the contrary, according to the testimony of the Scriptures (Isaiah 53:2–4), to be subjected to persecution is often an effect and reminder of the prophetic condition.

In tying Isaiah's words to Jewish destiny, the bishops again were able to understand Jews as Jews understand themselves, whereas in Christian tradition these statements had been regarded as a prophetic description of the persecution and suffering of Christ.

In their statement, "the dispersion of the Jewish people ought to be understood in the light of its own history," the bishops attempt to see the restoration of Israel as Jews see it, yet in full awareness of the problems this return poses for the Church both theologically and politically. In Israel, sanctification of space would be joined with sanctification of time as God promised the Land to the people in time.

> It is, at present, more than ever, difficult to pronounce a serene theological judgment on the movement of return of the Jewish people on "its" land. In this context, we cannot forget as Christians the gift once made by God to the People of Israel of a land where it was called to be reunited (see Genesis 12:7, 26:3–4, 28:13; Isaiah 43:5–7; Jeremiah 16:15).
>
> All through history Jewish existence has been constantly divided between life among the nations and the wish of national existence on this land. The aspiration poses numerous problems even to Jewish conscience. In order to understand this aspiration and the debate which results from it in all dimensions, Christians ought not let themselves be carried away by the exegesis that would ignore the forms of communal and religious life of Judaism or by a political position that might be generous but nonetheless hasty. They must take into account the interpretation which Jews give to their ingathering around Jerusalem, who, in the name of their faith consider it as a benediction.
>
> By this return and its repercussions, justice is put as a test on the political plane. There is, on the political level, confrontation of various exigencies of justice. Beyond the legitimate divergencies of political appeals, universal conscience cannot refuse to the Jewish people, who were submitted to vicissitudes in the course of history, the right and the means of political existence. Also, this right and possibility of existence cannot be refused to those who following the local conflicts resulting from this return are now victims of grave situations of injustice. So let us turn our eyes with attention toward this land visited by God and let us have the lively hope that it will be a place where can live in peace all its inhabitants, Jews and non-Jews. It is an essential question faced by Christians in the same manner as the Jewish people, to know whether the reassembly of the dispersal of the Jewish people, which took place under the constraint of persecution and by the play of political forces, will finally be or not, in spite of so many dreams, one of the ways of God's justice for the Jewish people and at the same time for all the peoples of the earth. How can Christians remain indifferent to what is actually on this land?

The next section calls for mutual esteem and knowledge, appealing to both clergy and people.

> The first condition is that all Christians have always respect for the Jew, whatever his manner of being Jewish. That they seek to understand the Jew

as he understands himself, instead of judging by their own ways of thoughts. They should esteem his convictions, his aspirations, his rites, and the attachment to them. They should also admit that there can be different fashions of being a Jew or to recognize oneself as Jewish without detriment to the fundamental unity of Jewish existence.

This is an important statement. It warns Christians against favoring one form of Jewish expression against another.

The second condition is that in encounters between Christians and Jews there should be recognized the right of each to give full testimony of his faith without being suspected of trying to detach a person in a disloyal manner from his community and to attach it to his own.

As a stern warning against proselytizing, the bishops address themselves specifically to the pastors:

The reason is that the Jewish people are a people of an "Eternal Alliance" [Covenant] without which the new Alliance [Covenant] could never exist. Also, far from envisaging the disappearance of the Jewish community, the Church recognizes itself in search for a living bond with it.

The issue of respect for the other's religion should be taken to heart by Jews as well. Individual conversion, on the basis of a person's convictions, is naturally legitimate; the effort to convert a people is not.

Finally, the statement addresses itself to "The Church and the Jewish People." It states:

The Jewish people are considered as having received through its particular vocation a universal mission with regard to the nations. The Church, for its part, estimates that its own mission can only be inscribed in the same universal message of salvation.

The function of Judaism has not come to an end. It is not simply the forerunner of Christianity.

Israel and the Church are not complementary institutions. The permanence of the vis-a-vis of Israel and the Church is a sign of the incompletion of God's design. The Jewish people and the Christian people are thus in a reciprocal contestation or as St. Paul said, of "jealousy" in view of unity (Romans 11: 14; see also Deuteronomy 32:21).

Christian theologians have asked: Is there a continuity of the Jewish function, or has it ceased with the coming of Christ? The bishops expressed themselves for continuity and for an eternal vying between Church and Synagogue. Why this is so is left to the will and wisdom of God; that it is so has to be acknowledged. It appears that the bishops, in contrast to Paul, hold that the Church must become "jealous" of the Jews just as the Jews are to be "jealous" of the Church. Paul speaks only of the "jealousy" of the Jews.

Basing their ideas on the teachings of Jesus and Paul, who both testified to the role of the Jewish people in the accomplishment of humanity's final unity, the bishops state:

> . . . the search that is being made today by Judaism for its unity cannot be strange to the message of salvation by God.

And in conclusion, the bishops affirm:

> But if the Jews and Christians accomplish their vocation along distinct roads, history shows that their paths are constantly crossing each other. Isn't their joint concern messianic times? One must express the wish that they enter finally the road of mutual acceptance and comprehension and that, repudiating their ancient enmity, they will turn towards the Father in the same movement of hope which will be a promise for the entire world.

Without raising the issue of humanity's being redeemed or un-redeemed, the bishops stress the task of toiling for a messianic future—messianic *times*—just as the Jew is concerned with the time, the new age of the Messiah. Instead of speaking, as did Vatican II, of the day when all people will address the Lord in a single voice, which could well be taken as a hope that they will all be Christians, the bishops express the hope that enmity will cease, that Jews will understand the good will of Christians, and that they will continue to turn to God in hope. The Jewish people is seen as eternal.

We have discussed the bishops' statement at great length, although it was not implemented, because it is a comprehensive statement, and a wise and bold document. It shows how far the Church can go without compromising its own integrity. The bishops' statement deeply influenced later pronouncements, including the guidelines issued by the Vatican, to which we shall now turn.

The Vatican Guidelines and Suggestions for Implementing the Conciliar Declaration "Nostra Aetate" are of special significance for various reasons: First, given at Rome, the pronouncement is of worldwide impact; second, resting on the experiences of ten years of interfaith dialogue, it sets the stage for the future; and third, it clarifies those points that had created apprehensions among Jews. For instance, Jews had felt that "deploring" anti-Semitism was too weak after all that had happened in the Holocaust. The guidelines straightforwardly proclaim:

> The spiritual bonds and historical links binding the Church to Judaism condemn all forms of anti-Semitism and discrimination, which in any case the dignity of the human person alone would suffice to condemn. . . . (All guideline quotes are from a pamphlet issued by the Commission for Religious Relations with the Jews, Rome, 1974, 7 pages.)

The links and relationships between Judaism and Catholicism render better mutual understanding and renewed mutual esteem obligatory.

> On the practical level in particular, Christians must therefore strive to acquire a better knowledge of the basic components of the religious tradition of Judaism; they must strive to learn by what essential traits the Jews define themselves in the light of their own religious experience.

With due respect for such matters of principle, we simply propose some first practical applications in different essential areas of the Church's life, with a view to launching or developing sound relations between Catholics and their Jewish brothers.

The section of the guidelines on *dialogue* takes cognizance of the tragic conditions of the past, when dialogue really was Christian monologue, and of the suspicion still existing among Jews, specifically in regard to the Church's intent in engaging in dialogue. Not triumphalism but care is to be the hallmark of the Christian attitude.

To tell the truth, such relations as there have been between Jew and Christian have scarcely ever risen above the level of monologue. From now on, real dialogue must be established.

Dialogue presupposes that each side wishes to know the other, and wishes to increase and deepen its knowledge of the other. It constitutes a particularly suitable means of favouring a better mutual knowledge and, especially in the case of dialogue between Jews and Christians, of probing the riches of one's own tradition. Dialogue demands respect for the other as he is; above all, respect for his faith and his religious convictions.

In virtue of her divine mission, and her very nature, the Church must preach Jesus Christ to the world (*Ad Gentes*, 2). Lest the witness of Catholics to Jesus Christ should give offence to Jews, they must take care to live and spread their Christian faith while maintaining the strictest respect for religious liberty in line with the teaching of the Second Vatican Council (Declaration *Dignitatis Humanae*). They will likewise strive to understand the difficulties which arise for the Jewish soul—rightly imbued with an extremely high, pure notion of the divine transcendence—when faced with the mystery of the incarnate Word.

While it is true that a widespread air of suspicion, inspired by an unfortunate past, is still dominant in this particular area, Christians, for their part, will be able to see to what extent the responsibility is theirs and deduce practical conclusions for the future.

In addition to friendly talks, competent people will be encouraged to meet and to study together the many problems deriving from the fundamental convictions of Judaism and of Christianity. In order not to hurt (even involuntarily) those taking part, it will be vital to guarantee, not only tact, but a great openness of spirit and diffidence with respect to one's own prejudices.

In whatever circumstances as shall prove possible and mutually acceptable, one might encourage a common meeting in the presence of God, in prayer and silent meditation, a highly efficacious way of finding that humility, that openness of heart and mind, necessary prerequisites for a deep knowledge of oneself and of others. In particular, that will be done in connection with great causes such as the struggle for peace and justice.

This leads to *liturgy*.

The existing links between the Christian liturgy and the Jewish liturgy will be borne in mind. The idea of a living community in the service of God, and in the service of men for the love of God, such as it is realized in the liturgy, is just as characteristic of the Jewish liturgy as it is of the Christian one. To improve Jewish-Christian relations, it is important to take cognizance of those common elements of the liturgical life (formulas, feasts, rites, etc.) in which the Bible holds an essential place.

Maintaining as Christians that the New Testament brings out the full meaning of the Old, efforts have to be made to acquire a better understanding of those elements in the Old Testament that have retained their perpetual value in accordance with Christian teaching.

> This is all the more important since liturgical reform is now bringing the text of the Old Testament ever more frequently to the attention of Christians.
>
> When commenting on biblical texts, emphasis will be laid on the continuity of our faith with that of the earlier Covenant, in the perspective of the promises, without minimizing those elements of Christianity which are original. We believe that those promises were fulfilled with the first coming of Christ. But it is none the less true that we still await their perfect fulfilment in his glorious return at the end of time.
>
> With respect to liturgical readings, care will be taken to see that homilies based on them will not distort their meaning, especially when it is a question of passages which seem to show the Jewish people as such in an unfavourable light. Efforts will be made so to instruct the Christian people that they will understand the true interpretation of all the texts and their meaning for the contemporary believer.
>
> Commissions entrusted with the task of liturgical translation will pay particular attention to the way in which they express those phrases and passages which Christians, if not well informed, might misunderstand because of prejudice. Obviously, one cannot alter the text of the Bible. The point is that, with a version destined for liturgical use, there should be an overriding preoccupation to bring out explicitly the meaning of a text,* while taking scriptural studies into account.
>
> The preceding remarks also apply to introductions to biblical readings, to the Prayer of the Faithful, and to commentaries printed in missals used by the laity.

The same principles must apply to *teaching and education*, discussed in the following section of the document. It is the same God,

> "inspirer and author of the books of both Testaments," (*Dei Verbum*, 16), who speaks both in the old and new Covenants.
>
> —Judaism in the time of Christ and the Apostles was a complex reality, embracing many different trends, many spiritual, religious, social and cultural values.
>
> —The Old Testament and the Jewish tradition founded upon it must not be set against the New Testament in such a way that the former seems to constitute a religion of only justice, fear and legalism, with no appeal to the love of God and neighbour (cf. Deut. 6:5; Lev. 19:18; Matt. 22:34–40).

---

*Thus the formula "the Jews", in St. John, sometimes according to the context means "the leaders of the Jews", or "the adversaries of Jesus", terms which express better the thought of the evangelist and avoid appearing to arraign the Jewish people as such. Another example is the use of the words "pharisee" and "pharisaism" which have taken on a largely pejorative meaning. (Footnote on p. 4 of the guidelines.)

—Jesus was born of the Jewish people, as were his Apostles and a large number of his first disciples. When he revealed himself as the Messiah and Son of God (cf. Matt. 16:16), the bearer of the new Gospel message, he did so as the fulfilment and perfection of the earlier Revelation. And, although his teaching had a profoundly new character, Christ, nevertheless, in many instances, took his stand on the teaching of the Old Testament. The New Testament is profoundly marked by its relation to the Old. As the Second Vatican Council declared: "God, the inspirer and author of the books of both Testaments, wisely arranged that the New Testament be hidden in the Old and the Old be made manifest in the New" (*Dei Verbum*, 16). Jesus also used teaching methods similar to those employed by the rabbis of his time.

—With regard to the trial and death of Jesus, the Council recalled that "what happened in his passion cannot be blamed upon all the Jews then living, without distinction, nor upon the Jews of today" (*Nostra Aetate*, 4).

—The history of Judaism did not end with the destruction of Jerusalem, but rather went on to develop a religous tradition. And, although we believe that the importance and meaning of that tradition were deeply affected by the coming of Christ, it is still nonetheless rich in religious values.

—With the prophets and the apostle Paul, "the Church awaits the day, known to God alone, on which all peoples will address the Lord in a single voice and 'serve him with one accord' (Soph. 3:9)" (*Nostra Aetate*, 4).

Information concerning these questions is important at all levels of Christian instruction and education. Among sources of information, special attention should be paid to the following:

—catechisms and religious textbooks
—history books
—the mass-media (press, radio, cinema, television).

The effective use of these means presupposes the thorough formation of instructors and educators in training schools, seminaries and universities.

Research into the problems bearing on Judaism and Jewish-Christian relations will be encouraged among specialists, particularly in the fields of exegesis, theology, history and sociology. Higher institutions of Catholic research, in association if possible with other similar Christian institutions and experts, are invited to contribute to the solution of such problems. Wherever possible, chairs of Jewish studies will be created, and collaboration with Jewish scholars encouraged.

The best way for people to know and respect each other is to join in common endeavors for others. This is recognized in the section on *joint social action*.

Jewish and Christian tradition, founded on the Word of God, is aware of the value of the human person, the image of God. Love of the same God must show itself in effective action for the good of mankind. In the spirit of the prophets, Jews and Christians will work willingly together, seeking social justice and peace at every level—local, national and international.

At the same time, such collaboration can do much to foster mutual understanding and esteem.

In conclusion, the statement admits that "there is still a long road ahead." But the Church, for its own sake, needs to concern itself with Judaism.

The problem of Jewish-Christian relations concerns the Church as such, since it is when "pondering her own mystery" that she encounters the mystery of Israel. Therefore, even in areas where no Jewish communities exist, this remains an important problem. . . .

Implementation of the guidelines is entrusted to the bishops. They are to create commissions or secretariats on national or regional levels, or to appoint suitable representatives to implement the mandate of the council. Therefore,

on October 22, 1974, the Holy Father instituted for the universal Church this Commission for Religious Relations with the Jews, joined in the Secretariat for Promoting Christian Unity.

This last sentence reveals a significant transformation in outlook. At the Council itself, the section on Judaism had been removed from the proposed inclusion in the chapter on "Christian Unity" and inserted in "Relations with Other Religions." Now it was affirmed that relations with Judaism were indeed an aspect of Christian unity.

The German *"Working paper: Basic Theological Issues of the Jewish-Christian Dialogue"* is the result of actual Christian-Jewish dialogue. It addresses both Christians and Jews.

The paper finds dialogue essential, as "their interest in each other is in itself an act of adoring God." Both

will have to work very hard on behalf of one another . . . trusting one another and revealing themselves to the other. . . .

The dialogue cannot succeed if the Christian sees in Judaism merely a memorial of his own past—of the time of Jesus and of the Apostles . . . if the Jewish partner can discover in the essential Jewish elements within the Christian faith nothing but the effects of a past condition which did indeed obtain within the first Christian communities, but nowadays no longer obtain. In both of those cases the one partner does not yet take the contemporaneousness of the other seriously. Instead he makes him into a mere mirror of his own past. . . .

The Jewish partner cannot be satisfied if, in a conversation with Christians, he is regarded merely as a surviving witness of the so-called Old Testament and of the period in which the Christian communities originated. Conversely, the Christian partner cannot be satisfied if the Jewish partner thinks that only he has something to say to the Christian which is essential to the Christian's faith, while that which the Christian has to say to the Jew has no essential meaning for the faith of the Jew. . . . The Christian Church, calling herself "People of God", must not forget that the present existence of Judaism is testimony to the fact that, still today, the same God is in faithfulness committed to that Election through which He became Israel's God, and through which He had made Israel His people. That is why the Christian does not adequately understand his own dignity and election if he does not take notice of, nor seeks to understand the dignity and the election of the Judaism of today. But in order to do so, he needs to familiarize himself with the Jewish faith and the Jewish existence to which his Jewish partners in the dialogue offer testimony.

When the Jew, rightly so, calls himself a "son of Abraham", he cannot forget—he can at most suppress it—that not only the first Christians in the distant past were sons of Abraham, but that also today nobody can be a Christian without acknowledging Abraham as the "father of all those who believe." Furthermore, the Jewish community is certain of the promise of a renewal of its covenant, as it is written: "Behold, the days are coming, says the Lord, when I will make a new covenant with the house of Israel and the house of Judah, not like the covenant which I made with their fathers when I took them by the hand to bring them out of the land of Egypt" (Jer. 31:31 f.). The Jewish community, therefore, must not forget that there would never have been a community of the Christians if the latter had not known the call from the same God into his "New Covenant". That is why the Jew does not completely understand the manner in which Abraham became the "father of a multitude of nations" (Gen. 17), if he does not take notice of, nor seeks to understand the faith of today's Christian. But in order to do so, he needs to familiarize himself with the Christian faith and the Christian existence to which his Christian partners in the dialogue offer testimony.

Once the meaning of that which binds them together in history has entered their consciousness and has been acknowledged, there is a chance that both partners in the dialogue might let themselves be called to a responsibility for each other. Each becomes a witness for the other to those mighty acts of God which are the cause of his living as a Jew or as a Christian at the present time. (Quotes from "Basic Theological Issues of the Jewish Christian Dialogue," translated by Elizabeth Petuchowski; Aachen: Central Committee of Roman Catholics in Germany, 1979.)

As companions in the work for God's rulership, Jews and Christians have to understand the elements of agreement between them but also the elements of divergence. Jews must see in Christianity a divine dispensation; Christians must recognize that the Jews' interest in Christianity is in no way to be construed as an inclination to accept the Christian faith as their own. Jews have the right to evaluate the Christian faith on the basis of the Christian's deeds in "the service of righteousness and peace," for Jesus himself taught it thus.

For the Christian, the goal of God's saving rulership, promised in Israel's Bible, is mediated by the Jew Jesus. Already here, not only the dividing but also the uniting function of Jesus shows itself: Through the Jew Jesus, the Torah remains effective within Christianity. Through him, its realization becomes the task of the Christians—as God's promise and commandment. The Jew, on the other hand, does not first have to get to know Jesus in order to love the Torah. As a Jew, he has this love as his heritage. Of course, a dialogue of Jews and Christians can take place seriously only when the Jewish partner, too, begins with the assumption that God caused something to happen in Christianity, which concerns him "for God's sake"—even though he may not see in it a way on which he himself can or must go. That is why Christians ask whether the living presence of essential Jewish elements in the Christian divine service, in the Christian proclamation, in the Christian understanding of Scripture, and in Christian theology, does not make possible a Jewish interest in Christian faith and life—over and above a mere taking note from the distance. Conversely, Christians must grant the Jews that a Jewish interest in Christianity can be an interest "for the sake of the Kingdom of Heaven"—even though it does not lead to Jews becoming Christians. A possibility of understanding the Jewish interest in Christianity was expressed by the Jewish philosopher of religion, Franz Rosenzweig (1886–1929), when he said: "Whether Jesus was the Messiah will be shown when the Messiah comes." Such an ambiguous formulation does not, however, mean that Jews and Christians are free to postpone until "the Last Day" their conversation about the hope which unites them, and the question about the Messiah which divides them.

In the mutual questioning, some recognition of the salvific meaning of the other way can, therefore, most certainly be expressed. Jews can acknowledge that, for the Christians, Jesus has become the way on which they find Israel's God. But they will make their evaluation of the Christian way dependent upon this, that the faith of the Christians in the salvation granted to them through God's messiah who came from the Jews does not diminish, but rather demand their obligation to act in the service of righteousness and peace. Christians understand Jesus as the fulfilment of the Law and the promise only when they follow him "for the sake of the Kingdom of Heaven," and when doing so, they listen to his word: "Not every one who says to me 'Lord, Lord,' shall enter the kingdom of heaven, but he who does the will of my Father who is in heaven" (Mtt. 7:21).

A fundamental difference between Judaism and Christianity centers around the approach to Jesus. But as both are called by God, it is forbidden to each to sway the other.

> The mutual evaluation of each other's way is thus indivisibly united with considerable divergencies in the approach to Jesus, and to the question, whether he is God's messiah. But this compels neither Jews nor Christians to dissolve the fundamental bracket of contents of the one commanding will of God. That is why it is fundamentally prohibited to Jews and to Christians to seek to move the other to become disloyal to the call of God which he has received. It is not to be thought that this prohibition is based on tactical calculations. Reasons of humane tolerance and respect for the freedom of religion, too, are not solely decisive in this. The deepest reason must rather be seen in this: that it is the same God by whom both Jews and Christians know themselves to have been called. Christians, on the basis of their own under-standing of the faith, cannot forego to testify to Jesus as the Christ also vis-a-vis the Jews. Jews, on the basis of their self-understanding, cannot refrain from stressing the non-abrogation of the Torah also vis-a-vis the Christians. In either case, this includes the hope that, by means of this testimony, the other's loyalty to the call he has received from God might increase, and that the mutual understanding might be deepened. On the other hand, the ex-pectation should not be included that the other may renege on his "yes" to his call or weaken it.

Christians must cast off any notion, based on the elevated humanity of Jesus the man, that "the Christians are the better Israelites after all." Jews must appreciate that the Christian concept "the Son of God having become man" does not dilute the oneness of God. " . . . it was precisely Jesus who mediated and represented to them the one and unique God of Israel. For Christians, God's becoming man is by no means a negation of the unity and uniqueness of God but rather its confirmation." In becoming man, God reveals His near-ness to humankind. The "Working Paper" points out that this same character-istic of God is proclaimed in Judaism independently of Christianity. This statement corrects the impression created by other Christian documents that Jews have known God only in His transcendence, not in His nearness.

> Indeed, God's becoming man presupposes that the one and unique God of Israel is not an isolated God without relationships, but a God who turns towards humankind and who is also affected by human destiny. This characteristic of God, according to the testimony of the Talmudim and the Midrashim—albeit without reference to, or connection with, Jesus—is likewise known to Rabbinic Judaism. Rabbinic Judaism, too, obviously knows that the one and unique God of Israel does not only "dwell" in transcendence, but also in the midst of His people, subjected to distress and persecution—as Lord, Father, Companion and Redeemer. The Christian-Jewish dialogue about the living God of Israel is, therefore, a great sign of hope.

As Germans, the authors of the "Working Paper" had to address themselves to the Holocaust and the State of Israel. The document recognizes that there can be no theological answers; the question must produce an action response.

The contemporary world has become polytheistic—we might even add atheistic. If there is a meaning to this trend, it can only be to call Christians and Jews to the task of witnessing to God in a world still fighting wars of religion thinly disguised as wars of ideology.

> In spite of the disagreement in agreement, which has not been glossed over, Jews and Christians are united by their having received the commission to act and to testify jointly in the world. Examples of essential tasks which, for the sake of the future, they will jointly have to undertake are the following:
>
> —How, in the face of the mass murder which has been committed against the Jews and the attempted destruction of the Jewish people, is it still possible to believe in God? How is it possible to bear guilt and suffering in the presence of God, instead of suppressing or fixating them? What meaning is there for Jews and Christians, and for their mutual encounter, in the systematic extermination of large segments of European Jewry, and in the founding of the State of Israel? How, in the face of the founding of the State of Israel as a central event in recent Jewish history, is it possible to combine the millennial Jewish hope in God's salvation with concrete political action in the present, without advocating either a religiously grounded ideologizing of politics or a politization of religion?
>
> —What is the meaning of the fact that, in a world which is as polytheistic as ever before (it is simply that the gods are given different names today), Jews and Christians believe in the One God? Is it not possible, indeed, is it not mandatory for Jews and Christians, on the basis of their revelation, jointly to develop a critique of ideology—in a world which still fights wars which essentially are wars of religion (which becomes clear when we substitute the word "ideology" for the word "religion")?
>
> —Do not Jews and Christians have the common obligation, in the face of world conditions which threaten the survival of humankind, to demonstrate and to show through personal example what the Bible understands by righteousness and liberty?
>
> —The basic demand of biblical Revelation, common to Jews and Christians,

is the absolute respect of the life of another human being. They should jointly specify the consequences which follow from this today for the maintenance of human dignity and human rights. In particular, they should, for example, together develop an ethics of the sciences, of technology, and of a concern for the future. (People who live after the year 2000 are also our "neighbors.")

—What concrete consequences can be drawn from the conviction, common to Jews and Christians, that man has been created in God's image? What obligations follow from the commandment, common to Jews and Christians, of unrestricted love? (cf. Lev. 19:18 and Mark 12:30f.)

Finally, the document addresses the grave danger arising from the misunderstanding that Jews believe in "justification by works" and that Christians might be "seduced" by their faith in grace to deny their responsibility for action in the world and for the world. This results in an actual reinterpretation of Paul, a "Reconsidering the Controversy about Law and Grace."

The encounter of Jews and Christians will also lead both sides to a clearer perception of the questions put to one another.

Jews can convincingly reject the Christian reproach that they believe in "justification by works" only if they do not deny the danger which could follow from their position. All the more so since they know that a warning against "justification by works" is part of their own religious tradition. The fact that the Torah claims the whole life of man does not prevent his being dependent upon God's mercy. Liturgical texts, like those which characterize the celebration of the Day of Atonement, the most important High Holy Day in the Jewish year, could afford Christians an intimate view of this aspect of Jewish life.

Christians can convincingly reject the Jewish reproach that they suffer from a "loss of ethics" only if they do not deny the danger which could follow from the possibility that their hope for grace might seduce them from their responsibility in and for the world. All the more so since they know that a warning against this danger is included in their own religious tradition. Ecclesiastical texts concerning the relationship between faith and works (cf. the Council of Trent), and already the Pauline admonition about "faith working through love" (Gal. 5:6) are eloquent examples of this.

Jewish and Christian criticism of "justification by works," and Jewish and Christian "rejoicing in the Law" (rejoicing is shared also by the Christian, as Paul expressly acknowledges in Rom. 7:12) have a common goal: to preserve the ability to pray and to praise God. That is why Jews and Christians find their way to the dialogue only when they together acknowledge what is said daily in the Jewish morning service: "We do not rely upon our own righteousness, but on Your great mercy" (Dan. 9:18).

From Pronouncement to Action

The "Working Paper" concludes with the admonition "that the Jewish-Christian dialogue must no longer remain the monopoly of a few interested specialists, it must engage all; clergy, educators, pastoral workers, the media—both Christian and Jewish."

In fact, the Catholic Church has forged ahead. An office for Catholic-Jewish relations was established at the Vatican and a U.S. Secretariat for

Catholic-Jewish Relations in the United States. Most dioceses have offices dealing with Catholic-Jewish relations. Official statements have faced the problems that may impede the dialogue, including the issue of the State of Israel, and have called for an understanding approach. Numerous Catholic universities provide courses in Jewish studies, and high schools have invited local rabbis to present Judaism to Catholic youth. Curricula have been developed on subjects including the Holocaust. Conferences and lecture series have been common. Texts have been subjected to scrutiny in order to eliminate items derogatory to Jews. Cordial personal contacts have developed or deepened.

We have dwelt at great length on the pronouncements of the Catholic Church for several reasons: By its organization, the Church is able to make pronouncements for all its faithful and give directions with a certain assurance that they will be implemented. By its size and its impact on Christianity as a whole, it can influence other Christian denominations with which it has an ongoing ecumenical relationship.

The documents reveal a profound concern with Jewish beliefs, sensitivities, and anxieties. They reveal that another faith *can* see the partner from the partner's own perspective. In doing so, the documents illuminate Judaism itself, in many ways as it is perceived by the Jews. The documents read together are an interpretation of Jewish religion and peoplehood as a living organism, meaningful for the world today.

PROTESTANTISM

Protestant churches of various denominations, their leaders, and many scholars have also spoken out on relations with the Jews. Franklin Littell, a leading Protestant theologian and formerly president of Iowa Wesleyan College, has been committed to confronting Christianity with its past, calling for acknowledgment of its guilt and for its active renewal.

During the tensions of 1967, when Israel was in grave danger and Jews throughout the world were terrified at the possibility of another Holocaust, questions arose in Jewish minds: Was the Church unconcerned? Was it tied to the concept of the Jews as homeless wanderers? Was it afraid that its missionary activities in the Third World might be jeopardized by any support for Israel?

The questions were echoed by two Christian theologians, A. Roy Eckhardt and Alice L. Eckhardt, in their joint work, *The Silence of the Churches*. But other church leaders disagreed strongly with them. They pointed to the work the Church had done during the crisis. The controversy itself proved to be beneficial. Perhaps the Jews were too sensitive and expected too much from a dialogue barely begun; perhaps they were partly justified. Christians argued the issue. A deeper commitment to the new spirit of the dialogue and wider and more active concern developed. The dialogue might have come to an end; instead, the crisis called for a maturing of expectations and of conscience on all sides, and increased awareness and renewed effort on a deeper level of understanding and cooperation.

One fact became very clear: The basic principles of theological dialogue must be carried into the arena of human events.

In the ensuing years, a significant dialogue developed with those churches that see in the return of the Jews to their Land a fulfillment of prophecy heralding the second coming of Christ. Dr. Billy Graham and the Southern Baptists belong to the group of fundamentalist churches that take such a position. (The Mormons, in the words of Joseph Smith, proclaimed this theology as early as 1843.) In 1969, the Reverend Robert C. Dodds, Director of Ecumenical Affairs of the National Council of Churches, pointed out that contact with Israel will help Christians to recover the full authenticity of their own faith by understanding Jews of a generation that had not known the humiliations by the Christian majority, the youth of Israel.

The misunderstanding of 1967 revealed the need for giving the dialogue a better foundation in understanding and forbearance. In 1973, church leaders widely condemned Egypt's and Syria's attack on Israel and their profanation of Judaism in their choice of Yom Kippur for the attack. Some church organizations were equivocal, however.

In 1965, 1968, 1969, and since, the leadership of the World Council of Churches, composed of Protestant, Anglican, and Greek Orthodox churches, met informally with a Jewish group of consultants. As a result, a Jewish consultative council was formally organized, meeting for the first time in 1970. Again, the question of Israel, with its close links to the Third World nations, was being debated. Israel has a large population of non-European Jews and has the desire and the means of aiding new nations in their development. Ways of cooperation in the Middle East may well be worked out in such a council of religions. This would call for a combined meeting involving not only Catholics, Protestants, and Jews, but also Muslim leaders.

In 1980, the Evangelical Synod of the German State of Rhineland, the official governing body of the Lutheran Church of that state, issued an ordinance, binding on all its affiliated churches, entitled "Synodal Ordinance toward Renewal of the Relationship between Christians and Jews." *Renewal* is the key term. The ordinance thus clearly admits that age-old teachings of Christianity were the basis of "Christian co-responsibility and guilt in regard to the Holocaust, the degradation, persecution and murder of the Jews" in Hitler's Germany. The Holocaust, in fact, constitutes a crisis in civilization, culture, politics, and religion, all of which contributed to it. In addition, Christians in Germany live "under the curse that Hitler's policies of Judenreinheit have been almost fully realized." The church must *repent* actively. The Synod prays that Jews may be willing to join with Christians in the work of renewal.

Because both Jews and Christians are witnesses to the everlasting One God, Christian missionary activity among Jews is to be rejected as contrary to the will of God, who has ordained Jewish survival and who loves Israel. The

New Testament must not be presented as standing in contrast to the Old; Christians are advised to speak of the "Hebrew Bible" rather than "Old Testament." Statements hostile to Jews and Judaism in the New Testament must be reinterpreted. Jesus must be recognized as a Jew. Christians must know that for both Christianity and Judaism God is God of *both* love and justice.

The restoration of the State of Israel as a "sign of God's historical faithfulness to His people" reveals His abiding concern. The question of a *theodicee*—a justification of God's actions—exists for Christians as for Jews. There cannot be a satisfactory explanation for God's actions, but there can and must be a common affirmation of God in the world.

Christians and Jews are bound together in love as *one* people; in different ways, they have received God's mandate. Jointly, they must explore God's word, as found in Scripture, and carry His mandate as His witnesses in the world. Practical ways of cooperation are outlined, including committees for common study and work on the local level and the establishment of a program of Judaic studies at one of the universities within the region. The Synod's statement invokes the spirit of Karl Barth, who declared that ecumenicity is possible only if the Jews are part of it.

A SENSE OF THINGS TO COME

Over the centuries, Christians, acting out of a very inadequate understanding of Judaism, have seen the Jews as a people to be indoctrinated and converted. In our time, this position seems to be changing, though not universally among Christian churches. As we saw from the discussion in the previous sections of this chapter, however, the official pronouncements of the great churches reject it. No one position dominates Christian thinking today; various perspectives are evident. Reinhold Niebuhr, for instance, has pointed out:

> If we measure the two faiths by their moral fruits the Jewish faith does not fall short. . . . [Missionary] activities among Jews . . . are wrong . . . not only because they are futile and have little fruit to boast for their exertions. They are wrong because . . . the two faiths, despite differences, are sufficiently alike for the Jew to find God more easily in terms of his own religious heritage than by subjecting himself to the hazards of guilt feelings involved in a conversion to a faith, which, whatever its excellencies, must appear to him as a symbol of an oppressive majority culture. (*Pious and Secular America*; New York: Charles Scribner's Sons, 1958, pp. 107ff.)

The evangelist Dr. Billy Graham takes a middle position. He opposes "proselytizing that is coercive," and rejects "gimmicks, coercion and intimidation," but feels committed to approach "all men concerning personal faith in Jesus Christ." He also affirmed that "in my evangelical efforts I have never been called to single out Jews as Jews," holding, along with most evangelical Christians, that "God has always had a special relationship with the Jewish people, as Paul suggests in the Book of Romans (Romans 9)."

At the same time, a number of groups in various Protestant churches and in newly emerging sects still regard conversion of Jews as a primary duty of the Church.

Although the Jewish masters throughout the ages have regarded Christianity as a divine dispensation, Jewish knowledge of Christianity has been scant indeed. As Jews reach a better knowledge of Christians—just as the opposite comes about—their fears will be dispelled, and the apprehensions mentioned in the German "Working Paper" can be set to rest. For this to happen, a concentrated effort is required on both sides—something that may be difficult in the near future.

Both Jews and Christians have so many internal tasks that a dialogue between them must necessarily take second place in the total program of instruction and education. Widespread laxity among Christians makes strengthening the faith the first priority of the leadership. Still, elimination of pejorative statements, corrections in texts, and reinterpretation of Scripture have already had profound and salutary results.

Recognizing the lack of knowledge about Judaism among Jews them-selves, Jewish leadership has to devote efforts to its cure. The situation is complicated by the fact that Jews live in a Christian environment. As Franz Rosenzweig has stated, the Jew who drifts out of Judaism moves not into a neutral sphere but into a Christian one. Strengthening Jewish commitment thus becomes even more difficult than it is for Christians to strengthen Christian commitment. But the task of opening up Jewish minds to the dialogue has begun.

Ambiguity concerning Israel has sometimes been a source of tension between Christians and Jews. Liberal Protestantism appears to favor the Arabs in the name of equal justice, whereas fundamentalist churches have been supportive of Israel, seeing in the return of the Jews to the homeland a prelude to the second coming of Christ. As understanding between Christians and Jews has improved a new challenge may have been placed on Christianity: The official relationship between Christianity and Islam has been better than that of Jews with Islam; Christianity may well be called upon to be the advocate of Judaism and Israel among Muslims.

Many of the Third World nations, especially in Africa, have become Christian. To them, Judaism is an unknown faith. They identify it with what they hear of Israel in a political context, often very hostile. In this situation, too, the Church can be advocate, helping the Third World to know what Judaism is.

The Christian-Jewish dialogue has made the greatest progress in the Western countries, especially the United States. In Germany, it suffers from the absence of a numerically strong and spiritually creative Jewry. In Israel, times and conditions have as yet not permitted a true concern with it, although the Hebrew University, through a number of its professors, has become a center of studies of other religions. Where Jews are a small minority, the dialogue will be more difficult as it may not appear pressing for the majority. But minorities, more than majorities, need the comforting support and understanding of their fellows.

DIALOGUE WITH ISLAM

Islam was long neglected by the West, which felt, mistakenly, that there was nothing to learn from it. Islamic religious leaders saw no need for a dialogue either, as for Islam the Quran holds the entire truth. Such a dialogue is still not carried on in the Islamic world, although there may be indications of a beginning interchange of ideas in Egypt. In addition, Jewry saw its first priority as dialogue with Christianity. But Vatican II, opening the gates for Christian-Jewish cooperation, also declared that much can be learned from Islam (and other religions) and that an interchange of ideas is highly desirable. The primary impetus, however, came with the new impact of the Muslim world on the West and the development of "diaspora" Islamic communities throughout the West. Mosques were built in Europe and America, and scholars became available.

There are some problems with a Muslim-Jewish interchange. Dialogue requires reassessment of sacred Scriptures; this is strongly resisted in Islamic lands. Muslim scholars living and teaching in the West may be regarded with suspicion by their fellow Muslims, having been "contaminated" by Western culture. If they are too bold, they may be excommunicated.

Nevertheless, the dialogue is showing signs of unfolding. For example, some Islamic scholars have held that there exists a difference between the portions of the Quran written at Mecca and those written at Medina: The former contain Mohammed's ethical pronouncements and conciliatory statements toward other religions. They have abiding authority. The latter reflect his conflicts with opponents, his vexations, and conditions of war; they were meaningful for their time but are not binding in the present. This critical approach to the Quran may be rejected by a majority of Muslims, but it is indicative of a new openness.

Timid as the beginnings may be, they are of vital importance. As dialogue expands, fellowship and peace are promoted. As Mohammed stated, "None of you is truly faithful as long as he does not desire for his brother what he himself loves."

CONTACTS WITH FAR EASTERN RELIGIONS

To this day, Judaism has given little attention to the religions of the Far East. Jews have had little occasion to relate to them, as there were few Jews in the regions where these religions prevail. In India the small Jewish community seems to be phasing itself out by emigration. Another Jewish community, in Kaifeng, China, died out in the nineteenth century after existing for almost one thousand years. Contact between these Jews and the rest of Jewry was scant.

Discovered in the seventeenth century by Jesuits, they sparked the interest of Christians, who believed that these Jews owned Torah scrolls so old that they were written before the rabbis could expunge prophecies relating to the coming of Christ from the Hebrew Scriptures, as they were supposed to have done. No such references were found, but Christian missionaires described the life of these Jews and have given us a picture of their ways. Unlike Christianity and Islam, Far Eastern religions did not emerge out of Judaism and thus have had no reason to disparage their mother religion. Partly as a result of the small number of Jews in the Far East, partly because Far Eastern religions are un-related to Judaism, and partly because Eastern faiths have a generally greater tolerance for other beliefs, no anti-Jewish sentiment developed in this region.

Eastern religions such as Hinduism and Buddhism essentially call on the human being to get away from the illusions of the world by withdrawal from it. In the eyes of the Western observer, taught by his faith to enter the world and make it better for all humanity, this Eastern attitude may be the reason why there has been little social progress. The West can influence the East, therefore, through Western religious tradition, by leading it toward ever-greater awareness of human social duties. At the same time, the East can teach the West that the frantic search for achievement, status, power, and goods of consumption may be a chase toward illusions, bringing no happiness and causing much suffering. A study of Eastern faiths can also encourage the faithful of Western religions to find deeper values in their own traditions. The contact with these religions deserves to be deepened.

II

WELLSPRINGS OF THE JEWISH SPIRIT

12

TENAKH: HOLY SCRIPTURES

In the introduction, we discussed the internal forces that have shaped Judaism, and in Part I we sketched in bare outline the basic currents of Jewish history. History and the various environments in which Jews have lived became the stage for the dramatic unfolding of Jewish ideas interacting with those of the surrounding world.

In the following chapters, we shall discuss Judaism's own spiritual and literary creations, emerging out of the genius of the people and its heritage—above all, Torah, both written and oral. This will enable us to understand the creative tensions and the blending of internal ideas and external forces, and the emergence of new forms and theological concepts held by all or some of the Jews in the contemporary world.

Although the Jews have made many contributions, they are best known for having given to the world the Holy Scriptures of the Bible. Christians call it The Old Testament; Jews, who do not use the New Testament, simply call it the Holy Scriptures, or look at it as the Bible. In ecumenical dialogue, discerning Christians have come to refer to it as the Hebrew Scriptures. A Hebrew word for this work is *Tenakh,* an abbreviation of three words—*Torah, Nebee-im, Ketubim*—the three sections making up Holy Scriptures. Torah (in this specific connotation) stands for the Five Books of Moses, the Pentateuch. Nebee-im (Prophets) contains the messages of the great prophets of Israel, but also the history leading up to their ministry. Ketubim (Collected Writings) is an anthology of a variety of works, including Psalms; Job; and the "Five Scrolls" of Song of Songs, Ruth, Lamentations, Ecclesiastes, and Esther.

This chapter will show how the Tenakh became to the Jews the source of their theology and orientation. By revealing to them the divine origin of the universe and of humanity, it led them to the duties that emerge from these facts. Tenakh discloses to the Jews the meaning of Jewish existence, keeps alive within them the spirit of *emunah* by making the Covenant manifest. It is the source of wisdom and the ladder of ascent in prayer.

For this reason, Tenakh has become the Jew's companion and is read to the congregation in worship. We have included in this chapter the selections appointed for special occasions of the liturgical year and the reasons that prompted their choice. We have also included some commentaries, both ancient and modern, to demonstrate how the Tenakh reveals ever-new meanings to the searching mind. We have consciously omitted the results of biblical criticism, in this context, as they did not affect Jewish thought throughout the ages.

TORAH

The Torah, or Five Books of Moses, is the central source of Jewish law and ethics, guidepost for thought and conduct and for the relationships between God and humanity and among people. Hence it is read to the people regularly during the cycle of the year, on Sabbath days, holy days, and every Monday and Thursday (once market days when the farmers came to town and thus could receive instruction in conjunction with their business). It is recited from a handwritten parchment scroll, which is stored in the Ark and removed for recital of its message. The congregation stands in reverence as it is carried to the reading desk.

Genesis

Bereshit (Genesis) is the first book of Torah, dealing with creation and the lives of the patriarchs. Bereshit is the Prelude. Here the destiny of the people as people of the Covenant is anticipated and founded. The story of creation emphasizes the divine origin of the universe, and humanity's stewardship in it.

Rashi, in his commentary to the first verse of Genesis, points in an equally important, different direction: God tells Israel and the world that He is the Creator and, therefore, the owner of His creation, entitled to distribute it as He pleases. "Should the world therefore say: you are robbers, having conquered the Land of Israel from the peoples that dwelt in it, then you may tell them: the Land, like all the world, belongs to God who made it, and He has assigned it to us" (Rashi: Commentary to Genesis 1:1). Thus in the consciousness of the Jewish people, the Land of Israel is woven into the very first utterance of Torah. Bereshit sets up an historical awareness. The God of creation is God of history.

The very first chapters equally establish the principle of human equality: All humanity is equal before God, and all people must be so treated. "God created *one* man only," says the Talmud (Mishnah Sanhedrin 4:5), "to teach you that he who destroys one single soul is deemed as having destroyed a whole world." Furthermore, the rabbis say, "God created only one person to promote peace in the world, that no one may say to his neighbor, my ancestors were more distinguished than yours" (Mishnah Sanhedrin 4:5). In this spirit, history must be fashioned.

The first commandment is given, and the significance of law and commandment as tools for moral decision is clearly demonstrated. Adam and

Torah Scroll, *open to Leviticus 19, including the commandment "You shall love your neighbor as yourself."* (Photo of author's Torah scroll by the author.)

Eve are not to eat from the tree of knowledge. In subsequent generations, only Noah recognizes this obligation. He is therefore rescued when the Great Flood destroys a wicked society. As he emerges from the Ark after the flood, God makes a Covenant with him, the sign of which is the rainbow.

Speaking to one individual, deserving of the Covenant on account of his obedience, God includes all of humanity in the Covenant. Individualism and universalism are joined in Jewish thought.

The patriarchs appear on the scene; Abraham, confessing the one God, is commanded to migrate to the land which is promised to his children. Abraham is told to leave his homeland. In Ur of the Chaldaeans, his birthplace, the king is absolute; Abraham has to become a sojourner. As such, he has to subject himself immediately and exclusively to God's kingship. When he makes a covenant with an earthly king, it is with one who recognizes God as supreme ruler—Melchizedek, the righteous king, ruler of Shalem, which, in popular etymology, came to mean city of Shalom, of peace* (Genesis 14:18–20). *God's* kingship is established.

God makes a Covenant with Abraham, "I *have given* this land to your descendants" (Genesis 15:18); the fact *is accomplished.* In return, circumcision is the seal his descendants affix to themselves—B'rit Milah, the Covenant of Circumcision (Genesis 17); it cannot be eradicated. He who fails to enter it is "cut off from his kin; he has broken My Covenant" (Genesis 17:14).

Then Abraham is tested. He is to sacrifice his son Isaac. The sacrifice was not consummated. After Isaac had been bound by his father, God stayed

---

*Shalem actually means "the foundation for the god Shalem, or Shalmon"; *Shulmany* in Assyrian.

Ark open, Temple Emanu-El, San Francisco. *Each of the three Torah scrolls has a crown, breastplate, and pointer. On the mantle are the letters "KT," for Keter Torah, the Torah is a crown. On the breastplates are the windows for insertion of the plaque indicating the occasion for which the scroll is rolled. The mantle on the center scroll is white in preparation for the High Holy Days. Its embroidered inscription states: "It [Torah] is a tree of life to them that hold on to it" (Proverbs 3:13).* (Photo by the author, reproduced courtesy of Congregation Emanu-El and Rabbi Joseph Asher.)

the knife in Abraham's hand; Abraham had stood the test. Interpreters have dwelt on the exemplary faith of Abraham that transcended the agony of a father called upon to sacrifice his son to God, for there is no greater agony and there is no greater affirmation of faith. In Jewish tradition, the *Akeda,* the binding, became symbolic of Israel's fate, for in every generation Jews have been willing to give their own lives and those of their children in expression of their love of God.

Isaac became the symbol of the Jew. Hence this story is read on Rosh Hashanah, a call to the people to pledge their fullest measure of devotion to God. Many penitential prayers have been written elaborating on the subject; they are called Akeda, the Binding, and during the penitential days the plea is repeated: "Remember the Covenant with Abraham and the Binding of Isaac, and bring back the remnant of the children of Jacob."

Torah Ornaments. *Torah crowns* (rimmonim) *(Padua, nineteenth century), breastplate, and pointer (silver). Note the small window on the breastplate with the plaque showing the occasion for which the scroll has been set.* (Photo by Kathie Minami, reproduced courtesy of Judah L. Magnes Memorial Museum, Jewish Museum of the West, Berkeley, California.)

A second element of the story is equally remembered. Abraham, like his contemporaries, believed that God actually called for human sacrifices. In rejecting the sacrifice, God taught him that He demands the response of the living, respect for life, and love; He does not call for death. A new level in humanity's God-awareness had been reached. Hence the congregation pleads "that God who desires life, may grant life." Many have died at the hands of those who showed no such reverence; let the test be over.

Knowing that Canaan is the place where his seed was to grow into an organic society, Abraham and his successors actually spent large portions of their lives abroad. The Land can exert its influence even as an idea, once its spiritual significance is recognized. Jacob and Joseph, dying abroad and aware of the symbolism of their own lives for their descendants, request to be buried "with their fathers." These men and women are individualists; they have to be in order to stand their ground against the society in which they dwell. They hear God's call, and, in individual response, act upon it. However, with individualism inevitably goes human error, and these people show themselves all too human on many occasions.

The greatness of the patriarchs rests in the fact that they had *emunah,* trust in God, though they had no tangible evidence that He would keep His promise. "He trusted in God, and He accorded it to him as merit" (Genesis 15:6). Said of Abraham, it also applies to Isaac and Jacob. In this manner, "the deeds of the fathers became the guideposts for the children," as the Talmud points out.

Exodus

The second book of Torah, *Shemot* (Exodus), presents the transposition of the lives of their ancestors into the collective experience of the emerging people. They are molded within a hostile environment in Egypt, where they have been made slaves; they are tested in their perseverance. They are to be a collective individual, composed of individualists. They are shown the differences between God-centered individualism, which leads to salvation, and human-centered, selfish individualism, which leads to destruction. Moses and Pharaoh are the two great protagonists: Moses speaking in the name of God; the other, Pharaoh, an absolutist who considers himself divine. Then the people are redeemed to find their way back to the Land of Promise.

No people can live without law; as a God-centered people, they are to receive a God-given law. Ten Commandments form the core of this law, encompassing the relationship of humanity to both God and fellow:

1. I the LORD am your God who brought you out of the land of Egypt, the house of bondage. [God is to be worshipped as God of history, of time, creative, dynamic; hence:]

2. You shall have no other gods beside Me. You shall not make for yourself a sculptured image, or any likeness of what is in the heavens above, or on the earth below, or in the waters under the earth. You shall not bow down to them or serve them. For I the LORD your God am an impassioned God, visiting the guilt of the fathers upon the children, upon the third and upon the fourth generations of those who reject Me, but showing kindness to the thousandth generation of those who love Me and keep My commandments. [Recognition of other gods denies divine omnipotence; graven images render Him as static. The image is also stationary; a representation of gods linked to a locale, to space; but God is everywhere, He goes with Israel.]

3. You shall not take in vain the name of the LORD your God; for the LORD will not clear one who takes His name in vain. [It denies His all-knowingness and desecrates His majesty.]

4. Remember the Sabbath day and keep it holy. Six days you shall labor and do all your work, but the seventh day is a Sabbath of the LORD your God: you shall not do any work—you, your son or daughter, your male or female slave, or your cattle, or the stranger who is within your settlements.

For in six days the LORD made heaven and earth and sea, and all that is in them, and He rested on the seventh day; therefore the LORD blessed the Sabbath day and hallowed it. [God's creatorship is thus affirmed; He owns the universe and may enjoin people from work on it. But the equality of humanity is equally established; no one under another's influence may be compelled to work; all are entitled to rest from toil.]

5.   Honor your father and your mother, that you may long endure on the land which the LORD your God is giving you. [Having brought you into the world, they are next to God.]

As we turn to the second half of these commandments, we note that they apply to human relations in terms parallel to those of the first five relating humanity to God.

6.   You shall not murder. [Even as God is unique and His living presence inviolate, so is every human person unique, and his life is inviolate and holy.]

7.   You shall not commit adultery. [As God may not be compromised by worship of other gods, even so is the creative unity of humans holy and may not be diluted.]

8.   You shall not steal. [It would mean considering other people's possessions to be expendable; the name attached to their possessions may not be taken away in vain, even as the name of God, owner of the world, may not be taken in vain.]

9.   You shall not bear false witness against your neighbor. [As Sabbath rest makes you a true witness of God's omnipotence as creator, so must evidence against our fellow human beings be true.]

10. You shall not covet your neighbor's house: you shall not covet your neighbor's wife, or his male or female slave, or his ox or his ass, or anything that is your neighbor's. [Both the fifth and tenth commandments go beyond visible actions and appeal to thought, intent, and ethical principles. Honor of parents may express itself in outward forms, but ultimately it is a matter of the soul's commitment. The prohibition of envy appeals equally to thoughts.]

The Ten Commandments are found twice in the Pentateuch—in Exodus (20:1–14) and in Deuteronomy (5:6–18). The versions differ slightly, but the differences are significant, especially in regard to the Sabbath commandment. In Exodus, the reason given for the observance of the Sabbath is religious: ". . . for in six days the Lord made heaven and earth and sea and all that is in them . . ."; in Deuteronomy, the reason given is social: ". . . so that your male and female servant may rest as you do. Remember that you were a slave in Egypt and the Lord your God freed you from there. . . ." Religious observance that does not grow into social justice is without meaning; social action that is not based on the religious concept of human dignity under God will easily go astray.

In connection with the revelation of the Ten Commandments, a Covenant is made with the people, making them God's treasured possession among all peoples, and constituting them a kingdom of priests and a holy people (Exodus 19:5–6). It is worth noting that this Covenant was not made in connection with a special dispensation of grace or of obligations, but in conjunction with commandments that were universal. Israel's position then was established as the priestly servant of all humanity, all of which is God's possession. The rabbis actually told the legend that God offered the Ten Commandments to the peoples of the world first, entrusting them into the care of Israel only after all the others had rejected them for reasons of expediency. The revelation took place in no-man's-land (Mount Sinai), the rabbis explain, to show that it belongs to all and is not connected with any country or nation. Jews have thus seen themselves as missionaries, not of their religion, but of the Ten Commandments.

Archaeology has not verified the event at Sinai, and biblical scholarship has shown that the religion of Israel took centuries to mature. Yet Sinai was a great religious experience. To the Jews, Sinai has been the moment when the people and their faith were fashioned as one. They therefore are one. To Jews, Sinai has always been a living experience. It has been true.

Encompassing God and humanity, action and thought, law and ethical motivations, the Ten Commandments are indeed the core of Torah.

Immediately, Exodus goes into case law, leading up to ethical conduct: You must assist your enemy, you may not discriminate against the stranger. As eternal reminders of your relationship to God and your fellows, you shall observe specific festivals throughout the year.

Individualism, doubt, and uncertainty lead the people astray to make themselves a golden calf, turning their back on Him. Yet God forgives and, in forgiving, reveals to Moses the attributes of His Being: merciful and gracious, long-suffering and forgiving (Exodus 34:6ff.), and He bids Moses to make a sanctuary, a visible sign that He dwells within the people. Centered around the sanctuary, the people's life has meaning.

Leviticus

Vayikra (Leviticus), the third book of Torah, sets up the sacrificial service which is entrusted to the priests, the descendants of Aaron, who are assisted in secondary functions by the Levites. The ceremonies at the consecration of both the sanctuary and the priests are described. A terrible tragedy happens: Nadab and Abihu, Aaron's elder sons, present an offering that is not prescribed and are felled by a devouring fire.

Having been elevated, they may have seen in their office a stepping stone to power and a means to unbridled individualism; it destroyed them. Priests and people must learn that their distinction lies only in serving obedience. Dietary laws are then handed to the people, who partake of the "royal table," and the priests are specially entrusted with the service of healing and of isolating communicable diseases and their bearers. Sexual purity is enjoined.

Now the book of Leviticus turns to a second command: You shall become holy. How can they become holy? By careful attendance to universal commands, by attuning their hearts as well as their actions to the will of God:

revere mother and father; keep the Sabbath; provide for the poor; consider your neighbor by dealing with him in absolute honesty. Even though he may never be aware of any deceitful act, you will have sinned. He may be deaf or dumb or blind regarding all of these, but God knows it. "You shall not hate your brother in your heart," nor take vengeance, nor bear a grudge, but must guide him. "You shall love your neighbor as yourself" (Leviticus 19:18). This observance of God's unchanging law makes human beings holy; it is a universal commandment. Through absolute honesty in weight and measure and in compassionate concern for the equal treatment of the stranger, the spirit of holiness is universally revealed and individually implemented. Holy days, once more, are explained. And finally, the law of the jubilee year is proclaimed.

At the beginning of this year, all agricultural property returned to its original owner, and all the bondsmen went free. In purchasing crop land during the fifty-year period, the purchaser paid in accordance with the years left in the cycle. If he bought in the fifteenth year, for instance, he paid for the thirty-five remaining years (Leviticus 25:8–17). While keyed to an agricultural society, the regulation holds a basic principle for all societies: It strikes a balance between free enterprise and social planning. The wealthy may acquire the land of a needy seller and utilize it for their own gain and profit, but only for a limited period. Eventually, the land returns to its original owner, the bondsman is free. Exploitation on a permanent basis is curbed.

The clarion call for freedom, connected with the proclamation of the year of the jubilee, came to be inscribed on the American Liberty Bell: "Proclaim liberty throughout the land for all the inhabitants thereof" (Leviticus 25:10).

> For the children of Israel are servants to *Me*, they are My servants whom I freed out of the land of Egypt, I am the Lord their God. (Leviticus 25:55)

As the rabbis explain: "My servants and not servants to other servants" (Kiddushin 22b).

Obedience to these laws and principles spells prosperity, the people are finally warned, and disobedience leads to punishment and disaster. But even though they may be dispersed to the lands of enemies, it will not be forever. The Covenant endures.

> I will remember My Covenant with Jacob, and My Covenant with Isaac and My Covenant with Abraham will I remember; and I will remember the Land. . . . And even then, when they are in the land of their enemies, I will not reject them nor spurn them to destroy them, breaking My Covenant with them, for I, the Lord, am their God. I will remember in their behalf the Covenant with their ancestors, whom I freed from the land of Egypt in the sight of the nations, that I should be their God; I the Lord. (Leviticus 26:42, 44, 45)

Numbers

The fourth book, *Bamidbar* (Numbers), starts with the assumption that the people are now ready for their march into the Promised Land. Their multitudes are numbered; the marching orders are given. The solemn blessing which the priests are to pronounce in God's name is exactly formulated. They may not bless on their own terms, nor "adjust" their blessings to their individual preferences, but must invoke God's name upon the people, that God—and not the priest—may bless them. This blessing has become universal:

> The Lord bless you and keep you;
> The Lord make His face to shine upon you and be
> gracious unto you;
> The Lord lift up His face upon you and give you
> peace. (Numbers 6:24–27)

The princes of the twelve tribes are now permitted to present their gifts to the sanctuary. They must all be identical so that there may be no envy and distinction, and—as a symbol of their equality and the equality of the tribes they represent—all the gifts are recorded in detail, though they are all alike.

Spies are sent out to scout the land. They are men of distinction but of small faith. One man is chosen from each tribe, twelve in all; but ten are convinced that even God cannot sufficiently sustain the people in battle against the fortified cities of the mighty enemy. In endorsing their views, the people prove that theirs is still the spirit of fainthearted slaves; hence they are not yet ready to enter the land. A whole generation must remain in the desert for a total of forty years, until all the fainthearted have died. A new generation, under the leadership of the two men of faith, one of whom was Joshua, may enter the land.

The people become restive under their enforced leisure and homelessness. Rebellion breaks out against Moses. Korah, a member of the tribe of Levi like Moses, joined by friends, accuses Moses of self-centered love of power. Moses has to be vindicated or else his whole ministry as God's servant will remain misunderstood by the people.

Slowly the years pass. The people begin to move again. The conquest begins. Then, Balak, King of Moab, fearing them, devises a plan. He invites Balaam to hurl a curse against the people and destroy them. Yet Balaam's curse turns to a blessing in his mouth as he looks down from the mountain heights upon the people in the valley. He cannot curse where God has blessed, and the people, by the purity of their lives, have deserved God's blessing. Thus did the Jews learn that God is indeed the mighty fortress, and obedience to Him a bulwark against the forces of destruction from without. They saw it even more clearly after they had fallen for another ruse: They had yielded to heathen orgies, weakening themselves in sexual license by joining the rites of those whom they had beaten. Their inner decay led many to defeat and death and weakened the very fabric of the nation. It was Phineas who redeemed them by his passion for God. There was no leadership; thus, in true individualism, he went ahead and stabbed the licentious couple who had set the pattern. A covenant is made with him and his descendants: "Behold I give to him my convenant of peace . . . the covenant of priesthood" (Numbers 26:12–13).

The rabbis dwell on the greatness and inspiration granted to Balaam, a seer and diviner; it approached that of Moses himself. But Balaam misused his power, being a man of hate. God's spirit and the gift of prophecy was not granted to Israel alone, the rabbis point out; it was given equally to those of all nations and all faiths, in order that all humanity might find its way to God and follow His commandments, and be a blessing (Bamidbar Rabba 14).

In preparation for entry into the land, the festive offerings are once more explained. All seems to be ready; Moses views the land from the distance and apportions it. A census of the new generation is taken. Aaron and Miriam (Moses's sister) have already been called to their rest; Moses knows he too must soon die and abandon his people. On God's behest, he ordains Joshua as his successor. A new era is about to begin.

Deuteronomy

Debarim (Deuteronomy), the fifth book, has been adjudged by biblical criticism to be of later date, but Jewish tradition has seen it as Moses's great farewell speech to his people. He relates to them their whole past, not glossing over his own shortcomings. He impresses upon them that they must not let the past fade from their minds and never make graven images or worship idols. Once more, he reviews the Ten Commandments for them.

His great affirmation, which has remained central in Jewish life and worship, is significant in every word:

> Hear, O Israel! The LORD our God, the LORD is One. You must love the LORD your God with all your heart and with all your soul and with all your might. Take to heart these words with which I charge you this day. Impress them upon your children. Recite them when you stay at home and when you are away, when you lie down and when you get up. Bind them as a sign on your hand and let them serve as frontlets between your eyes; inscribe them on the doorposts of your house and on your gates. (Deuteronomy 6:4–9)

This divine plea for love calls for an emotional response (all your heart), a total commitment even of life (all your soul), and a consecration of every act and human possession (all your might). Thus in every performance of Mitzvah, there must be found not merely the action in itself but the attunement of the heart. "God the All-merciful wants the heart," is the conclusion the rabbis draw (see also pp. 35–81). Love cannot be commanded; it can only be a plea of one who, in turn, is full of responding love. It is made clear to the people that God loves them dearly and tenderly and unconditionally. This love did not result from their strength and numbers, but is truly God's freely extended gift. Out of this love, we can understand God's "jealousness." He does not want His love to be diluted. Out of this love, we understand the blessing He will give the people, if they will but respond; the penalties He imposes in an effort to lead them back if they have gone astray; and His readiness to pardon graciously and fully when they return. In this love is enshrined the variety of forces which have fashioned Israel (Deuteronomy 11:13–21).

God-Torah-Mitzvot-Land form an indivisible unit, safeguarding survival. As the text shifts from an appeal to the people as a whole to a direct plea to every individual, the collective future of the people becomes the responsibility of every single person. Yet we assure ourselves of our own survival only as we remain linked in duty, obligation, and kinship to the whole.

As children of God, the people are warned against self-mutilation, enjoined once more to abide by the dietary laws. In His service, they are to tithe themselves and, equally in His service, remit the debts of debtors every seventh year, to allow the debtor a new start in life on equal footing with all the others.

The festivals are once again reviewed, and the organization of government and proceedings in court are outlined, followed by a most significant statement: In all disputes, the people shall be guided by the decision of their magistrates, duly appointed at any given time (Deuteronomy 17:8ff.). The rabbis saw in this injunction the basic justification for the evolution of Torah. Bound by conscience and tradition, the ordained leaders have the right and duty to adjust Torah to the conditions of the times. Thus Torah could not become ossified; by being keyed to life, it kept the people alive.

The king, if there was one, was to read the Torah throughout his life, that he might never come to rule by his own whim or regard his position as a tool to autocratic government. Later follows the command that the king read the Torah to the whole people once every seven years, in order that they know what the law is, thus preventing the ruler from deviating from it. Arbitrariness and self-centered individualism were thereby excluded.

Laws of war are enunciated; no action may be taken without a preceding offer of peaceful settlement (Deuteronomy 20:10). Greater emphasis, however, is placed on laws of peace, the relationships among the people. The concern is shown in such detail as this: "When you build a new house, you shall make a parapet for your roof, so that you do not bring bloodguilt on your house if anyone should fall from it" (Deuteronomy 22:8). "You shall not turn over to his master a slave who seeks refuge with you from his master" (Deuteronomy 23:16). The latter was a law of great significance in the United States in pre–Civil War days, when it was a source of controversy in practice between North and South.

With a solemn blessing, Moses parts from his people. Like Jacob before him, he has an individual benediction for each of the tribes, based on his deep knowledge of their abilities, shortcomings, and potentials. Each of them is given a specific task. Each is to make a specific contribution to the whole.

Moses is emphatic as he speaks to his people: "You stand this day before the Lord, your God . . . your children, your wives, even the stranger . . . to enter into the Covenant of the Lord to lead you into the land. . . . Not with you alone do I make this Covenant but with those who are standing here with us today before the Lord our God and with those who are not with us" (Deuteronomy 29:9–14).

The Covenant is to safeguard them and the Land. And as the rabbis explain, "those not with us" are the coming generations, not yet here, but included in the Covenant, *in* the people.

Then Moses steps up to Mount Nebo, is given a glimpse of the Land which he is not to enter, and is called to rest. God Himself buries him, that no one may know his grave. Israel is not to make saints of anyone, even Moses: The living spirit is the monument.

The rabbis find an additional message in this final story. Torah begins with charity, as God Himself fashions clothes to cover the nakedness of Adam and Eve; it ends with charity, as He buries His servant Moses. All of Torah is thus wrapped in the spirit of divine charity. In seeking God through Torah, humanity must imitate Him.

NEBEE-IM

Nebee-im (Prophets), the second section of the Tenakh, is divided into two basic parts: *Early Prophets,* including the books of Joshua, Judges, Samuel I and II, and Kings I and II; and *Later Prophets*, including the preserved records of the messages handed to the people by the literary prophets.

Only portions of these writings are regularly used in the worship of the synagogue. On holy days and special occasions, a portion of Prophets is appointed to be read after the reading of Torah. It is called **Haftarah**, and its subject matter is chosen either in relation to the Torah portion or to convey the special significance of the day. For instance, on the Sabbath day when the story of the death of Jacob is recited from the Torah scroll, the Haftarah deals with the death of David. On the Day of Atonement, the meaning of the fast is explained in the words of Isaiah 58. Social action is the message of the fast: "to loose the fetters of wickedness, to undo the bands of the yoke. . . ."

Early Prophets

This part of the Tenakh contains the historical books, whose events we have discussed, covering the period from the people's arrival in the Land of Canaan through the destiny of the two kingdoms. The struggle they have to engage in is twofold: with the nations they have to conquer and enemies they have to repel, and with themselves. They arrive before the mighty walls of Jericho and make them fall without raising a hand in battle. Preceded by the Ark containing the tables of the Ten Commandments, they surround the mighty fortress in procession, invoking the name of God, and the walls tumble. It might be a symbol to them that God is to be their King, that in serving Him they will prevail. The symbolic message fails. The unity of the people breaks down under the strain of self-centered antagonism, and their spirit erodes as they yield to the idolatrous and licentious practices of their neighbors.

Martin Buber has seen in the events during the times of the judges and in the conflict between prophets and kings a basic issue. To him, it was a struggle between the people's concept of their destiny and God's design for their existence.

Buber explains that, under the Covenant of Sinai, God desired to be the people's only King. To transmit His demands, God might appoint messengers and leaders, who would disappear from the scene when their limited mission had been accomplished. God was opposed to any monarchy under which one man would acquire personal power, hold on to it in his own right, and bequeath it to his descendants. God made it quite clear: "You shall be unto Me a kingdom" (Exodus 19:6), or, in Moses's words: "He was King in Jeshurun" (Deuteronomy 33:5). The unity of the people rested in God. But in the days of the judges, great conflicts arose; enemies from without overpowered the people, the unity under the spirit of God dissolved, and the demand for unity under a monarch, in opposition to the rule of God, became insistent and dominant (see Buber, *Kingship of God,* pp. 121ff., 136ff.). Therefore, God said to Samuel, who grieved in the belief that his leadership had been rejected: "They have not rejected you, but have rejected Me, that I should not be King over them" (I Samuel 8:7).

In the end, Israel's first king, Saul, suffered disastrous defeat. The Ark of the Covenant, receptacle of the tablets of the Commandments, was captured by the enemy. It had been carried into battle to ensure the king's victory by means of magically forcing God to sustain the earthly monarch. Since Saul had come to regard himself as absolute, and ceased to see his function as only a divine messenger, he had forfeited his claim to rulership; not even the Ark could help him. The people were plunged into complete defeat.

In David, the struggle of a man with himself parallels that of a king against the outward foes of the people. His victory is twofold—the outward one the result of his ever-renewed inner regeneration in repentance.

Solomon is described as the "wisest of men." Wisdom—*Sophia* of the Greeks—came to be seen as a divine power. To the writers of the Tenakh, wisdom meant Torah. By their obedience to Torah, the message of written text and prophetic message, kings are judged.

After Solomon's rule, decay sets in once more, resulting in political and spiritual division and in weakness, defeat, and destruction. The people fail to see that the land is to be a laboratory of the spirit; settledness is to be a challenge. Their failure means not that they are worse than other nations, but that they are no better. Theirs is but a kingdom, when it should have been unto God a kingdom of priests. They desire to be simply a nation when they are supposed to live as a holy nation.

Again we have interpreted the events not as the historian might, but as the authors and editors of Scripture did, frequently slanting events to convey an ethical message and spiritual idea. We have followed this interpretation, for it is the way the Jewish people have come to understand these events as a lesson for themselves throughout the centuries.

This period is distinguished by the emergence of the prophets. They, not the kings, are God's messengers, and they have therefore given their names to these books. The movement started as a kind of school, as people banded together, linked to each other by a certain spirit of ecstasy. To the people, the prophets were just diviners who could foretell the future. But out of their bands there emerged individuals who rejected the narrow scope of the organization. They did not wish to be "fortune tellers." They had a message to deliver; they had a burden placed upon them by God; they stood out as individuals in strength and indomitable courage.

The Hebrew word for prophet is *Nabee,* which William F. Albright explains from its Accadian source to mean "the one who is called" by God (*From the Stone Age to Christianity*; New York: Doubleday Anchor, 1957, p. 303). Prophets thus receive their call from God. They have to rebuke the people; have to warn them; call for rebirth of spirit, return, and repentance; and assure them of the ever-present love of God and His everlasting willingness to receive them back into His grace.

In this spirit, Samuel faces the people who want a king, warning them against dependence on human leadership and advising them to place their faith in God. He yields when God acquiesces in the fact that they have denied Him (I Samuel). Emboldened by his divine mission to rebuke if need be, the prophet Nathan approaches David at the height of the king's power, accusing him to his face of having committed a shameful crime deserving death (II Samuel 11–12). (David had seduced his neighbor's wife, Bathsheba, and sent her husband to his death in battle.)

In a later period, Elijah predicts doom to King Ahab, the sinful king of Israel, and has to flee from his wrath. Yet later Elijah returns to face all of Israel, including the king. The people, smitten by a drought, have made their appeal to both God and Baal, a compromise of expedience that called for "other gods before Him." There can be no compromise, Elijah makes clear: "How long will you keep hopping between two opinions? If the Lord be God, follow Him; but if Baal, follow him!" (I Kings 18:21). For the people in their weakness, Elijah provides a visible sign of God's power. But the prophet himself learns that it is not in storms or quakes that God makes Himself manifest, but rather in the still, small voice of conscience and inner vision that God is revealed, and this voice people must follow (I Kings 19). The vision of the divine may be granted more poignantly to the prophet, but it is granted to all humanity. The prophet, like the midwife, releases that which lies implanted in every human being, placed there by God Himself. This will be evident in the Later Prophets, whose utterances we possess, at least in part. Of the speeches of the earlier ones, we have no verbatim record.

Later Prophets

Traditionally, we count three major prophets and twelve minor ones. Those of whose works major portions have been preserved are called major prophets; they include Isaiah, Jeremiah, and Ezekiel. Although only minor portions of their works exist, the minor prophets are of equal significance. They include Hosea, Joel, Amos, Obadiah, Jonah, Micah, Nahum, Habakkuk, Zephaniah, Haggai, Zechariah, and Malachi. (The Book of Daniel, being quite late, is included in the third portion of the Tenakh.) We know that some of the books ascribed to these men, such as Isaiah, were actually written by several authors. We also know that some of the names were not the true names of the authors. (For instance, Malachi simply means "My Messenger.") Here we shall be concerned only with some of their major ideas, as they interpret, adapt, and evolve Torah.

These prophets came from all strata of society. Isaiah came from the ranks of the highest nobility, Amos was a lowly farmer, Hosea belonged to the middle class of comfortable burghers, Jeremiah and Ezekiel were priests. The northern as well as the southern kingdom were their spheres of action. And, like Ezekiel, they served as pastors to the people in Babylonian exile.

Amos (750 B.C.E.), compelled by the urgency of his call to lay down his plow, applies farmer's logic to his message: "As you sow so shall you reap." If you plant righteousness, your harvest will be good; if you sow wickedness, evil will befall you. This is universal; hence Amos is aware of the fact that the providence of the universal God of all time and space, which rests equally upon all the farmers' toil throughout the world, extends in equal measure to all His children, regardless of their race. "Are you not unto me like the children of the Ethiopians?" (Amos 9:7). He speaks of dark-skinned Ethiopians and lighter-skinned Philistines and Israelites in the same terms. Humanity is one. If Israel holds any specific place, it is to set an example of true living under God and to assume higher responsibility for which it will be held to account. "You only have I known of all the families of the earth; therefore will I visit upon you all of your iniquities" (Amos 3:2). The "chosenness" of the Jew does not spell privilege, for all humanity is equally privileged before God; rather, it demands higher performance. In this sense, every nation is chosen to contribute in fullest measure of its strength those goods which by endowment and education it is best equipped to give to humanity.

The prophets' opposition to a self-serving "establishment" is revealed in the encounter of Amos with the high priest Amaziah of the royal sanctuary of the northern kingdom. Amos interrupted a solemn service at the royal sanctuary, crying out in God's name: "I hate, I despise your feasts . . . nor will I look upon the peace offerings of your fatted beasts. . . . But let justice roll down as waters, and righteousness as a mighty stream" (Amos 5:21–25). Otherwise the sanctuary will be destroyed and Israel will fall (3:14–15). Amos's demonstration created a scandal, and the prophet was expelled from the sanctuary and the northern kingdom—yet he was proven right.

Hosea (ca. 745 B.C.E.) was equally severe in his rebukes, but he also emphasized divine love.

The prophet takes back his errant wife after she has had many adventures. This act of forgiveness symbolizes God's never-ceasing love for His people, though they may have gone astray. His call to repentance (Hosea 14) is read in the synagogue as Haftarah on the Sabbath between Rosh Hashanah and Yom Kippur, the period of repentance: "Return, O Israel, unto the Lord, for you have stumbled in your iniquity. Take with you words, and return unto the Lord. Say unto Him: Forgive all iniquity, and accept that which is good, and we will render instead of bullocks [the words of] our lips" (Hosea 14:2–3). Prayer—the words of the lips—is better than animal sacrifices; thus has Judaism interpreted the verse.

First Isaiah (742 B.C.E.) (comprising chapters 1–39) and *Micah* (740 B.C.E.). Both of these books are concerned with social injustice. In scathing words, Isaiah condemns ritual that is merely empty performance of rites and is not undergirded by social justice; if it is carried out by the very same people who oppress their fellows, then ritual turns into blasphemy, blessing into a mockery of God. He will have none of it. Isaiah demands not only penitence but "wash yourselves clean; remove the evil of your doings from before My eyes; cease to do evil, learn to do good; seek justice, correct oppression, defend the fatherless, plead for the widow" (Isaiah 1:16–17). Only then will the prayer of contrition have meaning. Micah has the same message.

The whole tenor of Isaiah's prophecies appears already in the account of his call:

> I saw the Lord sitting upon His throne, high and lifted up, and his train filled the Temple. Above Him stood the seraphim. . . . And one called to another and said: "Holy, holy, holy is the Lord of hosts, the whole earth is full of His glory." And the foundations of the thresholds [of the Temple] shook at the voice of Him who called, and the house was filled with smoke. (Isaiah 6:1–4)

God is *not* in the Temple; He is in the whole earth. The actions of society have to proclaim His holiness. It is a vain hope to assume that Temple ritual will be meaningful to Him without social responsibility. The same theme is taken up at the very end of the second Isaiah:

> Thus says the Lord: Heaven is My throne and the earth is my footstool; what is the house which you would build for Me, and what is the place of My rest? . . . This is the man to whom I will look, he that is humble and contrite in spirit, and trembles at My word. . . . He who sacrifices a lamb [is] like one who breaks a dog's neck. (Isaiah 66:1–3)

The true response is for humanity to offer itself, to unite under God's kingship, to establish peace and justice. Then God will choose His priests from among all nations. The whole world will have become a kingdom of priests, a holy people; only thus can ritual—the symbolic expression of true worship— be meaningful and acceptable. This world will be realized in the time of the Messiah. It is foretold by both Isaiah (2:2–4) and Micah (4:1–5):

> And it shall come to pass in the end of days, that the mountain of the Lord's house shall be established as the top of the mountains, and shall be exalted above the hills; and all nations shall flow unto it. And many peoples shall go and say: "Come, let us go up to the Mount of the Lord, to the House of the God of Jacob; and He will teach us of His ways, and we will walk in His paths." For out of Zion shall go forth Torah, and the word of the Lord from Jerusalem. And He shall judge between nations, and shall decide for many

peoples; and they shall beat their swords into plowshares and their spears into pruning hooks; nation shall not lift up sword against nation, neither shall they learn war any more.

As this time is not yet, Israel has the task to prepare for it by example: "O House of Jacob come let us walk by the light of the Lord" (Isaiah 2:5). All this will take place simply as the result of humanity coming to its senses. It calls for no miracles, only a simple awareness on the part of individuals and nations that God is the center, justice humanity's best weapon in the struggle for survival, and peace the most precious goal and treasure. Yet it may bring about a complete transformation of habits, practices, and attitudes. It will be like the wolf dwelling with the lamb, as national jealousies will depart. Thus it will come to pass under a truly chosen ruler, and Isaiah finds him in thinking of David:

> There shall come forth a shoot out of the stock of Jesse [David's father] . . . and the spirit of the Lord shall rest upon him, the spirit of wisdom and understanding, the spirit of counsel and might, the spirit of knowledge and of the fear of the Lord. (Isaiah 11:1–2)

In such manner is the Messiah seen, and the messianic age conceived; there will be no obstacles to Torah and Mitzvot in their widest meaning. This portion of Isaiah is traditionally recited as Haftarah on the very last day of Passover, the festival of redemption from bondage. It makes the march through history a pilgrimage of free people toward universal freedom, and it releases the Jew from holy days to daily rounds with a challenge and obligation.

In a similar spirit, Isaiah 58 has become the Haftarah in the morning service of Yom Kippur, the Day of Atonement. Not in chastisement, or in one-day prayer can God truly be worshipped, or even in the house of worship, but only through social justice.

Micah truly sums it up: "Wherewith shall I come before the Lord. . . . Shall I come before Him with burnt offerings? . . . He has told you O man, what is good, and what the Lord requires of you: Only to do justice, and to love mercy, and to walk humbly with your God" (Micah 6:6–8). The theme is carried through all the prophets.

Jeremiah (626–587 B.C.E.) tells the people in no uncertain words how meaningless the Temple really can become, how its existence holds no magical power of survival; that power lies in the conduct of the people (Jeremiah 7). In spite of terrible persecution, Jeremiah never gives up his faith in the regenerative powers that lie within the people, and neither do any of the other prophets. But he has to face trials much more severe than any others and, in the end, witnesses the destruction of the Temple, which he foresaw. He transforms defeat into victory: Exile may be the challenge which will bring about the regeneration; hence his letter to the Jews in Babylonia (Jeremiah 29:1–7). With the fall of the Temple—the loss of the unifying agency—*individual re-*

sponsibility grows. The people are no longer able to pass responsibility from the individual to the "government."

Ezekiel (593–573 B.C.E.) thus becomes the preacher of *individual* and *mutual* responsibility. Every one is responsible for his own destiny, yet accountable for the conduct of those whom he may influence. Ezekiel synthesizes individualism and collective destiny. He equally reminds the exiled of the eternal Covenant:

> I will remember My Covenant I made with you in the days of your youth, and I will establish it with you as a Covenant for all eternity. (Ezekiel 16:60–1)

Ezekiel is a visionary and has powerful revelations in Babylonia, as if to say, God's glory is indeed filling the whole earth; He reveals Himself everywhere. "Blessed by the glory of God from *His* place" (Ezekiel 3:12). Through the spirit of God, the dead bones of a decayed society can be made to live again; the hopeless can restore their trust, and even the Land can be restored to them (Ezekiel 37:1–15). This chapter, too, is recited as Haftarah on Passover, the festival of regeneration. Humanity can gain rebirth by guiding itself by His spirit.

Second Isaiah, Chapters 40–66 (c. 540 B.C.E.), is a prophet of hope. "Comfort ye, comfort ye my people, says your God" (Isaiah 40:1ff.) is the Haftarah recited after the mournful fast of Ab, commemorating the fall of the Temple. Israel is God's witness in the world (Isaiah 43:10–12), "a light to the nations to open eyes that are blind" (Isaiah 42:6–7) by its example. This entails suffering, as the servant of God, despised, disfigured, and mocked, upholds his ideals; may their heart be strong, for God will redeem them, and the entire human family will be benefited (Isaiah 53). True to his belief that the Jew serves the world, Isaiah welcomes converts who have joined the people and cleave to God; they, too, have a share in the future of Israel (Isaiah 44:5–56:3).

Haggai is the gadfly to the homecoming people. He wants a second Temple to be built, to be a symbol of the people's willingness to sacrifice. May they give of their substance, even though it hurts, to restore a visible center of divine presence; and may they be undismayed at the smallness of the new building, for its true glory may surpass the splendor of the ancient one.

Zechariah makes it clear that victory comes, "not by might, nor by power, but by My spirit" (Zechariah 4:6). Zechariah no longer shares the hope that reason alone will lead humanity to unity. Wars and cataclysmic events will precede the "Day of the Lord." Here we find one of the eschatological prophecies. Yet victory and peace are assured those who fight with God (Zechariah 14:1–21), and Israel will dwell in safety amid a reborn humanity. This portion is read on Sukkot, the festival when God's protection is symbolized.

Malachi points out the way and the goal. The goal is attained when "the hearts of the fathers are turned to their children, and the hearts of the children to their fathers" (Malachi 4:5). Even the natural conflict of the generations will have ceased. The road is Torah: "Remember the Torah of my servant Moses" (Malachi 4:4). Before redemption, there will be conflict; nations will be arrayed against each other.

Of *Jonah*, we have no historical background. His mission was placed by the book's author before the seventh century B.C.E., since the setting is Nineveh at the time when Assyria was still a mighty power. (Nineveh was destroyed in 612.) Jonah is told to call the Assyrians to repentance, but he refuses to go, for this would mean redeeming Israel's enemy by his appeal. After many adventures (including three days in the belly of a great fish), Jonah agrees to do God's will. He calls for repentance; the king and people of Nineveh listen, they have a change of heart, and the city is saved.

What is truly significant is the way in which Jews have come to think of their enemies and of God's concern for non-Jews; they are all His children, they are all deserving of life and a second chance, especially those "who know not their right hand from their left hand" (Jonah 4:11). It is the Jews' task to extend their help, their insights, their strength and life to them; and if the Jews refuse, God will see to it that it is done through them anyway, if they have the power to influence others for good.

The story is recited as Haftarah on the afternoon of Yom Kippur. It reminds the Jews that they are not singularly chosen for God's special attention and mercy, which He extends to all. Jews must consider themselves the world's servants, though they suffer in serving. Judaism's concept of God and humanity is universalistic.

The prophets of Israel are no philosophers. Calm, critical analysis is not theirs; they are moved by great and overpowering emotions, which spring from a dual source: the absolute conviction of God's mastery of the world (for He has created it, and He shapes its history) and the equally strong conviction that people can serve the purposes of the divine only by raising the standards of ethical conduct toward the absolute of complete social justice. Without this, ritual is meaningless mockery.

But these men do not speak in generalities. They address themselves to concrete situations in life, rebuke the people for failing to live up to the highest ideals in everyday conduct, and call on Israel to be holy, which means to be an example. They rebuke Israel not for being worse than other peoples, but for being no better than the rest, for not being an example. For this, Israel was created; hence it must endure, to find its reward in God's own time. Setting for all humanity the highest ethical goals and speaking in language of supreme grandeur, the prophets have remained the world's greatest and, in fact, only heralds of the truly good society under God, a society in which conviction will overcome expediency. They do not abrogate Torah and Mitzvot; they clarify their purpose.

KETUBIM

Ketubim (Collected Writings) constitutes the third portion of the Tenakh. As the title indicates, it is composed of a variety of different works. It includes the Psalms, Proverbs, Job, Song of Songs (Song of Solomon), Ruth, Lamentations, Ecclesiastes, Esther, Daniel, Ezra, Nehemiah, and Chronicles I and II. They are used in Jewish worship at a variety of occasions, which we shall mention in connection with the works themselves.

The *Psalms* are a collection of 150 poems, some of them lengthy, others very short. A good many of them have attached to them the names of the supposed authors, ranging from Moses to the sons of Korah and Solomon; the majority, however, are ascribed to David. A number of them have musical annotations, including the instruments to be used in accompaniment when they were recited in public worship in the ancient Temple.

Several poetic forms are employed. Parallelism is used frequently (as it is in other Hebrew poetry); that is, the second verse is a paraphrase of the first: "Lord, who shall sojourn in Your tabernacle? Who shall dwell upon Your holy mountain?" (Psalm 15:1). The alphabetic acrostic is also frequently employed, each verse beginning with a letter of the alphabet (Psalms 34 and 145). In Psalm 119, each letter is used eight times. Some psalms are arranged for antiphonal responses (Psalm 24). The Psalms of Ascents (120–134), as the title indicates, were sung when the people ascended in solemn procession to the hill on which the Temple stood.

In content, the Psalms range from glorification of God to outcry and lamentation, from meditation to jubilant praise, from individual prayer to choral hymn, "Hallelujah, Praise the Lord." They speak of encompassing "foes," and as the foe is not characterized, every individual may substitute personal need and distress as the "foe" when the psalm is offered as prayer. They may be framed in the singular form, yet the "I" may stand for an individual person or for the people as a whole.

The Psalms have been guide and comforter, a source of strength and renewed faith for the Jews and for Christians throughout history. The Psalms have upheld the people in sickness, distress, and trial, expressed the deepest yearning of their hearts, instructed them in the way of God, and put in words the spirit of gratitude welling up in human souls, which less gifted persons might never hope to express to equal perfection. In Hebrew, the Psalms are called **Tehillim** (praises), for even the outcry directed to God affirms Him as ever present and ever powerful to rescue; it affirms our trust in Him, that He does right, even though we do not understand the reason for His actions. Thus Psalms are praise in affliction as in victory.

Jewish tradition has divided the Psalms into five books, corresponding to the Five Books of Moses. Actually, they are a human response to Torah, witnessing to the fact that the Jews have understood it, accepted it, and made it their own.

In the ancient Temple, a special psalm was assigned for choral presentation every day of the week. (They are still used in the worship of the synagogue.) Psalm 92, sung on the Sabbath, reflects on God's work of creation, too deep for people to understand, yet culminating in the victory of the good, who shall be planted in the house of the Lord. On holy days, Psalms 113–118, called the **Hallel** (Praise), are recited in synagogue worship: God is recognized as God of nature and of nations; He rescued Israel from Egyptian bondage; may people give thanks to His Name. Calling on Him in distress, man shall always find rescue; hence he need not fear the devices of his enemies. As he moves in His direction he shall be blessed from His House: Therefore "Praise the Lord, His goodness endureth forever."

Jewish worship always opens with Psalms, and the Sabbath is especially welcomed with them. The affirmation of God as Sustainer is expressed daily by reciting Psalm 145. The Scroll of Torah is removed from the Ark and returned to it as Psalms rise in glorification of its Giver. Psalm 6 expresses the spirit of contrition and hope in Him; it is prefaced in daily prayer by the words: "Merciful and compassionate God, I have sinned before You."

In prayer for the sick, the name of the afflicted is presented to God as those verses of Psalm 119 which spell his name are being recited. Verses of the Psalms are woven into the prayers of the liturgy. Millions have turned to the Psalms in hours of need and of joy. In opening their hearts to God, they found comfort in the knowledge that "the Lord is my shepherd, I shall not want" (Psalm 23).

The Psalms have sustained the Jews, their faith and their hope, even as they are one of Judaism's greatest gifts to humanity.

Proverbs, Ecclesiastes, and *Job* offer worldly wisdom or philosophical discussion and are therefore called Wisdom books. Wisdom (**Hokhmah**) is actually personified at times. This worldly wisdom was equated with Torah; Torah is wisdom, and all wisdom, as Jews have seen it, is an extension of Torah, enshrined in it. Proverbs is a collection of short maxims, affording guidance in life. Ecclesiastes is a pessimistic reflection on life's vanity, redeemed only by the concluding sentence, added later, affirming God's ever-present will.

Job is a book that has fascinated philosophers, theologians, poets, and writers throughout the ages. We do not know who wrote the work. The rabbis are in disagreement as to whether Job was a Jew or a Gentile. Some rabbis hold that the whole poem is just a fictional dialogue, serving as a work of instruction, and that Job never lived.

Job is a good man, a simple man, who is blessed by God and daily renders thanks to Him. Unbeknown to him, a wager takes place between God and Satan: Will Job remain righteous under severe afflictions? God believes he will. Job is tested. In his agonies, he cries out in protest against God who has chastised him without reason. But he also proclaims: "Though he slay me, yet will I trust in Him" (13:15). His friends come to him to comfort him. They feel he must have sinned, for why else would God punish him so severely? But against the strongest arguments of his friends, Job maintains that he has not sinned, hence his suffering is not the wages of sin. He equally affirms that there is a God who must have willed it. He rejects the suggestion that world and humanity might be subject to a purely accidental chain of events. Job turns in violent rebellion against God. The rabbis, however, sought to excuse him and claim he never weakened in his affirmation of God. In the end, God appears to Job.

This is dual vindication: It proves that there is a God; it also proves that Job has not sinned, for God does not reveal Himself to sinners. Job has to learn, however, that the ways of God are hidden to people, whose life span is too short to comprehend the overall design of the deity and the tests God inflicts. One rabbinical interpretation is that Job prays for his friends (43:10), and his fortunes are restored as he makes up with his adversaries.

The following five books, the Five Scrolls or **Megillot** (plural of **Megillah**), were originally written, each on a separate scroll, Megillah, for public reading at various times during the liturgical year. In traditional congregations they are still recited at these occasions, but from the festival prayer book and silently. Only the Book of Esther is still read publicly from a handwritten, separate scroll; it has come to be known as "the Megillah."

The Song of Songs, the first Scroll, is a fervid love song. It has been interpreted as symbolic of God's love for Israel. It is recited on Passover, the festival of spring. Nature, like a bride in all her beauty, forecasts rich blessings; God is the groom. Should not Israel and all humanity equally prepare themselves, link themselves to God's love, and bring to fruition the blessings He has implanted within them?

Ruth, the second Scroll, is recited on Shabuot, the festival commemorating the revelation at Sinai, the giving of Torah. It is an idyllic story. Ruth, a Moabite convert, cleaves to Torah and to the people of Israel, and no adversity can weaken her determination: "Whither you go I will go." A desperately poor immigrant from abroad, she is eventually permitted the peaceful life of the happy farmer's wife in the Land, but this is only one part of her reward. Marrying a man of distinction, she becomes the great-grandmother of King David. The faith of Ruth in adversity is to become a guiding light to the people to cling to Torah as she did.

Lamentations, the third Scroll, is recited on the Fast of Ab, commemorating the fall of the Temple. It expresses the numb terror and despondency as well as the hope that springs eternal within the people, even as disasters grow to unbearable proportions.

Ecclesiastes, the fourth Scroll (also one of the Wisdom books, as we have seen), recited on Sukkot, reflects and mitigates the sense of frustration and pessimism at the approach of a bleak winter's season. Obey His commandments, it says, for this is the meaning of being human.

Esther, the fifth Scroll, is recited on Purim. It is a strange book, a rather fantastic and quite thrilling story, which never mentions the name of God. The scene is laid outside Palestine, in Persia. Perhaps it means to tell that God does work everywhere, though we may not be aware of His presence. The Jews in the story transgress against Torah. Even the story's chief protagonist, Esther, marries outside her faith. Yet as they return to Him in repentance, willing to give their lives for Him, they are spared, and a vicious plan to exterminate them comes to naught. The book gave hope to many in modern extermination camps, for they knew that though they might perish as individuals, the Jewish people would surely survive.

The Book of Daniel is found in Christian Bibles among the prophetic books, and in the Hebrew Bible among the Ketubim (Collected Writing). This in itself indicates the difference in status accorded the work in the two traditions. Its narrative is placed in the period of Nebuchadnezzar, which is the time of the Babylonian Exile of the Jews (sixth century B.C.E.). Biblical scholars believe, however, that the book is of much later origin, possibly of the period of the Maccabean revolt (second century B.C.E.). During both of these periods Jewish religion was under great pressure, and might have come to extinction had it not been for the faith and courage of dedicated leaders. The Maccabees furnished such leadership, and Daniel is depicted as a man prepared to give his life for his faith. The book was designed to give hope and guidance to Jews in difficult times; it showed them how previous generations had faced and overcome serious problems, and it armed them for the problems that lay ahead in their own time. The wisdom of Daniel is extolled, as is his prayerful devotion to God, even at a time when prayer to God was forbidden on penalty of death.

Several characteristics reveal the work to have originated at a time much later than the narrative would have us assume. First, portions of the book are written in Aramaic, a language closely related to Hebrew. Second, the Book of Daniel contains significant apocalyptic portions dealing with eschatology. (The term *apocalyptic* will be explained in detail in the section of Jewish apocalyptic literature [see page 214].) Apocalyptic utterances are usually cryptic, enigmatic, and deal with symbolic forms of statement. Eschatology deals with the end of times and the cataclysmic events that will bring it about.

In order to understand why the Book of Daniel was placed differently in the Christian and Hebrew Bibles, we have to know that the Hebrew Bible was edited and authorized by the pharisaic rabbis of the Mishnah. They decided which books of the many then current should be admitted, and which should be excluded. This was a lengthy undertaking. Most likely, the rabbis felt that the Book of Daniel had sufficient merit to be included, for it told of Daniel's faith and could inspire the Jews never to abandon their holy tradition. Also, there were among the rabbis men who were interested in apocalyptic literature. At the same time, however, it was a recent book. And, above all, it was apocalyptic and eschatological. Its study might lead to "calculations for the end," of which the rabbis disapproved as a subject of general study. If they were proven wrong, these speculations might weaken the faith. (In spite of the rabbis' warnings against eschatological speculations, these continued to have a place among many Jews.) Also, in contrast to the clearly understandable language of the prophets, Daniel spoke in symbolic terms; such language would allow for interpretations that might be subversive. The rabbis finally arrived at a compromise. They included the book in the canon, but not among the prophetic books.

Among Christians, however, the book assumed great importance. The New Testament Book of Revelations contains similar speculations, and may have been influenced by Daniel. Daniel's remarks dealing with cataclysmic eschatological events have inspired many Christians to speculations on the ultimate future, not shared by Jews. The Book of Daniel assumed an importance that warranted its inclusion in the prophetic section of Christian Bibles.

Daniel will be mentioned further in the section on Jewish apocalyptic literature.

Ezra and *Nehemiah* relate the trials of the people in rebuilding their land and Temple after the Babylonian Exile. Surrounded by the dangers of contamination, Jews withdraw from contact with the world, renewing their Covenant with God and Torah and Land.

Chronicles I and II review history once more, emphasizing the line of tradition that has come down through the generations and the religious significance of the events of Jewish history.

THE APOCRYPHA

The books of the Tenakh were collected, edited, and approved by the Pharisees. The Hebrew Bible is what the Pharisees decided it should be.

Some of the material reviewed by the rabbis for consideration was excluded from the canon because the rabbis considered it repetitious or felt that its message was not significantly in line with the educational objectives of Torah. Some of it was excluded simply because it was of too recent origin. But the people had used these books for inspiration. The Septuagint had translated some of them for the use of Diaspora Jewry who spoke Greek. The books had therefore acquired a degree of holiness and could not be destroyed. They remained but were withdrawn—hidden—from use in public worship. They were called *Genuzim,* hidden books, or, in Greek, **Apocrypha**. They were not explicitly forbidden reading.

In this manner, a distinction could be made between the portions of the fixed canon, designed for use in public worship, and works not to be read in public worship and therefore of limited distribution. Mistakes about the place of these works in tradition could thereby be avoided.

About fourteen or fifteen books have been designated as Apocrypha.

Maccabees I (written between 135 and 65 B.C.E.), is in general a reliable report of the Maccabean uprising, and *Maccabees II* (composed between 125 and 25 B.C.E.) covers much of the material of Maccabees I, but with a strongly religious message. These two books are a primary source for the events surrounding the festival of Hanukkah.

Ecclesiasticus, or *The Wisdom of Jesus (Joshua) ben Sirah,* was written by a deeply religious author in 180 B.C.E.; it offers practical ethical wisdom. Ben Sirah's grandson translated the work from Hebrew into Greek.

Judith (written about 150 B.C.E.) is fiction. It may have been inspired by the story of Jael, who cut off the head of the enemy Sisera, found in Judges.

Esdras (Ezra) I, a fragment of a Greek translation (around 150 B.C.E.), offers variations to the Ezra-Nehemiah reports in the canon.

Esdras (Ezra) II is an apocalyptic work. Chapters 3–14 are assumed to have been written in Hebrew or Aramaic near the end of the first century C.E.; chapters 1, 2, 15, and 16 are regarded as being composed by Christian authors.

Esdras III and IV were added from existing sources to the Bible in the translation of St. Jerome (the Vulgate). Here we also find apocalyptic sections.

The *Wisdom of Solomon* was written by two authors. One wrote Chapters 1–9, in Hebrew; the other translated the first part into Greek and added the rest. It is conjectured that the work was composed late in the first pre-Christian century. The work praises wisdom, calls for faithful adherence to God, and offers a review of history, showing Judaism superior to paganism.

The Catholic Church has included the Apocrypha in the canon; Luther regarded them as useful reading. Parts of the Apocrypha, particularly the Book of Enoch, contain eschatological speculations and prophecies that have had a significant impact upon Christian theology and Jewish mysticism. For scholarship tracing the events in the period between the Old and New Testament, the Apocrypha have been a rich source of knowlege. Their exploration has continued. In Judaism they have held a generally very minor place.

JEWISH APOCALYPTIC LITERATURE

Apocalyptic literature refers to works that originated after prophetic revelation had ceased. These works began to appear in the second pre-Christian century, although there are apocalyptic sections in the prophetic writings as well. Some rabbis were interested in apocalyptic pronouncements. They admitted the Book of Daniel into the canon.

We can discern two major forms of apocalyptic writing: descriptions of heaven and hell, the realm beyond our world, and predictions regarding the future, specifically the end of days. The prophecies are couched in highly symbolic and allegorical form.

Among the Jewish apocalyptic works are The Book of Enoch, The Fourth Book of Ezra, The Testament of the Twelve Patriarchs, The Abraham Apocalypse, The Barukh Apocalypse, and several chapters (chapter 3, and possibly 4 and parts of 5) of The Sibylline Oracles. Study of the various versions that have come down to us is a task by itself.

As we can see from the titles of the works, they were ascribed to earlier personalities—patriarchs and prophets—in order to give them greater value. They may have been written to meet the need of the people, now deprived of prophetic guidance, showing them that the events of their time, and the outcome of these events, was foreordained and stood under divine providence. At the same time, there was a greater distance between God and His creatures.

Apocalyptic literature deals with visions heretofore not made known: the secrets of the world beyond. God is surrounded by a heavenly court—angels, whose names and functions are described. With God, created from the beginning, the Messiah dwells—"Son of Man" (Enoch), who will be sent to earth when the time has come. The fallen angels have plunged into hell, where they dwell, or they may roam as demons, afflicting humanity with sickness and destruction. The humans, dwelling between heaven and hell, are to be assigned after death either to paradise or to **Gehinnom** (Gehenna, namely purgatory; Gehinnom was originally a valley near Jerusalem), depending on their actions.

Apocalyptic literature also deals with eschatology, the end of days and the events surrounding this end. Cataclysmic, cosmic wars will engulf humanity and the universe before the end. The terrors that are the signs of the end are symbolically described. Then a new messianic age will come about, and the dead will be resurrected. These concepts deeply affected both Jews and Christians, especially in the struggle against Rome in the days of Jesus, and in the thinking of the early Church regarding Jesus. Throughout history, they have occupied Christian thought and have also had a profound impact on Jewish beliefs. They came to be incorporated in the Midrash—which means that the rabbis selectively adopted and adjusted them—and such concepts as resurrection are now basic principles of Jewish faith. Other apocalyptic concepts have been retained in popular and even officially ordained traditional belief, especially in the Jewish mystical tradition.

TRADITION AND BIBLICAL CRITICISM

The Torah is the word of God, but was it actually dictated by God and written at the time, or close to it, when the events described occurred? Did the prophets whose names are attached to various books really write all their books, even when they lived long before the events to which they refer, or when their language shows traces of later usage, or when their messages do not seem consistent?

Orthodox Jews and fundamentalist Christians have firmly maintained that the text as we have it is God's literal Word in every aspect. The "scientists" among the Bible scholars have felt differently. They called for critical analysis of texts and for historical evidence to sustain the events related in Scripture. In their enthusiasm, the nineteenth-century Bible critics went far in dismembering Scripture. Twentieth-century archaeology has proven the Bible accurate on many points previously considered fiction or legend.

It must be remembered that the Bible is essentially a message, not a historical work, and that facts are frequently adjusted to sustain the message. Furthermore, a great deal of the written material had been transmitted by word of mouth for a long time before it was put into writing and so was subject to embroidery. It is held widely that oral tradition was essentially accurate and that it is *generally* trustworthy. This applies to both the Old Testament and the New Testament. However, ideas and even stories and poetry from other sources did find their way into it, and at times individual biases influenced the final versions.

The reader must realize that "older" parts of Scripture often were actually written later than the "newer" ones. The epistles of Paul, in the New Testament, precede the Gospels. The prophets precede parts of the Five Books of Moses.

Biblical criticism tells us that the Book of Amos was written by several people, with material added later; this conclusion is based on inconsistencies and contradictions in the various ideas expressed. The Book of Isaiah had several authors; it may, in fact, be an anthology of writings. It is certain that chapters 40–66 were written by a different author from the one who wrote the first part, but there is grave doubt that all the earlier chapters were written by one man. It is also doubtful that all the chapters in Isaiah II were written by one man. The order of the chapters may have been changed as well, as they were by different hands and in wrong sequence. The "utopia" of "the end of days" (Isaiah 2:2–4; Micah 4:1–5) is found in Isaiah and in Micah but was probably written by neither; the chapters of "the suffering servant" (Isaiah 35, 40–55) are said to belong to another author. The Psalms are again an anthology; even the names attached to some of them may not be the authors' names but those of the choral groups to whose repertoires they belonged. The Book of Daniel was written in retrospect and after the success of the Maccabean uprising which proved God's redeeming help; this places the book around 165 B.C.E. We are merely citing examples; biblical scholarship, which has encompassed the entire Old and New Testaments, continues.

Most important has been research into the Pentateuch, based in part on the critical analyses by two Protestant scholars of the nineteenth century, Graf and Wellhausen. The two men were puzzled by the use of two terms for the name of God—YHVH and Elohim—in the earliest chapters of Genesis. In addition, the creation story is given twice and with different slants in Chapters 1 and 2. To the critics, this indicated several authors, not only for Genesis, but for the entire Scripture. They arrived at the conclusion that there was one author who used the term YHVH for God (or, in German, JHWH); they called him the J author. Another author, using the term Elohim, was called E. Another author, concerned with priestly functions and privileges, was called P (Priest). The book of Deuteronomy was written by still another author, D, who reflected the ethics of the prophets.

It is now assumed that a "redactor," R, combined the J and E traditions into one manuscript, RJE. The J manuscript originated in approximately the tenth or ninth century B.C.E.; the E manuscript approximately the ninth or eighth century B.C.E. The RJE manuscript combined both.

D, the author of Deuteronomy, actually wrote more than this book. Deuteronomy was composed only in part by him; some parts were written after the Babylonian exile. D was concerned with showing that the entire world is God's, Who acts in behalf of Israel. He places his major emphasis on ethics, as the prophets had done. The books from Deuteronomy through Kings reflect his spirit and authorship.

But then came P, around the sixth or fifth century B.C.E. He wrote an entire manuscript of his own, and *then* incorporated the edited elements of J and E without changing them. This has led to contradictions in the text itself. P was concerned with law, both religious and civil, and his influence is noted in the first four books of the Pentateuch. In order to present his viewpoint, P also wrote Chronicles as a balance to the D books of history. He also wrote Ezra and Nehemiah. The tenor of the writings serves as clues to authorship. We note, therefore, that parts of Deuteronomy were written before Leviticus. One effect of this is that the holiest day of the Jewish Year, Yom Kippur, mentioned in Leviticus, would be of the most recent origin among the festivals.

We would now have to arrange final versions of the historical books of Hebrew Scriptures thus:

P: Books 1, 2, 3, 4 of the Pentateuch, Chronicles, Ezra, Nehemiah
D: Book 5 of the Pentateuch, and the rest of the historical books

How deeply did these results of critical research affect Jewish life? In some ways, they have affected it deeply in modern times. Reform saw no need for the observance of all the details of Mitzvot, as they had simply emerged in the course of time and need not be considered the literal command of God. Conservative Judaism saw in the variations the key to its religious outlook: It retained that which the people had accepted and declared holy, but it emphasized the evolutionary process that may still go on. Orthodoxy rejected biblical criticism. The division in religious Jewry is, to a large degree, based on critical Bible research.

On the other hand, research did not affect Jewish life. Yom Kippur may have been introduced late in biblical times, but it is universally observed and regarded as the holiest day of the Jewish year. Isaiah's and Micah's "utopia" may rest on other sources. But the very fact of its incorporation in the messages of two prophets indicates that it was either a widespread or a highly regarded tradition, or both. This increases its value instead of diminishing it.

Finally, Jewry through most of its Diaspora was Orthodox. Many modern Jews have been more deeply influenced by the heritage of their family past than by scientific analysis of Scripture.

The impact of biblical criticism must be seen in the perspective of the evolution of the Jewish people and its contemporary results.

13

OF ORAL TORAH

TRADITION

Judaism is not identical with biblical Hebrew religion. It rests on the Talmud, which was created in the period between roughly 100 B.C.E. and 500 C.E., and has evolved on talmudic foundations. We may say, therefore, that Judaism attained its normative form about the same time Christianity did; it is not a forerunner but a contemporary of Christianity.

The major part of the Talmud originated after the fall of the Second Temple. Yet the Talmud contains extended debates on issues relating to Temple worship and the Land, whose possession had been taken away from the Jews. This reveals that the hope for a return was never abandoned. The Messiah might come at any time, so they must be prepared. In the meanwhile, the Talmud transported the Jews into another world, far away from the exile in which they had to live. In the pages of the Talmud, it was as if the Temple still existed and Israel dwelt on its own soil as sovereign nation.

Thus study of the Talmud became both a form of worship and an "escape." Studying it brought the sacred service of Temple times into the immediacy of troubled lives, and was seen as equivalent to this service. This vision and this fulfillment were balm for deeply troubled souls; they were beyond this world. Being often a sufferer within history, the Jew could now transcend it. As he immersed himself in the Talmud, he was at the goal. This way of life allowed for survival.

The medieval Church attacked the Talmud on the grounds that it contained anti-Christian statements. The anti-Semites, down to Hitler's times, maligned it as a blueprint for depravity. In the thirteenth century, the copies that could be found by the authorities in France were burnt. Originally, the portion of the Talmud now called Gemara was simply called Talmud. The Jew studied Mishnah and Talmud; under outside pressure, however, the term *Gemara*, which meant nothing to the non-Jewish world had to be substituted. As understood today, Talmud comprises both Mishnah and Gemara.

Why this hatred? The Talmud does not contain any significant disparagements of Christianity, though a few remarks could be found and were excised by the Christian censors without affecting the work as a whole. But the Talmud was essentially Jewish. The Hebrew Scriptures could not be attacked as they were part of the Christian heritage; the Talmud was not. The Talmud, by its very existence, proved that Jews and Judaism had not ceased to be creative under the guidance of God, that Judaism had continued to evolve, that it was alive. Even more, the Talmud kept the future alive in the Messiah, yet to come, and the return to the Land. Thus the Talmud was a weapon of resistance, a denial of Christian triumphalism, as its disparagers were indeed aware. Today, the Talmud has drawn the interest of scholars and lay persons, both Christians and Jews, as one of the great achievements of the human spirit.

The rabbis held that Moses received from God both a written Torah and verbal instructions to be transmitted orally, Oral Torah. Written Torah offered hints that an oral tradition accompanied the written word. A clear instance could be seen in the verse of Torah: ". . . you shall slaughter any of your cattle or sheep . . . as I have instructed you" (Deuteronomy 12:21). As there were no instructions regarding the slaughter of animals in written Torah, the verse must refer to an orally given commandment. Torah was thus transmitted from generation to generation:

> Moses received the Torah from Sinai and transmitted it to Joshua, and Joshua to the elders, and the elders to the prophets, and the prophets transmitted it to the Men of the Great Assembly (Abot 1:1).

The relationship of written and Oral Torah is explained in a simple parable found in a medieval Jewish work, *Seder Eliyahu Suta* (82). To a doubter of the validity of Oral Law, the rabbi answers:

> Both were given at Sinai, as a king presents a gift to faithful servants. Once there were two servants, a wise one and a foolish one, and both received from their king a measure of wheat and a bundle of flax. The foolish one put them away in a chest, that they remain forever unchanged; the wise servant spun the flax into a cloth and made precious bread out of the wheat. Placing the bread on the cloth, he invited the king to be his honored guest.

Thus human concern, wisdom, and love of the Supreme King transform divine gifts of Torah into *Shulhan Arukh*, a well-prepared table. Without oral law, evolution is impossible, and God is not served.

The masters of the Talmud were the Pharisees and their successors, who saw themselves as entrusted with the divine task of carrying tradition forward and felt sustained by the presence of God's holy spirit.

Following rabbinic teaching, Judaism holds that prophecy came to an end with Malachi at the time of Ezra, who is regarded as the founder of the Great Assembly (whose members are founders of rabbinic tradition). The rabbis did not consider themselves as equal to the prophets, but as their legitimate heirs in the unfolding of traditon. "This Torah is not in the heavens . . . [it] is . . . in your mouth and in your heart to observe it" (Deuteronomy 30:12–14). This implies authority of interpretation.

Method of Interpretation

In order to arrive at the full meaning of the written Torah, the rabbis pay attention to every nuance of the written word, for nothing is to be regarded as superfluous in Scripture. They note spelling, grammar, and contradictions, and compare similar statements in various sections. But they also consider the practical needs of the people. The rabbis follow what Professor Harry L. Wolfson of Harvard has called the "hypothetico-deductive method," which is used in scientific work, but they apply it to the sacred word. Considering the Torah as the word of God, and thus timeless, the rabbis did not accept that portions of it could be superseded by later interpretation. The following example may explain the rabbinical method somewhat.

We read in the Ten Commandments: "Honor your father and your mother" (Exodus 20:12). The Hebrew text reads: "kabed et avikha ve-et imekha." The *et* is grammatically superfluous, but it is repeatedly used. The rabbis explain that the first *et* is introduced to include the father's wife, even if she is not the mother; the second *et* is to include the mother's husband, even if he is not the father; the *ve* is included to extend the duty of rendering honor to the elder brother, who has certain responsibilities in the upbringing of the younger children. They all must be given their due honor and respect (Ketubot 103a).

Furthermore, we read: "Everyone shall respect his mother and his father" (Leviticus 19:3). The rabbis note that whereas previously the father was mentioned before the mother, now the mother is mentioned before the father. There must be a reason for such a difference. They explain: Children are wont to love and honor their mother more than their father for all her kindnesses to them. The first verse (in Exodus) places the father first, because you may be inclined to honor him less than your mother, so you must make an effort to honor him more than your inclination compels you, in order that both be equally honored. The second verse (in Leviticus) deals with the equally strong inclination of children to respect their father more than their more yielding mother. Therefore, you must transcend your inclination and respect her as you do your father. Thus the rabbis find that the two verses indicate that both are to be *equally* honored *and* respected (Kiddushin 31a).

Another *et* and its interpretation are revealing. We read in Torah: "You shall respect the Lord your God and worship Him . . ." (Deuteronomy 6:13)—in Hebrew, "*Et* Adonai Elohekha tira . . ." The Talmud explains that Rabbi Simon Imsani, who had interpreted every *et* in the Torah, stopped when he came to this verse. Then "came Rabbi Akiba and interpreted it: 'Et' includes the disciples of the wise [the rabbis, who deserve respect]" (Pessahim 22b). Later interpreters asked: "Why did this answer not occur to Rabbi Simon?" They reply that, in reading the whole verse, he had to abstain because we may not worship any human beings. Rabbi Akiba simply put in punctuation marks that excluded the *et* from the second part of the verse, which reads "You shall respect the Lord your God—and worship [only] Him and swear [only] by His Name." The first part includes the rabbis; the second does not.

THE MASTERS OF THE TALMUD

The task of evolving Torah calls for integrity, humility, knowledge and wisdom, and a deep love of God and humanity. The Pharisees, their disciples, and the rabbis of the Talmud possessed all of these; theirs is indeed the spirit of the prophets, whose successors they are in both time and spirit. We recognize this spirit in the teachings and maxims of their lives. As it says in Shabbat 88b:

> The Rabbis taught: Those that accept humiliation without ever humiliating others, hear their disparagement without retorting, act always out of love, and joyfully accept chastisement, of them Scripture says: "They who love Him are like the sun as he rises in his might" (Judges 5:31).

Hillel's love of God and humanity came to be proverbial:

> Be of the disciples of Aaron, loving peace and pursuing peace, loving all men and leading them to Torah.
>
> He who aggrandizes his name destroys it; he who does not grow [in knowledge and wisdom] decreases; he who does not wish to learn deserves death [he withers away]; and he who puts the crown [of Torah and position] to selfish use shall perish.
>
> If I am not for my self [doing the work, if need be alone], who will be for me? If I am for myself only, what am I? [My work is without meaning.] And if not now, when [will it be done]? (Abot 1:12–14)

Rabbi Eleazar places a good heart above all other qualities, for all of them are included therein (Abot 2:13), and counsels:

> Let the honor of your fellow man be as dear to you as your own; don't be easily angered; return [to God in repentance] one day before your death [that is, every day]. (Abot 2:15)

Rabbi Gamaliel warns against selfish ambition as he pleads for civic responsibility: "May all who work in behalf of the community work *with them* for the sake of Heaven" (Abot 2:2).

"The decisive thing is not study but the deed" (Abot 1:17), is Rabbi Simeon ben Gamaliel's word of advice. He also pointed out: "The world rests on three things: truth, justice, and peace" (Abot 1:18). And Shammai, Hillel's intellectual antagonist, proclaimed as the rule for his life: "Make your study of Torah a well-appointed practice, say' little and do much, and receive every person with a cheerful face" (Abot 1:15). Yet the decision in all religious matters follows the School of Hillel:

> A heavenly voice was heard at Jabneh: "The words of both are the words of
> the living God, but the decision must follow the School of Hillel." In dis-
> cussion it was asked, "If both are the words of the living God, why was the
> decision accorded to the School of Hillel?" The answer was: "Because they
> were kindly and peaceful, always studied both their own views and those of
> the School of Shammai, and even presented words of the School of Shammai
> before their own," which teaches that he who humbles himself, God raises
> him up, and he who looks for aggrandizement, God humbles him. He who
> chases after recognition finds it running away from him; he who strives to
> avoid it, finds it following him. He who pushes his objectives will find himself
> pressured by them, he who puts them aside finds himself aided by destiny.
> (Erubin 13b)

Life, as the rabbis saw it, must be imitation of God.

> Rabbi Hama, son of Rabbi Hanina, said: "Follow none but the Lord your
> God" (Deuteronomy 13:5). But can man follow God? It means that we must
> follow God's acts. As He clothes the naked, so shall you clothe the naked
> (Genesis 3:21); as the Holy One—Blessed be He—visited the sick (Genesis
> 18:1), so shall you visit the sick. Even as He . . . comforts those who mourn
> (Genesis 25:11) so shall you comfort those who are in mourning. As the Holy
> One . . . buries the dead (Deuteronomy 34:6) even so shall you bury the
> dead. . . . The Torah begins with deeds of kindness—as God made clothes for
> Adam and Eve—and it ends with kindness, as it is written: "He buried [Moses]
> in the valley." (Sota 14a)

These were the principles held by the men who developed the
Talmud—the *Tannaim* (teachers), who were the masters of the Mishnah, and
the **Amoraim** (speakers), who carried on the discussions and made the decisions laid down in Gemara (the Completion). By their ordinances (**Takkanot**),
they erected the fence around Torah; by their preachments, they conveyed
ethical teachings. Their legal decisions, directing the Jews' path in life, are
called *Halakhah*, meaning walk; their preaching became known as **Aggadah**,
which means preaching. In Mishnah and Gemara, both are interwoven, but we
find Aggadah also in separate works arranged as a commentary to Scripture,
called **Midrash**, or the "search" for meaning. Law and ethics, Halakhah and
Aggadah, cannot be separated. Judaism, as a religion of action, has always seen
the law as an instrument of ethics and as an ethical ideal to be pursued. The
Torah does not say, for instance, "You shall love your enemies." It says
instead, "If you see the ass of your enemy lying under its burden and would
like to refrain from raising it, you must nevertheless help him to lift it up"
(Exodus 23:5). This is not a general injunction to love but a concrete, specific
act, which, in turn, cannot help but promote love among two former enemies.
As a piece of general legislation, it will eventually create a society whose
members feel an inner obligation to help each other, thus overcoming ani-
mosities.

Halakhah is practical and practiced ethics and must be understood as
such—Mitzvot become Torah, namely instruction. Judaism denies the often-
heard argument that we cannot legislate morality. We may actually have to
start with legislation so that, out of its observance, disagreeable as it may

appear to us at the beginning, a new spirit may emerge. Halakhah fortified by Aggadah may achieve it.

ORGANIZATION OF THE TALMUD

The Talmud is divided into six *orders*. Each order consists of a number of tractates. The tractates are subdivided into chapters and paragraphs. An individual Mishnah constitutes a paragraph, which is therefore simply called *Mishnah*.

1. The first order, *Zeraim* (Seeds), deals with the laws of agriculture. Since it is a duty to give thanks to God for the gifts of nature, the order opens with the Tractate *Berakhot* (Blessings), dealing with worship in general.

2. The second order, *Moed* (Appointed Times), discusses the rules and regulations pertaining to holy days. Among its tractates we find *Shabbat* (Sabbath), concerning the observance of the Sabbath; *Yom Tob* (Holy Day), dealing with the rules regulating the other holy days; and several tractates laying down Halakhah regarding specific holy seasons, such as *Yoma* (The Day of Atonement), Sukkah (Festival of Sukkot), and Pessahim (Feast of Passover).

3. The third order, *Nashim* (Women), contains marriage and divorce laws. Among its tractates are *Kiddushin* (Sanctification of Marriage), *Ketubot* (Civil Laws of Marriage), and *Gitin* (Laws of Divorce).

4. The fourth order, *Nezikin* (Damages), forms the code of civil and criminal law, which were public laws when Israel was a nation of old and during the Middle Ages, when Jews had their own civil jurisdiction.

Talmud, open. *The opened page gives the text analyzed in this chapter (tractate Berakhot 10b, 11). Note Rashi's commentary on the inner margin, Tosafot on the outer margin, and references, etc., on the sides.* (Photo by the author from Vol. I of his own 18-volume Vilna edition, 1896.)

5. The fifth order, *Kadashim* (Holy Things), deals with laws of Temple sacrifices in times of old and also lays down the dietary laws (*Hulin*).

6. The sixth order, *Taharot* (Purifications), states the laws of ritual purity whose observance was required as prerequisite for entry and service in the Temple of old.

In opening one of the heavy tomes of the Talmud, we find first of all that, regardless of edition, its pages are numbered identically. Otherwise we would never find an indicated quotation or discussion. At the beginning, we shall find the Mishnah; it will be followed by the Gemara, which discusses and analyzes it, to be followed in turn by another Mishnah. This text is found in a column in the center of the page, surrounded on the inner margin by the commentary of Rashi and, on the outer, by Tosafot (the additions made by Rashi's successors). Super-commentaries and cross-indexes may be found on the side or bottom of the page, witnessing to the fact that Torah and Talmud are not a closed book but are continuously developing.

Oral Torah did not come to an end with the compilation of the Talmud. It led to further commentaries and to codes, such as that of Maimonides, the Turim (see p. 75), and the *Shulhan Arukh*. On the basis of the accumulated material and precedents, the Orthodox rabbi has to decide individual cases brought to him. Throughout the ages, a number of these decisions, called *Responsa*, were collected; they serve a rabbi in the same way court decisions guide judges and attorneys. The authority to hand down these decisions is granted the rabbi by his ordination. Modern rabbis are trained in many fields and serve in many areas of life, being teachers, preachers, and counselors. The ancient and medieval rabbi was simply a scholar and teacher and, above all, the vested authority of Jewish law. Traditional rabbis still fulfill this function, but (as in England and sometimes in the United States) a group of rabbis who are specialists in Jewish law may be appointed to deal with the more difficult cases. Such a body is called a **Beth Din** (court of law). The Israeli rabbinate operates almost exclusively as an agency of religious law.

THE COMMENTARIES AND CODES

To understand the use of the rabbinical commentaries and codes, we shall follow the development of one small item of law from its source to the codes. We will look for the sources from which the rabbis drew their conclusions and see how they did it, understand their controversies on the basis of different readings of the sources, follow their mutual critique based on logic, and end with the final practical decision by the codifiers. Our procedure will follow five steps: (1) Find the source in the written Torah and study it; (2) study Rashi's commentary to the verse in written Torah; (3) turn to the Talmud and first study the Mishnah; (4) follow the comments of the Gemara. At each of these steps, Rashi's commentary will aid us. We may also study additional commentaries, such as Tosafot.

At this point, we will (5) turn to the codes, which give us the accepted decisions. (It is not always necessary to consult all of the codes. In easy cases, it may be sufficient to turn to the *Shulhan Arukh*, or even to one of the digests written later. In difficult cases, however, a rabbi may consult other codes and commentaries as well.) We can choose the code written by Maimonides, his *Mishneh Torah*. We may follow it by the *Tur*, the code of Rabbi Jacob ben Asher, who arranged the law in the four "Rows" or *Turim*. We shall certainly consult the *Shulhan Arukh* by Rabbi Joseph Karo, which is the authoritative code for traditional Jewish practice. Following the *Tur*, Joseph Karo arranged the code in four sections: (1) *Orah Hayim* (The Way of Life), containing laws of worship and holy days; (2) *Yore Deah* (The Teacher of Knowledge), dealing with dietary laws; (3) *Eben ha-Ezer* (The Stone of Help), containing the rules of family relationships, marriage, divorce, and so on; and (4) *Hoshen Mishpat* (The Breastplate of Judgment), dealing with civil laws and similar items.

Interpretation of the Shema

Our selection deals with the recital of the Affirmation of Faith, beginning with the words, "Hear, O Israel! the Lord our God, the Lord is One." The first word, *Hear*, is *Shema* in Hebrew; hence the whole paragraph is called the **Shema**.

Our source in written Torah is Deuteronomy 6:4–9, quoted here with the usual verse numbers to aid in the discussion:

> 4Hear, O Israel! The Lord our God, the Lord is One. 5You must love the Lord your God with all your heart and with all your soul and with all your might. 6Take to heart these words with which I charge you this day. 7Impress them upon your children. Recite them when you stay at home and when you are away, when you lie down and when you get up. 8Bind them as a sign on your hand and let them serve as frontlets between your eyes; 9inscribe them on the doorposts of your house and on your gates.

Rashi explains, citing midrashic and talmudic sources:

> "You must love" (Verse 5): Do His bidding out of love, for he who acts out of love cannot be compared to him who acts [only] out of fear. . . . "With all your heart": With both your inclinations (toward good or evil), or another explanation: do not act half-heartedly in relationship to God. "And with all your soul": Even if He takes your soul [life]. "And with all your might" (citing Tractate Berakhot): With all your substance or money. There are people to whom their money is more precious than their person, hence it is stated: "and with all your substance." Another explanation: With all your capacities. . . . And how does this love express itself? "These words . . . take them to heart" (Verse 6); through it, he recognizes God and cleaves to His ways. . . . "Recite them" (Verse 7): Your basic talk shall be about them. Make them your basic concern and not merely a side issue. "When you lie down": I might have thought even if he lies down in the middle of the day [he would have to recite them], hence Torah says: "When you get up." I might have thought, even if he rises up in the middle of the night, hence Torah says: "When you stay at home and when you are away." The Torah speaks of the

customary usage, the usual time of lying down and the usual time of rising up.

As we turn to the Talmud, we find the Mishnah in the Tractate Berakhot, Chapter 1, Mishnah 3. This is followed by the Gemara. The Mishnah and the following discussion of Gemara are found on pages 10b and 11a in all editions of the Talmud.

In Tractate Berakhot, Chapter 1, Mishnah 3, we read:

> The School of Shammai teaches: In the evening one must recite the Shema in a reclining position, and in the morning standing up, for it is said: when you lie down and when you get up. The School of Hillel teaches: One may read it in any position, for it also says: When you are away [literally, when you *walk* on the way]. [Torah simply says, you must recite it wherever you are and whatever you do.] Why does [Scripture] say: When you lie down and when you get up? This refers to the hour of the day when people lie down, and the hour when they rise up. Rabbi Tarphon told: "Once, when on the road, I reclined to recite the Shema in accordance with the teaching of the School of Shammai, and I was almost attacked by robbers." They retorted: "You deserved to get into trouble, having transgressed against the words of the School of Hillel."

And in the Gemara we find:

> The School of Hillel has indeed explained its reason and refuted the School of Shammai; but why, then, did the School of Shammai refuse to yield? It could argue [from the verse]: Scripture should have stated "in the morning and in the evening" [then the School of Hillel would be right]; but it states "when you lie down and when you get up." It must mean that at the time of evening rest a leaning position is required, and at the time of getting up, a standing position is required.
>
> The Rabbis taught: The School of Hillel says: one may recite it leaning, or standing, or sitting or reclining, or while walking on the way, or during one's work. Once, Rabbi Yishmael and Rabbi Eleazar, Son of Azariah, were together. Rabbi Yishmael was reclining, Rabbi Eleazar standing. When the time for Shema came in the evening, Rabbi Eleazar reclined and the Rabbi Yishmael stood up. Rabbi Eleazar said to Rabbi Yishmael, "Brother Yishmael . . . while I was standing you were reclining, now that I am reclining you stand." [Why?] He answered, "Because I followed the decision of the School of Hillel [which permits the recital in any position; therefore I stood up, even in the evening]; you followed the opinion of the School of Shammai. Furthermore [had I not stood up], the disciples might have observed it and established Halakhah in that manner." What did he mean by the second statement? According to the School of Hillel, one may recite the Shema while reclining, provided that one finds himself in a reclining position. Until now, you were standing, then sat down and reclined [to recite the Shema]. [I was reclining, and had I continued to recite, the disciples would have seen both of us reclining, and] therefore one would have believed that both of us followed the decision of the School of Shammai. Noticing it, the disciples might have fixed Halakhah permanently [according to Shammai]. [Hence I stood up.] (10b–11a)

In other words, one of the rabbis had been reclining already, and the other sat down before reciting the Shema. According to Hillel, the first one could have remained in his position, but this might have created the wrong impression that both followed Shammai; hence Rabbi Yishmael stood up. Now the disciples knew that the Shema could be recited in any position.

The overriding issue was the principle. There must be no doubt in the disciples' minds that the School of Hillel must always be followed because this principle had implications in numerous fields of Halakhah. In addition, the masters were aware of their obligation to teach not only by their words, but equally by their actions. Conduct is instruction; teaching and practice must go hand in hand. Example is more important than preachment. The disciples would recognize in the performance of their masters that they took in utter seriousness not only the *act* of reciting the affirmation of faith and of love of God, but the *meaning* of their affirmation, as well, in preparation and in recital, in adjustment of body and direction of heart. The two rabbis knew that in the presence of their disciples their action spelled out both a legal precedent and an inspiration in faith. Seen in this manner, the concern of these men is not a dwelling on trivialities and hairsplitting, but an act of guidance. No one ever knows how deep the impression of his actions may be, though they may appear insignificant to himself. It is only in this manner that we can fully understand the great concern of the rabbis with the exact performance of every Mitzvah.

Now we turn to Maimonides's *Mishneh Torah*, Book 2, and find the following:

> Twice a day one must recite the Shema, in the evening and in the morning, as Scripture says, "when you lie down, and when you get up," at the hour when people lie down, namely at night, and at the hour when people rise up, namely at daytime. (Chapter 1, Par. 1)
>
> He who recites the Shema without directing his heart [to God] . . . has not done his duty. (Chapter 2, Par. 1)
>
> Everyone may recite it in his prevailing position, standing or walking or sitting or riding on an animal. Yet it is forbidden to recite the Shema stretched out, facing downward or upward; but he may recite it resting on his side. If he is obese or sick and cannot turn on his side, let him turn a bit sidewise and recite it. (Chapter 2, par. 2)
>
> If he is walking, he shall stop during the first verse; the rest he may recite walking. If he is asleep . . . one must wake him up. (Chapter 2, Par. 3)
>
> He must wash his hands before he recites it. . . . (Chapter 3, Par. 1)

The regulations regarding the Shema will be found in the Orah Hayim section of *Tur* and *Shulhan Arukh*. In the Orah Hayim of *Tur*, Chapters 61 and 63, we read:

> He shall recite it in awe and attunement to God . . . everyone shall consider it a new royal proclamation, newly issued, whenever he recites it. . . . It is God's proclamation. Thus do we find it in the Midrash . . . when a king of flesh and blood issues a proclamation to his provinces, all the people receive it standing up . . . but the Holy One . . . said to Israel: . . . "I will not burden you by commanding you to stand up when you recite it . . . you may do so even while walking on the way, but must do so in awe and reverence."
>
> He may read it either walking or standing or sitting down, but not lying down

on his back, as Maimonides points out [here Maimonides is quoted]. Anyone who wishes to impose upon himself a special burden by standing up when he had been sitting down does wrong, and is actually called a sinner.

[Commentary by Joseph Karo:] For in daytime he transgresses against the decision of the School of Hillel and appears to be following the School of Shammai . . . and at night he follows neither school. He is called a sinner, for we find in [Tractate] Shabbat [40a] that he who transgresses against the rulings of the Rabbis is called a sinner.

Finally, we read in the Orah Hayim section of the *Shulhan Arukh*, Chapters 61 and 63:

He must recite the Shema with attunement to God, in awe and reverence. "Which I charge you this day" [is cited in Scripture] to tell you that it must be new to you every day, and not be like something often heard and habitual. It has been a custom to recite the first verse aloud, in order to arouse the "Kavanah" [attunement].

It has been a custom to place the hands over the face during the recital of the first verse, in order that he may not be distracted from his Kavanah by extraneous impressions.

He shall prolong the pronouncement of the letters of the word "One" in reflection on God's Kingship in heaven and on earth and to call to mind that God is One and Only in the universe, ruling over its entire expanse.

After the first verse he shall recite: Blessed be His Name, His glorious Kingdom is for ever and ever. [This sentence is not part of the verses in Deuteronomy.]

After these first verses he shall pause for a brief instant [before continuing "and love . . ."] to indicate [and reflect on] the distinction between "Acceptance of the Kingdom of Heaven" [contained in the first and second verse, which are the foundation of Jewish life and all its Mitzvot] and the Mitzvot ["love," which derive from it]. He may recite it walking, or standing, reclining, or riding on an animal, but not lying stretched out, facing downward or upward; yet he may recite it lying on his side [note: if he is lying down already, and it would be a burden for him to get up]. If he is obese and cannot turn to his side, or sick, let him turn a bit to the side and recite it.

He who wants to make it hard on himself and stands up after he has been sitting, to recite it standing up, he is called a sinner.

If he is walking and wants to recite the Shema, he shall stop at the first verse.

If he is asleep one must wake him up, even if it troubles him.

In these developments, we see the respect for written Torah—every word in it is regarded as significant. Fluid interpretation at the beginning of the development yields to terse regulation at the end. We should remember that Hillel and Shammai lived at a time when the Land constituted a unifying force. Maimonides balanced strictness in observance by freely speculating in philosophy, as Torah permitted. The *Shulhan Arukh*, at the end of the development, was written to unite the people and strengthen their will to live through Mitzvot. Immersion in Mitzvot gave the people the sense of closeness to God and to one another. The elements of God-Torah-Land-Mitzvot are all there, yet emphasis is placed differently as outward conditons weakened the

Land as living soil of a people, and as persecution drew them ever more deeply into the shell of minute performance.

A Midrashic Section

The following excerpts are from the Tractate Makkot, folio 23b/24. I have added the commentary of Rashi wherever appropriate. I have also added some observations of my own, which are introduced with the initials "LT."

> Rav Simlai taught: 613 Mitzvot were told to Moses, 365 prohibitions corresponding to the days of the sun year, and 248 duties of performance, corresponding to the limbs of the human body.
>
> > Rashi: Every day he is thereby admonished not to transgress.
> >
> > LT: The figures given reveal the ethical character of Torah and its commandments: Every day of the year demands anew that the Jew keep desires in check. At the same time, every limb of the human body must be placed in active service to make God manifest in the world.
>
> Rav Hamnuna said: Which verse in Torah points to this [the 613 commandments]? It is: "Moses charged us with Torah as the heritage of the congregation of Jacob" (Deuteronomy 33:4). The numerical value of the word "Torah" is 611, and the commandments "I am the Lord your God, who brought you out of the land of Egypt" (Exodus 20:2) and "You shall have no other gods beside Me" (Exodus 20:3), we heard from the mouth of the Almighty. [This brings the total to 613.]
>
> > Rashi: 611 came from Moses, therefore it is written: "Torah" (613) did Moses charge us, two came out of the Almighty, a total of 613.
> >
> > LT: The Rabbis did not count the commandments; they gave the figure of 613 as an ethical guideline, as we saw. Now Rav Hamnuna looks for text in Scripture as reinforcement. He finds it by adding the numerical value of the letters in the word *Torah* [Each Hebrew letter has a numerical value] and arriving at 611. Now we find in Exodus 20:15–16 that the people fell back; they were overpowered by the voice of God and pleaded with Moses to speak to them and give them God's word. By tradition, this happened after the first two commandments were spoken by God Himself; the first two they heard from God's mouth directly. Thus Moses wrote *Torah*, 611, and God spoke 2, for a total of 613. This play with numbers reinforces the rabbinic statement. We have to assume, however, that the number 613 came first and was based on the addition of the days of the year and the limbs of the body (as known to the rabbis), to teach the lesson of faith symbolically. Then came the "proof."
>
> Then came David and reduced them (the 613 commandments) to 11; as we read: "A Psalm of David. Lord who may stay in Your tent, who may reside on Your holy mountain? (1) He who lives without blame, (2) who does what is right, (3) and in his heart acknowledges the truth, (4) whose tongue is not given to evil, (5) who has never done harm to his fellow, (6) or borne reproach for [his acts toward] his neighbor, (7) for whom a contemptible man is abhorrent, (8) but who honors those who fear the Lord; (9) who stands by his oath even to his hurt; (10) who has never lent money at interest, (11) or accepted

a bribe against the innocent; the man who acts thus shall never be shaken (Psalm 15)."

(1) "He who lives without blame": This is our father Abraham, of whom it is said: "[God said to him] 'Walk in My ways and be blameless' ";

(2) "who does what is right": as for instance Abba Hilkiyahu, a man of scrupulous integrity (Taanit 23a/b);

(3) "and in his heart acknowledges the truth": as for instance, Rabbi Safra;

(4) "whose tongue is not given to evil": This is our father Jacob, as it is written: [when his mother Rebecca ordered him to put the fleece of a lamb on his arm to appear like Esau at the touch of his blind father Isaac, and receive the blessing destined for Esau] "if my father touches me, I shall appear to him like a trickster and bring upon myself a curse, not a blessing" (Genesis 27:12). [He therefore did not want to do it.]

(5) "who has never done harm to his fellow": He does not cut into the business of his neighbor [undercutting him];

(6) "or borne reproach for [his acts toward] his neighbor": He brings close those near to him [coming to their aid];

(7) "for whom a contemptible man is abhorrent": This is King Hezekiah, who dragged the bones [even] of his father on a rope ladder [He set an example of the fate awaiting the sinners even after death; his father Ahaz was very evil and even sacrificed a son to the idols; he was abhorrent to Hezekiah; see II Kings 16 for all of Ahaz's evil deeds.];

(8) "but who honors those who fear the Lord": This is Yehoshafat, king of Judah; when he saw a disciple of the wise, he rose from his throne, embraced and kissed him and called him: My father, my master, my teacher;

(9) "who stands by his oath even to his hurt: as, for instance, Rabbi Johanan, who said once: 'I shall keep my fast until I get home'" [a pledge that was not binding, but, having once made it, he kept it];

(10) "who has never lent money at interest": even to a heathen [which Torah permits (Deuteronomy 23:20–21)];

(11) "or accepted a bribe against the innocent": as, for instance, Rabbi Ishmael ben Yose;

As Rabbi Gamaliel came to the verse, "The man who acts thus shall never be shaken," he wept. As he said, "[Only] he who does *all* of these will not be shaken [a task beyond the capacity of a human being], but he who does only one of these, will be shaken." They [his colleagues] replied: "Is it stated 'He who does *all* of these'? In fact, he who does *but one* of these, will not be shaken."

Rashi
(excerpts):   *"David reduced them to 11"*: In the beginning they were all Zaddikim, and could take upon themselves the yoke of many Mitzvot, but later generations were no such perfect Zaddikim, and if they were to observe all of them, no one would be able to be meritorious; hence David came and reduced them, in order that they might gain merit by observing these 11 Mitzvot, and thus, as generations get less distinguished, one reduces them [the number of Mitzvot]. *"or accepted a bribe against the innocent"*: Even if it was permissible to do so, as, for instance Rabbi Ishmael ben Yose, whose tenant farmer brought him what he owed him *ahead of time*, and he did not wish to accept it, as he might be his judge [in some future litigation, and then feel biased in his favor].

> LT: The passage reveals the intent of the rabbis. It is not the number of Mitzvot that counts, but the spirit. No generation has to carry more than it can. Following God means not simply remaining within the letter of the law, but going beyond it, in spirit and in action toward the human neighbor, Jew or non-Jew. *One* such action establishes the person, makes the person human and thus beloved by God.

The text continues in the same manner, and the essence of Torah is further distilled.

> Then came Isaiah and reduced them [the commandments] to six, as it is written: (1) He who walks in righteousness; (2) speaks uprightly; (3) spurns profit from fraudulent dealings; (4) waves away a bribe instead of grasping it; (5) stops his ears against listening to infamy; (6) shuts his eyes against looking at evil—such a one shall dwell in lofty security . . . (Isaiah 33:15–16).

> Then came Micah and reduced them to three: "He has told you, O man, what is good and what the Lord requires of you: (1) only to do justice, and (2) to love goodness, and (3) to walk modestly with your God; then will your name achieve wisdom" (Micah 6:8–9).

>> (1) to do justice: establishing justice
>> (2) to love goodness: doing good deeds of loving kindness to others
>> (3) to walk modestly: burying the dead and providing for a bride.

> Then came Isaiah and reduced them to two, as it is stated: "Thus said the Lord: (1) observe what is right and (2) do what is just, for soon My salvation shall come" (Isaiah 56:1).

> Then came Amos and reduced them (the commandments) to one, as it is said: "Seek Me, and you will live" (Amos 5:4).

Here we recognize the rabbis as teachers of ethics, establishing the ultimate meaning of Mitzvot. They arrive at the number of Mitzvot not by counting them but by the primary concern that Mitzvot be understood as guides for every day of the year, teaching self-discipline and motivating the use of every limb of the body to promote God's will in the world. After arriving at their conclusion, they link it up with scriptural pronouncements. To the rabbis the ultimate measure of a good Jew is not simply the performance of laws but the spirit, the ethics, that go beyond the laws. In performance, the spirit of the laws is made manifest. It should be noted that most of the actions that establish a good Jew are deeds of kindness and concern for fellow human beings. The rabbis give us to understand that the "yoke of Torah" is adjusted to the capacities of each generation, but the principle is not affected.

The rabbis used several methods in their interpretations. *Gematria* is the counting of the numerical value of the letters of a word for interpretative purposes. *Kal va-homer*, one of the hermeneutic principles, is a conclusion drawn "a foritiore" from a less involved to a heavier or more involved situation (for example, if theft is a crime, then theft plus murder is a crime, the latter situation being "heavier").

The rabbis were, of course, convinced that the word of Torah was literally divinely given, yet they had no hesitation in regarding themselves as the divinely authorized interpreters. We must recognize the power the rabbis assumed for themselves. If necessary they interpreted to meet peoples' needs and *then* found the basis for their interpretation in Torah. They demanded respect for their decisions. At the same time they were aware of their human frailty and inadequacy: Rabbi Gamaliel wept, recognizing his own short-comings; his colleagues comforted him in compassion. In choosing examples of perfect living, they did not confine themselves to personalities of the past, but drew from the lives of men living at their own time, as if to say: Jewish living in the true spirit of Torah is possible today, for it rests on the spirit.

Consulting the Talmud on a Controversial Modern Issue

A final example may show us how the rabbis deal with an ancient issue that is currently the subject of great controversy in American society—namely, abortion. We shall cite the Mishnah, discuss how its conclusions were reached, and see that the explanations of the great commentators of the Middle Ages can lead to divergent practical conclusions. At the same time, we get a glimpse at the rabbis' deep concern with human life. We begin with the Mishnah, found in Ohalim 7:2:

> A woman has severe trouble in giving birth: We have to dismember the child in her womb and bring it out limb by limb, for her life takes precedence over its life. If the greater part of the child has emerged, we are not to touch it, because we may not take one life for another life.

Obviously, we are dealing with a birth that jeopardizes the mother's life. The question arises, Why may we take the living child, still in the womb, whereas we may not touch it once it has partially emerged?

There is no Gemara to this tractate, but the Talmud deals with the issue in Sanhedrin 72–73. The rabbis start with a general discussion: May a person kill another person who is in pursuit of a third person with the intent of killing him? The answer is: He may. We find a similar situation in Scripture: "If the thief is seized while tunneling [under a wall for the purpose of housebreaking], and he is beaten to death, there is no bloodguilt in his case" (Exodus 22:1). It is to be assumed that the thief is prepared to kill any person he comes upon by surprise, and we may anticipate this fact.

The rabbis are aware that the case is not identical with the one under discussion. But it serves another purpose. In their concern for human life, the rabbis have laid down the rule that no one may be put to death unless he has been warned by bystanders immediately before commiting his act that he was engaging in the grievous crime of taking a human life. The criminal must have done his deed with full knowledge of its gravity. What about the man who breaks in? "His act of breaking in is his warning." In other words, he knew what he was doing. The general conclusion, therefore, is that there are cases when warning is not required.

Now we have to consider another principle. The prospective mur-
derer, the pursuer, is about to commit two crimes: He is about to wipe out a
human life *and* he destroys his own life in the eyes of God, who will hold him
to account. We may prevent that.

Ultimately, the rabbis base their decision on another verse in Scripture: "If a man comes upon a betrothed girl in the open country, and the man
lies with her by force, only the man who lay with her shall die, but you shall
do nothing to the girl. The girl is not guilty of a capital offence, for this case
is like that of a man attacking another and murdering him" (Deuteronomy
22:25–26). In cases of rape and murder, it is necessary that the criminal be
killed.

These, in general, are the principles underlying the statement of the
Mishnah in Sanhedrin: "The following may be restrained by [the taking of
their] life: He who pursues another in order to kill him . . . he who pursues a
betrothed young woman. . . ." Now we turn to the case of childbirth:

> Rav Hona stated: A minor, who pursues another person: we save him through
> [taking] his life. He therefore holds the opinion that the pursuer need not be
> given any warning. Rav Hisda argued against Rav Hona: [We have learned:]
> If the head has emerged, we may not touch it [the child], because we may not
> sacrifice one life for another. Why not, if [the child] is a pursuer? The reply:
> This is different, for the pursuit comes from Heaven [God].

To clarify: Rav Hona holds that one may kill a child who pursues
another person. Rav Hisda argues against him: The child to be born is a
pursuer, about to destroy his mother. Under these circumstances, it should be
permitted to kill the child even after his head has emerged, as we are em-
powered to destroy a fully developed, independent human being who is in
pursuit of another. But the Mishnah forbids the taking of life once the child has
emerged. Should we not conclude that we may *not* kill a pursuing minor? The
reply is: We may kill a pursuing minor, but this situation is different; in this
situation God, not the child, is the pursuer.

From this interpretation another question arises, with which the later
masters take issue: If God is the pursuer, why may we take the life of the child
before it has emerged? After the child has emerged, we may not sacrifice one
life for another. Does that mean that before the child was not considered to
have life?

Maimonides decides: "The sages have ruled: A woman in childbirth,
who has severe trouble giving birth: it is permitted to dismember the child in
her womb by either medication or by hand, because it is like a pursuer, being
after her. Has its head emerged we may not touch it, for we may not displace
one life for another" (Mishneh Torah, Hilhot Rotseah 1:9). Rabbi Joseph Karo,
in the *Shulhan Arukh*, adopts the same ruling (Hoshen Mishpat 424:12). Rashi,
however, offers a different interpretation in his commentary to the section in
Sanhedrin. The salient points are italicized:

> We are dealing with a woman, who has severe trouble in giving birth, and whose life is in danger; then the midwife may stretch out her hand, dismember it [the unborn] and bring it out limb by limb, *for as long as it has not emerged into the world, it is not a living being* [literally, soul], and we may slay it to save its mother; has its head emerged, we may not touch it, for it is like a child, and we may not displace one life for another. [Rashi could refer to Exodus 21:22: an embryo is not equal to a living being.]
> When men scuffle, and one pushes a woman with child, and her child is aborted, but the worst does not happen [the woman does not die] he shall be fined, as the woman's husband shall impose on him, according to judgment; but if the worst does happen [the woman dies], then you shall give life for life. (Exodus 21:22–23)

The fetus is not here regarded as a human being; the guilty merely pays damages; if the mother dies, he is guilty of manslaughter.

The differences among the commentators are highly consequential. Maimonides obviously regards the unborn fetus as a *human being* that may be killed if it is a pursuer. He would therefore prohibit abortion for any other reason. [However, Maimonides holds that a premature child is not to be regarded as a viable human being until after the child has lived for thirty days (Maimonides, Mishneh Torah, Hilhot Rotseah 2:6)]. Rashi, on the other hand, seems to regard the unborn fetus as *not a living being at all*. This leads us to ask what his stand would be on abortions for other reasons (Tay-Sachs disease, for instance)? Contemporary rabbis and rabbinical bodies thus have to wrestle with two viewpoints of the highest authority. Rabbinical opinion may conflict, or a rabbi may be guided by one or the other in individual circumstances.   Let us briefly summarize the entire argument:

1. A person pursuing another person's life is to be restrained even by being put to death; the fetus is such a "pursuer" putting his mother's life in jeopardy, and must be destroyed.
2. In such an emergency "due process of law" is impossible and therefore suspended.
3. In destroying the pursuer we prevent him from committing grievous sin, in this case the inadvertent killing of the mother by the fetus.
4. A significant difference exists between other "pursuits" and childbirth; in the former, a living human being may be put to death, in childbirth the largely emerged child may not be destroyed, for God is the pursuer.
5. Destruction of the unborn is required, according to Maimonides and others, because it is life against life, and the mother has precedence; according to Rashi, because the fetus in the womb is not a "living being."
6. Full viability is attained after thirty days.

We have sketched in very broad lines the development of Jewish law in one instance, seeing how it ultimately rests on Scripture, interpreted by the rabbis. We have noted their concern for human life. We have recognized the evolution of Jewish law, which is open-ended. Orthodox, Conservative, or Reform rabbis, may come to different conclusions yet all rest on recognized authorities, as long as they are within the area of Halakhah.

14

DEFINITIONS AND SYMBOLS: GOD, HUMANITY, AND ETERNITY

GOD: CONCEPTS AND THEOLOGICAL ISSUES

The Scripture uses many names for God. We found that the names **YHVH** and **Elohim** served the various schools of higher biblical criticism in their investigation of the origin and authorship of the various sections of the Bible.* A quotation from Scripture may guide us.

> And God spoke to Moses, He said to him: "I am YHVH. I appeared to Abraham, Isaac and Jacob as *El Shaddai*, but I did not make Myself known to them by My name YHVH" (Exodus 6:2). Now . . . Moses drove the flock into the wilderness. . . . He gazed: there, the bush blazing in fire, yet the bush was not consumed. . . . And God called him out of the bush . . . and said: "I am the God of your father, the God of Abraham, the God of Isaac, the God of Jacob. . . . I will send you to Pharaoh to lead my people, the children of Israel, out of Egypt." And Moses said, "When I come to the children of Israel and say to them, 'The God of your fathers has sent me to you,' and they ask me, 'What is His name?', what shall I say to them?" And God said to Moses *"Ehyeh-Asher-Ehyeh*," and He said: "You shall say to the children of Israel, 'Ehyeh sends me to you.'" (Exodus 3:1–14)

The several names of God in this passage are left untranslated; they will be explained in our discussion.

Ehyeh-Asher-Ehyeh has been translated as "I Am That I Am," or "I Am Who I Am," or "I Will Be What I Will Be" or "I Am Who Brings Into Being." The root of the word is *hayah*, being. The name YHVH is derived from the same root and related to the definition God gives Himself.

Basically, the term speaks of God as *Being*—absolute, unchanging Being. We have to understand that clearly. A human being, and all of nature, changes. From the day of birth to the day of death, cells are created and cells

---

*The development of the Jewish God concept out of Egyptian, Canaanite, and Mesopotamian sources offers a fascinating study, as does the origin of the Jewish festivals and rites of passage. The scope of our text does not permit such a discussion here; however, several works dealing with these subjects are listed in the bibliography.

die. God, in contrast, says of Himself that He is Absolute Being. He is What He is, always; he does not change, does not age, has no limit in time or space.

God is beyond human comprehension. The Jews have therefore refrained from pronouncing the word YHVH, in which there is expressed something unfathomable. Were they to pronounce it, they might drag the name of God down to the level of human comprehension; they would diminish His Being. Therefore, the word is pronounced **Adonai**, *the Lord*. This means Jews know there is only *one Lord*, and no one, divinity or human being, could possibly be mistaken for *the Lord*. This is as far as human comprehension can go. Since God is Being, there can be only One God; He is not subject to change. God cannot be said to ever assume human form, because this would limit His Oneness and His absolute Being.

What about the beings in the world—stars and stones and humans? They could not have any being independent of God; therefore God is He who Brings Into Being; He is the Creator.

What about time? There cannot be time that is outside of God. God is the Creator of Time and the God of History. Isaiah states: "I am the first and I am the last and there is no God but Me (44:6)."

What about space? There cannot be any space outside God. "Holy, holy, holy is the Lord of hosts, the whole earth [universe] is full of His presence" (Isaiah 6:3).

As every place is God's, the rabbis used the term **Makom**, Place, as a name of God.

God is therefore incomparable. "To whom then can you liken Me, to whom can I be compared? says the Holy One" (Isaiah 40:25). There is *nothing* but God (Isaiah 45:6).

(This should not be confused with pantheism. Pantheism states that the totality of nature is God; Judaism states that God created the totality of nature and fills it. He is more than this totality.)

At the Burning Bush, God talks with Moses. This means God is a person, and He has been so understood generally. We must understand, however, that this does not mean He has a body. He is a person in the sense that He acts freely and relates freely, something the forces of nature cannot do. Maimonides warns against ascribing to God any physical attributes and maintains that terms such as "the arm of God" and "the voice of God," which we find in the Bible, refer only to the effect of God's action that was perceived by human beings. God as a person is a unique person; there is no other person like Him. As God of history, God also knows of human frailties; He is therefore the God of compassion.

In Exodus, God revealed Himself to Moses as El-Shaddai. This is a dual term. We shall turn first to **El**.

The Canaanites knew a deity El; hence Abraham may have called God by this name. Generally, the term has been used in a different form: Elohim, a plural to which the verb is always affixed in *singular* form when speaking of God. Elohim also means judge. The term thus means God is the sum total of power and justice: He unites all power and justice into One. He metes out judgment and enforces it.

God, as One, combines power and majesty with graciousness and kindness, judgment with mercy. In any other being, this would be a contradiction; in God's Being it is not. "I am, nothing beside Me: Who forms the light and creates the darkness, Who makes peace and creates woe, I, the Lord am doing all these" (Isaiah 45:6). There are no contradictions in God's being. Noting the terms Elohim and YHVH, found in the story of creation in Genesis, the rabbis have given their use a meaning quite different from that applied by biblical criticism. They say that in the beginning God decided to rule the world by strict justice (Elohim), but He realized that it could not exist when judged by the absolute standard of justice. He added the attribute of His compassion, prepared to permit mercy to mitigate justice—hence the two Names (YHVH Elohim). Ultimately, he found that even tempered justice was too much for humanity and world, and He based His rule entirely on mercy (YHVH). We find, therefore, that in the pronouncement of His attributes (Exodus 34:6–7) the term El, God of justice, is intimately linked to *Rahum*, a term derived from *Rehem*, the mother's womb. He is concerned with justice, but He is abundantly compassionate, sheltering His people in absolute loving security. In an attempt to understand some facets of God's Being, Rabbi Johanan says in Megillah 31a of the Talmud:

> Whenever you find the greatness of God expressed in Scripture, you equally find expressed His humility. Thus it is recorded in Torah, repeated in Nebeeim, and again, for the third time, in Ketubim. In Torah (Deuteronomy 10:17–18) we read: "For the Lord your God, He is God of gods, and Lord of lords, the great God, the mighty, and the awesome, who shows no favor and takes no bribe . . . but upholds the case of the fatherless and the widow." In Prophets (Isaiah 57:15) we read: "For thus says the High and Lofty One that inhabiteth eternity, whose Name is Holy: I dwell . . . with him that is of a contrite and humble spirit, to revive the spirit of the humble, and to revive the heart of the contrite ones." Repeated a third time in Ketubim (Psalm 68:5–6), it reads: "Extol Him that rideth upon the skies, whose name is the Lord," followed by, [He is] "a father of the fatherless, an advocate of the widows."

The Jew, recognizing the holiness and absoluteness of God, is confidently sure that God's power will be but the instrument of His mercy. This synthesis is expressed in the designation of God as "our Father." A father has power and dominion, which is exercised in behalf of his love. "Blessed art thou, O Israel," exclaims Akiba, "for He who cleanses you of all your sins, and before Whom you cleanse yourselves, it is your Father who is in heaven."

On the Days of Awe, the great prayer of petition (in which Jews ask for a year of health, sustenance, forgiveness of sins, and blessings) appeals to God as "Our Father, our King." Trusting in Him as "our Father," secure in His eternal love, their appeal is directed to Him as "our King," all-powerful to supply all needs.

As King, He must judge all humanity, for without justice the world could not endure; as Father, he waits for people and urges them to repent, and never ceases pleading with them to the moment of their death that they may return. And if they do repent, He will immediately receive them in affection as His beloved children. Even in judging, He is aware of human frailties and deals with humanity kindly, as the Father who has given life and knows the weaknesses of his children. Therefore, Jews have realized that divine love is never withdrawn from them in prosperity or in adversity; they praise Him even in moments of deepest sorrow and distress.

The patriarchs knew God as **Shaddai**. The etymology of the term is not clear. Some scholars of the school of biblical criticism explain the term as meaning God of the Mountains; Jews have given it a different etymological derivation.

Benno Jacob, a German rabbi and writer, holds that Shaddai stands for the God who goes with His people wherever they may be; the patriarchs, strangers in a land not yet their own, wandering abroad from time to time, found strength in this God-awareness. This Name of God is also affixed to the **Mezuzah**, designating Jewish homes throughout the world. This may have been the source of Jacob's interpretation. Maimonides explains the term as *Yesh* lo *day*—He was self-sufficient to create the world; he needs no other force and no assistance as Creator.

The term **Shekhinah** has been used to signify God's presence, His resting, dwelling among the people and in the world. "They shall make me a sanctuary and I shall dwell (*shakhanti*) in their midst" (Exodus 25:8), "I shall dwell in their midst forever" (Ezekiel 43:9), etc.

Jews have also applied to Him the term **Shalom**, meaning Absolute Perfection. (*Shalom* means peace, which is the sum of perfection.)

We shall deal further with the concept of God in discussing Jewish theology, and see, for instance, that Mordecai Kaplan does not conceive of God as a person. This is legitimate, since Judaism recognizes the inability of human beings to fathom God. To see God in terms other than *absolute* unity, or to hold that He assumed the form of man, is illegitimate in Judaism.

HUMANITY

Rabbi Akiba used to say, "Beloved is man, as he was created in the image [of God], and an even greater love was accorded him in being made aware that he is created in the image of God" (Abot 3:18). Thus he becomes God's co-worker, and all men are equal. The creation of but one man underscores this fact: No one can say that his ancestors were better than those of his neighbor (Sanhedrin 4:5). Created in the image of God, and endowed with a divine soul, human beings have worth and dignity beyond any other work of God's creation, even though they are a product of the earth, to which they must return, weak, frail, and insignificant. This dual character is expressed by the Psalmist:

> When I behold the heavens, the work of Your fingers, the moon and the stars which You have established; what is man that You are mindful of him, and the son of man that You take account of him? Yet You have made him but little lower than the angels, and have crowned him with glory and honor. You have made him to have dominion over the works of Your hands. . . . (Psalm 8:4–6)

Man thus is "son of man," but he is also "son of God" (Deuteronomy 14:1); the choice is his. Man bears the characteristics of his divinity and the characteristics of his animal character, the rabbis point out. Like any animal, he eats and drinks, excretes, multiplies, and dies. As a divine being, he stands erect, speaks, reasons, and sees straight. If he is worthy, he precedes the angels, is *higher* than the Psalmist thinks; if he is unworthy, every insect may remind him, "I was created before you and take precedence over you."

The first questions addressed to man as he appears before God in final judgment of his life are these:

> Have you dealt faithfully with your fellowman; have you appointed regular periods for [the study of] Torah [that it be a guide to conduct]; have you brought children into the world; have you looked forward to redemption . . . ? If the fear of God is his treasure, it will be well with him, otherwise not. (Shabbat 31a)

The work of human beings in the world—our striving for redemption, and our actions in behalf of God as we carry out our daily rounds—these assure our life of worth. Not in Mitzvot toward God, but in those toward our fellows do we primarily earn our salvation. This entails a decent love for one's own self. Of Hillel it is said that he considered the care of his body a Mitzvah. Judaism has never believed in the merits of asceticism and has even stated that people must account for the decent joys in life which God has placed in their way and which they declined (Jerushalmi Kiddushin 4). Joined to this self-respect must be humility. Moses was deigned worthy by God to receive the Torah because he was humble (Shabbat 67a).

These principles entail also an unconditional love of neighbors, even of enemies. We must help them and may not even bear any grudge against them (Exodus 23:4–5; Leviticus 19:17). We must consider the dignity of all and may never put anyone to shame. Only in secret may we give our support to the poor, lest they feel embarrassed. Charity in Hebrew is called **Tzedaka,** righteousness; it is simply right living that we support those with whom destiny has dealt harshly:

> Better than charity is the loan given to the needy, which helps set him up; better even a partnership with him, that allows him to draw on your experience as well as your resources. (Abot deRabbi Nathan 41:66a)

> Let the honor of your fellow man be as dear to you as your own; and let the property of your fellow man be as dear to you as your own. (Abot 2:15, 17)

This applies not only to Jews, but to all people, regardless of faith or race or color:

> I call heaven and earth to witness that on every person, be he Jew or non-Jew, man or woman, or servant, the divine spirit rests on him according to his deeds. The heathen is your neighbor, your brother, to do him wrong is a sin. (Tanna debe Eliyahu 207, 284)

The Jew, therefore, respects the right of all to find their way to God in their own fashion. Judaism did exclude the heathendom of old with its immoral practices, but solemnly declares that "the righteous among the peoples of the world will have a share in the world to come" (Yalkut Shimoni to Prophets 296). "The just among the peoples of the world are priests of God" (Eliyahu Sutah 20).

Judaism accords respect to all ethical faiths and, finding that they all lead to salvation, does not engage in missionary work. Nevertheless, Judaism would consider it unfair to deny to any person the right to join the faith and destiny of the Jewish people. If, in full conviction, a person feels that Judaism gives him true spiritual fulfillment, he has a right to find it. Having thus affiliated himself, the convert becomes a full-fledged member of the Jewish people, beloved by God and his newly found fellows in faith.

In Judaism, not one single soul is considered expendable. God is the Father, and every human being is a child of God upon whom the holy spirit rests. Only through sin may the holy spirit depart from us, as David found out. Invoked in grievous sin, he therefore cries out: "Do not take Your holy spirit from me" (Psalm 51:13). In return to God through repentance, we find this spirit restored to us.

Why People Sin

Every human being is endowed by God with a soul. This soul is given to us pure. Daily prayer affirms, "The soul which You, God, have given me is pure." Nevertheless we sin. Sin is the rejection or evasion of God's command. We sin when we transgress against those ordinances that relate us to God; we sin more grievously when we wrong our fellows. In the latter case, we both thwart God's will *and* hurt our neighbor. The human intent determines the severity of a sin: We may sin inadvertently, for such is the human condition that "there is no man who does not sin" (I Kings 8:46), or we may commit a sin deliberately.

There are various terms in Hebrew connoting sin: **Het**, which actually means missing the mark that Torah has established, or failing it. Error in judgment or lack of determination may be the causes. This term is used in the confession on Yom Kippur when sins against one's fellows are being repentantly admitted before God. **Aberah** means transgressing, stepping out of the boundaries God has set. Why do we sin? Why did God give human beings the capacity to sin? This has been a difficult question for the rabbis. God is all powerful; nevertheless, "all is in the hands of Heaven (God), except the fear of Heaven" (Berakhot 33b).

God placed the inclination to do evil into all of His creation, including human beings. It is called *Yetzer ha-Ra*, or simply **Yetzer**, the Drive: "The drive of man's heart is evil from his youth" (Genesis 8:21). This Yetzer *was already* in Adam and *prompted* him to transgress against God's command in the Garden of Eden. By his transgression, Adam brought death into the world. But no one dies on account of Adam's sin; he dies on account of his own. "Adam sinned and died, Elijah did not sin, therefore he did not die" (Pesikta 76a). The rabbis tell that God caused all future generations to state accusingly to Adam, "You have caused us death!" When Adam was deeply disturbed at being the cause of all death, God comforted him: "They do not die on account of your sin, but all on account of their own!" (Tanhuma, Bereshit 29).

It was stated that God was sorry He created the Yetzer; but the rabbis also said God saw it as very good (Bereshit Rabba 9:17). Without the Yetzer, understood, for instance, as the sex drive, there would be no procreation. Thus sex, within its rightful confines, becomes good. The Yetzer, a force released in us by outside temptation, can equally release in us the power of will to conquer it; doing so, we grow in our humanity. "Surely, if you do right, there is uplift. But if you do not right sin is the demon at the door, whose urge is toward you, but you can be his master" (Genesis 4:7). The power to do evil is a condition of our freedom to do good, and of our responsibility.

The tragedy in yielding to the Yetzer lies in the fact that one sin begets another "until it becomes permitted in [the sinner's] eyes" (Kiddushin 40a). With every act, the sinner unknowingly removes himself further and further from the grace of God and the fellowship with others.

Judaism holds that all sin *as* Adam sinned and not *because* Adam sinned. We are told in the Talmud that Adam's *physical* beauty was taken from him after his transgression (Bereshit Rabba 12:6), but his state of ethical awareness did not undergo any change; it resides in humanity as it did in the first progenitor. In this sense, there is no Original Sin.

We are armed in two ways against sin. One is **Teshuvah**, repentance, literally *return* to God's domain from which we have strayed. Better is the effort to avoid sinning. Torah is the way.

> Torah can be compared to a remedy; like a man who has hit his son and wounded him, and then gives him a tape for his wound, telling him: "My son, as long as the tape is on the wound you may eat, drink, bathe, and have no fear; but if you remove it, you will get infected." Even so God speaks: "My children, I have created the Yetzer ha-ra, but I have created Torah as its antidote; occupy yourselves with Torah and you will not fall into its hand . . . but if you do not occupy yourselves with Torah, you will be delivered into its hand. . . . (Kiddushin 30b)

SUPERNATURAL BEINGS

According to Jewish tradition, the work of human beings in the service of God can be aided or impeded by supernatural beings, specifically angels and satanic forces. Humanity's struggle will culminate and be resolved with the coming of the Messiah, who is not a supernatural being but is sent by God and filled with God's spirit. The individual's striving in life will find its reward in the World to Come.

We shall briefly discuss these forces that interact with human beings during their lifetimes, and the hope held out for the future that gives human beings direction.

Angels

Malakh (angel) simply means messenger. Whoever carries God's message in the world becomes His angel. Significantly, the messengers of God in the narrower sense of His Angels, are simply called "man." Three men (angels) appear to Abraham to predict, among other things, the birth of Isaac (Genesis 18). Samson's mother, to whom an angel predicts a son who will rescue his people, recognizes him simply as a man of God (Judges 13:2–6).

In time, angels came to be considered special creatures, serving as specific messengers of God, surrounding Him as a heavenly court (Isaiah 6), performing functions specifically entrusted to them by God Himself. The names given them are evidence of their functions: *Raphael*, God heals; *Uriel*, God is my light; *Michael*, Who is like God. It is an angel who relays God's message to Abraham, telling him not to sacrifice his son (Genesis 22:11ff.).

In later writings, the idea of guardian angels is developed. Michael is Israel's guardian angel, who will lead Israel in the conflict with the enemies of God in the battle at the end of days (Daniel 12).

The fact that Jewish thought recognizes angels should not obscure their minor position: To God alone prayer is offered and from Him alone help is expected. "For His angels will He put in charge over you to guard you . . . because he has set his love on Me, *I* will deliver him" (Psalm 91:11–14).

Satan

The concept of Satan entered Jewish beliefs from Persian thought. The Persian philosopher Zoroaster believed in a conflict between light and darkness, good and evil, which would continue throughout the ages, until, at the very end, God, the light of the world, would triumph over the forces of darkness and evil. God was surrounded by a heavenly host, the angels; His adversary, Satan, by his minions of evil.

This form of dualism came under attack. The second Isaiah makes it clear that God alone creates light and darkness, fashions peace as well as evil (Isaiah 45:7). Satan was demoted and became a kind of prosecuting attorney, as in the book of Job, where he levels his accusation against Job and is given the right to test him. From then on, he no longer appears in the book. It is God who settles the issue and determines Job's fate. Yet even as the accuser, doing his duty, Satan is rebuked. Has he no compassion with the remnant of Israel, "a brand plucked out of the fire?" (Zechariah 3:1ff.).

A belief in Satan and his power can be traced through Jewish history to the present. Fear of demonic forces led to widespread use of amulets among the common folk, especially in Eastern Europe. And it was thought that the gaze of another person could bring "the evil eye," especially upon children, and lead them to harm. Satan could disturb the worshipper's concentration or prevent the sounding of the shofar. Magical formulas were used to dispel him.

Thus recognized, Satan never did attain equal power with God. God could always repel him. In Conservative, Reform, and Reconstructionist Judaism, Satan plays no role. Even in those circles of Orthodox Jewry where the concept may still be held, it is affirmed that to God alone belongs the ultimate power. He alone, providentially watching over humanity as a whole and over every individual, is their merciful and living shield, protector, and guardian; He may chastise, but only in love, and He will redeem. Satan is also seen as personification of Yetzer, and then the accuser. God eventually will wipe him out.

The Messiah

Plagued by adversity, setbacks, and disappointments, subjected to tyranny, yet convinced that God, Master of History, would lead the world to redemption, the Jews came to envision the day when peace and fellowship would reign, when no further obstacles would prevent the full enjoyment of the Land and the wholehearted response to the divine call in Mitzvah. This was the day of the **Messiah**. As David once had been Israel's ideal king, so would his descendant establish a perfect society. Isaiah's utopia—the time when the lion and lamb would dwell together, and the "shoot of the trunk of Jesse" would rule in righteousness (Isaiah 11)—was transposed into the future as both goal and challenge. In the forecast of Malachi, this Messiah, God's anointed (*messiah* means anointed) would be preceded by Elijah, the prophet, who had never died but had gone bodily to heaven (II Kings 2:11–12). Elijah had been the foe of compromise, the champion of integrity; he would create the unity of love between the generations which would assure the coming of the messianic age (Malachi 3:23–24).

The *messianic age*, more than the person of the Messiah, has been Judaism's basic concern and longing. Its ideal has inspired Jews' dedication to social justice.

When will the Messiah come? "Today, if you will hearken to my voice," quote the rabbis (Psalm 95:7). Maimonides warns against any eschatological predictions. The times calculated for the end of days, Maimonides points out, will pass without fulfillment; the end is concealed, speculation regarding it prohibited by the rabbis. "For the vision is yet for the appointed time. . . . Though it tarry, wait for it; because it will surely come, it will not delay" (Habakkuk 2:3). Thus the messianic age is not a subject for calculations, but an eternal task and challenge to grow toward it. What will this end be? Again, Maimonides answers:

> The world will not change its accustomed order, but Israel will dwell secure, and mankind will find that true faith which will prevent them from making

war and carrying destruction. Israel will not become exalted over mankind, or wield power, but will be undisturbed to follow Torah, study it, perform its Mitzvot. No longer will there be war in the world; all mankind will enjoy peace and prosperity; and all will search for that wisdom which God alone can give. (Mishneh Torah XI, XII)

Orthodox Jews believe in a personal Messiah, a man who will actually arrive. Reform Jews, by contrast, see in the messianic age the symbol of a future in which all humanity will be united. The modern philosopher Hermann Cohen, as a liberal Jew, eliminates the belief in a personal Messiah yet considers the Messiah idea as the most powerful lever in history and Judaism's most significant contribution to the vision of the future. As Cohen puts it:

> The future, which the prophets have painted in the symbol of the Messiah, is the future of world history. It is the goal, it is the meaning of history. . . .
>
> It is humanity itself which has to bring about this age of the Messiah. Men and cultures must learn to think and hope for the ideal of human life, the ideal of individuals and nations, the future of the Messiah as something in the *future* of the human race. The realization of morality on earth, its tasks and its eternal goal, this, and nothing else is the meaning of the Messiah for us. . . .
>
> The Kingdom of the Messiah is the kingdom of God. Not a personal ruler is this Messiah, not a hero, but the spirit of God rests upon him and he brings justice to the peoples. . . . (*Jüdische Schriften* III, p. 173ff.) .

The significance of the messianic idea in Judaism can hardly be over-emphasized. It differs from the Christian idea, as it is directed to the future. It has sustained Jews in times of trials and inspired them to work for the kingdom of God on earth, not for themselves but for all humanity.

Resurrection

Many pious and devoted workers for the great consummation of history will die before the event happens. Should they not be rewarded? These considerations may have prompted the belief in resurrection. Daniel (12:2) mentions the awakening of those who sleep in the dust, some to their rewards, others to their punishment. The idea is not found in the Five Books of Moses, but the Pharisees believed so firmly in the resurrection that they interpreted the Song at the Red Sea (Exodus 15:1) to refer not only to the rescue which Israel had just felt but also to the future. "Then sang Moses and the children of Israel" can also be grammatically construed as, "Then will Moses . . . sing." According to rabbinic comment, this refers to the day of their resurrection.

But Jews have not been preoccupied in daily living with the question of resurrection. Reform Jews denied it at one time. As far as punishment is concerned, Jews, in the words of Hillel, maintain that God is altogether too merciful to impose eternal punishment for the temporary aberrations of weak human beings during their lifetime. He will be gracious to all humanity.

The World to Come

As Judaism firmly believes in the God-given soul, bestowed pure on every man and woman, it also maintains a firm faith in **Olam Haba**, the world to come. This is not the same as the time of the Messiah, or the resurrection. It is the sheltering of souls in God's eternal dwelling forever. There they will share the joys of their closeness to the divine Glory.

The Talmud warns against any particular formulation: "All the prophets have prophesied only regarding the days of the Messiah; concerning Olam Haba [it is stated]: 'No eye has seen it, O God, but Thine' (Isaiah 64:3)" (Berakhot 34b; Sanhedrin 99a). Judaism does not devote excessive thought to the question of the "salvation" of souls. "All of Israel will have a share in the world to come"; "All the righteous of the peoples of the world have a share in it."

While the idea of a temporary punishment or purgatory—the **Gehinnom**—can be found in Judaism, that of eternal damnation would run counter to the Jewish concept of an all-loving God. Gehinnom expiates the sins of humanity's temporary stay on earth, but sinners will find rest every Sabbath. "The punishment of the wicked in Gehinnom lasts for twelve months; for it has been written: 'It will be from month to [the same] month' [of the following year] (Isaiah 66:23)" (Mishnah Ediyot 2:10). Even Gehinnom is severely limited in time.

The task is here and now. Jews are to devote themselves to it and leave to God the ultimate determination of the future. "Rabbi Jacob used to say, 'This world is like an antechamber of the world to come; prepare yourself in the antechamber that you may enter into the chamber.' He also used to say, 'Better is one hour of repentance and of good deeds in this world than the whole life of the world to come; and better is one hour of bliss in the world to come than all of life in this world'" (Mishnah Abot IV: 21–22). Our great moments of giving of ourselves fully are experiences that surpass even the world to come, yet the anticipation of the world to come may lead us on in life.

SOME SYMBOLS

A symbol is a visible object or an act that conveys a message greater than itself. Every Mitzvah is, in a sense, a symbol. It stands for the presence of God to whom response is rendered, and it links every Jew to the community of Israel, past, present, and future. It speaks of Torah, upon which it is based, and reveals the sanctity of life. A few special symbols will be mentioned here.

The **menorah** is the seven-branched candelabrum which was once the lamp in the sanctuary (as ordained in Torah) and is now the coat of arms of the State of Israel. Zechariah sees a seven-branched menorah in a vision and is told, "Not by might, nor by power, but by My spirit" [will you prevail] (Zechariah 4:6). The seven branches reflect the seven directions of the universe, East,

West, North, South, Above, Below, and humanity's place itself. All of them are to be illuminated by the light of the holy spirit.

The windows in the Temple of old were so constructed that the light did not fall into its precincts from the outside, but was shed abroad from the menorah within. The menorah thus stands for the illumination that shall go forth from Zion. It represents Israel's function as a light to the nations; it envisions the day when all will walk in God's light; and it assures Jews that by the spirit of God they will prevail against the forces of adversity. (The Hanukkah menorah has nine branches and should be distinguished from the one in the ancient Temple. It will be explained in Chapter 20.)

The **Magen David**, Shield of David, is a six-pointed star. We do not know if David's shield actually had this form. As symbol, the Shield of David emerged later than the menorah. The synagogue in Capernaum, Israel (second century C.E.), features the menorah prominently and the Magen David only incidentally. It may have been a charm, repelling evil spirits, even as the five-pointed star was used in the Middle Ages. The explanation that Franz Rosenzweig offers holds a great deal of poetic meaning (see Chapter 15).

A yellow star had to be worn by the Jews under Nazi oppression so they would be easily recognizable and subject to derision and mob attack. The color of this star was yellow, after the yellow badge the Jews had to wear in some Islamic countries and later, during long periods of the Middle Ages, in Europe.

The Magen David has become the emblem on the flag of Israel. There, in the form of blue bars, it is superimposed on a white background with blue, horizontal stripes. The colors, white and blue, are derived from the colors of the Tzitzit, ordained in Torah, as will be explained in Chapter 20.

Wearing a head covering is a late symbol. For many centuries, the practice was fluid. It might signify the fact that "the glory of God resides above and I humbly cover myself before it," indicating the limitations of the human mind (Kiddushin 31a). Yet it may also stand as a symbol of Jewish self-respect and hope. Paul declared: "Every man praying or prophesying having his head covered, dishonoreth his head" (I Corinthians 11:4). At that time, in Jewish custom men might or might not cover their heads (Nedarim 30b). It might have hardened as a distinctive feature of Judaism as opposed to Christianity. The world forced a grotesque, horn-like hat upon the medieval Jew to symbolize his demonic character: The Jew, son of the devil, wore horns. But the Jew, never doubting the love of God and convinced of his redemption in the day of the Messiah, wore it proudly. First he wore it only during worship, then always. At the time, royal princes were distinguished at court by wearing head coverings in the presence of the king. Abused by the world, the Jew affirmed that he was a prince in God's sight and, like a prince, might let his head remain covered in the presence of the King of Kings. To the degree that degradation increased, the wearing of the hat became universal. As a symbol of self-respect, it was truly Mitzvah, enshrining God's presence, Torah, and commandments, and a permanent reminder of redemption.

The custom has had a deep emotional hold on Jews. Today, the head covering in the form of a skull cap has become recognized in the general society as the distinguishing mark of the Jew in worship. Reform Judaism has ruled that heads need no longer be covered in worship since times, symbols, and customs have changed. At one time, covering the head was prohibited in Reform synagogues. Reform Judaism was heatedly attacked for this ruling, however; so, it makes the wearing of a skullcap optional today. Over time, Jews, especially in non-Orthodox Judaism, have quietly discarded many laws of the Torah. But the head covering has remained; it is an expression of Jewish self-affirmation.

*Interior of Temple Emanu-El, San Francisco, California. Note the dominant position of the Ark, reached by steps on each side. Above it is the eternal light. The Ark is placed under a canopy, or **huppah**. Below on the platform is the reading desk of the cantor, flanked by two seven-branched candlesticks. (Photo by the author, courtesy of Congregation Emanu-El and Rabbi Joseph Asher.)*

15

THEOLOGICAL ISSUES

Theology is the systematic study of God, humanity, and the meaning of human existence under God. The Scripture deals with theological concepts. The Book of Job, for instance, asks: Why do the good have to suffer; how can a loving God permit it? The prophets spoke of God and what He demands of humanity, but theirs is no systematic theology. Fulfilling God's Mitzvot was "living theology." The Talmud points out: "[If there were a choice], better they forgot Me [says God] but kept my Mitzvot" (Jerushalmi, Hagiga 1:7). For in Mitzvot, He is made manifest. God and Mitzvah thus are linked inseparably as call and response. Halakhah is living theology. Those who respond cannot forget the Caller.

Jewish theology derives from Written and Oral Torah, but throughout much of their history the Jews did not engage in systematic theology, which emerges from the confrontation between various philosophies that may create doubt in the mind of the faithful or from events that demand an explanation of God's actions. In the following section, we shall consider a few Jewish philosophers and theologians who have left a lasting impact on the shaping of the Jewish mind. Our treatment of Jewish theology will become more extended as we reach the present, culminating with the Holocaust theologians.

SOME EARLY THEOLOGIANS AND PHILOSOPHERS

Philo of Alexandria, a deeply religious Jew and leader of the Jewish community of Alexandria, Egypt, lived in the first century B.C.E. He deserves our attention here although his contribution to Jewish theology has not been significant. His work reveals the relationship between Christian theology and Jewish thought. We shall mention three elements of Philo's thought.

First, Philo had to come to grips with Hellenistic thought. Just as Greek thinkers interpreted Homer's great poems, the *Iliad* and the *Odyssey*, symbolically in order to make them meaningful for their own time, so Philo did for Torah. By so doing, he may have succeeded in keeping some of his contemporaries faithful to the Jewish faith.

Second, Philo's concept of the *Logos* came to have fundamental significance in Christian thought. Philo held that God fashioned an intermediary, the *Logos* or *Word*, in creating the universe. This Logos shaped the world to spare God contact with its finite inadequateness. Philo does not explain clearly whether this Logos was of God, or a divine creation, or both. His idea is reflected in the first verses of the Gospel of John: "In the beginning was the Logos, and the Logos was with God and the Logos was God. He was in the beginning with God. All things were made through him . . ." (John 1:1 ff.). This formulation came to be basic for Christian theological understanding of the triune God. (Some similarities to Philo's thought can be found in Jewish mystical writings.)

Third, Philo determined the character of all medieval philosophy: Jewish, Christian, and Islamic. For the Greek, philosophy was the exercise of the independent human mind, which was free to follow its own direction to whatever the conclusions might be. Philo established philosophy as the handmaiden of revelation; that is, he made it subject to the truth made manifest by revelation and limited by it. This was of fundamental significance for the future development of philosophy.

Another Jewish philosopher, *Benedict* (Barukh) *Spinoza* (1632–1677), severed the link between religious revelation and philosophy. He restored the latter's independence, seeing in it a critical evaluator of sacred scriptures and the truths proclaimed in them. As he severed the bond, Spinoza was read out of Judaism and, most likely, approved of this breaking of ties. Spinoza's pantheism "deus sive natura," God and nature are one, may rest on the Jewish concept of God's absolute unity, although he denies the existence of a freely creating, transcendent God.

Saadia (882–942 C.E.) claimed Judaism as religion of reason. Nothing in Torah is beyond reason. Whereas Christianity's great theologian St. Thomas Aquinas held that some of the divinely revealed truths will forever remain beyond human understanding, Saadia posited that even divinely revealed truth is entirely based on reason. God merely revealed it in advance, in order that Jews might live by divine truth while still searching for its understanding. He compared the Jews to children, whom the teacher gives the answer to a problem in order that they may apply it in daily life while trying to reason it out for themselves. Mainstream Judaism has emphasized its character as a religion of reason.

Judah Halevi (1080–1140) stressed the singularity and uniqueness of the Jewish people, chosen by God from all the peoples of the world. In each generation from Adam to Jacob God picked one person, endowed with the most perfect soul and highest intellect, and this special gift descended on all of Jacob's progeny, the entire Jewish people. They were therefore given God's chosen Land on earth and were granted the abundance of Mitzvot by which they are to live. But this special election does not make them masters; it makes them servants of humanity.

Halevi saw Israel as "the heart of humanity," and the first organ to be afflicted by the disorders in the body. Whenever Israel is afflicted, it is a symptom of disease in the entire organism of humanity. Jews as a whole have not accepted this almost biological concept of hereditary election, but they have learned from Halevi to regard themselves as the "barometer" of human conditions: Throughout the ages, persecution of Jews revealed deep-seated ills in society.

Another point emerges from Halevi's thoughts: The Jewish people is unique and so is its contribution to the world given in unique fashion. But the world, from early times to the present, has judged and evaluated the Jews by the world's standards and concepts not by Jewish self-perception. Jews are "good" in term of meeting the expectations of the non-Jewish world. Halevi held that Jews must be seen and judged by what they are themselves. Being themselves, they can in their unique way serve as humanity's heart.

Moses Maimonides (1135–1204) was both codifier of Jewish law and philosopher. After his death, serious arguments arose as to whether he had truly fused both, or whether he was simply Aristotelian as philosophical thinker. At times, his *Guide for the Perplexed* was banned. To Maimonides, the study of philosophy was a *duty*, the highest rung on the ascent to God.

Maimonides, in what has been called *negative theology*, maintained that, although we know *that* God exists, we shall never know *what* He is. His Oneness surpasses any human concept of oneness. When we speak of one thing, we nevertheless can conceive that two of the same kind may be possible or that the one thing, let us say a body, is composed of parts. None of this can be held of God. When the Bible uses anthropomorphisms, such as the hand of God or the voice of God, it merely speaks of the effect God had on human beings, as if His guiding hand had led them or His voice spoken. Human limitations are absolute.

Torah, Maimonides held, was given us by God to develop our intellect and to improve human relations through law. When human intellect finds its limits, Torah provides answers. The world cannot have existed for all eternity, as Aristotle held, for the laws of nature and time itself had to be created by God. They offer no proof regarding beginnings. Recognizing our limitations, we must follow holy traditions: God created the world and the time in which it unfolds. Why He did so and why He chose a certain moment is beyond our capacity to understand.

On the other hand, Maimonides held that many of the miracles reported in Scripture were ordinary events that were simply seen as miracles by the people. Others were ordained from the beginning of creation as part of the world's course; they were not introduced as a divine "afterthought." The sacrificial cult was God's concession to Israel; He permitted it in *one* place, the Temple, in order not to deprive the people of a form of worship practiced by all other peoples. The true worship is prayer, which can be offered everywhere. Since we cannot know God's reasons, we must recognize His will in the emergence of Christianity and Islam, through which humanity was lifted from paganism to monotheism and from which it will advance further.

The Ashkenasic masters of Judaism rejected philosophical pursuits for hundreds of years. Not until the period of the Emancipation did it recur in any significant degree.

Moses Mendelssohn (1729–1786) showed boldness similar to that of Maimonides. Judaism was divinely ordained *law*; the mind was otherwise free to speculate.

Samson Raphael Hirsch (1808–1888), founder of Neo-Orthodoxy, though close in spirit to Maimonides, criticized him strongly for living in two worlds. Worldly knowledge must always be subservient to the Word of Torah. But in denying Maimonides, Hirsch reveals the master's impact on him and, through him, on Neo-Orthodoxy.

TWENTIETH-CENTURY THEOLOGY AND PHILOSOPHY

In the twentieth century, the situation of Western Jews was similar to that in Spain in the Middle Ages. Western thought and life attracted and permeated Judaism.

Herman Cohen (1842–1918)

Cohen was a Kantian, founder of the Neo-Kantian school at Marburg. His work *Religion of Reason from the Sources of Judaism* reveals by its title that he affirmed the rational character of Judaism. To Kant, God was unknowable, "thing-in-itself" due to the structural limitations of the human mind. To Cohen, God was equally forever removed from our grasp. But, as a stone thrown into a pond forms ever wider circles in the water, so does every partial knowledge of God lead us toward new knowledge of Him, endlessly.

Can we prove the idea of God as *One* God? It is manifest in the fact that nature and moral conduct are keyed to each other. They must therefore have *one* single source. According to Cohen, we must strive for a world where perfect moral action corresponds to the perfection of nature. This is contained in the concept of the Messiah—the symbol of the future for which we must ever strive and which we shall never reach; the ideal of humanity and society perfectly attuned to nature. Today we can recognize how true this is, as through ethical acts we preserve nature, and, as we act upon it, nature reacts and allows us to exist.

While ethics is a road toward this future, religion holds a higher place, for religion evokes the spirit of compassion. Compassion is the hallmark of religion. Jews and Judaism are necessary for the world. Mitzvot, in response to God, create an everlasting attunement. Being a small minority in the world, Jews offer humanity an opportunity to show compassion with the weak and numerically small in its midst. Jews are humanity's challenge to be religious by being compassionate and to be human by striving for the messianic future.

Herman Cohen reflected the thinking of German Jewry—and its grievous error. Committed to reason, he believed that reason would guide people and that Germany, a nation of thinkers, might lead the movement. He was to be disappointed in his own life, and German Jewry was to suffer greatly for its error. Sigmund Freud was closer to the mark when he posited that human beings are motivated not by reason but by subterranean irrational passions. Such passions were to sweep German and European Jewry away. Cohen's philosophy reflects the noble "weakness" of German Jewry.

Franz Rosenzweig (1886–1929)

Cohen's disciple, Rosenzweig has remained one of the most significant influences on contemporary Jewish theology. He was influenced by Hegel, from whom he had learned that history is in a constant process of unfolding, the unfolding of the Absolute. Rosenzweig concluded that humanity is moving toward God. Christianity is entrusted with the task of bringing humanity to God. But how can Christianity be certain that its efforts will bring humanity to God? Perhaps God cannot be reached at all. To show humanity that it can come to God, the Jewish people exist. They have come to God, are already with Him. Therefore, the rest of the world can come to Him also.

Rosenzweig thus sees Judaism and Christianity as complementary. Judaism has come to God, thereby proving that human beings can reach Him and find shelter in Him. This knowledge is to inspire Christianity to engage in the arduous task of bringing the rest of mankind to God, where Judaism already dwells. Rosenzweig finds a source for this interpretation in the verse: "No one comes to the Father, except through me [the Son]" (John 14:6). He explains: no one comes to God except through Christ, the Son. This provides the challenge for Christians to bring the rest of humanity to God through Christianity. But then Rosenzweig continues stating, "no one comes," but he who is already with the Father, namely the Jews, need no longer come. This means the Jews do not need Christ, as their pilgrimage to God has already been completed. Rosenzweig maintained that Christianity must move forward leading the world, but Judaism must rest inactive, showing the goal and the possibility of reaching it. The two religions, divinely created, depend on each other. Here, for the first time, we find a Jewish thinker speaking of the *necessity* for Christianity to exist and do its missionary work. Rosenzweig could not foresee that Judaism was to emerge once again from its isolation outside history and return into history, especially with the emergence of the State of Israel.

To Rosenzweig, Judaism remains in itself, its life revolving around its inner core of Mitzvot. It is with God. Out of this concept Rosenzweig developed a significant interpretation of the Jewish star in his work *Star of Redemption*. The elements of the universe are *God* at the apex, and *world* and *man* at the base of a triangle; world and man are facing each other. The dynamic forces resulting in evolution are *creation* (God fashions the world), *revelation* (God teaches man his task), and *redemption* (man as steward of the world under God's command brings about the unity of all). This process, taking shape among the peoples of the world, is completed in Judaism. Thus we have the Star of Redemption.

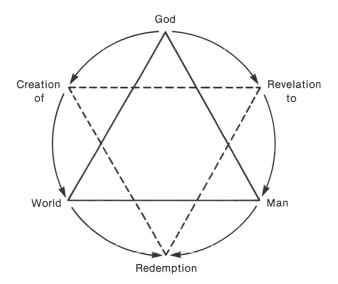

Rosenzweig's greatest impact on contemporary non-Orthodox Jewry rests on his own life. He found in hard thinking the road from the periphery of Jewish life to its core through the performance of Mitzvot. He did not observe any Mitzvah, he did not understand, but strove to understand it, in order to observe it. This distinguishes him from Orthodoxy, for whom the fulfillment of Mitzvot in their entirety is mandatory. Asked whether he was performing a certain Mitzvah, he replied "not yet." This "not-yet" has guided many Jews and brought about a return to the practice of Mitzvot in large segments of liberal Jewry. It has particularly influenced the direction taken by Reform Judaism toward greater, more meaningful traditionalism.

Martin Buber (1878-1965)

Buber has influenced Christian thought as much as Jewish thought. In his fundamental work, *I and Thou*, he explained that I can relate to my fellow man as an It—using him as my tool—or as a Thou—a subject, equal to me, influencing me, engaging me in dialogue in which both he and I will grow. This same dialogue must go on between man and God. Studying theology makes God an It. Theology will not lead to a live commitment to God. I must listen to whatever God has to say to me. He will tell me at every moment, how He wishes me to relate in *action dialogue* to my fellow man. As I act in true I and Thou fashion toward my neighbor, I am in dialogue with God as well. Why do I need God? As God has revealed that every human being is to Him a Thou, he has taught me that every human being is equal to me, as he is equal before God. The most direct way to God, therefore, leads through society.

Buber regarded Judaism as a necessary paradigm of the I and Thou spirit in the world. To be able to fulfill this task, Israel must dwell on its own land—Israel—forming its own society, dedicated to the vision of the future. Paradoxically, Buber saw in the fulfillment of Mitzvot—in fact, of all ritual—a wall of separation between God and man; the dialogue was no longer immediate. While Buber's basic concept of I and Thou, his Zionism, and his search for peace between Arab and Jew have deeply influenced modern Jewish thought, his denial of Mitzvot has been hard for Jews to understand. As we saw earlier, Buber was deeply influenced by Hasidism. Ernst Simon, an outstanding thinker, educator, and deeply observant Jew, and Buber's colleague and dedicated disciple for many decades, has permitted us a glimpse at Buber's motivations:

> I told him [Buber] of my personal experience with the Jewish form of life. In spite of the objective danger of its ossification and the subjective danger of compulsion neuroses, it had yet become for me a daily opportunity to serve God, in which I placed my confidence. "Exactly this confidence is what I lack," was Buber's reply. At that we have then left it. (*Entscheidung zum Judentum*; Frankfurt am Main: Suhrkamp Verlag, 1980, pp.154–155; my translation)

Leo Baeck (1873–1956)

A heroic leader of German Jewry during the Holocaust, Baeck rests his thought on that of Cohen, Buber, and Rosenzweig. His emphasis is the Covenant: God made a Covenant with nature, with man, with Israel. The Bible is the Book of the Covenant. Noah is under the Covenant, and with him mankind (Genesis 9:9–13); Abraham is under the Covenant (Genesis 17:1–11); the Covenant with Israel is established at Sinai (Exodus 31:16–17) and repeated throughout Scripture. Nature, subjected to natural law, is compelled to follow the Covenant. Man is brought under the Covenant by the command given him by God: You shall, you shall not. But man is free to abide by the Covenant or to reject it. God therefore saw the need of creating a people that would serve as an example to humanity. Mysterious in His Being and actions, He created the Jewish people, which is to find the reason for its existence in living under the Covenant. Jews are "*this people* which I formed for Myself that they might tell of My praise" (Isaiah 43:21). Jewish history reflects Jewish striving toward fulfillment of this special mission, its backsliding, and its return to its task. By its character and function, it is often at odds with a self-centered society and therefore subjected to derision and persecution. But the Jewish people must live. Set apart, Israel serves humanity. *Faith* for the Jew means the decision of will and deed to respond to God's command.

The awareness of **B'rit**—the covenantal character of Judaism—has thus been given a central position in current Jewish thought.

Abraham Heschel (1907–1972)

Heschel was a Jewish thinker who also found widespread response among Christian theologians. A master of the English language, Heschel goes back to his own experiences in the unhappily lost environment of the Jewish communities of Eastern Europe. Life in Torah and Mitzvot filled the Jews of Eastern Europe with an awareness of God. Their heart and emotions provided the answers to their quest for God; life was response to God's call. The whole world was filled with God's glory, testifying to Him; Torah revealed Him in its sacred pages; and Mitzvot made Him manifest in life. Heschel therefore sees three trails that lead to God: We must sensitize ourselves to God's presence in the *world*, in things; feel His presence in the *Bible*; experience His presence in sacred *deeds*. Heschel analyzes these phenomena, deals with the essence of the prophets' consciousness of God, shows the meaning of the Sabbath as an experience, and arrives at the conclusion that the function of Judaism is to sanctify *time*, while that of the world is to penetrate *space*.

In moving language, Heschel wishes to guide Jewry toward an actual experience of Judaism as he knew it in his childhood. The living God is not found in philosophical analysis. Ultimately, Jews will have to take the leap to God in performance of Mitzvot, for these are the response to a God who calls them. The insights gained from sensing God in nature, Scripture, prayer, and deeds are not granted to Jews alone; they must serve as directives for all peoples and for all times. Then the living God who speaks out of the Bible and speaks today, to whom all shall respond, can show us the way in our troubled world and give us, as His children, true human dignity. Yet Heschel held out a challenge to Jewry. While fully remaining in touch with the whole of Western civilization, Jews are to evolve their way of life out of their own inner forces. At the same time, Heschel was extremely active in movements of social justice and in interfaith dialogues. Christians as well as Jews have acknowledged him as their teacher and spokesman.

Mordecai Kaplan (born 1881)

Mordecai Kaplan's thinking has influenced all of non-Orthodox Jewry. His school has developed into a full-fledged Jewish "denomination," with its own rabbinical college and its congregations: Reconstructionism.

Kaplan sees the Jews as a people not in any way chosen but simply imbued with the will to live and to contribute to the welfare of humanity. Judaism is not simply a religion, but an "evolving religious civilization." This civilization enhances the lives of its followers, making them more meaningful. It is religion, for it is impossible to remove religion from it as religion is expressed in every one of its facets. It is civilization, for it expresses itself in a totality of forms—in language, literature, art, music, even cuisine. It never stands still but evolves to make a contribution toward the individual's and society's salvation, not in a world to come, but here and now.

Kaplan has been influenced by American Pragmatism. He has equally acknowledged the influence of the French sociologist Emile Durkheim (1858–1917) upon his thought. But Kaplan himself is an original thinker who has endlessly refined his ideas. He has brought about a "galilean revolution" in placing the root of the Jewish God concept in the Jewish people, rather than seeing the people as constituted by God.

In *The Elementary Forms of the Religious Life*, Durkheim defines religion as

> a unified system of beliefs and practices relative to sacred things which unite into one . . . single, moral community . . . all those who adhere to them. . . . Before all, it is a system of ideas with which the individuals represent to themselves the society of which they are members and the obscure but intimate relations they have with it . . . for it is an eternal truth that outside of us there exists something greater than us, with which we enter into communion. (New York: Free Press, 1965, p. 62, p. 257)

A society is therefore more than the sum of its individual members, more than the soil upon which it lives. It exists by the *spirit* which it has created and which it fosters. Every member of society partakes of this spirit and, in turn, shapes it. This spirit emerges from the *collective* ideals of a given society and the *values* it holds. These pull the members of society toward higher ideals. Pursuing values, the members transcend themselves and society evolves. Kaplan accepts these principles and points out that values come into being as a result of an organic society that is closely united. Values are not facts, but they are factors. The value of a dollar, in the economic realm, is based on the agreement of the American society that a piece of paper (in itself without value) can be exchanged for a certain amount of goods and services. The value of the currency is based on societal agreement on the means of meeting its economic needs. This value has been established as a result of society's experience.

By partaking of the spirit of society, the individual achieves self-transcendence. The spirit of the Jewish people discovered behind nature a force that brings about harmony in the universe. This force is God. God is not identical with nature (Kaplan rejects pantheism); He is transnatural. He shapes nature's balance. In the human realm, Israel, out of its own spirit, made another discovery: the God creating harmony among people and nations, the God of ethics. This God, YHVH, became the people's challenge, calling for ethical nationhood. The essence of Judaism is the striving for ethical nationhood. We cannot say, therefore, that God created the people; rather, we must say that the people, out of its collective spirit, discovered God. God then becomes a force that exerts a constant pull. Kaplan points out that we have to distinguish between that which *is*, that which *ought* to be, and the *means* that bring the ought to fruition. We all have *reason*; it reveals to us what the world is like. We ought to have *wisdom* to lead a life of meaning. The instrument that leads us from reason to wisdom is *intelligence*. Wisdom, hokhmah, enabled the Jewish people to discover God. The eternal law of nature and of humanity was understood by Jews as B'rit, as Covenant. The striving for self-transcendence was expressed by Jews as striving for holiness. "You shall be holy [transcend yourselves], for I, the Lord your God am holy [transnatural]" (Leviticus 19:2).

How is the collective spirit of a people created and maintained? It is done by common history and heroes, common teachings and laws, common celebrations and observances. These Kaplan calls *sancta*, holy symbols. The Mitzvot are sancta. For Jews as Americans, the flag is also sanctum, as are national holidays. If a Mitzvah loses its character as a sanctum, it can be discarded; new sancta may equally emerge out of the people's spirit. The Jews therefore find fulfillment within the confines of an organic Jewish people. As Americans, they have to immerse themselves in the civilization of America as well; they live in two civilizations that must mutually influence and strengthen each other.

The Jews must strive to promote ethics in human society. The Jewish concept of salvation, as Kaplan sees it, is not a salvation in a hereafter, but a "salvation" of society here. Thus the Sabbath is a sanctum, bringing to mind the duty of every Jew to fight for the human rights of everyone, such as the right to rest from work and the opportunity for recreation. The State of Israel and its people can collectively promote the ideal of ethical nationhood. Israel is therefore important; it is central. From Israel insights go out to the Diaspora, and from the Diaspora similar insights go out toward Israel. It is a two-way street.

The Jewish people is not a chosen people, but a people like others, with an individual insight, just as others have individual insights. The Jewish people makes a contribution to the world. Jewish religion then emerges from the totality of Jewish civilization. Judaism is an *evolving religious civilization*. Jews who in some manner identify with this civilization, regardless of denomination or even secular outlook, are to be regarded as living a legitimately Jewish life: they contribute to the civilization.

Scripture is never completed; every generation adds to it out of the total experience of the Jewish people and enlarges it. With the elimination of its literal meaning, it has to be demythologized. Prayer is to call forth the power within worshippers to recognize ultimate values, and to release within themselves the power of self-transcendence, the divine that leads them from the *is* to the *ought*, the humanization of people through ethics.

16

ATTEMPTS AT HOLOCAUST THEOLOGY

Holocaust theology is a difficult undertaking. Theology tries to interpret God's ways by means of human reason. The Holocaust is so unique in human history that any endeavor to explain God's "reasons" must fail. Therefore, any attempts must be seen as tentative. Such attempts can truly be made only by Jews, trying to understand the event from their inner perception of God. Yet all dialogue with other religions must rest on the fact that it takes place over the graves of six million murdered Jews and in the recognition of the State of Israel as a theological fact. In this spirit, a new generation of Jewish theologians has tried to come to grips with the events in Jewish history, both shattering and reviving. They have followed in the footsteps of the **existentialism** of Buber, Rosenzweig, and Baeck, or the naturalism of Kaplan.

Emil Fackenheim

Fackenheim was born in Halle, Germany, in 1916. He received his rabbinical education and ordination at the liberal Hochschule für die Wissenschaft des Judentums at Berlin. In 1938, he was confined to the Nazi concentration camp at Sachsenhausen. After his release, he studied in England and Canada; for many years he has been professor of philosophy at the University of Toronto. Among his Jewish works are *In Quest of Past and Future, Encounter between Judaism and Modern Philosophy, God's Presence in History,* and *Jewish Return into History.*

Auschwitz, he points out, has shaken Jewish existence to the core. The believing Jew has been confronted by the question, has God abrogated His Covenant with Israel? The unbelieving Jew cannot but ask, has liberalism failed? Seeing man as the measure of all things, liberalism started out as a benevolent humanism and ended up by making one man, Hitler, the measure of all things. Will the Secular City lead in the same direction, since it does not demand that humanity account to a transcendent God for its actions? Perhaps God is dead, asks the questioner, and religion only an emotion? In response, *the emergence of Israel gives evidence of the Jews' unparalleled will to live* in the face of the most concerted effort ever made in history to exterminate them. Does the victory of this will point to a God who sustained it and brought it to fruition?

Reason offers no answer to these questions. But existentially they must be answered—for the sake of the Jews who must retain their balance and for the sake of humanity. The answer can only be an existential affirmation of God. He is not dead, although He may have gone into eclipse, may have hidden Himself.

The existential affirmation of God rests on several existential needs. *Were the Jews to deny God, they would be giving Hitler a posthumous victory.* This may not be. The world as a whole cannot expect to find its way without God either. Self-transcendence is not enough, since no person or society can truly go beyond that which it is. Jews and all peoples must once again consider themselves accountable to a transcendent God of justice. Such an affirmation does not resolve the perplexity of the Jews who have to face up to the two soul-shaking events that took place within one decade, and to their juxtaposition. But they are stabilized in the knowledge that the living God has willed them, even though His thoughts are incomprehensible. As God lives, the events created by Him have meaning. With the affirmation of the living God for existential reasons goes obedience. God has spoken and speaks, demanding response and obedience. Jews must subject themselves once again to Mitzvah. The body of Mitzvot should be seen not as law but as command. Law is an impersonal force, but command, Mitzvah, points to a *Metzaveh*, a commander. It creates the relationship between the person who issues the command and the person who obeys it. This is the position of Franz Rosenzweig. The Jews are called to be a witness of the living God. Their will to live in the face of Auschwitz, resulting in the rebirth of Israel, testifies already to their trust in God. But Jews must exhibit it consciously. They must inject the living God into the Secular City; they must be a witness. Otherwise this City, humanity, may lose itself again in nihilism.

The talmudic rabbis enumerated 613 commandments binding on the Jews. Fackenheim postulates a 614th: survival.

> Because after the Nazi celebration of death life has acquired a new dimension of sanctity. . . . Because insanity had ruled the kingdom of darkness, hence sanity, once a gift, has now become a holy commandment. Why hold fast to mere Jewishness? Because Jewish survival after Auschwitz is not "mere" but in itself and without any further reasons or theological justifications a sacred testimony to all mankind that life and love, not death and hate, shall prevail.

Why did the surviving Jews seek the danger of the State of Israel, rather than live in peaceful forgetfulness in other parts of the world? Because

> the state of Israel is a collective testimony against the groundless hate which has erupted in this century in the heart of Europe. Its watchword is: Am Yisrael Chai—"the people Israel lives" (*The Jewish Return into History*; New York: Schocken, 1978, pp. 96–97).

American Jews in particular face contradictions. Narrowly removed from Auschwitz, they enjoy great freedom. They see many of their fellows subjected to persecution and suffering, and they live in a world in which the exaltation of human autonomy has brought about both human betterment and deepest human suffering. The Jews have to live with these contradictions; they have to live *in* the world and *for* the world. They may not despair of it. On account of what has happened to them, they must open the quest of Jeremiah and Job. But while asking "why," they may despair neither of God nor of the world. Out of their existential confrontation with the living God, the Jews must rather do their share, as Jews, witnesses and workers, to bring about humanity's renewal. The world must come to a direct confrontation with God, recognizing Him in action. The Jews aware of the encounter, must once again see Sinai as a real meeting point of God and humanity and accept its imperative, the commitment to the Covenant.

Fackenheim's thoughts have been seconded by a number of his colleagues in the liberal rabbinate, such as Eugene Borowitz and others who have contributed to the swing toward Mitzvot and Halakhah evident in Reform Judaism.

Richard L. Rubenstein

Rubenstein had to find his way painfully. He came from a home where Jewish tradition was deliberately belittled. After studying at the Jewish Theological Seminary at New York, where he was a disciple of Mordecai M. Kaplan, he served as rabbi in Hillel Foundations, the Jewish student foundations at universities. He now teaches Judaism at Florida State University, Tallahassee.

As the title of his work, *After Auschwitz* (Indianapolis: Bobbs-Merrill, 1966), indicates, he too sees in Auschwitz, and also in the restoration of Israel, the key elements of Jewish destiny in our time. Believing, with Mordecai Kaplan, that the Jewish God concept is the result of the collective Jewish people's consciousness, he arrives at conclusions completely at variance with Kaplan's optimism. The Jewish God was the God of history, and the Jewish people were placed in the world to promote its progress toward an ethical future. This had been normative belief for over two thousand years. Auschwitz proved, however, that the concept was an error and the experiment of improving human ethics a failure. Jews should therefore realize, according to Rubenstein, that with the restoration of Israel the end of their historical function has been reached; it is "realized eschatology." Humanity cannot be improved: The lesson of Auschwitz is that it remains savage. Israel therefore abandons its self-assumed missionary task and returns from a religion of history to a religion of nature. Peasants live by the cycle of the year, as nature provides it; their view of life is cyclical. This is "paganism," in contrast to traditional Judaism and Christianity, which live by the time-line of history. Jews must return to this archaic paganism; as a matter of fact, they have already done so in Israel, where the festivals of Judaism are observed with new forms—

namely, as festivals of sacred moments throughout the seasons of the year. The Jews, like the pagans of old, are to follow the cycle of the year from spring through summer, fall and winter, then start over again. The Jewish people steps out of history: "The straight line of Jewish history has become the circle of eternal return" (p. 142). Israel has come home, and the joy at the Western Wall, the last remnant of the Temple, was the joy of homecoming after nineteen hundred years of Diaspora.

But turning from the God of history to the God of nature does not entail the elimination of traditional ritual; it actually reinforces it. In traditional ritual, the archaic and mythic elements of Judaism are contained, and in their observance the link with the ancient past of the people is forged. "The European catastrophe marks the death of the God of History . . . an insightful paganism, utilizing the forms of traditional Jewish religion, is the only meaningful religious option remaining to Jews after Auschwitz and the rebirth of Israel" (p. 130).

By "insightful paganism," Rubenstein does not call for a return to pagan gods and goddesses but rather seems to call for recognition of some pagan insights. He states:

> In the religion of history, only man and God are alive. Nature is dead and serves only as the material of tool-making man's obsessive projects. . . . In the religion of nature, a historical, cyclical religion, man is once more at home with nature and its divinities, sharing their life, their limits, and their joys (p.136).

Perhaps Rubenstein thinks of *deus sive natura*, God as nature, in ways that are reminiscent of Spinoza. He can therefore maintain that the Jews must accept nature and the world without illusions, knowing that, being of the earth, they will return to it and must be true to it. People cannot hope for survival; birth and death are the boundaries of their existence. With the God of history, all messianic hope, even that of seeing in the Messiah simply the symbol of a humanity at peace, has to be given up. Only death releases people from toil and trouble—only death is the "Messiah."

In a later work, *The Cunning of History*, Rubenstein assesses history and the future of humanity in the light of the Holocaust. Throughout the ages, people always found ways to exterminate the unwanted masses. The Nazi brought to this process of population control a hitherto unknown efficiency, and, above all, a wholly detached and highly effective bureaucracy. It is horrifying to contemplate what may be done in the future to get rid of the undesired and superfluous. Having learned the methods of the Nazi, people can improve on them by use of computers.

It is fallacious to assume that civilization spells growth of rationality and of humanitarian spirit. Civilization is an organic process of unfolding, in which reason, beauty, love, and compassion on the one hand, and cruelty, destructiveness, and savagery on the other are necessarily found—the thesis and antithesis in the unfolding of civilization.

Judeo–Christian tradition holds no assurances either. In fact, this very tradition may be implicated in the events. Judeo–Christian tradition established the division between the elect, who will have life, and the damned, who deserve to be exterminated. The Nazi simply carried these theological ideas into the secular world and created the caricature of the biblical idea of the "chosen people," proclaiming themselves as *Herrenvolk*, the master race. They alone had the right and duty to survive, which meant extermination of the "damned."

The tenor and impact of Rubenstein's book is deeply pessimistic; the Holocaust has left its mark on him.

Elie Wiesel (born 1928)

Taken shortly after his Bar Mitzvah from his hometown, Sighet, in Transylvania, Elie Wiesel endured the years until liberation in various Nazi concentration camps. After liberation, he became a writer and journalist in Paris. He subsequently came to the United States, where he serves as professor of humanities at Boston University. Recently he was appointed chairman of the President's Commission on the Holocaust. His numerous books, which give us a panorama of the Holocaust, are regarded as "midrashic"—trying to convey the deeper meaning of the event.

For instance, he writes of the hanging of a young boy and two adults by the Nazis in Auschwitz, to which the entire prisoner population had been summoned.

> All eyes were on the child. He was lividly pale, almost calm, biting his lips. . . . The three victims mounted together on the chairs. The three necks were placed at the same moment within the nooses. "Long live liberty" cried the two adults. But the child was silent. "Where is God? Where is He?", someone behind me asked. At a sign from the head of the camp, the three chairs tipped over. . . . I heard a voice within me answer . . .: "Where is He? He is hanging on this gallows. . . ." (*Night*, New York: Avon Books, 1972, pp. 75ff.)

Later, Wiesel was to say to François Mauriac: "I knew Jewish children every one of whom suffered a thousand times more, six million times more, than Christ on the cross. And we don't speak about them . . . " (*A Jew Today*, New York: Vintage Books, 1979, p. 22).

Wiesel has stated: "Holocaust literature there cannot be. Auschwitz negates all literature as it negates all theories and doctrines; to lock it into philosophy means to restrict it. . . . The concept of a theology of Auschwitz is blasphemous for both the non–believer and the believer . . . " (*A Jew Today* p. 234). Yet the memory of Auschwitz must be kept alive for humanity's sake. Judaism must be alive—the Jewish people must live, and Israel must live. The theological contradictions are unsurmountable. But life holds the answer. As the epigraph of his book *A Jew Today*, Wiesel uses something he was told by a wise man in 1944: "You are Jewish, your task is to remain Jewish. The rest is up to God."

Eliezer Berkowitz

In his younger years rabbi in the Orthodox synagogues of the Berlin congregation, later professor at the Hebrew Theological College at Skokie, Illinois, and now a resident of Israel, Berkowitz represents an Orthodox position. God may choose to "hide His face," allowing humans to choose freely between good and evil. God may decide to reward the sufferers for the pain they have borne, but God is not committed to grant such a reward. He has done so in allowing the restoration of Israel.

III

LIFE AS MITZVAH

17

PRAYER AND THE HOUSE
OF THE LORD

The term *Mitzvah* is so broad that it allows diverging emphases in observance. Orthodox Jewry has seen in Mitzvah essentially the observance of religious commandments, whereas Reform Jewry has laid stress on social justice and social action as Mitzvah. Neither, of course, has disregarded the total aspect of Mitzvah.

The same applies to the term *Covenant*, which Mitzvah makes manifest. To some, it is the bond linking Jews to God; to others, it is simply a term expressing belongingness.

Ideally, in traditional perspective, the totality of life is to be a witness to God, an all-encompassing Mitzvah through which God will be made manifest and the people of Israel sustained.

The *Shulhan Arukh* states it clearly:

> Man shall make himself strong as a lion as he arises in the morning to serve his Creator. (Note by Rabbi Moses Isserles: "I have set the Lord always before me" (Psalm 16:8) is one of the basic principles of Torah; it is one of the virtues of the righteous who walk before Him at all times. . . . Let man take to heart that the Great King, God—whose glory fills the whole earth—stands over him and watches over all his actions. . . . This awareness will immediately fill him with reverence, humility, and awe before Him, Blessed be His Name. . . . May he never feel ashamed before those people who make mock of him on account of his service to God, His Name be Blessed (Orah Hayim 1:1).)

> If he cannot study without an afternoon nap, let him take a nap, but not drag it out. . . . Even in as small a matter as that, may his intentions be not to give pleasure to his body, but to return his body to the service of Him whose Name be Blessed. The same applies to all the enjoyments in this world; not pleasure be his intention, but service to his Creator, Blessed be He, as it is written, "In all your ways recognize Him" (Proverbs 3:6), to which our sages have commented: "May all your actions be for the sake of Heaven" (Abot 2:12). Even his unregulated actions, such as eating and drinking, walking and sitting, standing, intercourse, talk, and all the needs of the body, every one of them should be directed to the service of his Creator, or as a means leading to service unto Him. Thus, if he be hungry or thirsty and eats or drinks simply for his enjoyment, his acts are not praiseworthy; rather shall his intention be to eat

and drink for the preservation of his life, in order that he may serve his Creator. . . . The same goes for intercourse, the marital duties ordained in Torah. If he performs them to appease his desires or for the enjoyment of his body, he should be ashamed; even if his intentions are to have children who may eventually help him and ultimately take his place, that too is not praiseworthy. His intention shall be to have children who will serve his Creator; or better yet, his intention shall be to fulfill the commandment of marital duty like a man who pays a debt. The same applies to talk. . . . All in all: He must turn his sight and heart toward his road, weigh all his actions on the scales of his intellect. If he sees something leading him to an opportunity of serving his Creator, Blessed be He, let him do it; otherwise, may he not do it. He who conducts himself in this fashion serves his Creator always. (Orah Hayim 231:1)

We may readily admit that such a life is impossible for the average person even if he is Orthodox. Many Jews lead committed Jewish lives, without being bound by all these rules. By the time the *Shulhan Arukh* was written, Mitzvah had become *the* pillar of Judaism; we may see in its statement a guideline and goal affecting every action, and affording a yardstick by which daily routine may be measured. We note that nothing is excluded from being a Mitzvah; there is no dualism of spirit and flesh. All depends on the intent. Sex may be a Mitzvah, while simple rest, under certain circumstances, may not be.

Since everything from enjoyment to suffering must be given a meaning in God's plan, it is essential that we be aware of our actions as we perform them; then they will become Mitzvah.

THE BERAKHAH (BLESSING)

All of life ideally should be Mitzvah. The rabbis of the Talmud ordained, therefore, that every act be preceded by a spoken affirmation that it is done "for the sake of Heaven." Every pleasure must be savored in adoration of its Creator. Thus the unit of prayer was formulated in order that Jews might clothe the promptings of their hearts in a structured garment. This unit is **Berakhah**, the Benediction. The Psalmist had used it: "Blessed are You, O Lord, teach me Your statutes" (Psalm 119:12).

The Talmud teaches:

Over fruit growing on trees one says [before eating them]: "Blessed are You, God our Lord, King of the Universe, He who creates the fruit of the tree." . . . Over wine one says: "Blessed . . . who creates the fruit of the vine." . . . Over fruits of the ground one speaks: "Blessed . . . who creates the fruit of the ground." Over bread one pronounces: "Blessed . . . who brings forth bread from the earth." Over anything which does not grow from the earth one says: "Blessed . . . by whose word all was created." . . . After a meal everyone shall say grace. (Mishnah Berkhot 6:1, 3, 6)

Over comets, earthquakes, thunder, storm, and lightnings, over mountains, hills, oceans, rivers, and deserts [a blessing is pronounced by the beholder]. . . . Over rain and on getting happy news one says: "Blessed . . . who is good and is doing good." On receiving evil tidings one recites: "Blessed . . . the true judge." . . . It is man's duty to bless God for the ills that befall him holding hidden good, even as he gives blessing for the good that comes to him, though it hold hidden ills. . . . Has he built a new house or bought new clothes, he shall pronounce praise: "Blessed . . . who has kept us alive, has sustained us, and has brought us to this time." (Mishnah Berakhot 9:2, 3, 5)

Our thoughts thus revolve constantly about God. The world is truly the Lord's, and the fullness thereof. What we own may be legally ours; ideally, it is God's. The Berakhah is our request for permission to use it, joined to our pledge to make use of it for God's glory, in order that God may be made manifest. The totality of life thus becomes worship; it is Mitzvah.

Understanding the character and purpose of Berakhah, we may arrive at an understanding of Jewish prayer in general, which is built on Berakhah.

PRAYER AND ITS STRUCTURE

The Hebrew term for prayer is **Tefillah**, from the verb *palal*, meaning "to judge; to plead; to concentrate." Prayer is concentration on the abiding. Ernst Simon, a leading contemporary thinker, has given us the traditional view of prayer in general and Jewish prayer in particular ("On the Meaning of Prayer," in *Tradition and Contemporary Experience*, New York: Schocken, 1970; pp. 269–273). He points out that prayer in general is based on three suppositions: the belief in a *personal God*, our faith that this personal God *cares* for His children, and our conviction that *we may turn to God* with praises and thanks without wishing to flatter Him, and to approach Him with our supplications without wishing to force Him to do our bidding.

Jewish prayer has four additional features: First, *it is communal prayer*. The Jews were the first to introduce communal prayer, and peoplehood occupies a legitimate place in the Jewish faith. Second, *it is formulated prayer*. Judaism knows individual, spontaneous prayer. But a man is not only an individual; he is part of a community, of the Jewish people. Communal prayer must be formulated prayer. Third, *it employs a multitude of external symbols*: the Tallit, the phylacteries, the shofar. These are designed to sanctify every act of life; to promote constant awareness of God's presence; to discipline our thoughts, emotions, and actions; and to link us with our people. Finally, *study and worship are equated*. Both are prayer. In praise, Jews turn to the God of creation; in supplication, to the God of compassion and justice; and in study, to the God of revelation. And they listen to what God has to say.

Prayer must therefore be offered not as routine, but with *kavanah*, attunement of heart (Berakhot 4:4). It must acknowledge that God's will be done, not man's. Many prayers begin with the words "May it be Your will."

Formal prayer is to be preceded by meditation, leading the worshipper into tune with God's will.

Formal prayer accompanies all of life. For every day of the week, Jewish law has appointed three orders of prayer: **Shaharit**, the morning prayer, **Minhah**, the afternoon prayer, and **Maariv**, the evening prayer. On holy days, a special prayer, the **Mussaf** (Additional Prayer), reflecting on the significance of the day, is added. These prayers are uniform throughout the year, as far as their core is concerned; morning, noon, and evening prayers are the same for every day. This is significant. Structured prayer, first of all, expresses our feelings better than we could in our own words. It offers the vehicle for our own thoughts, as we fill the familiar words with ever-renewed meaning. (In addition, it links us to the community.)

The repetition of identical prayers actually corresponds to the eternal course of time, which is always the same, from sunrise to sunset, yet ever renewed. The worshipper who endows the unchanging words with ever-new meaning is thus drawn to the fact that, though life is uniform, it may not be routine. Day follows day, but each day is a new creation, challenging us to renew ourselves in spirit and in action, and never to lose our wonderment at the miracle which is evident in the orderliness of nature. This finds clear expression in one of the Berakhot that is part of every worship:

> We gratefully acknowledge unto You that You are the Lord our God, and the God of our fathers unto all eternity. You are the Rock of our life, shield of our salvation from generation to generation. We give thanks unto You and declare Your praise for our lives committed unto Your hand, for our souls entrusted unto You, for Your miracles that are with us daily, Your wondrous deeds and acts of goodness that are with us at all times, evening, morning, and afternoon. You are good, for Your mercies never fail; compassionate, for the acts of Your loving kindness never cease. We hope in You forever. For all this Your name be blessed and exalted, You, our King, always and forever. May all the living offer laud unto You, and praise Your Name in truth, God of our salvation and of our help. Blessed are You, O Lord, "The Good" is Your Name, and to You it is proper to render thanks. (Daily Amida, eighteenth benediction)

Under God, every moment of life becomes a miracle. He is God of time (history) and space. The knowledge that He *is* gives hope. All that live express His praise, being witness to His creative power.

Of the three prayers, the morning and evening prayers have their source in the Shema itself: Rehearse the words of God's unity and the call to love every evening and every morning. Morning prayer prepares for the road in life; evening prayer calls to account. The afternoon prayer, at the time when the afternoon offering was once presented in the Temple, calls for pause and reflection: How much has been achieved? What may yet be done to transform the work of the day into a Mitzvah?

We may compare the worshipper's appearance before God to an audience before a king. Its structure reflects this thought.

The Daily and Additional Prayers

Shaharit   (Morning Prayer)

1. On arising, the individual, grateful for his reborn strength, prepares himself for the meeting; even as he puts on his clothes, he is aware of God's beneficence in clothing him, in feeding him, in giving him bodily vigor.

2. In meditation and psalm, the worshipper puts himself in tune with the occasion.

3. Individuals form a group to meet the King. Public worship opens with the call to worship, "Bless the Lord to whom all blessing belongs." The congregation responds, "Blessed be the Lord to whom all blessing belongs, unto all eternity."

4. The people affirm God's greatness, love, and majesty:
   a) He is the Creator of day and night, the Lord of nature.
   b) He is the source of all wisdom, who has given his Torah to His people.
   c) He is One, calling for love: the Shema Yisrael is recited.
   d) He is the God of history, who has rescued Israel from all enemies, and will help all humanity.

5. Trusting in Him, the worshipper offers his petitions to Him, asking for wisdom, health, forgiveness of sins, his daily bread, and restoration. But he begins and concludes with praise. This prayer is recited standing and is called **Amidah**. The petitionary prayer is first offered in silent devotion and then publicly repeated by the reader (during morning and afternoon worship), with insertion of the sanctification, **Kedushah**, proclaiming His divine majesty: "Holy, holy, holy is the Lord of hosts, the whole earth is full of His glory." The wording of the final petition closely resembles the affirmation of faith in its wording. The affirmation had started with: *Shema Yisrael, Adonai Elohenu,* "Hear, O Israel, the Lord our God." The petition begins with: *Shema kolenu, Adonai Elohenu,* "Hear our voice, O Lord, our God . . . and accept graciously our petition." The same rhythm that proclaims Him expresses the plea, for it emerges out of recognition and simply evokes reciprocal love.

6. The individual confesses his sins in awareness that he is truly unworthy to petition, much less to receive the divine mercies for which he has asked.

7. The word of the King is heard. The Torah is read on appointed days of the week and on special days.

8. With a final affirmation, **Alenu**, and remembrance of the departed (that their memory be a guide), the congregation takes its leave.

Minhah   (Afternoon Prayer). The afternoon prayer is short. Since the recital of the Shema is not ordained, it is omitted. Psalm 145 (which speaks of God's goodness to all) creates the mood of worship. God is the Sustainer; may we be mindful of it whether the day so far has been successful or a failure. Then the Amidah is recited and repeated. Confession of sin and final affirmation conclude the worship.

Maariv   (Evening Prayer). Parallel to morning worship, the evening worship, after an introductory psalm, starts with the call to worship. Then God is praised as (a) Creator of night and (b) author of Torah, source of all wisdom. Then (c) the Shema is recited. (d) God is revered as Master of history. (e) Now a special prayer for protection throughout the night is included. (f) The Amidah is recited silently, after which, with affirmation, worship is completed.

A prayer at bedtime concludes the day.

On Sabbath days and holy days, all petitions are omitted; sheltered in God's peace, Jews should forget their cares on these days. Confession of sin is also omitted; nothing should dim the joy of God's day, not even the knowledge of sinfulness.

On festivals of joy, the Hallel (Psalms 113–118) are recited by the people in gratitude for God's special dispensations of help.

Mussaf (Additional Prayer). To commemorate the special festive occasion in remembrance of the ancient service in the Temple, a special prayer is added on holy days, the Mussaf, Addition. It is recited after the reading of Torah and keynotes the special occasion and its sacrifices in the Temple of Jerusalem. (Reform Judaism has eliminated it.)

The prayers are not simply read, but rendered in the form of a recitative which is very old. The reading of the Torah and Haftarah follows a prescribed pattern of modes, which the reader must know. While every Jew with ability and moral character may serve as "the congregation's messenger," leading them in prayer, Jews have always had a great love for music (a dynamic force, in contrast to sculpture), demanding a well-trained **chazan** (cantor) with a good voice, who might endow the words with added meaning, expressing in song the yearning of the heart and conveying in music the message of a special day. Thus over the years a great body of liturgical music has developed. Each holy day has its own song. Compositions were frequently influenced by the musical taste of the general environment. Today, leading Jewish composers are writing liturgical music in modern idiom.

The Prayer Book

In the morning two [Berakhot] are to be recited before [the Shema], and one after [the Shema]; in the evening two before [the Shema] and two after [the Shema and preceding the Amidah]. (Berakhot 1:4)

We have seen that this formal arrangement is still followed, and we can recognize in it the great age of formal Jewish prayer. Indeed, the text is very old; tradition traces the origin of its key skeletal portions to Ezra and his contemporaries and immediate successors, a body of unidentified teachers called the Men of the Great Assembly. The Prayer Book is thus the second oldest literary work still in constant use in the Western world, the oldest being the Bible (and both of them are of Jewish origin). Transmitted by word of mouth, the prayers were edited in the ninth century, and editions with slight variations appeared throughout the centuries.

Actually, the **Siddur** (the prayer book) reflects the evolution and destiny of the Jewish people. The fate of Sefardic and Ashkenasic Jewry is reflected in the variations in the Siddur used by either group. Yet the variations are small and do not prevent a worshipper brought up in one tradition from following easily in the prayer book of the other, or in fact from feeling at home in either worship. While the basic core always remained unchanged, poets and singers throughout the Middle Ages were free to add poetry of their own, especially for worship on holy days. Thus variety in uniformity was achieved, the new tied in with the old. It was the printing press that gave the Siddur its unchanging character; prayers and poems included in the printed Siddur found the widest acceptance and, once printed, could not easily be changed.

Throughout the ages, the Orthodox prayer book has undergone hardly any changes, although modern translations have been produced, and a number of additional and optional readings have recently been included in some editions. Reform, Conservatism, and Reconstructionism, however, effected certain basic revisions.

Reform was the most radical. Realizing the inability of the people to understand Hebrew, it emphasized prayer in the vernacular, leaving only a few basic Hebrew prayers and arranging the book itself to read from left to right, following the English practice, rather than from right to left, which would have acknowledged the primacy of Hebrew, as Hebrew is read from right to left. The prayers for the Land of Israel were eliminated in the belief that Emancipation had brought full freedom for all Jews in the countries where they lived, and a hope for restoration of Zion could be safely abolished. The Mussaf, dealing with the sacrifices of ancient times, was eliminated. In recent years, however, new editions of the Reform prayer book have reintroduced numerous traditional portions, including prayers for Zion, the 1974 edition being quite "conservative."

The Conservative prayer book shows only slight changes in the Hebrew text. The hope for the rebuilding of the Land of Israel is powerfully expressed, but the sacrificial service in the Temple, as of old, is presented merely as a recollection of the pattern of worship which once prevailed. A great many English responses are added, to offer variety in the service and permit it to be keyed to special religious as well as civic and national American observances.

The Reconstructionist prayer book, following basic Conservative principles, has adjusted the text to naturalistic Reconstructionist theology; references to the "chosenness" of Israel are also omitted. The link to the Land of Israel and to Hebrew is as strongly maintained, as in the Conservative Siddur.

Numerous efforts have been made, and are being made, to key the Siddur to the needs of the people and to modern philosophy. None has fully succeeded. In none of the prayer books, however, has the basic pattern, hallowed by tradition, been broken.

It cannot be denied that the use of different prayer books has split Jewry. Yet there is still sufficient uniformity transcending the differences to make the prayer book a unifying element among the Jewish people.

The Congregation

Prayers may be offered by every individual in private. Yet it is better if they rise from a united congregation. The congregation is symbol of the people, a united society before God, and forecasts the united society of humanity under God. In addition, the congregation sustains the individual; each worshipper aids, upholds, and strengthens the next; selfishness departs; responsibility grows.

To constitute a congregation for the purposes of public worship, a quorum of ten, or **minyan,** is required. Why ten? The ordinance goes back to ancient times and gives us an insight into the scriptural interpretation of the Talmud by the rabbis. Twelve men were sent by Moses to scout out the land; ten came back with an evil report, and only two were confident that God's help would permit Israel to overcome the enemy. To the ten, who had conspired for evil, God calls out in indignation, "How long shall I bear with this evil *congregation?*" (Numbers 14:26). Ten once formed a congregation of rebellion; may ten form a congregation expressing faith and obedience, upholding each other in this spirit. Orthodox Jewry insists on a minyan of ten males who are Bar Mitzvah.

Reform and Reconstructionism do not insist on the minyan. They have also given women equal status in the congregation, and both have ordained women as rabbis. The Conservative rabbinate has granted women equality. They may be part of the minyan, form a minyan, lead public worship in all its facets, and assume spiritual and educational leadership in accordance with their personal qualifications. Rabbinical ordination was approved in principle in 1980. Implementation rests, however, on the decision of the individual congregation and rabbi.

Physical Reminders

The Tallit.   The ancient Jews, like the Bedouins of today, used to wear a large, four-cornered robe, which they wrapped about themselves. It was their only garment. To remind them of the constant presence of God and keep them from going astray in their daily pursuits, Torah commanded that they place fringes, like tassels, on the corners of the garment, which, swaying at every step, would remind them of God's presence. They were to remember that all of life could and should be a Mitzvah: "Ye shall see them and remember all of God's Mitzvot and do them; and not go astray . . . and be holy unto your God" (Numbers 15:37–41). Modern men no longer wear such a garment, but it became the **tallit,** a four-cornered robe with tassels **(tzitzit)** on it. It is worn in worship during day hours (the time of day when the tzitzit can be seen in natural light, as Torah commands). It may be a big garment, which may cover the worshipper entirely and which he may even draw over his head when he wishes to commune with God in complete concentration and absorption, or it may be simply a stole, or prayer shawl. The stole in Christian worship is derived from it. The cantor or leader at worship will wear it even at nighttime. He approaches God, symbolically wrapped up in Mitzvah. The tallit is the garment symbolically clothing the worshipper in the robe of responsibility; his life, in every step, must be walked in God's presence. The wearing of a small four-cornered garment beneath the suit is practiced in Orthodox groups. Some permit the tzitzit to be visible.

The Tefillin. "Bind them as a sign on your hand, let them be for frontlets between your eyes." These injunctions contained in the Shema (see p. 198) simply mean that our minds and actions must be guided by the love of God. Yet the commandment was also taken literally, and has led to the **tefillin,**

Tallit and Tefillin. Note the tassels on the tallit's corners (the fringe along the side is not required). The tefillin for head and arm consist of the cubes containing the parchment scrolls, and the leather straps. (Photo by the author from his own collection.)

or phylacteries, as visible symbols. A small leather container in the form of a cube, containing several selections from Scripture, is attached to a leather strap and placed on the left upper arm, opposite the heart; the remainder of the strap is wrapped about the arm and hand. Another container is similarly placed on the head. Thus are head (seat of the mind), heart (traditionally the source of will), and hand (the instrument of action) encircled by His word and His love. The word of God sets our limitations and lifts us up.

Each cube of the tefillin holds four sections of Scripture, including the Shema (Deuteronomy 6:4–9; Deuteronomy 11:13–20; Exodus 13:11–16; Exodus 13: 1–10). Every one of these selections contains the injunction to place God's word on hand and head. The selections speak of God's deliverance, His providence, and His promise to return Israel to its Land. They also spell out the duties of humankind to make Him manifest through the word of education and the example of a life dedicated to Him.

The tefillin are a visible sign of convenantal love that binds God and Israel. They are worn during the morning service on weekdays. On Sabbath and holy days, the tefillin are not worn. These days, in themselves, are reminders of God's nearness; to add more symbols might obscure their true meaning as guides to ideas.

The Mezuzah. "Write them on the doorposts" (see p. 198). A small scroll, the **mezuzah,** containing several of the same selections as the tefillin, including the Shema (Deuteronomy 6:4–9; 11:13–20), is placed on doorposts of Jewish homes. Thus the Shema is the last greeting and admonition to those who leave the house; may their lives be guided by its ideals. The Shema is our first welcome home; may we place our home, and our thoughts and actions within it, under the instruction of God's Torah. On the back of the scroll, visible when it is rolled up, is written the word *Shaddai:* God who is everywhere with the people in all their habitations.

Like the scroll of Torah itself, the scrolls in tefillin and mezuzah must be handwritten on parchment by pious men who dedicate their lives to this holy art; they also make the containers and straps of the tefillin, following special regulations. No special rules apply to the container in which the mezuzah is kept, and many artistic designs have been fashioned for it.

THE HOUSE OF THE LORD

In Chapter 2, we saw that in ancient times the Jews were the first to transform the small dwelling place of the deity into a meeting place where people met in the presence of God to sustain each other as they affirmed Him in solemn assembly. The religious meeting house is a Jewish invention. Originally, it was called **proseuche,** the term **synagogue** standing for the gathering of the people rather than for a building. Eventually the latter term was applied to the building, subtly reminding the congregation that it is the people who

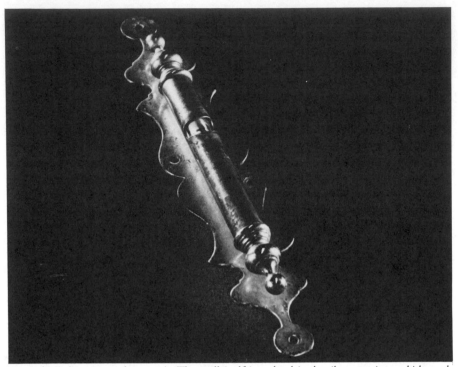

Mezuzah *(India, nineteenth century). The scroll itself is enclosed in the silver container, which can be attached to the doorpost.* (Photo by Kathie Minami, reproduced by courtesy of Judah L. Magnes Memorial Museum, Jewish Museum of the West, Berkeley, California.)

give it meaning and purpose. The term *temple* came to be used in modern times under the influence of Reform. It was to indicate that the individual synagogue had now assumed the place of the ancient temple, once and for all, as no restoration of the Land was anticipated. Over the years, however, the term lost this connotation, and we find *temple* and *synagogue* used interchangeably without any real difference between the terms.

In ancient Israel, during the period of the Second Temple, we find synagogues in many communities operating simultaneously with the national sanctuary. The synagogue was the House of Prayer (*Bet ha-Tefilah*). It was also the House of Study (*Bet ha-Midrash*), and the ancient synagogue of Capernaum in Israel shows a large educational annex attached to the central sanctuary. Finally, it was the House of the People (**Bet Am**), their assembly hall. This threefold function has been retained and has actually been strengthened in modern times. All synagogues have religious school facilities, and most of them are equipped for social gatherings in a religious atmosphere.

Structurally, the synagogue translated some of the features of the ancient Temple into its different character and purpose, while diverging from others. At the same time, individual traditions and general taste have made for variety of design in various countries. The ancient Temple had three sections: the court where the people assembled, the sanctuary where the menorah and other holy vessels were found, and the holy of holies, separated from the sanctuary by a curtain, containing (during the period of the first Temple) the Ark with the Tables of the Ten Commandments. This area was only entered once a year by the high priest. The synagogue, too, has three sections: the people's pews; the pulpit; and the Ark, *Aron hakodesh*—the shrine, frequently separated by a curtain, in which the Torah Scrolls (plural: Sifre Torah; singular **Sefer Torah**) are kept.

The differences are equally significant. In ancient and many contemporary Orthodox synagogues, the **bimah,** or reading pulpit for the Torah, is found in the center, and the scroll is carried there for reading. The people once again surround Torah, as they did when it was first bestowed upon them at Mount Sinai. Modern synagogues have placed the bimah in front of the Ark

Ark closed, Temple Emanu-El, San Francisco. *This freestanding Ark is unique in synagogue architecture. It is inspired by the Ark of the Covenant of the ancient Temple, although it does not follow that design. On its sides, it has the symbols of the twelve tribes of Israel. The Hebrew inscription means "Know before Whom you stand," an admonition to the worshippers to remind them that they stand before God. This inscription is found in most synagogues.* (Photo by the author, reproduced courtesy of Congregation Emanu-El and Rabbi Joseph Asher.)

(partly to save space). With the Emancipation in the spirit of adaptation to the Protestant Church, additional changes were introduced: decorum, the rabbinical robe, the reintroduction of the sermon, now in modern form, and so on. Traditionally, the reader of the service faced the Ark and stood on the same level as the people. He was not a priest but one of them, their "messenger," offering their prayers while standing in their midst. In Conservative and Reform congregations, he generally faces the people, to be better heard. The Torah is elevated; steps lead up to the Ark, in which the Sefer Torah is kept, and to the center bimah (when it is retained), from which it is recited as divine instruction. Some modern synagogues have two reading desks in front (one

Torah Curtain *(India, nineteenth century). The embroidery features the letters "K–T" in Hebrew, an abbreviation of* Keter Torah, Torah is a crown. (Photo by Kathie Minami, reproduced courtesy of Judah L. Magnes Memorial Museum, Jewish Museum of the West, Berkeley, California.)

sometimes of higher elevation). One is used for reading of the Torah, while the other (lower) is used by the reader leading the congregation.

The Ark and bimah are the centers of worship, combined into one in modern synagogues. As once in the Temple, an eternal light burns in the sanctuary, signifying the presence of God and the eternal illumination going forth from His word. The menorah may also be in use, as in the Temple. But there is another, invisible, worship center. Synagogues should be so oriented that the worshipper faces Jerusalem in prayer. God–People–Torah–Mitzvah–Land thus are fused into an indivisible unit, their oneness symbolically expressed.

The entrance hall was designed for the people to put themselves in the

A breastplate of German manufacture, *showing two "lions of Judah" holding the Tablets*. (Photo by Kathie Minami, reproduced courtesy of Judah L. Magnes Memorial Museum, Jewish Museum of the West, Berkeley, California.)

mood of reverence. In traditional synagogues, a wash basin and water pitcher may be found there for the worshippers to cleanse their hands symbolically before entering the sanctuary. (This is not holy water, however, although the holy water font in the entrance area of Catholic churches may be derived from it, or be an adaptation of the laver in the court of the Temple where the priests purified themselves. Furthermore, water once used may not be used again.) From this hall, a step would sometimes lead down into the synagogue proper (although we do not usually find it today) to signify "Out of the depths I call upon You, O Lord!" (Psalm 130:1). The synagogue has to have windows. It is not to be removed from the world, but rather must be a place from which the world is to be reviewed in the light of God's design.

In line with a practice emerging during the time of the Mishnah, it became customary to separate men and women worshippers by placing the women in a gallery (which was eventually curtained) in order to eliminate wordly temptations during worship. Conservative and Reform synagogues have seen a greater value in keeping families together in worship and have instituted mixed seating.

While the rabbis ordained quiet and grave decorum in the synagogue, their advice was frequently not followed. This was the people's place, their second home; here they celebrated the joyful events of life and reflected on their afflictions; here they gathered for many purposes; and, above all, here the voices of children and adults could be heard in study, recital, and discussion. To this day, a synagogue is called a **Shul,** a school, by the people. Consequently, conduct was rather informal, and some of it has remained so.

By Jewish law, the synagogue must rise above the roofs of the houses in the town. During the Middle Ages, this was specifically prohibited by the Christian authorities. As a symbol, therefore, Jews sometimes attached a high pole to the roof of their house of worship, surmounting it by the Star of David, a practice which may have brought the star into widespread use.

There are no specific rules regarding synagogue architecture. Old synagogues frequently followed the general style of the time. Often we find Moorish architecture used to distinguish synagogues from Christian houses of worship. In modern times, this freedom from restrictions has inspired architects to fashion buildings in a modern style, some of them of great beauty and daring design.

18

THE MITZVAH OF PHYSICAL CONSECRATION: DIETARY LAWS

As daily worship and study of Torah bring mind and soul into attunement with God, the **dietary laws** consecrate the body. Judaism has never made the distinction between body (as weak) and soul (as strong and divine). Both must serve God; both are holy.

The dietary laws may well have emerged from numerous taboos of antiquity or from health considerations; their hygienic character is in many instances self-evident. Pious Jews have looked at them in a different light. Truly devout Jews see in them simply God's law: He has commanded their observance, to "sanctify us by His commandments," and He knows their purpose. Yet these laws may also be considered a means of preserving Israel's uniqueness, linking the members of the Household of Israel to closer unity. Jews could and would associate only with those who shared the practices of life and table and were barred from primary contact with those who did not. These laws may also be viewed as symbolic of belonging to a group, binding the members in fellowship (as a handshake may bind the members of a fraternal order), reminding them of their tradition, history, and aspirations.

Depending on the emphasis placed by individual Jews on these various points of interpretation, patterns of observance have varied among modern Jews. Orthodox Jews will make the greatest sacrifices, denying themselves many contacts with friends in order to observe strictly the God–ordained rules. Others may wish to honor their basic principles, without being concerned about minute details, as unifying bonds to God and fellow Jews. Again, many Jews may observe them in their homes, in order that any Jew may join their table, yet feel free to disregard them when eating out. Their homes must be hallowed; in the home, Israel's eternity under God must be expressed, symbolized, and transmitted. Some Jews will observe but a few of the laws as a matter of discipline and a symbol of belonging; for instance, they may refrain from eating pork. Finally, there are those who see no purpose and spiritual meaning in the dietary laws and do not feel bound by them in any way. They cannot accept the doctrine that Torah was literally dictated by God and cannot see any spiritually sustaining symbolic power in the dietary regulations. Of course, there are many who are simply backsliders, lax in any observance. But to millions of Jews, the dietary laws are precious; they will deny themselves food rather than break them, even under difficult conditions, and will cheerfully accept the many sacrifices, including comparative isolation in society, they entail.

Prohibited Foods

There is no prohibition against any vegetables. Regarding animal food, the Scripture sets definite rules (Leviticus 11; Deuteronomy 14):

1. It permits whatever animal that "has true hoofs, with clefts through the hoofs, and that chews the cud" (Leviticus 11:3), listing among the permitted ones the ox, the sheep, the hart, and the gazelle (Deuteronomy 14:4–5). If either of these two characteristics is missing, the animal may not be eaten. This forbids the pig, which has clefts through the hoofs but does not chew cud, and the rabbit, which chews cud but has paws rather than hoofs.

2. It prohibits a number of birds. Since the exact meaning of the ancient Hebrew terms for the birds is not known, only those birds which have traditionally been eaten may be consumed. This includes chickens, ducks, geese, pigeons, and turkeys as "clean."

3. Fish must have fins *and* scales (Leviticus 11:9; Deuteronomy 14:9), which excludes all shellfish as well as eel and sturgeon.

4. "Swarming things" are equally prohibited, from mice to crocodiles to most insects. Certain locusts and grasshoppers were once scripturally permitted, but today no insects are permitted, as the identity of those mentioned in scripture is no longer clear (Leviticus 11:20–23, 29–30).

Thus all animals that live by destruction of others are excluded, as are birds of prey—a reminder, perhaps, to strive for peace.

Restrictions on Permitted Foods

Even permitted animals may be consumed only under certain conditions. The following are prohibited: animals that have died on their own (Leviticus 11:39; Deuteronomy 14:21); animals that have been torn by others (Exodus 22:30); all blood (Leviticus 7:26); certain animal fats (Leviticus 3:17); and certain sinews (Genesis 32:33). Torn animals are "**terefah,**" a term more generally applied to all forms of forbidden food. None of these restrictions, or any of those following, apply to fish.

Preparation of Meat.   Any animal not slaughtered by a method approved by Jewish law, or found diseased, is not suitable for consumption.

1. Animals must therefore be slaughtered by a man trained in Jewish law, a *Shohet*. Using a very sharp knife which may not have any nicks in it, he must cut the animal's throat, severing arteries, veins, and windpipe in one continuous stroke without exerting downward pressure. This is the act of **Shehitah**. In this manner, the brain is so rapidly drained of blood that no

pain sensation occurs. (It takes some time to feel pain, as we know when we cut ourselves with a very sharp knife; physiological research has shown that the Jewish method of slaughter is the most humane one. In addition, rapid drainage of blood makes the meat better fit for preservation.) After the slaughter, the shohet must examine the animal for disease, and if he finds damage in the lungs, an ulcerated stomach, or discoloration of the brain, the animal may not be eaten.

2. The Jewish butcher, who must be an observant and knowledgeable Jew, then removes the sinews. Since those of the hindquarters are difficult to remove, this part is frequently not used at all unless the butcher has special, certified skill in preparing it.

3. Elimination of the blood becomes the task of the housewife. The meat must be fresh; if it has been stored for three days, the blood has congealed to the point where it cannot be removed and the meat cannot be used (unless it has been soaked once in water during this period to keep it soft). The housewife soaks the meat in water for about one-half hour, then covers it with salt on all sides, leaving it in the salt for about one hour, and then washes off the salt. Another method is to broil the meat over an open fire, permitting the blood to flow out freely; this method must be used for liver. After this procedure, the meat is **kosher**, which means it is "all right."

4. Kitchen utensils that have been used in connection with forbidden foods cannot be used in a kosher household. Neither can foods that have admixtures of nonkosher ingredients. Soap containing animal fats cannot be used for washing dishes; detergents, being inorganic chemicals, can be used. The Union of Orthodox Congregations therefore has a service of certification. On many products regularly obtainable in food stores, a "U" in a circle—Ⓤ—certifies that they can be used in kosher households. Other Orthodox certification services use a variety of certification marks.

Meat and Milk. At three different places in Scripture, we find the injunction: "You shall not seethe the kid in the milk of his mother" (Exodus 23:19, 34:25; Deuteronomy 14:2). This was interpreted as containing three prohibitions: against eating meat and milk products together, against cooking them together, and against using any mixture of them. These products may therefore not be served together; for example, butter and milk may not be found at a meal that offers meat. After eating meat, a person has to wait several hours before eating milk products. Furthermore, different utensils have to be used for meat and for milk. This requires a kosher family to have two complete sets of dishes, silverware, and cooking utensils. (A third set for neutral food, such as fruit, may also be found in the home.) If these become mixed up, they may occasionally be cleansed by either boiling or burning out the food by bringing the utensils to red heat. Otherwise, the utensils become useless. The decision in this matter rests with the rabbi, whom the family will consult. In addition, the kosher family will need two other complete sets of dishes for Passover, when those having come in touch with leavened food during the year may not be used.

The laws of *kashrut* (kosher laws) call for thoroughly trained rabbis to supervise and decide problems, learned *shohetim* and conscientious butchers, and vigilance and devotion from every housewife (although practices become second nature with the years). Above all, they set God always before all Jews, as they discipline themselves to accept or deny the pleasures of food and even its life-sustaining gifts. This is Mitzvah, a daily and constant response to God, promoting inner strength, and the joyful conviction in observant Jews that they follow the will of God with body as with soul.

19

SABBATH, DAY OF RE-CREATION

Daily observance is the pulse beat supplying Jews with the lifeblood of the divine. The Sabbath re-creates them, giving them the strength for meaningful daily living. It is linked to God's creative act itself (Genesis 2:1–4). God rested from His work and hallowed the Sabbath. It is the only holy day ordained in the Ten Commandments, both in Exodus (20:8–11) and in Deuteronomy (5:12–15). But God needs no rest; the meaning of the term lies deeper. God ceased from making the world all by Himself; henceforth people must be His co-workers. As Creator, God is the world's owner and may ordain rest for those who toil in His domain. In obeying this command, Jews acknowledge God's ownership of the world and constitute themselves not its master but its stewards.

They are to become aware that people are called to carry on God's work during the six days of labor. This task has two distinct features: First, nature and all its produce must be utilized for beneficent purposes; we may neither squander its riches nor selfishly claim them all for ourselves. Hence the commandment emphasizes that God is nature's creator. Secondly, society and every one of its members is equally God's; all humankind must be given that dignity which comes from being God's children. Servants, too, must be allowed to rest, as is doubly emphasized in the version of the Commandments found in Deuteronomy, "that your servants may rest as well as you." The meaning of the Sabbath thus synthesizes the religious element and the social element, the spiritualizing of daily work and the promotion of humanity's basic rights. Judaism considers one without the other to be meaningless.

To Jews, the Sabbath has become not merely a day of rest, but a day of spiritual re-creation for the tasks which form the functions of the week's labor. As such, it has given the Jews strength, hope, and confidence. Truly, human beings, so charged with a divine duty, are dear to God. The Sabbath became a Covenant between God and Israel (Exodus 13:12–17); its desecration spells denial of God Himself and His creatorship (Numbers 15:32–36). It guarantees Israel's eternity, for the servant's life has meaning as long as the Master's work needs to be done, and this work is eternal. It has given Jews the strength to endure and preserve their mental balance. In the terms of the German poet (of Jewish background) Heinrich Heine: a dog during the week, the Jew is restored to his true character as a prince of God one day a week. If he must, he can return to the degradation the world may impose upon him, for he knows his true identity. According to the rabbis, the Sabbath thus provides Jews with "a taste of the world to come." Sagely, they remark: "As Israel has kept the Sabbath, the Sabbath has kept Israel alive."

Prohibition of Work

The meaning of *rest* had to be defined, lest a person rationalize that his work, or that imposed upon his servants, could not really be called work. A simple yardstick was used in this definition. All of God's world is His sanctuary; as His co-workers, Israel once built a sanctuary in the desert, a small symbol of His presence, though He pervades the entire universe. All types of work once connected with the building of the tabernacle in the desert are therefore prohibited. In this manner, the principle of rest in God's behest is realized by those who are called to build the greater sanctuary of a God-centered society.

This led to the prohibition of thirty-nine basic kinds of work, arranged in several general categories: (1) the growing and preparation of food (eleven prohibitions); (2) clothing in all its processes (thirteen prohibitions); (3) leather work and writing (nine prohibitions); (4) the building of shelter (two prohibitions); (5) the use of fire (two prohibitions); (6) work completion, the final hammer stroke (one prohibition); and (7) transportation (one prohibition). Around these primary prohibitions, the rabbis added secondary ones to prevent violation of the basic ones. Thus the Sabbath became a day of complete spirituality. The toil of daily living fell away, and thoughts and preoccupation with daily events were completely banished. A truly divine peace settled upon those who fully observed it.

Observance of the Sabbath

The Jewish Day of Rest always starts with the preceding evening. Scripture states: "It was evening and it was morning" (Genesis 1), putting the night before the day. This is a natural arrangement also for the farmer and artisan, whose days end when the sun sets; their thoughts then turn to the morrow. All Jewish holy days begin with the preceding evening.

Friday evening thus becomes a night of solemn observance. The food is prepared during the day, the body beautified, a festive table is laid out.

Traditionally the mother, guardian of the home, kindles the Sabbath lights, blessing God and invoking His blessing upon her household. There must be at least two candles on the table—a double portion, compared to the single dim light that was once the only illumination during the week.

Also traditionally, the father would attend worship accompanied by only the male members of the family. The mother stayed at home with the female members and the infants. This gave her an hour of relaxation and meditation after strenuous Sabbath preparations, and refreshed her for the Sabbath meal that was to follow. Today, women frequently accompany their husbands to worship and the family prays together. It is also hoped that the men in the family assist the women in the Sabbath preparations.

After the opening Psalms, the welcome hymn to the Sabbath Bride is sung, and, following the habit of the mystics, the congregation turns to the door, welcoming the Bride. Sabbath Psalms (Psalms 92, 93) follow. The evening prayer is offered, followed by the Kiddush.

When the father returns home, the family welcome the Sabbath angels, which, according to tradition, accompany him home to bless his festive table. The father praises his wife, diligent mother, as a "woman of valor," knowing that the joyful family Sabbath is her work (Proverbs 31:10–31). Both parents bless their children with the biblical blessing (Numbers 6:25–26) and bestow upon them their Sabbath kiss.

On the table stands the cup of wine, and beside it lie two loaves of bread (**hallah**) covered by an embroidered cloth. The loaves are a reminder of the double portion of Manna, covered by a layer of dew, allotted Israel in the desert every Friday.

The father raises the cup, blessing God for the Sabbath. This is the **Kiddush**, the sanctification of the Sabbath. Every family member shares in the wine. He cuts the hallah, praising God for bread, and each member partakes of it. The festive meal follows, concluded by songs and grace.

The following morning, the family attends worship, which includes the reading of Torah, a special section for each week. Seven people are "called up" to follow the reader, who recites from the sacred scroll. Each offers a blessing of thanksgiving for the gift of Torah. An eighth person reads the Haftarah, the prophetic selection of the day. The service may also include a sermon, an interpretation of Torah.

The family then returns home for Kiddush and a joyful meal. The rest of the day belongs to the people, as the morning belonged to God. Torah study may be included. An afternoon nap after the midday meal has become an accepted folk habit. A leisurely stroll in nature can also be part of the observance.

The afternoon prayer calls the worshippers back to the synagogue. Torah is read again—the first section of next week's portion. In this manner, a bridge is built across the hardships of the week; a new Sabbath beckons.

The *Third Meal,* between the afternoon and evening prayers, was for the mystics a time of immersion into the eternal. It has been adapted in Israel and among some Jewish groups elsewhere as an hour of song, praise, and fellowship.

Evening worship commences when three stars have appeared in the sky: night has fallen. (Generally, the Jewish calendar gives the exact time.) **Habdalah** follows: the "separation" from the holy day. The cup is filled to overflowing, and a portion of the wine caught in a plate beneath it, symbolizing the hope that happiness may overflow during the week. A twisted candle is lit; it is held high by the youngest. The father begins to recite the Habdalah. He then takes a box filled with spices—often in the form of a tower, for God is tower of salvation—sniffs the sweet-smelling contents, and passes the box around. May each member of the family take a last whiff of the Sabbath aroma into the week.

The father speaks the blessing over the flame of the candle. This is the beginning of the first day of the week, when God created the light (Genesis 1). God is praised for the light. After giving thanks, he makes use of this light by watching the play of light and shadow on his hands. On conclusion of the Habdalah, the candle is dipped into the overflow of the wine to be extinguished.

The greeting of the Sabbath is "*Shabbat Shalom,*" or, in Yiddish, "*Gut Schabbes.*" After Habdalah, the wish expressed in greeting is "*Shabua tov,*" or, in Yiddish, "*A gute Woch*"—both meaning "a good week."

Habdalah Set—*including Kiddush cup, spice box (seventeenth-century, German) in the form of a tower, and twisted candle—on a plate for the overflow of the wine.* (Photo by Kathie Minami, reproduced courtesy of Judah L. Magnes Memorial Museum, Jewish Museum of the West, Berkeley, California.)

A short repast is offered, to "accompany the Queen (Sabbath)" on her retreat. Pleas for divine protection during the week are rendered to God. May Elijah, guardian of Israel, accompany the members of the family on their chores and soon herald the arrival of the Messiah.

In medieval times, Jewish families had a special "Sabbath lamp," lit only on the Sabbath, which could be lowered and raised. This led to a common saying: "As the lamp is lowered [on Friday], sorrow rises and vanishes; as the lamp is raised [after Habdalah], sorrow descends again."

The best expression of the essence of the Sabbath is perhaps found in the following paragraph from the Mussaf prayer:

> They who observe the Sabbath and call it a delight rejoice in Your kingdom. The people that hallow the seventh day are all sated and given delight out of Your goodness. For upon the seventh day You poured out Your grace and hallowed it; You called it the most precious of days, in remembrance of the works of creation.

Variations.   Having described the traditional observance at its most complete, we should note that there are many variations in Sabbath celebration and observance. For instance, many American congregations have instituted a late Friday night service for those who cannot observe the Sabbath in the home, followed by **Oneg Shabbat,** a fellowship hour. Reform Jews do not consider themselves bound by work prohibitions.

Of Wine and Bread.   Wine and bread are widely used in Jewish observances. They are indeed most precious gifts resulting from the partnership of God and human beings. The divine gifts of nature are transformed into perfect food through human ingenuity. In raising the cup of wine, the head of the house proclaims an even deeper meaning. **Kos,** the Hebrew word for cup, is derived from *kosas,* to measure out. It stands, therefore, for the gifts God has measured out, be they plentiful or scanty, pleasant or full of sorrow. As Jews raise the cup, they give thanks for all.

20

THE JEWISH CALENDAR
AND HOLY DAYS

As we walk through the year, the seasons of nature and the events of Israel's historical march from slavery to freedom under God are all remembered and given meaning in the observance of the Jewish holy days. In order to understand how these days of remembrance are fixed, we must briefly look at the Jewish calendar.

THE JEWISH CALENDAR

The Jewish years are numbered from the date of creation, arrived at by the ancients by adding up the years of the generations in Scripture. While we know that the report of Scripture does not coincide with scientific knowledge of the world's origin, there has been no change in the numbering; it recalls God's creatorship. Thus the year 1000 of the general calendar is equivalent to the year 4760 in the Jewish one, except that the Jewish years start in the fall.

The months of the Jewish year correspond to the cycle of the moon, beginning and ending with the new moon. In this sense, the year is lunar-oriented. When Israel dwelt in its own land under its own sovereignty, the Sanhedrin solemnly proclaimed the beginning of each month upon receiving testimony that the first sickle of the moon had appeared in the sky. Messengers were then sent out to all communities to give them the exact date, which was important for the observance of the holy days. But these messengers could traverse only the land of Israel itself in sufficient time before the festivals; the Jews in the Diaspora had no certification. These latter Jews, therefore, observed two days for each holy day to be certain that one of them was correct. To this day, Jews in Israel observe only one day of festivals, whereas Orthodox Jews in the world observe two, even though we have a firm calendar and know the exact dates. Reform Judaism has felt that there is no longer any need for a second day, since the exact dates are known; hence it observes only one day of every festival. Since 1969, Conservative Judaism has made the observance of the second day optional, thereby achieving a coordination of holy day observances with those of Israel. The second day of Rosh Hashanah is to remain compulsory, as it is observed in Israel.

The Jewish calendar was permanently fixed by Hillel II (about the middle of the fourth century C.E.) and has worked well through the centuries. It is based on a combination of solar and lunar years, in order that all festivals should occur during the same season of the year. The lunar year has only 354 days, 10 days fewer than the solar year; consequently, unless adjusted, its dates would recede, and festivals would run through all the seasons. This may not be. To adjust the two calendars, 7 leap years of 30 additional days each (one whole month) were included in every cycle of 19 years. (Nineteen moon years of 354 days equals 6,726 days; add to it 7 times 30 days, or 210 days, and we arrive at 6,936 days, the approximate equivalent of 19 sun years; other minor adjustments, in addition to leap years, take care of the variations in the sun year.) Thus Jewish holy days may move back and forth within the span of 30 days of the sun year, but they always fall in the same season.

It may help us in our discussion of the festivals, which accentuate the course of the Jewish calendar year, to list them in a table, giving their position in the seasons of the year, their length, and their biblical origin. Those that are observed as major holy days are underlined, and an asterisk marks those that are observed for only one day in Reform Judaism and in Israel. We shall start with the fall month of *Tishri*, beginning between September 6 and October 4 of the solar year.

The days of fasting commemorate tragic events in Jewish history and call Jews to repentance. They have no specific names and are simply called by the calendar date. The names of the months are of Persian derivation; Torah simply calls them "first month," "seventh month," etc., counting them from Nissan, the month of liberation, the beginning of Israel's freedom (Exodus 12:2).

The days of the year are accented by the Sabbath, which suspends their uniformity: Life must not become routine. The seasons of the year call man and woman to judgment by the success and failure of each season's harvest. The festivals provide the accents.

THE DAYS OF AWE

In the fall of the year, when the harvest is gathered, the farmers ponder: If the harvest is poor, where have they failed to sow and irrigate? If the harvest is good, how can they apply the same procedures again, and in other parts? They judge themselves, make their accounting. Translating this approach into spiritual terms, Judaism has appointed special days in the fall as days of judgment, divine and human. As the accounting at harvest time is a universal task, so is spiritual judgment seen as universal.

As the farmer's day ends at nightfall, so the Jewish calendar day also

Name of month	Hebrew date	Festival	Biblical origin	Observed and obligatory in Israel and Conservatism	In Reform
Tishri	1	Rosh Hashanah	Lev. 23:23–25	Yes	Yes
	2	Rosh Hashanah		Yes	No
	3	Fast of Gedaliah	II Kings 25:22–25 Zechariah 7:5; 8:19	Yes	No
	10	Yom Kippur	Lev. 23:26–32	Yes	Yes
	15	Sukkot*	Lev. 23:33–36 Deut. 16:13–17	Yes	Yes
	16	Sukkot		Yes in both, but not as major holiday in Israel and Reform	
	17–22	Sukkot		Yes	Yes
	22	Shemini Atzeret*		Yes	Yes
	23	Simhat Torah		No	No
Marheshvan					
Kislev	25	Hanukkah	Apocrypha: Maccabees	Yes in both; observed for 8 days	
Tebet	10	Fast day		Yes	No
Shebat	15	New Year's Day of Trees		Yes	Yes
Adar I (*additional month in leap years*)					
Adar II	13	Fast of Esther	Book of Esther	Yes	No
	14	Purim	Book of Esther	Yes	Yes
Nissan	15	Pessah*	Exod. 12; Lev. 23:4–8	Yes	Yes
	16	Pessah	Deut. 16:1–8	Yes in both, but not as major holiday in Israel and Reform	
	17–20	Pessah		Yes	Yes
	21	Pessah*		Yes	Yes
	22	Pessah		No	No
Iyar**					
Sivan	6	Shabuot*	Exod. 19–20	Yes	Yes
	7	Shabuot	Lev. 23:15–21 Deut. 16:9–12	No	No
Tammuz	17	Fast day	Zech. 7:5; 8:19	Yes	No
Ab	9	Fast day	Jeremiah 52	Yes	No
Elul					

*Observed for only 1 day in Israel and Reform Judaism and—optionally—in Conservative Judaism.

**Following the Holocaust and the restoration of the State of Israel, several days of minor observance have come into popular acceptance. These newly established days of popular observance fall into this period: Yom Ha-Shoa on the 27th of Nissan; Yom Ha-Atzmaut on the 5th of Iyar; and the emerging celebration of Yom Yerushalayim on the 27th of Iyar.

ends at nightfall, and a new day begins then. As the farmer's year ends at harvest time, so the Jewish year does the same.

Fall marks **Rosh Hashanah**, the Beginning of the Year, New Year's Day. "On the first of Tishri the calendar year begins" (Mishnah Rosh Hashanah 1:1). The opening period of the year is a time of great solemnity, sober judgment, and awesome awareness of God's power. It is a period of repentance, a return to God, of renewal. These are **Yamin Norain**, the Days of Awe.

Pious tradition linked this moment of renewal with the supposed date of the creation of the world; it must be a creative moment in the building of a better world. The Days of Awe open with the festival of Rosh Hashanah, followed by a week of repentance (when in daily pursuits Jews are bidden to put into action the resolutions they have made). They culminate in Yom Kippur, the Day of Atonement, when—in complete separation from the world, united with God for a full period of a night and day—Jews confess their shortcomings and ask for forgiveness, not only of God but equally of their fellows, and return to daily living with new confidence and a new purpose.

Rosh Hashanah

The Preparation. To awaken the faithful from the slumber of unexamined living, the **shofar** (ram's horn, the oldest musical instrument in use at any worship service in the Western world) is sounded in daily worship for an entire month preceding the festival. In the days preceding Rosh Hashanah, special services of intercession—Selihot (prayers for forgiveness)—are held at early morning hours. On the holy day itself, however, no confession is heard, no plea is yet offered. Confession of sins is preceded by the affirmation of God, to whom they are to be confessed; Rosh Hashanah is the day of affirmation. God is proclaimed as King, Judge, and Redeemer of all humanity, and the shofar is sounded in His honor.

The Eve. Evening services are simple. On returning to the festive meal in the evening, Jews find several symbols on the table in addition to the usual wine and bread. The hallah may be round, in the form of a wheel, for a wheel goes through the world, and those who are on top may be down before long and those who are low may be raised soon, as God's will may be. May all put trust in Him rather than in their own strength. A sweet apple is dipped into honey and consumed by the members of the family: May the year be sweet.

The Morning. Early in the morning, the people return to worship. Curtains, Torah covers, pulpit coverings are all white, symbol of purity. In Orthodox synagogues, the men wear the white garments in which they will some day be buried, a reminder of human frailty and equally of human equality. (Before God, all are alike, weak mortals; yet their very weakness evokes divine mercy and must lead them to be tolerant with one another.) On holy days a special prayer book called **Mahzor** is used. It contains the liturgy of the day, embellished by religious poems, the **Piyutim,** by various poets of various times. The morning prayer is followed by the scriptural reading. It tells of Abraham, prepared to give his son in obedience to God's will, and of how God set aside the sacrifice, a call to humanity to do its utmost, trusting in divine love.

The shofar's voice is heard. Its sound is weird, primitive, like the outcry of the human heart. In its piercing sound is enshrined the full message of the day. Maimonides explains it:

> Wake up, sleepers, from your sleep; and you that are in daze, arouse yourselves from your stupor. Reflect on your actions and return in repentance. Remember your Creator. Be not as those who forget truth in their chase after shadows, wasting their year wholly in vanities which neither help nor bring deliverance. Look into your soul, and mend your ways and deeds. Let everyone forsake his evil ways and worthless thoughts. (Teshubah 3, 4)

Four signals are sounded in succession: **Tekiah,** a long-drawn sound; **Shebarim,** a three-times broken sound; **Teruah,** a whimpering, nine-times broken sound; and, again, Tekiah. As the rabbis point out, Tekiah is the wakening call; Shebarim the sobbing of the contrite heart; Teruah the weeping of a heart aware of its guilt; and Tekiah the straight, awakening sound again.

Samson Raphael Hirsch has elaborated on the meaning by comparing the sounds to the signals alerting the people during their wanderings in the desert. Tekiah called them to attention in their daily routine, and thus it calls

Author sounding the Shofar. (Courtesy of Robert McKenzie, Napa.)

again. Shebarim and Teruah were signals commanding the people to break up camp; thus it becomes a call to break with the past and its errors. Tekiah once again called the people to start marching in a new direction; it enjoins change of direction in life toward holier goals ("Choreb," *Versuche über Jisroels Pflichten*, Altona, 1837, pp. 182ff.).

The Mussaf prayer brings the affirmation to its climax. Before the congregation proclaims God's holiness in Isaiah's words—"Holy, holy, holy, is the Lord of hosts, the whole earth is full of His glory"—it reflects on God's power in a symbolic hymn by Calonymus be Meshullam of Mainz (though ascribed by him to one of the earlier medieval martyrs of faith):

> Let us speak of the great holiness of this day, for it is indeed a day of awe and dread. On it Your kingdom is exalted, Your throne established in mercy, and You are enthroned upon it. In truth, You are judge and prosecutor, knower and witness, recorder and sealer. . . . You remember long forgotten deeds. You open the book of memories, and it tells its own story, for the seal of every man's hand is set to his act. The great Shofar is sounded, and a still, small voice is heard. The angels theselves are dismayed and gripped by fear and trembling. They affirm: See, the Day of Judgment that summons the whole heavenly host to judgment; for in Your judgment not even they are flawless. . . . And all that live You let pass before You as a flock of sheep. . . . On Rosh Hashanah the sentence is inscribed, on Yom Kippur it is sealed: how many shall pass away, and how many shall be born; who shall live and who shall die. . . . But Repentance, and Prayer, and Works of Goodness annul every severe decree . . . for . . . You do not desire the death of the guilty, rather that he turn from his way and live. To the very day of his death You wait for him. If he returns You will right away receive him. In truth, You are their Creator, know their urges, that they are but flesh and blood. After all, man's origin is dust, and his end is dust . . . but You are King, the Living, Everlasting God.

This hymn is regarded by some scholars as the source of "Dies Irae" in the Catholic Requiem Mass.

The Mussaf then moves to the threefold proclamation of God, using appropriate verses from Scripture:

Malkhiot: God is King: "Shema (Hear, O Israel)" is acknowledgment of His Kingship. Then the shofar is sounded in royal proclamation.

Zikhronot: He is the Judge who mercifully remembers all His creatures even while judging them, as He has done from Noah's days to ours. The Covenant God made with Noah, Abraham, Isaac, and Jacob is brought to mind. The section concludes with the words: "Praised be You, O God, who remembers the Covenant." The shofar is again sounded.

Shofarot: He is Redeemer, who, by the sound of the shofar, once gave His Ten Commandments, and who, by the sound of the shofar, will redeem humanity. The shofar is sounded once again, expressing trust in His redemptive power.

The Afternoon.   In the afternoon a quaint custom is observed, which may possibly stem from Christian usage (at least, Petrarch tells us of having observed it in the city of Cologne). The people go to the river, reciting verses from Micah: "And You will cast their sins into the depth of the sea" (7:19). May God do so unto the penitent, who symbolically express the desire to abandon sin to the waves.

The week following Rosh Hashanah is a period of implementation. Selihot are offered every day, early in the morning. The day immediately following Rosh Hashanah is a day of fasting, when no food or drink may be consumed. It is called the Fast of **Gedaliah.** Gedaliah was the Jewish governor placed in charge of the community in Palestine by the Babylonians after the destruction of the first Temple. Holding him responsible for their unhappy fate, the people murdered him, bringing the wrath of the king upon them, which forced them to give up their homeland in flight. The message is obvious. People must not blame others for their troubles, or try to find scapegoats for their fate, for the end of such an attitude spells disaster.

This whole period, including Rosh Hashanah and Yom Kippur, is called "The Ten Days of Repentance."

Yom Kippur

As Jews approach the holiest day of the year—the Day of Atonement, **Yom Kippur**—they must make up the wrongs done to their fellows, for without reconciliation among people, there can be no forgiveness from God. The rabbis ordain that all people must seek out their enemies again and again and, being approached by others, the offended parties must show generosity in forgiving and forgetting fully and graciously. Then they are ready for Yom Kippur.

For twenty-four hours no food or drink may touch the lips of the Jew, no earthly concerns enter his mind as he stands before God. In token of castigation, Orthodox Jews wear soft shoes instead of leather ones. Memorial lights are lit so that the memory of the departed may be an inspiration to their descendants, and the men stand in the garments of death. All prayers during the twenty-four-hour period include the confession of sin. It is recited privately, for only God to hear, but it is also repeated in unison, to acknowledge mutual responsibility one for another. The confession thus renews the spirit of the responsible kinship of all people. A plea to "Our Father, Our King" (throughout the Ten Days of Repentance, *Teshuvah*) is offered. May God grant health and sustenance, forgiveness, and peace.

Before departing for the Synagogue, the mother lights the holy day candles, speaking the blessing. The parents bless their children with a special blessing. A twenty-four-hour candle will shed its gleam upon the returning family later at night. Yom Kippur, though a fast, is a festival, a day of spiritual rejoicing.

Yom Kippur lacks the drama of the Shofar; it is all inwardness. In the synagogue, all the lamps burn bright; memorial candles flicker. The people are dressed in white and wear the tallit. They stand in awe as they face the white curtained Ark.

The Evening. Worship opens with the **Kol Nidre,** known for its haunting melody. In itself, the prayer is simply a declaration of dispensation from ascetic vows once made but not kept. The tune, however, expresses all the longing for God, the agony of those who pledged their lives to Him yet found it cut short in martyrdom. Immediately, the outcry finds answer: God says, "I have forgiven."

The regular evening service is offered, followed by Selihot, confession of sins, and the plea to "Our Father, Our King." It is a long service. Some will remain in the synagogue for most of the night, reciting the Book of Psalms in antiphon, followed by various meditations on God's greatness.

The Morning. The morning service starts early. The early hours of the day are seen as the most auspicious time for the plea for divine forgiveness by the people confessing their sins. Scripture reading follows. Its prophetic portion includes the following passage from Isaiah (58: 5–7), clarifying the message of the fast:

> Is not this the fast that I have chosen, to loose the fetters of the wickedness, to undo the bands of the yoke, to let the oppressed go free, and to break every yoke? Is it not to share your bread with the hungry, and that you bring the poor that are cast out to your house; when you see the naked that you cover him, and that you hide not yourself from your own flesh?

The message fits in well with the confession of sins, for in the formal confession the transgressions against God are not mentioned; only those toward humanity are mentioned.

Noon. The congregation enters the Mussaf prayer. In it, the ancient ritual of the service in the Temple is recited. As it reaches the portion which tells of the people prostrating themselves before God, the congregation kneels and proclaims, "Praised be His Name, His glorious Kingdom is forever and ever." During the year, Jews do not kneel, for the action might be misunderstood: Are they kneeling before God, or is the burden of life pressing them down? Now, in solitude before Him, away from the world, but having understood the message of Isaiah, the congregation becomes the symbol of a humanity unitedly bending the knee before Him. Trusting that this future will become a reality, pledging to work for it, the people kneel.

Afternoon. A second Scripture reading follows. To make clear that God's love and forgiveness and His kingdom are not reserved for Jews but are given to all humanity, the book of Jonah is recited as part of this Scripture reading. All are God's children, as Jonah learns:

> Should I not have pity on Nineveh [says God], that great city, in which there are more than a hundred and twenty thousand people who cannot discern between their right hand and their left hand, and much cattle, too? (Jonah 4:11)

The Minhah (afternoon) prayer follows. Its purpose throughout the year is to give pause for reflection on the course of the day so far. On Yom Kippur, it brings to mind those whose lives had been lived truly to the fullest, the martyrs. Together with a memorial service for the departed, which is part of the Yom Kippur service, it extends the link to the past from which the march toward a future can be charted. The individual thus stands between past and future, a link in an eternal chain.

The Twilight Hour. **Ne'eelah** (the closing prayer during the fading hours of the day), is a special prayer for Yom Kippur:

> Open unto us the gate, at the time that the gate is being closed,
> as day has almost waned.
> The day is waning, the sun is setting fast,
> let us enter Your gates!

Nightfall. As the stars rise in the sky, and the day is completed, the congregation stands in silence. This is the moment of affirmation, the moment of the vision of God's kingdom. Slowly, word by word, the people recite before the open Ark:

> Hear, O Israel, the Lord our God, the Lord is One!
> Blessed be His Name, His glorious Kingdom is forever and ever!
> The Lord, He is God!

The Ark is closed. The shofar is sounded—Tekiah! Onward into life! Finally, Habdalah is recited.

The road leads directly to *Sukkot,* the Festival of Thanksgiving for harvest and shelter that God has bestowed. Sukkot follows five days after Yom Kippur.

SUKKOT: COVENANT OF NATURE AND SOCIETY

The spiritual stocktaking of the Days of Awe has served as preparation for an accounting of the physical blessings in a spirit of gratitude rather than in simply economic terms; hence **Sukkot** immediately follows, a festival of joy before God who has blessed and "will bless all your crops and all your undertakings, and you will have nothing but joy" (Deuteronomy 16:15).

The Symbols of Sukkot

The Festive Bouquet. Scripture (Leviticus 23:40) ordains that a bouquet of four plants be brought to the sanctuary—citron (**etrog**), a branch of the date palm (**lulab**), myrtles (*Hadassim*), and willows of the brook (*arabot*). These

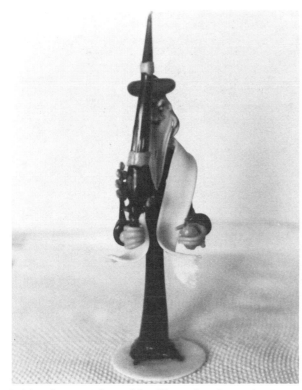

Lulab and Etrog. Whimsical handblown glass figurine by Gianni Toso of Venice. Note the additional plants (myrtles and willows) attached to the lulab (palm branch), held in the right hand, and the etrog (citron), held in the left. (Photo by the author from his own collection.)

four represent the variety of the produce of the earth: citron, an edible fruit of pleasant taste and smell; the date (the branches of which are presented), an edible fruit tasty without smell; myrtles, tasteless but of sweet smell; and willows, which have neither taste nor fragrance but are of use. All of these varities are essential for life; without any one of them, the bouquet is worthless. The rabbis saw in them a symbol of humanity itself: There are those who have both intelligence and human kindness (taste and smell); others who have but intelligence nourishing society without fully relating to their neighbors; those whose kindness sweetens the atmosphere about them though they be far from brilliant; and, finally, those who are in no way distinguished yet are needed in the framework of our society. No human being is expendable.

    These four plants are brought to the synagogue, and during the recitation of the Psalms of Thanksgiving (Psalms 113–118, the Hallel), they are pointed in six directions (the four directions of the compass and above and below) with the recital: "Praise the Lord for He is good, His goodness endureth forever." This expresses symbolically that God is found in all the directions of

Traditionally every Jew brings the Arba Minim to the synagogue for the festival prayer service. The Talmud notes that even "a child who knows how to shake the lulab is obligated to do so." The men wear the tallit in various ways. (Photo by Phyllis Friedman.)

the universe. We may see in this observance one of the reasons for the significance of the number seven: They are six directions, forming the sources of divine blessing, and finally human beings, the seventh point, who must gather them to make good use of them.

This human function is expressed at the end of the Mussaf service. Now, preceded by the Scroll of the Torah, the congregation, with the bouquets in hand, marches in procession through the sanctuary, as once they surrounded the altar in the Temple. (Guided by Torah, they take in hand the gifts of the world in procession through days and years.) The congregation intones, "Hoshanah, Save us, O God, we beseech You." (It is Jews and humanity on the move, in the best sense of the word, invoking God's help that their work be accomplished.)

The Sukkah.   As God must be Mover, He equally provides shelter and rest. This is expressed in the **Sukkah,** a small hut or booth covered with a roof of branches and leaves, in which the family takes its meals during the holiday, if the weather is good. Originally a shelter in the harvest fields, the Sukkah was endowed by Torah with a deeper meaning: God made the people dwell in

Family Celebrating the Sukkot Festival in the Sukkah (pewter, seventeenth-century Germany). Note the roof made of branches and decorations, including the Sabbath lamp. Inscription on the rim: "You shall dwell in Sukkat for seven days" (Lev:23:42). (Photo by Kathie Minami, reproduced courtesy of Judah L. Magnes Memorial Museum, Jewish Museum of the West, Berkeley, California.)

booths when He took them out of Egypt (Leviticus 23:42–43). He gives rest on the march toward the future. As long as twigs and branches form the roof, revealing the stars as witnesses to God's power, we may hope for peace, something concrete shelters implicitly deny. Rabbinic wisdom has explained that Jews go into the Sukkah in the fall, when others return to their homes, to show that they do so not for the sake of comfort in summer's heat but in obedience to Mitzvah. How truly this expresses the fate of the Jews, so often homeless and driven about when others dwelt secure, yet feeling protected by God. This spirit is underscored by the "guests" who are invited symbolically to dwell with the family in the beautifully decorated hut in order that their spirit be an inspiration. There are seven, one for each day: Abraham, Isaac, Jacob, Joseph, Moses, Aaron, and David. All rose to greatness through homelessness; rather than weakening their faith in divine protection or in their divine mission, their homelessness strengthened it.

Two elements are combined in the lesson of Sukkot. In ancient days, our greatest enemy was nature. It might withhold sustenance from us; failure of crops, storms, and natural disasters might lead to famine; epidemics might strike. In the festive bouquet, thanksgiving is expressed for harvest and, with it, for the preservation of life amid the natural hazards. In modern times, we have largely mastered nature, assured ourselves of abundant food, at least in

Western countries, and defeated many diseases. Technology has provided us with the means. But a new danger has arisen as a result of our technological progress; human beings themselves. Locked in conflicts while distances have shrunk, armed with the latest weapons of world destruction, we are greatly to be feared. Wars are getting to be ever more frightful and all-encompassing. The Sukkah, therefore, makes it clear that we can and must live together in an open society, finding shelter in the spirit of love, which is the imitation of God. Then it will dwell secure. The Jews are to maintain humanity's hope by their steadfast endurance throughout their historic wanderings. Sukkot serves as a contemporary reminder to us to preserve nature.

Yet the vision of the future may lead to skepticism: Can it ever come to pass? The people may well argue, "We have heard the message, but in a few days the festival will be over, and we will be back to the eternal, hopeless round of dreary toil and suffering." Fall and the onrush of winter, together with the events of the day, may speak more loudly than Torah and Mitzvot and holy days could. With psychological insight, the rabbis permitted the people to express these thoughts. On Sukkot, the Book of Ecclesiastes is read: "Vanity of vanities, all is vanity," all is hopeless. As the feelings are given vent, an opportunity for an answer is also given:

> The end of the matter, all having been heard; fear God, and keep his Mitzvot; for this is the whole man. For God shall bring every work into the judgment concerning every hidden thing, whether it be good or whether it be evil. (Ecclesiastes 12:13–14)

In Orthodox congregations, Sukkot ends with two days of celebration: **Sh'mini Atzeret,** the "Eighth Day, Feast of Conclusion," and **Simhat Torah.** Non-Orthodox congregations may celebrate only one day. On the last day of the Sukkot season (called **Simhat Torah,** Joy in Torah), the annual cycle of scripture readings from the Torah Scroll is completed and the new cycle started immediately. The Scrolls are carried in procession, followed by the children, who receive sweets. There is no end, there is always the beginning, and it is linked to ever new hope with every succeeding generation. With the Torah in their arms (literally), the Jews step out of the holy day season into the winter and the new year.

THE BEGINNING OF A MONTH

By biblical command, the beginning of a month is observed in special worship (Numbers 10:10, 28:11–15). It is announced on the preceding Sabbath with a prayer for divine help. In the ancient city of Mainz, where I grew up, this announcement was always recited in the theme song of whatever holy day might fall during the period of the next month. In announcement of Heshvan, the month following the fall festivals, the melody was adapted from the recitative usually employed in the study of the Talmud. The month of Heshvan has no holidays; the announcement sets the key for the month and the winter: The study and practice of Torah is to give it light. Only a few minor festivals occur during this period.

HANUKKAH

In midwinter, the festival of **Hanukkah** is observed for eight days. It is a very minor holiday, the only one that has no biblical source, as it is based on the story of the **Maccabees** related in the Apocrypha. In the year 167 C.E., Antiochus IV, Epiphanes, overlord of Syria (to which Judah belonged), introduced the worship of Greek gods as the state religion, ordained for himself divine recognition, desecrated the Temple, and prohibited the exercise of Jewish religion. A small band of heroic fighters, led by Judah the Maccabee, arose against him, prepared to give their lives for freedom of religion. As far as we know, this was the first time in history that men rose in a concerted, organized, popular movement in defense of their faith. They overcame the enemy and reconsecrated the Temple; *Hanukkah* means dedication.

This is the background of the observance, yet it does not celebrate a victory of arms, but that of the spirit. The rabbis tell a story: When the Maccabees entered the Temple, they found the menorah unusable; they took their spears, fashioning out of them a makeshift menorah, transforming the weapons of war into the implements of peace. They also found that there was left only one small cruse of oil, still bearing the seal of the high priest, just sufficient to light the menorah for one day. It would take eight days to prepare new oil, which is required for it by biblical injunction (Leviticus 24:1–4; see also Numbers 8:1–4). Miraculously, the oil supposedly burned for eight days, until a new supply had been prepared (Shabbat 21). It was then ordained that every year in every home the light be lit in memory and as inspiration.

Observance

A nine-branched menorah is used. There are some types of menorah in which oil is used, but candles are permitted and usual. The center light, set apart, is the **shamash,** the serving light, with which the others are kindled. Every evening, an additional candle is lighted, beginning with one and eventually reaching eight, even as the miracle grew day by day. It is the spiritual aspect that matters, not victory in war; and this is brought out in the Haftarah of the Sabbath during Hanukkah: "Not by might nor by power but by My spirit [will ye prevail]" (Zechariah 4:6).

The festival is minor, and there is no work prohibition. While the candles are burning, the family might engage in work which really is not work, such as playing cards. Children play with a *dreidel* (a little top, from the German *drehen,* to turn, spin). Four letters are engraved on it: *N* (which gives the child *n*othing), *G* (which allows him to *g*et all out of the kitty), *H* (which

Hanukkah Menorah (brass, seventeenth-century Dutch). The menorah shows in stylized form the cups and calixes that were hammered out of the seven-branched menorah of the Tabernacle (Exodus 37:17 ff.). (Photo by Kathie Minami, reproduced courtesy of Judah L. Magnes Memorial Museum, Jewish Museum of the West, Berkeley, California.)

gives him *h*alf), and *S* (which compels him to *s*et or put one—a nut or a chip or a penny—into the kitty). But the letters also form the initials of the sentence: *Nes Gadol Hayah Sham,* a Great Miracle Happened There. The children might get a few coins to play the game. This was the extent of gifts.

Hanukkah has become a much more important holiday in contemporary America. The house is decorated, and the children receive gifts every night of the feast. This "upgrading" of Hanukkah may be regarded as significant in several ways. Jewish practices evolve and change in accordance with popular consensus among Jews, a testimony to the character of Judaism as a living and unfolding civilization. Hanukkah unquestionably assumed a greater significance due to its proximity to Christmas. Both occur at roughly the same time; both are festivals of light. The increased emphasis on Hanukkah reflects a desire of many parents to give their children an occasion for celebration that is similar to that of their Christian friends. This change reveals the

Hanukkah Menorah, in form of a wall plaque for decorative use during the year (brass, nineteenth-century Dutch). The shamash (serving light) is elevated above a plaque with the Hebrew inscription "For Mitzvah is a lamp, Torah a light." This menorah burns oil. (Photo by Kathie Minami, reproduced courtesy of Judah L. Magnes Memorial Museum, Jewish Museum of the West, Berkeley, California.)

influence of the surrounding culture on the development of Jewish ways, and the ability of Judaism to absorb these influences into its own structure.

Hanukkah should not be regarded as a substitute for Christmas, however, nor should the menorah be viewed as a substitute for the Christmas tree. The celebration through light in both religious traditions goes back to ancient pagan rites that celebrated the winter solstice. Christians and Jews have adopted it and adjusted it, each in their own way, to celebrate the light of spiritual renewal. Thus is created a unity-in-difference that is of value to the adherents of both religions in their individual expressions and in their common endeavors.

Hanukkah reveals another side of Jewish religious practice as well. By permitting card playing and games at an appointed time, the rabbis built them into the structure of the faith itself, decreasing their temptation, which a blanket prohibition might increase. We shall see this again in connection with Purim, the Feast of Lots.

OTHER HOLY DAYS

The Tenth Day of Tebet, a fast day, commemorates the siege of Jerusalem. It may also serve to remind the card players that the time has come for a return to their duties.

The Fifteenth of Shebat, planting season in Israel, is observed by giving children various fruits, while the youth in Israel goes out to plant new trees. The link to the Land of Israel is thus made manifest.

The Fast of Esther, a day of reflection before merrymaking, about one month (in a leap year, two months) later, precedes Purim. Esther was called upon, according to the biblical book that bears her name, to plead for her people, whom a wicked enemy, Haman, had planned to destroy. She had to go to the king, unbidden, which could cost her her life, even though she was his wife. In prayer and fasting, she prepared herself. With courage, she approached to plead the cause of her kinfolk, was graciously received, and was permitted to bring deliverance to her people, while Haman was hanged. We have no historical evidence that the story ever happened, yet the spirit deserves emulation.

Purim is known as the Feast of Lots because Haman cast lots to ascertain the best day for the massacre of the Jews. Since **Purim** falls during the Christian carnival season, it has acquired many of its characteristics. In the evening and morning, the Book of Esther is recited from a special scroll, the Megillah. Children are armed with noisemakers and are permitted to rattle them whenever the name of Haman is mentioned, for the joyful sound of children dwelling in the house of God has always overcome the designs of Israel's foes. The morning is given over to the exchange of gifts. Esther commanded that all send gifts to their friends and to the poor; only this way can deliverance be celebrated. The poor cannot reject the gifts they are handed, not because they need them, but because they are from friends. No one can feel ashamed. The afternoon brings merrymaking. Masquerades were introduced during the Middle Ages. In Israel, there are great carnival parades. Purim is specially set aside as a day when getting drunk becomes a Mitzvah:

> He shall drink until he no longer knows whether Mordecai [who planned the rescue with Esther] is to be blessed or cursed, or whether Haman [the villain] is to be cursed or blessed. (*Shulhan Arukh*)

In Israel, the feast is therefore also called *Ad delo Yada,* "Till he knows no longer." Again, we note the psychological insight of the rabbis. By permitting drunkenness on one day, they eliminated the temptation of alcohol. Jews have always used alcohol in moderation, accompanying it with a prayer, which transforms the taking of a drink into a Mitzvah, or a toast, *L'hayim,* may it be unto life.

PESSAH (PASSOVER): THE BIRTH AND THE COVENANT OF FREEDOM

Pessah, the festival of spring, comes one month after Purim and marks the rebirth of nature in renewed strength and promise. In the Land of Israel, it is the season of the beginning harvest: The grain has grown, the lambs have developed to usefulness for human needs. From the earliest times, people have marked this moment in celebration, rejoicing in the harvest of early grain. Farmers linked their feasting to that of the shepherds, who saw the flock blessed. Pessah has remained a festival of nature, of gratitude for the land and for its yield, but Torah gave it an additional meaning. It has become the festival of freedom, commemorating the deliverance of Israel from Egyptian bondage, that the Jews be servants of God and not of men. The fusion of these ideas into the unity of God-Torah-Land-Mitzvah is most clearly expressed in Deuteronomy 16:1–4:

> Observe the "month of the green corn," and prepare a Passover unto the Lord your God, for in the month of green corn did the Lord your God lead you out of Egypt by night. [Note the linking of agriculture to a historical event.] Offer a Passover sacrifice of the flock and the herd in the place which the Lord will choose for His Name to reside there. [The shepherd's thanksgiving is fused with Mitzvah, a response to God.] You shall not eat leavened food with it; for seven days shall you eat *matzot* [unleavened bread], the bread of affliction; for in great hurry did you go forth from the Land of Egypt. [The historical significance of the feast is added to its agricultural and pastoral one.] Thus shall you remember the day of your departure from Egypt all the days of your life. [The event in all its implications calls for a commitment.] And there shall not be seen any leaven in all your domain for seven days. . . .

The Message.   Pessah makes God manifest as God of Nature and of History. Freedom is the principal message of Pessah; social conduct must make us deserving of it. Pessah and the Exodus from Egypt are therefore the key event and key challenge to the Jews. The Ten Commandments establish God as He "who brought you out of the Land of Egypt, out of the house of bondage." Every Sabbath and holy day worship includes the words "in remembrance of the Exodus of Egypt." Daily worship contains this remembrance as well. The Exodus revealed God as Master of history, making us His co-workers, in order that freedom might extend to all. "The stranger . . . you shall love . . . as yourself, for you were strangers in the land of Egypt: I am the Lord your God" (Leviticus 19:34).

Matzah.   It is too easy to forget this, and it is quite common for the poor, having become affluent, to *wish* to forget, and to think only of themselves. This may not be. On the festival of deliverance and harvest joy, the Jews may feast themselves not on pastry but on **matzah**—the unleavened bread, consumed in Egypt when slavery permitted little time to prepare decent bread. This matzah is the bread of liberty as well, symbol of freedom "because they were thrust out of Egypt and could not tarry" (Exodus 12:39) to bake real bread. Remembrance of enslavement provides the incentive to promote liberty. Matzah consists simply of flour and water baked quickly into a flat substance like a cracker, for it must not rise. The admixture of spices, which wealth can produce, is forbidden, an admonition that prosperity may never lead to that selfishness which forgets to love the stranger and further human welfare. By linking God–Torah–Mitzvah–Land, Judaism has made of a nature and historical festival a powerful call to righteousness. Pessah celebrates the redemption of a people.

Removing Leaven.   In preparation for the festival, all leavened items must be removed. This leaven, **hametz,** includes a great many varieties of bread and pastry, products made with starches, and grain alcohol. No hidden traces may be left. This called for a complete spring housecleaning, which may well have promoted health among the Jews of the Middle Ages, when the general population permitted dirt to accumulate and become a breeder of diseases. On the night before Pessah, "one must search for hametz by the flame of a light" (Pessahim 1:1). It is a custom still observed, a joyful march through the house, when children might gather small pieces of hametz (left on purpose) and be happy in this opportunity to share, learning the meaning of the feast by doing. Since the dishes used throughout the year have become permeated with hametz, Orthodox Jews will replace them by special ones which are used only during the holiday and stored throughout the year.

Ordination of the Seder.   So significant is the message of Pessah, immediately directed to every person, especially the child, that observance in removal of hametz and in the worship of the synagogue is not sufficient. "When, on this day at a future date, your child asks, 'what does this mean?' you [individually] shall *tell* him." (Exodus 13:14). A specific family celebration has thus come into being, truly a Lord's Supper, dedicated to Him on the eve of the holiday. It is based on the family gathering preceding the Exodus (Exodus 12:1–14), when God passed over (hence the name *Passover*) the homes of the Israelites while punishing the Egyptians. Ordained as a perpetual observance, it led to the offering of the paschal lamb in Temple days, which the family shared during the evening meal. Sacrifices are no longer offered in Judaism, but otherwise the **Seder** or "order" of the family service, outlined in the Mishnah (Pessahim), has remained.

The Seder

The Symbols on the Table.   To make the meaning clear to the child, symbols are used:

1. At each seat is a little book containing the story in its right order; it is called *Haggadah,* the story.
2. There is also a cup at each place, which will be filled with wine four times. Four promises of freedom are found in Exodus (6:6–7); four times the cup of deliverance is therefore passed. God says: "I will bring you out from

Seder Plate (silver, German, nineteenth century). The open doors reveal the three tiers for the matzot; the condiments and symbolic items are placed on top and in the ornamental containers. (Photo by Kathie Minami, reproduced courtesy of Judah L. Magnes Memorial Museum, Jewish Museum of the West, Berkeley, California.)

. . . Egypt; will deliver you from their bondage, will redeem you . . . and will take you to Me for a people."

3. An additional cup is placed at the hand of the leader, the father, who conducts the Seder. It reflects a fifth promise of ultimate redemption for all humanity. Traditionally, Elijah is the messenger of this blessed day (Malachi 3:22–24; Malachi 4:4–6, according to the King James version); the cup is thus called "Cup of Elijah." It is not drunk but used only as a reminder to speed the coming of the universal day of peace. The past reaches out to the future.

4. At the head of the table, three matzot are placed, symbol of the three groups in Israel's community who were liberated: Priests, Levites, and common folk, Israelites. They were all redeemed equally; they must all be mindful of the message of the matzah. These three matzot are covered with a cloth.

5. A roasted shankbone is a reminder of the Pessah offering of old (the Passover lamb), combining joy in nature with the spirit of dedication. It is not eaten; there are no more sacrifices.

6. An egg, symbol of nature's awakening, is placed next to it. It also commemorates ancient Temple sacrifices. It, too, is not eaten.

7. A dish of green vegetables (parsley) and a dish of salt water come next; the beauty of nature once was made bitter by the tears the slaves shed in their

toil, and again made glorious as, by God's help, they marched dry-shod through the salty waters of the Sea of Reeds (the Red Sea).

8. Bitter herbs (**maror**) including horseradish—reminders of slavery—and a dish containing a brownish-colored mixture of nuts, apples, wine, and cinnamon (*haroset*)—a reminder of the mortar which ancient Jews had to make for Pharaoh—are placed nearby.

The Service. Opening Ceremonies: Candles are lighted as on every festival. The members of the family recline in comfort; the Kiddush, sanctification of the day, is recited over the first cup of wine. Then parsley is dipped into salt water and distributed; it is a symbol of wealth, as ancient meals always would start with an aperitif, but woven into it is both the idea of spring and redemption and the memory of enslavement, the salty water of tears.

The head of the house breaks the middle matzah, putting aside one portion for later use, even as a poor man would reserve some of his bread for the future. He shows the rest to the family: "This is the bread of poverty our fathers ate in the land of Egypt." Immediately, he draws the relevant conclusion: "May those who are still cast out in the street come and join us in our celebration," that the family may promote the spirit of hospitality which will make humanity free.

The Events of the Past.   Now the child asks the questions of the day: "Why is this night different from all others, as we eat matzah and bitter herbs, dip herbs in condiments, and sit in special comfort?" With these questions, the actual story begins. The *past* is reviewed, a tale briefly interrupted by the father in an admonition to the adults. There are different kinds of children, bright ones and wild ones, average ones and simple ones; treat all children in accordance with their personality and abilities, then the past will become relevant, and the future of tradition will be preserved. Returning to the story of divine rescue in days gone by, the father makes clear the unity of the people: "In every generation each person must look at himself, as if *he* had been freed"; concludes the first part in thanksgiving. The second cup of wine, praising God for help in ages past, is consumed.

The Present.   The *present* enters. The matzah, whose meaning has by now been explained, is shared by all. The bitter herbs are dipped in haroset and consumed. Following the practice of Hillel, a sandwich is made of matzah and bitter herbs, an opportunity of bringing to mind Hillel's way of life and his teachings. He saw the essence of Torah in love of neighbor, and that is the essence of this celebration. The festive meal follows, concluded by the sharing of the matzah previously put aside, the *afikomen,* a reminder of the ancient paschal lamb. Previously the children have been permitted to steal the afikomen, perhaps to keep them entertained, perhaps to indicate that they should early "steal" the spirit of matzah from their elders and carry it into the next generation; they will now receive a small reward for returning it. After grace, the third cup is drunk, in gratitude for God's manifold gifts of the present.

The Future.   Now the thought turns to the *future,* the task ahead. The door is opened to welcome Elijah, symbolically expressing ultimate rescue. In the Middle Ages, this served an additional, tragic purpose. Jews were accused of using Christian blood for the Seder. This was a calumny once directed against Christians, who were accused by the heathens of using pagan blood in the mass, for the idea of the mass was not comprehended by the world. Now Christians, forgetting that they, too, had been outcasts, leveled it against the Jews, and the Jews looked outside to watch if there were any evil spies. The Seder then returns to hope for the future in song and praise, and even children's charades, concluding with the fourth and final cup of wine, a toast to the future. Since 1966, an additional ritual for the Seder has been enjoined on all Jews in America by the combined rabbinical organizations of all groups of American Jewry. A fourth matzah was added to the three traditional ones, the matzah commemorating Russian Jewry, to be distributed to the participants with the following declaration:

> This is the Matzah of Oppression. We set aside this *lechem oni*—this matzah of oppression—to remember the Jews of the Soviet Union. . . . They cannot learn of their Jewish past and hand it down to their children. They cannot learn the languages of their fathers and hand them down to their children. They cannot teach their children to be their teachers, their rabbis. . . .
>
> We shall be their voice, and our voices shall be joined by thousands of men of conscience aroused by the injustice imposed on Soviet Jews. Then shall they know that they have not been forgotten, and they that sit in darkness shall yet see a great light.

Morning Worship

Morning Worship follows the regular order, with special poetry for the festival. But, beginning with the third day of the Passover festival, a part of the Psalms of Praise, Hallel (Psalms 113–118), is omitted, out of compassion for the Egyptians. They suffered; therefore joy is diminished. "Rejoice not when Your enemy falls," says Scripture (Proverbs 24:17). The rabbis put the admonition into God's mouth: He rebuked the angels, who wished to break out in song at Pharaoh's destruction. "The works of My hands [the Egyptians] are drowned in the sea and you want to sing?" (Sanhedrin 39b).

The Song of Songs, which is recited on Pessah, strikes the positive note of thanksgiving for God's eternal love, shown both in nature and in His dealing with His people in history. The song, a fervid love song, has been seen by Jews as symbolic of God's love for the people.

THE PERIOD OF COUNTING

From the second day of Passover, when a measure, an *omer,* of grain was offered in the Temple of old, to the festival of Shabuot, the days are counted; this has been called the Omer Period. Passover spelled deliverance from slavery; Shabuot, commemorating the giving of the Ten Commandments, places the Jew under the freedom of obligation. The people counted the days leading to the freedom under God's "constitution," the one and only true guarantee of abiding liberty. The period between Pessah and Shabuot is considered a time of mourning. Tradition has it that the disciples of Rabbi Akiba died of a plague during this period, stricken as a result of their feuding, in spite of their knowledge. The Talmud mentions twelve thousand disciples (Yebamot 62b), suggesting to scholars that these disciples were actually slain in the Bar Kohkba rebellion against Rome. They may have had too many "leaders" with individual strategic plans. This is also the period of the great massacres of German Jewry during the crusades of 1096.

MODERN DAYS OF POPULAR OBSERVANCE

Yom Ha-Shoa ve-Ha-Gevurah (Holocaust and Resistance Day). In World War II, during the last days of Pessah, the Jews in the Warsaw Ghetto rose up against the Nazis. They knew that they could not win but wished to show their resistance. The battle was fierce and ended only after the Germans cut off the water supply to the ghetto and brought in flame throwers. But the myth of German invincibility had been destroyed; no longer did the uniform by itself invoke fear. The twenty-seventh of Nissan has therefore been chosen for a general observance in remembrance of Holocaust and Resistance. It is being ever more widely observed.

Yom Ha-Atzmaut (Israel Independence Day). On May 14, 1948 surrounded by the armies of their enemies, the leaders of Israel declared the State's independence, putting their trust in the "Rock of Israel." The event brought new pride to world Jewry, and an upsurge of self-confidence and self-affirmation. The day is observed on the fifth of Iyar. If this date falls on a Sabbath, the holiday is observed on the preceding Thursday.

Yom Yerushalayim, Jerusalem Day, commemorating the reunification of the Holy City in 1967, has recently come to be observed on the twenty-eighth of Iyar. From 1948 to 1967, the city of Jerusalem was divided. The "Old City," with its many shrines, was in Jordanian hands. During this period, Jews were denied access to their shrines, including the Western Wall, Judaism's holiest place of pilgrimage. When the city was reunited, the Jews discovered that ancient synagogues had been blown up, Jewish cemeteries had been desecrated, and gravestones had been used for latrines. Jewish determination not to permit these desecrations to happen again may be one reason for their tenacious refusal to cede half the city once again.

Further, Jerusalem has been capital of Israel since King David's times. As such, it is mentioned repeatedly in the Bible, and is remembered in daily prayers that express the hope that it be restored to its former position. Jerusalem is thus deeply enshrined in Jewish consciousness and love. Jerusalem, particularly the "Old City," which is filled with the monuments of Jewish history, is, in a sense, a "mother" for all Jews.

SHABUOT: COVENANT OF TORAH

The next major festival of the year is **Shabuot,** the Feast of Weeks; it falls seven weeks after Pessah. With Pessah and Sukkot, it is the third of the Pilgrimage Festivals. It commemorates the giving of the Ten Commandments, and is called in the Talmud *Atzeret,* concluding festival. The march to freedom was completed only with dedication to God's Covenant of Torah. In ancient times, the farmers brought their first fruits to the Temple on this day. Therefore, synagogues are decorated with trees and flowers, but there are no symbols. Nothing can symbolize Torah, revealed on this day.

The Torah reading is the Ten Commandments. The Book of Ruth is also recited, not simply because it tells of an event occurring during the harvest period of the year, but primarily to show that Torah is not only for Jews. Ruth, the Moabite, cleaving to God, becomes the great-grandmother of King David. Jews know of no distinction in races; they know only those who accept the divine charge of creative living and those who reject it. And those who live by it are truly worthy to bring about redemption—symbolized in David— regardless of their background. Many congregations have instituted a service of confirmation on this day, when young people (usually after completion of junior high school) confirm their lives in the Torah and tradition of the Jewish people.

THE THREE PILGRIMAGE FESTIVALS

Christian Parallels

Torah ordained that three times a year the men of Israel were to make a pilgrimage to Jerusalem: on the festivals of Passover, Shabuot, and Sukkot (Deuteronomy 16:16–17). By their pilgrimage and physical presence in the Temple at Jerusalem, the people gave expression to the indivisible unity of the Jewish people under God. The three pilgrimage festivals—*Shalosh Regalim*— clearly represent the unity of God-Torah-Mitzvot-Land.

These three festivals have been adapted by Christianity and American tradition. Pessah and Shabuot became Easter and Pentecost; Sukkot, the secular American Thanksgiving. Christian doctrine translated the social idea into individual terms. It has linked Easter to the Risen Christ and his redemptive work *for* humanity. Judaism connects the Passover feast with the "resurrection" of the Jewish people from Egyptian bondage, from which its task derives to help "redeem" humanity from injustice. Shabuot is dedicated to the giving of the Ten Commandments to the people; Pentecost recalls the outpouring of the Holy Spirit upon the disciples. The Thanksgiving observed in America by all faiths has been turned into a secular feast. It originated with the Puritans, who, well aware of the biblical holidays, may have drawn on Sukkot. The great holy days of Rosh Hashanah and Yom Kippur have no counterpart in other religions, though some of the liturgy was taken over into Holy Week of Christianity.

General Rules for Holy Day Observance

During the festivals, the same work prohibition applies as on the Sabbath, with one exception: The preparation of food and all that pertains to it is permitted (Exodus 12:16).

Pessah is ordained for seven days, of which the first and the last are full holy days with work prohibition. The intermediate days are half-holy days, when work is allowed. Diaspora Jews observe eight days, of which the first two and last two are full holy days. *Shabuot* is observed on one day, a full holy day, although two full holy days are observed in the Diaspora. *Sukkot* is ordained for eight days, of which the first and the last are full holy days. Diaspora Jewry observes the feast for nine days, the two first and two last days being full holy days.

SUMMER DAYS OF MOURNING

Two events once took place during the summer months that call for fasting and repentance.

The Seventeenth of Tammuz marks the time when the walls of Jerusalem were breached, and regular Temple worship came to an end. Three weeks later, the ninth of Ab marks the date of the destruction of both the first and the second Temple.

Tishah b'Ab, the **ninth of Ab,** is observed in deep mourning. For twenty-four hours, the congregation fasts. All the coverings are removed from Ark and pulpit. The people, like mourners for a dear one, sit on low stools. In the evening, the Book of Lamentations is recited. In the morning, dirges are sung, telling of Israel's tragic fate throughout the centuries.

Yet hope is expressed as well. Tradition will have it that the Messiah will be born on Tishah b'Ab. An understanding of the meaning of suffering will lead to the kind of conduct which will bring humanity's salvation.

Three weeks after Tishah b'Ab, the shofar summons the people to prepare themselves for a new year.

VARIATIONS

It should be noted that the various groups in Judaism follow different styles of observance. Reform, for instance, observes only one day of the festivals, and its members do not feel bound by the work prohibitions. In many non-Orthodox communities, only the synagogue may have a Sukkah for congregational fellowship, and there may be only one set of the festive bouquet for Sukkot. Torah readings vary in various rites.

The Seder of the Passover festival is widely observed, but nonreligious Jews may develop their own individual "Haggadah" dealing with human freedom in general and/or Israel in particular.

Various popular forms of celebration have emerged in Israel, in addition to the traditional ones or in their place. These, and other forms of expression and of celebration, reflect the varieties of Jewish belief among affirming Jews.

21

THE YEARS OF LIFE

As the transition from season to season is marked by special observances, the milestones in human life are similarly set aside for reflection, dedication, and commitment.

The rabbis of old gave clear expression to their conviction that every age group has its specific duty. Rabbi Judah ben Tema outlined it:

> At five years [the child is ready] for the study of Scripture,
> At ten for Mishnah,
> At thirteen for [responsibility in performance of] Mitzvot,
> At fifteen for Talmud,
> At eighteen [the youth is ready] for marriage,
> At twenty for the pursuit of a livelihood,
> At thirty [man reaches] strength,
> At forty full understanding,
> At fifty the ability to provide counsel,
> At sixty he enters his senior years,
> At seventy he attains old age,
> At eighty [his survival reflects] strength,
> At ninety bent in anticipation of the grave,
> At one-hundred he is as dead and past, withdrawn from the world
> (Mishnah Abot 5:24).

The life of a Jew starts with Torah, leading to Mitzvot, reaching its first fulfillment in marriage. From then on, his duty is to those around him, the children through whom he perpetuates the household of Israel, the family whose livelihood is his responsibility, and his society, to whom he must impart the wisdom he has acquired by guidance and counsel. Old age to him is a period not of rest but of reflection, as he gives thanks to God, who has permitted him to attain the span of "threescore years and ten, or even by reason of strength, fourscore years" (Psalm 90:10). Aware of his destiny to stand before his Maker, he faces death in calm submission. Should he live beyond the usual span of life, he must gain the wisdom of withdrawal, letting new generations face their problems in their own way, finding new solutions for their own time and needs.

Living in this fashion, he knows that his work on earth will not be without results, that he will pass on his name and achievements even after he himself has died. This is symbolically expressed in the fact that succeeding generations will bear his name, making a name for themselves by building upon the foundations of the past and the name their ancestors have made in the world.

THE JEWISH HOME AND JEWISH NAMES

The strength that safeguards Jewish life and survival rests on the Jewish home. The family covenanted within itself and, as a unit, with God and Israel, is the bulwark of the future. The congregation is, in a sense, a family of families and, at the same time, their protector. Judaism would be endangered were the family shattered.

This continuity is expressed in Jewish names. It is customary to give every child a Hebrew name in addition to his common one; by this name, he will be called to the Torah, recorded in the marriage certificate, remembered in prayer after death. There were no family names in Jewish usage. A son and daughter were known by their own names and that of their father. Moses thus would be called Mosheh ben (son of) Amram. The name of the biblical Miriam would be Miriam bat (daughter of) Amram. King David is known as Son of Jesse.

It is customary among Ashkenasim to name a child after a departed ancestor in order that the example of a fulfilled life may be a guide and that the eternal chain of the generations may be made visible. The Sefardim name their children after forebears who are still living in order that a child may look upon a living grandfather or grandmother as special guide and counselor in life. These names are bestowed upon boys at the time of circumcision and on girls in a special blessing in the synagogue shortly after birth.

The civic name given a child may, of course, be the same as the Hebrew name, as in the case of biblical names such as David, Ruth, or Michael. It may be a translation of a Hebrew name or of its meaning: Johanan becomes John; Miriam is given its latinized, common form of Mary; Judah, compared in Scripture to a "lion's whelp," becomes Leo. Most common, however, though least desirable, is the practice of using alliterations, making the civic name start with the same letter as the Hebrew one; thus Aaron becomes Alfred, Samuel becomes Seymour.

Family names were introduced under civic ordinances in the Napoleonic period. Frequently they are based on the cities from which the family originated, such as Oppenheimer (from the German city of Oppenheim on the Rhine), or Posner (from Posen, now Poznan, in Poland). Names may indicate the family's descent from the priests or Levites of old—for instance, Cohen (priest) of Cahn, or Katz, an abbreviation of *Ka*hen *Tz*edek, a righteous priest. Segal is an abbreviation of *Seg*an *L*evaya, overseer of Levites.

Hebrew names may be translated into modern languages. Today in Israel, they are being translated back into Hebrew.

In medieval times, various homes were distinguished by signs or special features, and the people dwelling in them were remembered by these. A house with a red shield bestowed upon its inhabitants the name *Rothschild;* one with a large flight of steps in front (a *treppe,* or *trepp* in earlier and colloquial German) resulted in the name *Trepp.* A great many names, however, were simply bestowed by officials upon the Jews by government decree. This led to abuses, as these officials were frequently corrupt. If a man were willing to pay well, he might get a beautiful name, such as *Blumenfeld* (a field of flowers) or *Rosenberg* (a mountain of roses); if not, some hideous name might be given him.

Many Jews whose names might be hard to pronounce in America have anglicized their names and have become indistinguishable. Unhappily, this had also to be done to escape discrimination.

ON JOINING THE HOUSEHOLD OF ISRAEL

A person becomes a member of the House of Israel either by birth or by conversion. By birth, he is considered a Jew if his mother is a Jew, even if his father is not. Reform and Reconstructionism will now recognize the child of a Jewish father and non-Jewish mother as a Jew if the child has been brought up as a Jew and become Bar Mitzvah or Bat Mitzvah. Conversion implies full acceptance of the duties and obligations of the Jewish faith and people. The convert must fully take upon himself "the yoke of Torah and Mitzvot" and cast his lot with that of the Jewish people. Judaism has not made conversion easy, although in recent years we find a greater readiness to accept converts.

Preceding conversion, the candidate has to discuss his resolve carefully with the rabbi, for his conversion must be from conviction. The rabbi outlines to him the privilege of joining the Jewish faith but also the disadvantages that are attached to being a Jew—the duties that it demands, the discrimination to which Jews have been exposed. He points out that from the standpoint of "salvation," a non-Jew is not considered in any way inferior or less privileged than a Jew, but that a Jew is obligated to perform the Mitzvot to attain that state which a non-Jew reaches by simple compliance with basic principles of ethics and of justice. Then the rabbi must send the candidate home, to give him an opportunity for a clear analysis without any pressure. If he is determined to convert, the postulant undergoes a period of study in order that he know what it is he is to accept. He is still free to withdraw.

The rite of final acceptance traditionally consists of circumcision for males plus immersion; for women, only immersion is required. The formal rite includes a declaration of acceptance of Judaism before a rabbinical court of three. Reform Judaism requires only this declaration and no other rites; however, its position toward traditional requirements is in a state of change. The convert is then given a Hebrew name. In the case of men, the name is usually Abraham; considered a son of the founder of Judaism, who brought many converts to the One God, he is called Abraham ben Abraham. Henceforth he enjoys all the rights of a Jew and bears full responsibility for the performance of mitzvot. A certificate testifies to his admission. No one may ever hold it against him that once he was not a member of the family of Israel (Talmud Baba Metzia 58b). On the contrary, "having left the environment of their childhood, they deserve our special respect and kindness" (Bamidbar Rabba 8:2); "they are beloved of God." Many of the great leaders of Jewry were themselves either proselytes or the immediate descendants of converts. "He may see his grandson be high priest" (Bereshit Rabba 70), even as Ruth saw her great-grandson David as king of Israel.

In our own time, problems have developed in Israel, resulting from the talmudic law on conversion. Religious and family matters have been placed in the hands of the strictly Orthodox rabbinate in Israel, which refuses to recognize conversions performed by non–Orthodox rabbis. While the rabbinate will recognize as a Jew the child of a mother converted by Orthodox rabbis in Israel and abroad, if the child has been born after conversion, it will not recognize the child of a mother converted by a non–Orthodox rabbi as a Jew. In many cases, immigrants from Russia found themselves in trouble. Married to non-Jewish women who had thrown in their lot with their husbands, they found that neither their wives nor their children were recognized as Jews. This often proved to be deeply humiliating to them; to their wives, who had faithfully stood with them in times of grave trials; and to their children, who regarded themselves as Jews. The State passed a law recognizing these wives and children as Jews, and also recognizing people converted by non-Orthodox rabbis *abroad,* but only for *immigration purposes.* All naturalization steps for non-Jews are waived; they are citizens, and, as such, all fall under rabbinical law regarding marriage and so on. Orthodoxy is politically fighting for repeal of this relief law.

Admission to Judaism can be and is granted to people of all races and colors by even the most Orthodox rabbis, and these converts become full-fledged members of the Jewish people. Orthodoxy generally makes conversion difficult, however, as a matter of principle.

Also under talmudic law, a member of the Jewish people never loses his status, even if he is not religious. The Supreme Court of Israel has ruled, however, that a person who consciously adopts another faith has made a choice electing another "family" and has relinquished Jewish allegiance and all it entails. Jews having joined non-Jewish sects, such as Jews for Jesus, cannot claim affiliation with the Jewish people and religion.

A proposal advanced by some prominent leaders that Jews once again become active in promoting conversion to Judaism—following the pattern of the talmudic period—has created serious debate within Jewry, even though such activity would extend only to those who are not affiliated with any religion and are seeking one. The reason for the idea has been that the Jewish people can profit from new members, especially after the losses during the Holocaust, and, at the same time can offer a spiritual home to many that are homeless. The objections have been that such activity would reverse a Jewish position that is of very long standing and that has influenced the theological and practical outlook of Jewry, as well as its relationship to other faiths. A change in position can also result in similar activities by other religious bodies directed toward Jews, with unforeseen consequences. The number of converts to Judaism in the United States is currently estimated at about twelve thousand per year.

Circumcision: The Covenant of Abraham

The covenant of circumcision (**B'rit Milah**) is the first mitzvah to which the newborn son is led. Its hygienic character has come to be recognized to the point where some physicians perform it almost routinely on all newborn boys, regardless of religious affiliation, simply as a health measure. (Medical studies seem to indicate that there is a much lower incidence of cancer of the penis when circumcision has been performed, and women married to circumcised men have a lower incidence of cervical cancer.) To the Jew, however, it is a religious act, patterned on the example of Abraham, into whose Covenant the child enters (Genesis 17:10ff.), and ordained in Scripture (Leviticus 12:3). It has been regarded as so significant that it was to be performed in the synagogue in the presence of the congregation. It is sufficiently important that the operation must be performed even on the Sabbath or Yom Kippur, when these days fall on the appointed eighth day after birth. Only when there is danger to a child's health may it be postponed. In no case should it be performed earlier, according to religious law.

Pious men, especially trained in the performance of the operation, are called to conduct it; such a man is called a **mohel.** It is an honor to be a mohel, and there are distinguished businessmen who, to the neglect of their own affairs, dedicate themselves to this mitzvah, naturally without pay. Lately it has become a paid profession.

Tradition calls for a quorum of ten (the legal minimum constituting a congregation) to be present. The grandmother or a close relative brings in the child, thus becoming his godmother; a close relative holds him during the operation, thus becoming his godfather. The godfather is seated on a chair next to which another chair is placed, symbolically for Elijah, guardian of Israel's Covenant with God. With a quick stroke, the mohel removes the foreskin of the penis, wipes off the blood, and secures the skin so it cannot grow back. The father speaks the blessing: "Blessed are You, O Lord . . . who has commanded us to enter him into the Covenant of our father Abraham." The people re-

Chair of Elijah (German-Jewish folk art, Rheda, Westphalia, Germany, 1803). This double-seated chair is used at circumcisions. The godfather, holding the child, sits on the left seat; Elijah, "guardian of the Covenant," symbolically sits on the right. (Photo by the author, reproduced courtesy of Jack H. Skirball Museum of the Hebrew Union College–Jewish Institute of Religion, Los Angeles, California.)

spond: "As he entered the Covenant, so may he enter into [the study and performance of] Torah, into marriage, and [the performance of] good deeds."

The name is then bestowed upon the child as the mohel raises the cup of salvation in prayer that it be a cup of happiness. A drop of wine is passed to the child's lips, and the father finishes it. A festive meal completes the observance.

Today, circumcision has frequently become a hurried affair, celebrated in the hospital with only the closest relatives present. This may be required by the rules of the hospital. In any case, circumcision should not be performed before the appointed time, and its religious character should be preserved. Hadassah Hospital in Jerusalem has a surgical section attached to its synagogue in order that the rite maybe performed under highest hygienic conditions and yet according to the traditional custom of Jewish religion.

In recognition of women's equality, non-Orthodox Jewry has instituted a rite for new-born girls. There is no operation, however. The child is brought into the gathering by the godmother and held by the godfather. The parents express their thanksgiving to God, the name is bestowed upon the child, and a festive meal follows.

Naming of children in the synagogue has also become widespread. In Orthodox congregations, the father is "called up" to the Torah on a date shortly after the girl's birth. This date is sometimes delayed until the mother can join him; her first departure from the house after confinement should be to the synagogue. After the father has followed the reading of the portion and recited the blessing, a special benediction is given to him, the mother and the child, at which time the girl's name is proclaimed.

In non-Orthodox congregations, both parents appear at the synagogue. Depending on the practice of the congregation, the child may also be brought. At a special blessing, the child's name is bestowed. The child, if present, is personally blessed by the rabbi, who places hands on the little one's head. This applies to boys and girls equally, but should not replace the B'rit. Above all, it should not be seen as a substitute for the circumcision rite—that is, allowing circumcision to be performed simply as a surgical operation at the date of the physician's choosing and without religious character.

BAR MITZVAH AND BAT MITZVAH

As early as possible, the child should learn his prayers, the affirmation of faith: "Hear O Israel, the Lord our God, the Lord is One," and should recognize the value of Torah: "The Torah which Moses commanded us is the heritage of the congregation of Jacob." Gradually, he is brought to know and understand and practice. The responsibility for this Jewish development rests upon the parents.

At the age of thirteen, theoretically the beginning of puberty, the boy becomes **Bar Mitzvah,** a (responsible) Son of the Mitzvah. The first mitzvah he performs is to give allegiance to Torah. Now that he may be counted as one of the minyan, he will be called to Torah to witness or, if he is able to read Hebrew, himself read a portion of it; to recite the Haftarah; and, above all, to pronounce the blessing which is a pledge to Him "who has given us the Torah of truth, thus planting eternal life in our midst." At this age, a Jewish child automatically enters the state of responsibility. No special rite is required, though it has been in practice throughout the ages, akin to ancient puberty rites. Today, as part of the worship service, the boy may be addressed by the rabbi. He is then given gifts at the joyful celebration which follows.

All too often, this celebration may be far too lavish, designed more for the parents and their friends than for the boy himself. While it may well express the parents' pride in having raised a child to conscious Jewish living, frequently it is totally secular. Worst of all, it may fail to impress the youngster that Bar Mitzvah is not the end of his training as a Jew but very much the beginning. It is the open door to responsible living. A correction of this abuse has been sternly demanded by the American rabbinate.

Recognizing the equality of women in our society, many congregations have instituted for girls **Bat Mitzvah** (Daughter of the Commandment) observances patterned after those of Bar Mitzvah.

Following the Christian custom of confirmation, a ceremony has found entrace in the synagogue that allows the young people after Bar or Bat Mitzvah to continue their education and to confirm their faith at the age of about sixteen when they have a greater awareness of their duties. As we have seen, it is held on Shabuot, the festival commemorating the giving of the Ten Commandments, the holiday of Torah, to which these young people are to give their allegiance.

MARRIAGE

Judaism believes in early marriage yet feels that a man should be able to support his family when he takes this important step. The Talmud advises careful thought in order that both partners be matched well physically and emotionally, in background and in outlook. The rabbis advise against any marriage in which the woman is of higher social status. They see the best assurance for a blessed home in a mother who is the daughter of a "disciple of the wise" (Yoma 71a); she has acquired the spirit of Torah and can transmit it to the children. It is prudent, even in our day, for young people to obtain the rabbi's guidance together with their parents' counseling before they enter the holy bond of marriage.

In antiquity, the young people were solemnly betrothed to each other one year before their final marriage vows; this wait allowed the future bride to prepare her trousseau and eliminated the man's fear "that someone else might get her." The betrothal ceremony has now become a part of the marriage.

The Traditional Wedding

Formalized in ancient Judaism, the wedding ceremony, by tradition, combines both legal and religious features. In Jewish law, a couple is married if the man gives a gift of some value to his bride with the intent of marrying her, and she accepts it in this spirit. This custom resulted in the wedding ring; hence a double-ring ceremony is not essential in Judaism. A second method of marrying was by contract, **Ketubah,** and a third by cohabitation. All these elements are present in the wedding rites. In addition, God's blessing is invoked.

The Service. In the center of the expectant congregation stands the **huppah,** the wedding canopy. There the rabbi, flanked by the witnesses, awaits the couple. To the strains of joyful song and music (often Psalms 118:26–29: Blessed who enters by the Name of the Lord, we bless you out of the house of the Lord), the groom enters, escorted by his father and his father-in-law. He waits for the bride, who will join him under the huppah, escorted by her mother and mother-in-law. Traditionally, the groom sees the bride before she is veiled on the wedding day to ascertain that she is indeed the one he has chosen as his life's companion. This saves him from the fate of the patriarch Jacob, who was deceived by his father-in-law, Laban (Genesis 29:16–25).

Upon ascertaining that the two wish to be married, the rabbi raises the first cup of wine and recites the blessings of betrothal. Groom and bride share the cup, which is put to their lips by their father and mother.

A Huppah (wedding canopy) with rabbi and couple under it in the whimsical style of the glassblower Gianni Toso of Venice. (Photo by the author.)

The groom places the ring on the index finger of the bride's right hand, saying: "Be you consecrated unto me by this ring according to the law of Moses and Israel." Willingly accepting the ring, the bride indicates her consent. The ketubah, a marriage contract signed by witnesses, is then read by the rabbi.

Raising the second cup of wine, the rabbi invokes upon the couple the "Seven Blessings." Again, groom and bride share the cup, as they will henceforth share the cup of life together. It is now put to their lips by their father-in-law and mother-in-law. At the end of the ceremony, a glass is broken as a reminder of Jewish suffering ever since the fall of the Temple. It may also serve as a reminder to the couple that love may break easily, that they must therefore treat each other tenderly. The rabbi's address and blessing are optional but customary. The congregation exclaims **"Mazel tov"**—may it be under a good constellation. Music has always been regarded as an essential part of the wedding celebration. Now the music strikes up.

The couple leaves the synagogue together. Ordinarily, they have to fast before their wedding, and before the ceremony each recites the confession of sins, as on Yom Kippur. Now they break their fast together in solitude.

Their togetherness now has an additional meaning: should they wish to do so, they could consummate their marriage. At the festive meal the Seven Benedictions are recited again. All the requirements have now been met: the gift (the ring), the contract (ketubah), and their "coming together."

Marriage and Divorce

The Jewish marriage ceremony is called sanctification, **Kiddushin;** in the home its spirit was truly fulfilled. The Jewish home was holy, a haven of peace, for it was a home with a purpose. The women knew that theirs was the greatest task of all—that of raising the children in Torah and Mitzvot. "Be fruitful and multiply" says Torah (Genesis 1:28), and the Talmud comments that each family should have at least one son and one daughter (Mishnah Yebamot 6:6). But mutual enjoyment of marriage is equally important, and the Talmud permits contraceptives under certain conditions—for instance, when a pregnancy would endanger either the health of the mother or the welfare of a previous child (for instance when the mother's milk would run dry too soon as a result of a new pregnancy). (Ketubot 39a.)

Another Jewish law may have added to the permanence of the home. Jewish law based on Torah prohibits intercourse during the period of menstruation and seven days thereafter; for about twelve days every month, husband and wife may not even touch each other. She is **Niddah,** ritually "Separated." Then the wife has to immerse herself in a ritual bath of purification, a **Mikveh,** before intercourse can again be permitted. As a matter of cleanliness and hygiene, this immersion was of great value, especially in the Middle Ages, when bathing was very rare in most other cultures. This commandment is strictly observed by Orthodox women to this day. Thus husband and wife can hardly get tired of each other physically, a factor greatly contributing to the stability of the home.

If a marriage does not work out, divorce is permitted. While the rabbis proclaim that the altar sheds tears when a home is broken (Gitin 90b), Judaism has been wise enough to permit divorce without requiring the proof of "guilt" on the part of either partner.

Before a rabbinical court of three, a bill of divorcement (*get*) is written in accordance with specific detailed regulations, purposely made difficult as a deterrent to divorce. The husband, who must request the get, then hands it to his wife, and as she accepts it in free will, she is divorced. She may remarry ninety days later (in order to avoid questions of paternity in case of an early pregnancy in her second marriage). A woman may remarry her husband, but only if she has not been married to another man after her divorce from him.

According to traditional Jewish law, the husband could divorce his wife, yet she could not divorce him (although in ancient times the Jewish court would force him to grant her a divorce when conditions warranted). This has created problems for modern Orthodox Jews. Conservative Jews include in the marriage contract a provision binding the man to grant his wife a religious divorce should the occasion arise. Conservatism also provides for annulment by a rabbinical court. Reform Jews require only the legal divorce granted by the state. Reconstructionism has provisions allowing the woman to initiate and obtain the divorce.

Today, no religious divorces may be granted until the final divorce has been obtained by the couple in the civil courts, in accordance with the law of the state. Under the talmudic law, "the law of The State is *the* [religious] law [as well]" (Talmud Baba Kamma 113b). However, women who have obtained only a court divorce are regarded as still married under traditional Jewish law; any second marriage is regarded by Orthodoxy as adultery and children out of it as bastards (*mamzerim*). In Jewish law, a bastard (*mamzer*) may marry only another bastard, down through the generations. This has created problems in Israel. A man who marries again on the basis of a court divorce has transgressed against the ordinance prohibiting polygamy, but not against the law of Torah, thus the children are not affected. Children born out of wedlock are *not* considered mamzerim. Conservative, Reform, and Reconstructionist Judaism have done away with the concept of mamzer.

THE POSITION OF WOMAN

Historically, the position of the Jewish woman has been one of dignity, with many rights, but not of equality with men. The rationale for this comes from the history of the people. A nomadic society in search of land and settlement is exposed to hazards: wild beasts, raiders, attacks by enemy armies. Repelling these attacks is the task of men, who have to be ready at a moment's notice. Israel emerged as such a society and, even during its settled life, was for centuries exposed to these emergencies. Men thus took a major burden in battle; women tended the home and the children. This led to male dominance in public life, even after the reasons for it had disappeared: Military leaders were men, priests were men, the teachers of Torah were men—and their power grew.

Male dominance was never absolute, however, nor was there absolute certainty about male superiority. In Torah, we find two versions of the creation of woman. The first gives her full equality: "And God created man in His image. . . . Male and female He created them" (Genesis 1:27). The second tells us that God created woman out of man's rib—out of *him,* deriving existence from him (Genesis 2:21–22). On one occasion, the doubts about women's legal rights were resolved by divine guidance. The daughters of Zelophehad came to Moses, claiming their share in the distribution of the land as heirs to their father, who had no son. Their demand was granted, setting a precedent: Women have property rights (Numbers 27:1–11).

As need arose, women took leadership positions: Moses's sister Miriam was an organizer and leader (Exodus 15:20); Deborah served as general and judge (Judges 4–5); Huldah was a prophetess (II Kings 22:14–20) and Esther a skilled diplomat (Book of Esther). However, the woman's domain was essentially the home. Here her power was absolute. Abraham answered the question "Where is your wife Sarah?": "There in the tent" (Genesis 18:9). When Sarah insisted that Ishmael, son of the concubine Hagar, be expelled as an unworthy companion to her own son Isaac, God told the unwilling Abraham: "Whatever Sarah tells you, do as she says" (Genesis 21:12). Another precedent had been set, granting the woman undisputed power in the home. Thus it has remained.

Even God's names reflect this division of functions. He is "Man of War" (Exodus 15:3). As He dwells within the people, however, He is spoken of in the feminine, *Shekhinah*, the indwelling: "As a mother comforts her son, so will I comfort you" (Isaiah 66:13). Divine wisdom is called "our sister" (Proverbs 7:4; Sota 11a). Once attained in public life, male power continued to assert itself as time went on. Mitzvot of performance tied to given moments were confined to men, who would not be burdened by pregnancies or the nursing of babies when duty arose.

These strictures became generalized: Women were not merely relieved of all duties of performance linked to certain times of the day or year, they were *not permitted* to perform these duties, among them the duty and the right to study Torah, even though it was not linked to a specific time. It was held that Torah stated "teach them [the words of Torah] to your son" [therefore, not your daughter] (Deuteronomy 11:19; Kiddushin 29b). Gradually women were restricted from wearing the tallit and the tefillin, and they could not be counted among the minyan. They were curtained off in the gallery of the synagogue. They came to be regarded as temptresses, whose hair, voice, and limbs threatened the purity of the men. They could be neither judges nor, in many (though not all) cases, witnesses.

According to the Talmud, women could, in principle, be called to the Torah during worship to read a section to the congregation. However, as there were males in the congregation who were incapable of reading from the lesson, it was held that the "dignity of the congregation" was disturbed if a woman showed a knowledge greater than that of some men (Megillah 23a; Berakhot 20b). Thus they could not become rabbis or cantors, or lay leaders in worship.

The greatest disadvantage of women rested on the scriptural statement " . . . he shall write her a bill of divorcement" (Deuteronomy 24:1). This was interpreted to mean that a man could divorce a woman, but she could not divorce him against his will. This problem was alleviated in times when Jews had sovereignty, as the courts would imprison a recalcitrant husband until he agreed to grant the divorce. Where this power did not exist, the woman had no recourse. Furthermore, a woman could not remarry if her husband had disappeared without any trace, or if his death had not been certified through witnesses, although a man could remarry in similar circumstances.

The traditional prayerbook contains a benediction for men: "Blessed are You, God . . . who has not made me a woman." Why did women accept this inferior status for so many centuries, and still accept it in Orthodox Jewry? There may be two reasons. The rabbis ascribed to them a greater sensitivity toward God's will; hence they were the rulers in the home and the primary force in the upbringing of their young children. The women saw this as an equitable distribution of functions; they insisted on their rights and gloried in their responsibilities. Perhaps they also realized that their husbands were frequently humiliated in the marketplace, and they wished to give them a sense of importance and power at home. In this manner, they preserved their husbands' self-respect. Some women did become active in business, permitting their husbands undisturbed time to study Torah.

But times have changed, and the inferior position of woman no longer corresponds to our sense of ethics. Non-Orthodox women have come to demand equality.

First of all, they demanded and obtained (in non-Orthodox Judaism) those rights that Jewish law (Halakhah) had originally granted them: the right to study Torah and Talmud (granted in Orthodoxy as well), the abolition of the woman's gallery, and the rights to be called to the Torah, wear tallit and tefillin, lead the service, and be counted among the minyan required for public worship.

More difficult was the issue of divorce. Reform Judaism does not require a religious divorce. Conservative Judaism does. To offer relief, it has ruled that any marriage is entered in accordance with the sense of the rabbis (Kiddushin 3a) and can therefore be annulled by the rabbinical court if the husband consistently refuses to grant a get, or if he has disappeared. Reconstructionism has equalized the positions of women and men.

Ordination of women was the most difficult question, as we saw in Chapter 7.

Wherever women have attained full equality with men, they have assumed a heavy responsibility: doing traditionally male work *and* being mothers.

SICKNESS AND DEATH

It is our duty to keep our bodies in good health, worthy instruments in the service of God. But sickness is the lot of all, and Jews must seek competent medical aid when it occurs. Jews may therefore not live in a town that has no physician (Jerushalmi, Kiddushin 4:12). When illness strikes, they turn to God and find strength in friends, whose duty it is to visit, but they must also do all that can humanly be done to restore their health.

As death approaches, family, and, above all, friends stay with the patient. They recite with them the confession of sins, or, if he is too far gone, do this for him. They repeat the affirmation of faith, "Hear O Israel, the Lord our God, the Lord is One," making an effort to time or repeat the affirmation of faith that the Oneness of God is proclaimed by the dying with his last living breath.

During these last stages of life, no manipulation of the dying is permitted beyond that which is medically required. It is believed that any touch might shorten his life, and we have no right to diminish this God-given span by even a moment.

These last acts of kindness are performed traditionally by the men and women of the "holy fellowship," the *Hevrah Kadishah*—a group of people distinguished by their piety, who perform this service as a voluntary act of free devotion, a true mitzvah, for which the departed can render no thanks; only God may. After death, they place the deceased on the earth (as symbol of his return to dust, whence he came); later they wash him and dress him in the simple white linen garments he may have worn on Yom Kippur and put a tallit around his shoulders. Women have similar white garments and are similarly attended by women in this ritual. The "fellows" make a simple wooden coffin and place the body in it, following the ordinances of Rabbi Gamaliel and the rabbis, who taught:

> Formerly, they used to serve in the house of mourning, the rich in crystal goblets, the poor in colored glasses. Formerly, they kept the faces of the rich uncovered, but covered those of the poor, which had been darkened from want; since the poor were thus put to shame, it was ordered that the faces [of the departed] be always covered, out of respect for the poor. Formerly, the rich were carried out on a specially made, bed-like coffin and the poor on a simple bier; since this put the poor to shame, it was ordered that all be carried on a simple bier. . . . Formerly, the funeral of the dead was harder on his family than his death [on account of the expense involved]; then Rabbi Gamaliel took action, ordering that he be treated in the plainest way, ruling that he be buried in linen garments. Thus the popular custom developed to bury the dead in linen garments. (Talmud Moed Katan 27a, b)

The equality of all in death is to be visibly demonstrated. The poor need not go into expensive arrangements, which might be too hard on them. The message seems to be particularly significant for our own time. No ostentation is allowed. The departed is to be laid to rest as quickly as possible. Embalming is to be avoided, unless the law requires it. Flowers should not be sent; rather, the money should be used for charitable purposes in honor of the departed.

Friends dig the grave. After a brief eulogy and prayer, they lower the coffin. Family and friends put the earth back. Thus does he return to the earth whence he came, as the spirit returns to God who gave it. (Cremation is not permitted in traditional Judaism.) At the moment of their bitterest grief, the mourners tear their garments. This is often done symbolically by tearing a ribbon attached to the garment. (Thus Judaism, in deep psychological insight, permits grief to be expressed freely, rather than be bottled up to lead to neuroses later on.) Then the children recite the **Kaddish.** As they leave to return home, they pass through the lines of their friends, who greet them with the words, "May God comfort you."

Upon their return, the mourners receive their first meal as a gift of friends, lest, in their grief, they forget to sustain their bodies. For seven days, they sit on low stools, receiving the consolations of their neighbors. Grief is expressed—it must be given an outlet to restore people to healthy living—and the friendship of their fellows sustains the mourners. After thirty days, life must return to normal; the period of mourning is over. The one exception is the death of a parent, for whom mourning lasts a full year; each morning and evening, the sons join the congregation in worship and recite the Kaddish for eleven months. On the Sabbath eve service after their bereavement, the mourners are received at the door of the synagogue by the rabbi with the word of comfort: May God comfort you . . . (There is no mourning on the Sabbath, which, however, is counted among the seven days.)

Funeral and mourning practices have been "modernized" in our time. A return to the simplicity of the Jewish funeral might be helpful to the bereaved and is in keeping with tradition. In Judaism, the mourners are permitted to utter their grief. Friends perform the Mitzvah of *levayat hamet,* accompanying the dead on his last journey, and offer the first food to the returning mourners, as tradition commands, lest the mourners forget to eat in their sorrow. The traditional service is simple: a psalm, a prayer, eulogy, Kaddish. The house of mourning in Jewish traditional practice becomes a place of quiet gathering, where friends truly comfort the mourners in quiet rehearsal of the departed's virtues and in meditation on God's merciful justice as they gather in worship during the days of **Shivah,** the seven days of mourning.

There is greatness in the uniformity of the Jewish service, its simplicity, the traditional robes for the dead, the wooden casket covered by its black shroud. In simplicity lies nobility and the source from which comfort springs.

Yahrzeit

As the years pass, the anniversary of the day of death is observed by the children. It is called **Yahrzeit** (from the German *Jahr*, year, and *Zeit*, time, meaning anniversary). A light is kindled for twenty-four hours, for the soul is a light of God. The children visit the grave of their parent, and, on parting, place a small stone on the tombstone. In ancient days, stone-hills marked the resting places of the dead, and each visitor placed a stone on them, thus maintaining them. The custom has remained, though Jewish cemeteries now have regular tombstones. Child and friend thus leave their "visiting card."

They offer their prayers to God at the cemetery, and, throughout the day, in worship, fasting, and charity, reflect upon the lives of their dear ones, and emulate their example of tzedakah (righteousness, charity). They hope that their lives reflect true honor upon those who brought them up. This is the meaning of the Kaddish, recited at the burial, during the year of mourning, and on Yahrzeit. It is not a prayer for the dead, but an affirmation of faith, and as such is used in other parts of the service. How better can children demonstrate the faith and strength bequeathed unto them by their parents than by affirming God in the hour of their deepest loss? How better can they honor them than by declaring before the assembled congregation:

> Magnified and sanctified be His Great Name throughout the world which He has created according to His will. May He establish His kingdom during your life and during your days and during the life of all the House of Israel. To this say ye Amen [so be it].

And the people respond, uplifted by the faith of those who are bereaved:

> Amen. May His great Name be blessed for ever and ever.

The declaration of trust continues, to conclude with the words:

> May He who establishes peace in the heavens above, make peace for us also, and for all of Israel. To this say ye Amen.

And the people respond:

> Amen.

In this prayer (source of Christian "Our Father") is enshrined the entire course of Jewish life, through days and seasons and years. It is appropriate that it conclude the lifetime of a Jew, linking it with those who follow, for it is indeed the motto of Jewish life: the "Sanctification of the Name."

VARIATIONS

The rites surrounding the stages of life vary in the different Jewish "denominations." A few examples, in addition to those we have seen already, may be given, but they do not cover the entire range of variations. Reform Judaism abbreviates the wedding ceremony and issues a certificate of religious marriage in place of a ketubah, whereas Conservative Judaism has changed the text of the Ketubah. In Reform Judaism, no special garments are required for the deceased, nor need there be a special coffin. The tearing of the garments, or black ribbon, is omitted. Observance of the days of mourning is left to the individual. In non-Orthodox congregations, women also recite the Kaddish.

What is more important than any specific differences is the unity that remains behind them. A Jew abiding by the traditions of the environment in which he or she has been brought up is to be regarded as a faithful Jew.

22

RETROSPECT AND PROSPECT

Jews, as individuals and as a people, are both exceptional and unexceptional. The liturgy of Sabbath afternoon reflects: "Is there like Your people Israel any other earth-tribe on earth?" The Hebrew word used for people, *Am,* emphasizes the exceptional; the term used for earth-tribe (a translation used by Martin Buber) is *Goy.* This term, often used colloquially by Jews in reference to non-Jews, is here applied to the Jews—denoting their character as an unexceptional family of people among other unexceptional families.

Jews share the characteristics of average people: their strengths and their weaknesses, their joys and their sorrows. Some Jews are bright; others are average. Some are wealthy, while others are very poor, even in America. Some belong to management of corporations; others are union members. Jews exhibit the varieties of political and social ideas and affiliations of their neighbors. They have borne the burdens and obligations of our country's call in war and peace with patriotism ever since the inception of the United States. There are also conscientious objectors and social revolutionaries among them.

Jews are exceptional by their history, their heritage, and their kinship. Within the last few generations, they have undergone several traumatic experiences. There exist hardly any American Jews who have not learned of Jewish persecution from immediate members of their family, even if they themselves do not bear its scars. Yet to many of the new generation, the Holocaust is but history to be learned and difficult to grasp. There are hardly any Jews at all who have not been uplifted in spirit by the rebirth of the State of Israel and have not been involved in its destiny.

Elements of prejudice still exist in society. Generally, Jews have found themselves free to move both economically and socially. They have moved into the suburbs. Most of their children go to college. Judaism has been seen as a religion. A young generation, reared as equals in society, has regarded religious barriers as minor—as have their non-Jewish contemporaries—with the result that interfaith marriages are more common. At the same time, conversions to Judaism, primarily for the sake of unifying a future family religiously, have reached an all-time high.

The young and the old both need education in Judaism, and this is happening. The day-school movement is growing, new materials for adults and children are being published, camps and camp institutes are flourishing, and experiments in new forms of worship are going on. Means are being sought to strengthen meaningful family observance, as the family is the core of Jewish life. The study of Hebrew has greatly expanded due to the impact of Israel, and pilgrimage to Israel has come to be regarded as essential by many American Jews. The existence of college courses in Judaism has motivated many to study Torah in an atmosphere that permits challenge and criticism and includes both Jews and Christians among the students.

Jews are a minority, a very small minority. Their contribution in the fields of religion, ethics, literature, science, and the arts has been greater than the proportion of their numerical strength. Their achievements have brought them recognition, but they have also earned them antagonism from some. As a group, contributing to the welfare of society as a whole, they deserve consideration for their ideals. Individually, however, Jews are neither altogether intelligent nor ethically outstanding. As it would be an error to stereotype them to their disadvantage, it would be unjustified to do so to their advantage. The individual Jew shares all the weaknesses and shortcomings of the human race. He stands in need and is entitled to the same forbearance on the part of his neighbors that all human beings can claim. He, in turn, is duty bound to accord this forbearance to all alike.

The birthrate among Jews is lower than that of the general population; thus they will become a smaller minority. This has created anxieties: A minority is never totally secure. Such a minority position may have been for the Jews one of the challenges leading to intellectual achievement. They have felt that recognition can come only from the ideas they produce. They know that they have to excel to compete for average opportunities. But by their emphasis on achievement, they have also exposed themselves to animosity. Black leaders have claimed that the same problem exists for their people as well.

Among the concerns of American and world Jewry is the anti-Semitism of the radical right and left. Disguised frequently as "anti-Zionism," it emerges at times in its full and ugly form of plain hatred for Jews. Jews have been particularly grieved to find two groups affected by this evil: some of their own youth and segments of the radical blacks. Some of the reasons have been described earlier. We may add that Jews have been traditionally both paternalistic and politically liberal; to the radical left this means "establishment" and "reaction." Radical young Jews may oppose the values of their parents in contempt of American society. Siding with the Third World, they have followed Marxist propaganda in regard to Israel, unaware that Israel is part of the Third World, and its institutions, such as the Kibbutzim, the all-inclusive labor union, and the like, are based on ethical concepts of social responsibility that have their roots in Jewish tradition.

There may be another reason for the anti-Jewish and anti-Israel stance of radical young Jews and radical blacks, perhaps unperceived by both of them, but sometimes recognized: the attempt to escape from the confines of the minority group. Radical Jews, by their radicalism, believe that they are aligning themselves with the majority of the new nations constituting the larger mass of the population of the world. Radical blacks may feel that they are joining the white majority, whom they perceive as anti-Jewish. In both cases, the collapse of existing values and lack of a stable society might be responsible.

But there exists another form of rebellion of youth against the establishment and against their parents so thoroughly enmeshed in it: a return to Jewish learning, Jewish values, and Jewish social action. Disillusioned with the materialistic spirit of America, some young Jews have returned to Orthodoxy, and many families have organized *haburot* (fellowships) dedicated to study and life in Jewish heritage. Some have even migrated to Israel. These movements are small, but they offer a positive rebellion against the existing society— positive in the sense that these Jews wish to recapture their inner autonomy by living an authentic Jewish life in creative rebellion. The same spirit can be observed among young Russian Jews who are affirming their Jewishness again, not merely against a spiritually empty life, but, in their case, also against the political repression society and government have imposed.

For those, comparatively very few, who actually migrate to Israel, this step has a twofold significance: It makes them "normal," transforming them into members of a majority *as Jews*. It also may be regarded as a sign of rebellion against their elders. Israel, in addition to being the fulfillment of Jewish prayers and hopes, has normalized the position of American and world Jews. No longer are they members of a strange group calling themselves a people and yet lacking a basic characteristic of normal nationhood, an independent country of their own. The establishment of the State of Israel remedied this situation; vicariously, it normalized Jews. Even the shortcomings of the State contributed to this normalization. Survivalist Jews are linked to Israel in spirit and in soul, as we have pointed out. But even marginal Jews derive from its existence a new spirit of self-assurance and pride, although they would never wish to go there (even as many religious Jews see no religious obligation to migrate to Israel).

Gravely afflicted by the loss of life in the Yom Kippur War, Israel appealed to world Jewry for assistance: aid to restore devastation; visits from as many as could come in witness of kinship; Aliyah by those prepared to spend their lives, or a period of life, replacing the fallen in rebuilding the Land. The initial response, in terms of aid, was universal and generous. It revealed Jewish hopes. Linked in kinship with the people of Israel, every Jew hopes that this tiny remnant of the Holocaust may be saved from persecution and prosper in freedom. American Jews, like many concerned non-Jewish Americans, feel that Israel is important for the United States; it is the only trustworthy ally and true democracy in the embattled area of the Middle East. Israel permits a fruitful exchange of ideas through which Judaism can evolve spiritually and culturally. It also has theological significance, as we have seen.

Another deep concern for American and world Jews is Russian Jewry. American Jewry will have to shoulder the burdens of relocation. It also has to keep up the pressure for full rights to be granted to those who may wish to remain in Russia while living as Jews.

Peace with the Arabs is another concern for the Jews. There is no hatred for the Arabs, especially as individuals. There is rather a desire to share with Islam the insights Muslim religion and Judaism have to offer each other.

Jewry is thus reaching out in many directions, past and future, in America and Israel, toward self-realization and dialogue with other faiths, in thought and in action. It is *Goy* and it is unique. Its cohesion is based ideally on both *religious* and *communal* association. As the people of the Covenant, Jews have to establish this synthesis. But as one form of association undergoes stresses, the other makes itself felt more strongly. The nineteenth century saw emphasis placed on *religion,* leading to the evolution of Judaism; the twentieth century has witnessed an unparalleled reemergence of the spirit of *communality* at a time when religion is in need of reevaluation in the light of historical events.

This communality is also religion, living theology. Strengthened by the Holocaust in their will to survive, Jews have been determined not to give Hitler his "posthumous victory," as Fackenheim termed it. This means that a vibrant Jewish life in Israel and the Diaspora is vital. Other nations were subjected to the violent destruction of war for the sake of political or economic reasons, their cities and population devastated as a "strategic necessity." Jews were exterminated as Jews. As long as there is a vestige of belief among non-Jews that Jews "deserve" to be homeless and oppressed, the world has not fully recognized its human obligation. It still dwells in ancient prejudice. Jews are concerned, not only for themselves, but for the world, its humanity. A meaningful dialogue between people of different faiths, backgrounds, races, and nationalities is imperative for humanity's future.

Humanity is the only answer to the Holocaust. By living, Jews continue to offer the challenge of true humanity to the entire world. By wresting victory out of utter defeat—Hitler and the world's silence—they perform a task. The Jews thus become and will remain *Am Olam*—the eternal people, and a people of and for the entire world, for all humanity.

BIBLIOGRAPHY

This bibliography is offered merely to provide the next step for the interested reader.

UAHC stands for the Union of American Hebrew Congregations. JPS is the abbreviation for the Jewish Publication Society of America.

Introduction to Judaism; Jewish Ideas

Baeck, Leo, *The Essence of Judaism.* New York: Schocken, 1961 to the present.
Buber, Martin, *Israel and the World.* New York: Schocken, 1948.
———, *On Judaism.* New York: Schocken, 1972.
Epstein, I., *The Faith of Judaism.* New York: Penguin, 1954.
Finkelstein, Louis (ed.), *The Jews: Their History, Culture, and Religion,* 3 vols. New York: Schocken, 1970–1971.
Herberg, Will, *Judaism and Modern Man.* New York, Atheneum, 1970.
Heschel, Abraham J., *God in Search of Man: A Philosophy of Judaism.* Philadelphia: JPS, 1954.
Kaplan, Mordecai M., *Judaism as a Civilization.* New York: Schocken, 1967.
———, *The Meaning of God in Modern Jewish Religion.* New York: Jewish Reconstructionist Press, 1962.
Roth, Cecil (ed.), *Encyclopedia Judaica,* 16 vols. Jerusalem: Keter, 1971.
———, *The Standard Jewish Encyclopedia.* New York: Doubleday, 1959.
Steinberg, Milton, *Basic Judaism.* New York: Harcourt Brace, 1947.
Trepp, Leo, *A History of The Jewish Experience: Eternal Faith, Eternal People.* New York: Behrman, 1973.

History

Bamberger, Bernard J., *The Story of Judaism.* New York: Schocken, 1970.
Ben-Sasson, H. H. (ed.), *A History of the Jewish People.* Cambridge, Mass.: Harvard University Press, 1976.
Eban, Abba, *My People—The Story of the Jew.* New York: Random House, 1978.
Flannery, Edward H., *The Anguish of the Jews: Twenty-Three Centuries of Anti-Semitism.* New York: Macmillan, 1965.
Margolis, Max L., and Alexander Marx, *History of the Jewish People.* Philadelphia: JPS, 1927; New York: Meridian Books, 1960.

Parkes, James, *A History of the Jewish People*. Baltimore: Penguin, 1969.

Potok, Chaim, *Wanderings*. New York: Random House, 1978.

Stillman, N., *Jews in Arab Lands*. Philadelphia: JPS, 1979.

Bible and the Biblical Period

The Holy Scriptures (standard translation). Philadelphia: JPS, 1917.

The Torah (standard translation of the Pentateuch, revised). Philadelphia: JPS, 1962.

The Book of Psalms, A New Translation. Philadelphia: JPS, 1972.

The Prophets, Nevi'im, A New Translation. Philadelphia: JPS, 1978.

Albright, William F., *The Archaeology of Palestine*. New York: Pelican, annually since 1949.

———, *The Biblical Period from Abraham to Ezra*. New York: Harper & Row, 1963.

Bamberger, Bernard J., *The Bible: A Modern Jewish Approach,* 2nd ed. New York: Schocken, 1963.

Bright, John, *A History of Israel*. Philadelphia: Westminster, 1959.

Buber, Martin, *Kingship of God*. New York: Harper & Row, 1972.

———, *Moses: The Revelation and The Covenant*. New York: Harper & Row, 1958.

———, *The Prophetic Faith*. New York: Harper & Row, 1960.

Cross, Frank, *Canaanite Myth and Hebrew Epic*. Cambridge, Mass.: Harvard University Press, 1973.

Glatzer, Nahum N. (ed.), *The Dimensions of Job*. New York: Schocken, 1969.

Heschel, Abraham, *The Prophets*. Philadelphia: JPS, 1962.

Kittel, Rudolph, *Great Men and Movements in Israel*. New York: Ktav, 1968.

Noth, Martin, *The History of Israel*. New York: Harper & Row, 1960.

Orlinsky, Harry M., *Ancient Israel*. Ithaca and London: Cornell University Press, 1971.

Sandmel, Samuel, *The Hebrew Scriptures: An Introduction*. New York: Knopf, 1962.

Vriezen, Th.C., *The Religion of Ancient Israel*. Philadelphia: Westminster, 1967.

Postbiblical and Talmudic Periods

Adler, Morris, *The World of the Talmud*. New York: Schocken, 1963.

Baeck, Leo, *The Pharisees and Other Essays*. New York: Schocken, 1947.

Baron, Salo, and Joseph L. Blau, *Judaism in the Post-Biblical and Talmudic Period*. New York: Liberal Arts Press, 1954.

Flavius, Josephus, *The Jewish War*. Baltimore: Penguin, 1959.

Gaster, Theodor H., *The Dead Sea Scriptures*. New York: Doubleday Anchor, 1957.

Ginzberg, Louis, *The Legends of the Jews*. Philadelphia: JPS, 1961.

Goldin, Judah, *The Living Talmud* (translation from Hebrew of *The Sayings of the Fathers*). New York: Mentor Books, 1957.

Hanson, Paul D., *The Dawn of Apocalyptic*. Philadelphia: Fortress Press, 1975.

Herford, R. Travers, *The Ethics of the Talmud: Sayings of the Fathers*. New York: Schocken, 1969.

————, *The Pharisees*. Boston: Beacon Press, 1962.

Kadushin, Max, *The Rabbinic Mind*. New York: Blaisdell, 1965.

Montefiore, Claude C., and H. Lowe, *A Rabbinic Anthology*. Philadelphia: JPS, 1960 to the present.

Moore, George Foot, *Judaism in the First Centuries of the Christian Era,* 2 vols. New York: Schocken, 1971.

Neusner, Jacob, *From Politics to Piety: The Emergence of Pharisaic Judaism*. New York: Ktav, no date.

Russell, David S., *The Method and Message of Jewish Apocalyptic*. Philadelphia: Westminster, 1964.

Sandmel, Samuel, *Philo of Alexandria*. New York: Oxford University Press, 1978.

Schuerer, Emil, *History of the Jewish People in the Time of Jesus*. New York: Schocken, 1961.

Stone, Michael, *Scriptures, Sects and Vision: A Profile of Judaism from Ezra to the Jewish Revolts*. Philadelphia: Fortress Press, 1980.

Strack, Herman L., *Introduction to the Talmud and Midrash*. Philadelphia: JPS, 1959; New York: Meridian Books, 1959.

Yadin, Yigael, *Masada*. New York: Random House, 1966.

Christianity

Baeck, Leo, *Judaism and Christianity*. New York: Atheneum, 1970.

Buber, Martin, *Two Types of Faith*. New York: Harper & Row Torchbook, 1961.

Carmichael, Joel, *The Death of Jesus*. New York: Macmillan, 1962.

Cohen, Arthur H., *The Myth of the Judeo-Christian Tradition*. New York: Schocken, 1971.

Eckardt, Roy A., *Elder and Younger Brothers—The Encounter of Jews and Christians*. New York: Schocken, 1973.

Flannery, Edward H., *The Anguish of the Jews*. New York: Macmillan, 1965.

Gilbert, Arthur, *The Vatican Council and the Jews*. Cleveland and New York: World Publishing, 1968.

Isaac, Jules, *The Teaching of Contempt: Christian Roots of Anti-Semitism*. New York: Holt, Rinehart and Winston, 1964.

Klausner, Joseph, *From Jesus to Paul,* New York: Humanities Press, 1956; Boston: Beacon Press, 1961.

————, *Jesus of Nazareth*. New York: Macmillan, 1953.

Klein, Charlotte, *Anti-Judaism in Christian Theology*. Philadelphia: Fortress Press, 1978.

Parker, James, *The Conflict of the Church and the Synagogue*. Philadelphia: JPS, 1969.

————, *Prelude to Dialogue: Jewish Christian Relationship*. New York: Schocken, 1969.

Rubenstein, Richard L., *My Brother Paul*. New York: Harper & Row, 1972.

Sanders, E. P., *Paul and Palestinian Judaism*. Philadelphia: Fortress Press, 1977.

Sandmel, Samuel, *Anti-Semitism in the New Testament*. Philadelphia: Fortress Press, 1978.

————, *The Genius of Paul*. New York: Farrar, Strauss, 1958; Boston: Beacon Press, 1961.

————, *A Jewish Understanding of the New Testament*. Cincinnati: Hebrew Union College Press, 1957.

————, *Judaism and Christian Beginnings*. New York: Oxford University Press, 1978.

————, *We Jews and Jesus*. New York: Oxford University Press, 1965.

Werner, Eric, *The Sacred Bridge, Liturgical Parallels in Synagogue and Early Church*. New York: Schocken, 1970.

Zeitlin, Solomon, *Who Crucified Jesus?* New York: Bloch, 1964.

Medieval and Modern Periods

Abrahams, Israel, *Jewish Life in the Middle Ages*. Philadelphia: JPS, 1960.

Altmann, Alexander, *Moses Mendelssohn*. University of Alabama Press, 1973.

Glatstein, Jacob, Israel Knox, and Samuel Margosches, *Anthology of Holocaust Literature*. Philadelphia: JPS, 1969.

Glatzer, Nahum N., *The Dynamics of Emancipation*. Boston: Beacon Press, 1965.

————, *Faith and Knowledge, A Medieval Reader*. Boston: Beacon Press, 1963.

Himmelfarb, Milton, *The Jews of Modernity*. Philadelphia: JPS, 1973.

Katz, Jacob, *Exclusiveness and Tolerance*. New York: Schocken, 1962.

Marcus, Jacob R., *The Jew in the Medieval World*. New York: UAHC, 1938; Meridian Books, 1960.

Parkes, James, *Anti-Semitism*. Chicago: Quadrangle, 1964.

Sachar, Howard M., *The Course of Modern Jewish History*. New York: Dell, 1963.

Scholem, Gershom, *The Messianic Idea in Judaism*. New York: Schocken, 1971.

————, *Sabbatai Sevi*. Princeton, N.J.: Princeton University Press, 1973.

Sklare, Marshall (ed.), *The Jews: Social Pattern of an American Group*. New York: Free Press of Glencoe, 1958.

Werblowsky, Zwi, *Joseph Karo*. Philadelphia, JPS, 1976.

Jewish Philosophy and Theology

Agus, Jacob B., *Modern Philosophies of Judaism*. New York: Behrman, 1971.

Bamberger, Bernard J., *The Search for Jewish Theology*. New York: Behrman, 1978.

Bergman, Samuel H., *Faith and Reason: An Introduction to Modern Jewish Thought*. Washington: B'nai B'rith Hillel Foundations, 1963.

Bokser, Ben Zion (trans.), *Abraham Isaac Kook—The Lights of Penitence, Lights of Holiness, The Moral Principles, Essays, Letters, and Poems.* New York: Paulist Press, 1978.

Borowitz, Eugene B., *How Can a Jew Speak of Faith Today?* Philadelphia: Westminster, 1969.

————, *A New Jewish Theology in the Making.* Philadelphia: Westminster, 1968.

Cohen, Arthur A., *The Natural and Supernatural Jew: A Historical and Theological Introduction.* New York: McGraw-Hill, 1962.

————, (ed.), *Arguments and Doctrines, A Reader of Jewish Thinking in the Aftermath of the Holocaust.* Philadelphia: JPS, 1970.

Cohen, Hermann, *Religion of Reason out of the Sources of Judaism.* Translated by Simon Kaplan. New York: Ungar, 1971.

Editors of *Commentary* magazine, *The Condition of Jewish Belief.* New York: Macmillan, 1966.

Fackenheim, Emil L., *Encounters Between Judaism and Modern Philosophy.* Philadelphia: JPS, 1973.

Glatzer, Nahum N., *Franz Rosenzweig, His Life and Thought.* Philadelphia: JPS, 1953.

Guttman, Julius, *Philosophies of Judaism.* New York: Schocken, 1973.

Herberg, Will, *The Writings of Martin Buber.* New York: Meridian Books, 1960.

Heschel, Abraham J., *Who Is Man?* Stanford, Calif.: Stanford University Press, 1966.

Husik, Isaac, *A History of Medieval Jewish Philosophy.* Philadelphia and New York: JPS and Meridian Books, 1958.

Jacobs, Louis, *Jewish Ethics, Philosophy and Mysticism.* New York: Behrman, 1969.

————, *A Jewish Theology.* New York: Behrman, 1973.

————, *Jewish Thought Today.* New York: Behrman, 1970.

Kaplan, Mordecai M., *The Purpose and Meaning of Jewish Existence* (A critique of Hermann Cohen). Philadelphia: JPS, 1964.

Kaplan, Mordecai M., and Arthur A. Cohen, *If Not Now, When?—Toward a Reconstruction of the Jewish People.* New York: Schocken, 1973.

Kaufman, William, *Contemporary Jewish Philosophies.* New York: Reconstructionist Press, 1976.

Lewry, Hans, Alexander Altmann, and Isaac Heinemann (eds.), *Three Jewish Philosophers (Philo, Saadia, and Judah Halevi): Readings and Introduction.* Philadelphia and New York: JPS and Meridian Books, 1960.

Maimonides, Moses, *The Guide of the Perplexed* (abridged). Translated by M. Friedlander. New York: Dover, 1962.

Rosenzweig, Franz, *Star of Redemption.* Translated by William Hallo. Boston: Beacon Press, 1972.

Rothenstreich, Nathan, *Jewish Philosophy in Modern Times.* New York: Holt, Rinehart and Winston, 1968.

Twersky, Isadore, *A Maimonides Reader*. New York: Behrman, 1972.
Wolf, Arnold J. (ed.), *Rediscovering Judaism*. Chicago: Quadrangle, 1965.

Jewish Mysticism and Hasidism

Buber, Martin, *The Legend of the Baal-Shem*. New York: Schocken, 1969.
———, *Tales of the Hasidim*. New York: Schocken, 1961.
———, *Ten Rungs: Hasidic Sayings*. New York: Schocken, 1962.
Jacobs, Louis, *Hasidic Prayer*. New York: Schocken, 1978.
———, *Hasidic Thought*. New York: Behrman, 1976.
Scholem, Gershom, *Major Trends in Jewish Mysticism*. New York: Schocken, 1963.
———, *On the Kabbalah and Its Symbolism*. New York: Schocken, 1965.

Holocaust and Theological Endeavors

Bauer, Yehudah, *The Holocaust in Historical Perspective*. Seattle: University of Washington Press, 1978.
Berkowitz, Eliezer, *Faith after the Holocaust*. New York: Ktav, 1973.
Cohen, Arthur A. (ed.), *Arguments and Doctrines: A Reader of Jewish Thinking in the Aftermath of the Holocaust*. Philadelphia: JPS, 1970.
Dawidowicz, Ludy, *A Holocaust Reader*. New York: Behrman, 1976.
———, *The War Against the Jews*. New York: Holt, Rinehart and Winston, 1975.
Epstein, Helen, *Children of the Holocaust*. New York: Putnam, 1978.
Fackenheim, Emil L., *The Jewish Return into History*. New York: Schocken, 1978.
———, *Quest for Past and Future*. Bloomington: Indiana University Press, 1968.
Hillberg, Raul, *The Destruction of the European Jews*. New York: Harper & Row, 1979.
Langer, Lawrence L., *The Holocasut and the Literary Imagination*. New Haven and London: Yale University Press, 1975.
Levin, Nora, *The Holocaust: The Destruction of European Jewry, 1933–1945*. New York: Schocken, 1973.
Rubenstein, Richard, *After Auschwitz*. Indianapolis, Ind.: Bobbs Merrill, 1966.
———, *The Cunning of History: Mass Death and the American Future*. New York: Harper & Row, 1975.
Sachs, Nelly, *O The Chimneys*. Philadelphia: JPS, 1968.
Wiesel, Elie, *The Gates of the Forest*. New York: Holt, Rinehart and Winston, 1966.
———, *A Jew Today*. New York: Vintage, 1978.
———, *The Jews of Silence*. New York: Holt, Rinehart and Winston, 1972.
———, *Night*. New York: Avon, 1972.

Judaism in America

The American Jewish Year Book. Philadelphia: JPS, annual.

Glazer, Nathan, *American Judaism*. Chicago: University of Chicago Press, 1959.

Glock, Charles Y., and Rodney Stark, *Religion and Anti-Semitism*. Berkeley: University of California Press, 1966.

Goldberg, M. Hirsch, *Just Because They Are Jewish*. New York: Stein and Day, 1978.

Herberg, Will, *Protestant, Catholic, Jew*. New York: Doubleday, 1955.

Heschel, Abraham J., *The Insecurity of Freedom*. Philadelphia: JPS, 1966.

Janowsky, A., *The American Jew, A Reappraisal*. Philadelphia: JPS, 1964.

Korn, Bertram W., *American Jewry and the Civil War*. Philadelphia: JPS, 1961.

Liebman, Charles, *The Ambivalent American Jew*. Philadelphia: JPS, 1973.

Neusner, Jacob, *American Judaism, Adventure in Modernity*. Englewood Cliffs, N.J.: Prentice-Hall, 1972.

Quinley, Harold E., and Charles Glock, *Anti-Semitism in America*. New York: Free Press, 1979.

Sidorsky, David (ed.), *The Future of the Jewish Community in America*. New York: Basic Books, 1973.

Sklare, Marshall, *The Jews, Social Pattern of an American Group*. Glencoe, Ill.: The Free Press, 1958.

Stark, Rodney, and Foster, Glock and Quinley, *Wayward Shepherds: Prejudice and The Protestant Clergy*. New York: Harper & Row, 1973.

Zborowsky, Mark, and Elizabeth Herzog, *Life is with People*. New York: Schocken, 1976.

Varieties of Religious Expression: Life and Law

Blau, Joseph L., *Modern Varieties of Judaism*. New York: Columbia University Press, 1966.

Bleich, J. David, *Contemporary Halakhic Problems* (Orthodox). New York: Ktav, 1977.

Borowitz, Eugene B., *Reform Judaism Today*. New York: Behrman, 1978.

Davis, Mosheh, *The Emergence of Conservative Judaism*. Philadelphia: JPS, 1963.

Freehof, Solomon B., *Responsa* (Reform), numerous volumes. New York: Ktav, 1955–1963; New York: Hebrew Union College, 1969–1974.

Kaplan, Mordecai M., *The Future of the American Jew* (Reconstructionist). New York: Macmillan, 1948.

———, *The Meaning of God in Modern Jewish Religion* (Reconstructionist). New York: Reconstructionist Press, 1937.

———, *Questions Jews Ask: Reconstructionist Answers*. New York: Reconstructionist Press, 1956.

Plaut, W. Gunther, *The Growth of Reform Judaism*. New York: World Union for Progressive Judaism, 1965.

————, *The Rise of Reform Judaism*. New York: World Union for Progressive Judaism, 1963.

Siegel, Seymor, *Conservative Judaism and Jewish Law*. New York: Ktav, 1977.

The Position of Jewish Women

Lacks, Roslyn, *Women and Judaism*. New York: Doubleday, 1980.

Meiselman, Mosheh, *Jewish Woman in Jewish Law*. New York: Ktav, 1978.

Priesand, Sally, *Judaism and the New Woman*. New York: Behrman, 1975.

Zionism

Bein, Alex, *Theodor Herzl*. New York: Atheneum, 1970.

Buber, Martin, *On Zion*. New York: Schocken, 1973.

Halkin, Hillel, *Letters to an American Friend*. Philadelphia: JPS, 1978.

Hertzberg, Arthur (ed.), *The Zionist Idea*. Philadelphia and New York: JPS and Meridian Books, 1960.

Heschel, Abraham J., *Israel*. New York: Farrar, Straus and Giroux, 1971.

Sachar, Howard, *A History of Israel from the Rise of Zionism to our Time*. Philadelphia: JPS, 1979.

Spiro, Melford E., *Kibbutz, Venture in Utopia*. New York: Schocken, 1963.

The Jewish Year in Worship and Art

Prayer Books and Aggadahs by the various denominational groups.

Philip Goodman has authored anthologies for every holiday, published by the Jewish Publication Society of America (Philadelphia).

Agnon, S. Y., *Days of Awe*. New York: Schocken, 1948.

Arzt, Max, *Justice and Mercy: Commentary on the Liturgy of the New Year and the Day of Atonement*. New York: Holt, Rinehart and Winston, 1963.

Gaster, Theodor H., *Festivals of the Jewish Year*. Philadelphia: JPS, 1953.

————, *Passover: Its History and Traditions*. Boston: Beacon Press, 1962.

Heinemann, Joseph, and Jakob J. Petuchowsky, *Literature of the Synagogue*. New York: Behrman, 1975.

Idelson, A.Z., *Jewish Liturgy*. New York: Schocken, 1967.

————, *Jewish Music*. New York: Schocken, 1944.

Kampf, Avram, *Contemporary Synagogue Art*. Philadelphia: JPS, 1966.

Millgram, Abraham, *The Sabbath, Day of Delight*. Philadelphia: JPS, 1944.

Roth, Cecil, *Jewish Art*. New York: New York Graphic Society, 1971.

Schauss, Hayyim, *The Jewish Festivals*. New York: UAHC, 1938.

Wischnitzer, Rachel L., *The Architecture of the European Synagogue*. Philadelphia: JPS, 1964.

————, *Synagogue Architecture in the United States*. Philadelphia: JPS, 1955.

Living as a Jew

Borowitz, Eugene B., *Choosing a Sex Ethic: A Jewish Inquiry*. New York: Schocken, 1970.

Brav, Stanley B., *Marriage and the Jewish Tradition*. New York: Philosophical Library, 1951.

Cahnman, Werner J., *Intermarriage and Jewish Life*. New York: Herzl Press, 1963.

Donin, Hayim Halevi, *To Be a Jew* (Orthodox). New York: Basic Books, 1972.

Klein, Isaac, *A Guide to Jewish Practice* (Conservative). New York: Ktav, 1978.

Siegel, Richard, Michael Strassfeld, and Sharon Strassfeld, *The First Jewish Catalogue—A Do-It-Yourself Kit*. Philadelphia: JPS, 1973.

Strassfeld, Sharon, and Michael Strassfeld, *The Second Jewish Catalogue— Sources and Resources*. Philadelphia: JPS, 1976.

Trepp, Leo, *The Complete Book of Jewish Observance*. New York: Behrman House—Summit Books, 1980.

Some Periodicals

The various synagogue and rabbinical bodies have regular periodicals for their constituents. B'nai B'rith issues *The National Jewish Monthly,* which is popular in style and has wide appeal beyond the membership, and *Jewish Heritage,* an educational quarterly. *Judaism* is a scholarly quarterly. The *Reconstructionist* deals with many subjects from the Reconstructionist point of view. *Commentary,* a monthly magazine issued by the American Jewish Committee, holds high prestige among Jewish and non-Jewish readers. *Sh'ma, A Journal of Jewish Responsibility,* deals with the issues of our time from the Jewish point of view; the journal is daringly innovative. *Tradition* is an excellent quarterly issued by the Orthodox Rabbinical Council of America. The national rabbinical and congregational organizations issue scholarly and popular journals. *Moment* is a magazine dealing with all aspects of Judaism. *Midstream* is a review published by the Herzl Institute. Other groups, as well as individual publishers, issue magazines and periodicals.

The larger Jewish communities have their own newspapers, usually dealing with local Jewish affairs, but often including wider coverage; they are usually weeklies and written in English.

GLOSSARY

Ab, ninth of—fast day mourning the fall of the Temple of Jerusalem both in 586 B.C.E. and in 70 C.E.

Aberah—transgression, sin.

Adonai—the Lord, speaking of God; replaces the tetragrammaton, YHVH, which is not pronounced by Jews.

Aggadah—the story; term for the homiletic portions of the Talmud, containing legends, parables, and ethics.

Alenu—concluding prayer of worship, named after its first word: *upon us* rests the duty to render praise.

Aliyah—going up; migration of Diaspora Jews to Israel.

Amen—see **emunah.**

Amidah—prayer of affirmation and petition recited three times daily while standing.

Amora—(pl. Amoraim) masters of the Gemara in Palestine and Babylonia (approx. 200–500 C.E.).

Apocrypha—books of semisacred character excluded from the canon of Hebrew Scriptures.

Ashkenasim—(pl. of *Ashkenas,* supposedly meaning *Germany*) Jews living in Germany, France, England, and later in Poland and Russia during a large part of their history, developing there a set of identifying religious practices and customs. The majority of American Jews are Ashkenasim.

Baal Shem—Master of the (Divine) Name; name given to the founder of Hasidism (Jewish mysticism) in Poland.

Bar Mitzvah—Son of Mitzvah, responsible for its fulfillment; a boy reaches this stage at the age of thirteen, when a ceremony underscores his passage from childhood to adult membership in the Jewish community.

Bat Mitzvah—Daughter of Mitzvah, responsible for its fulfillment. A ceremony of recent origin underscores this passage of girls from childhood to adult membership in the Jewish community.

B.C.E.—before the common era; used to designate dates preceding the Christian era.

Berakhah—benediction, blessing, praise; the unit of prayer.

Bet Am—house of the people; *Bet Hakneset*—house of assembly. Both are terms for synagogue.

Bet Din—rabbinical court, adjudicating cases arising from religious law (**Halakhah**).

Bimah—pulpit from which Torah is read to the people; used also for "chancel" in the synagogue.

B'nai B'rith—sons of the Covenant; worldwide fraternal order, founded in U.S.A.

B'rit—Covenant. God made a Covenant with nature, humanity, Israel. God never abrogates his Covenant, even at times when the partners fail to live up to it. *New Covenant:* Christianity.

B'rit Milah—Covenant of circumcision; act of circumcision.

C.E.—common era; designates dates of the Christian era.

Chazan—cantor, musically trained singer and leader of worship; today also frequently in charge of education.

Cheder—(school) room; primary school for Hebrew study in the Eastern European education system.

Conservatism, Conservative Judaism—Jewish denomination, basing itself on tradition but believing in the evolution of "positive historical Judaism" by the people's consent; Conservative Judaism endeavors to adapt Jewish law to modern conditions by means of reinterpretation.

Covenant—see *B'rit.*

Diaspora—the dispersion or scattering of the Jews; Jewish community outside Israel.

Dietary laws—laws based on Torah governing food permitted and forbidden to Jews.

Ecumenical—worldwide; a movement toward Christian unity but also taking into account Judaism and other non-Christian religions. The ecumenical spirit between Christians and Jews has grown, especially since the Second Vatican Council, which concluded in 1965.

El—name of God, in Jewish tradition emphasizing God's attribute of justice. The Canaanites of antiquity used this term as a designation of one of their deities.

Elohim—plural of El, but always used with a singular verb; the One God as Sum of all power and justice.

Emancipation—elimination of civic disabilities of Jews by modern states, requiring Jewish adjustment to western culture.

Emunah—faithfulness, trust; God's *faithfulness* in all times and conditions calls for humanity's *trust* in Him. The word *Amen* has the same root; it is an affirmation of trust, "so it shall be."

Eschatology—discourse about the last things, dealing with the end of days, ultimate judgment, and so on.

Etrog—citron; one of the four plants used in worship on Sukkot.

Existentialism—a philosophy and theology encompassing various schools. Instead of asking about the essence, the universal features of all things, existentialism asks: What must I, as a concrete human being, accept and believe, in order that my life will be authentic and have meaning? Existentialism calls for the individual human decision that has to be made by each person and has to be made anew in every situation. The religious existentialist hears the voice of God, revealing Himself out of God's grace and love; the individual then responds. Since science cannot offer proof of the truths arrived at existentially and individually, the individual must take the leap into faith, to God. But without this belief his life might be meaningless and desperate. Jewish theologians, such as Franz Rosenzweig and Martin Buber, developed Jewish existentialism. Emil Fackenheim writes that the issue of Auschwitz calls for an existential answer affirming God, else Jewish existence would not be bearable.

Galut—exile; life outside the Land of Israel, in oppression.

Gaon—Excellency. Title of the head of academy in Babylonia.

Gedaliah, Fast of—fast day immediately after Rosh Hashanah, named for the Jewish governor of Palestine murdered by his fellow Jews at the time of destruction of the first Temple (II Kings 25; Jeremiah 40:1).

Gehinnom—purgatory.

Geiger, Abraham—one of the founders of Reform Judaism in Germany (1810–1874).

Gemara—completion; record of extensive discussion of the rabbis, based on the *Mishnah*. *Mishnah* and *Gemara* together complete the *Talmud*, the compendium of learning.

Habdalah—prayer of *separation* of the Sabbath and holy days from the days of the week.

Haftarah—portion of Prophets appointed to be read after the reading of Torah on holy days and special occasions.

Haggadah—text used at celebration of the Passover Seder (see also **Aggadah**).

Halakhah—the path of life; law and the legal decisions of developers of Jewish law, guiding life and its activities; core of traditional observance.

Hallah—loaf of bread set on the table on Sabbath and holy days; after a blessing, thanking God for its gift, the family partakes of it.

Hallel—Psalms 113–118; Psalms of thanksgiving, recited on holy days of joy.

Hametz—leaven, and all items made with it, which must be removed from the house during Passover.

Hanukkah—midwinter festival of eight days, commemorating the reconsecration of the Temple after the victorious uprising of the Maccabees, for religious freedom.

Hasidism—mystical movement, particularly that founded by Rabbi Israel Baal Shem in Poland (1700–1760); in modern days, explored by Martin Buber and Gershom Scholem.

Haskalah—enlightenment movement among Jews in Eastern and Central Europe.

Hasmon—founder of the House of *Hasmonaeans,* the family of the Maccabees (see **Maccabees**).

Het—sin; "missing the mark" of God-ordained performance in life.

Herzl, Theodor—founder of political Zionism (1860–1904).

Hillel Foundations—Jewish student foundations at universities, named after Hillel, one of the greatest among the Pharisaic masters and known for his graciousness and love of humanity. They are a division of the **B'nai B'rith.**

Hokhmah—wisdom. Divine wisdom, *sophia,* is equated in scriptural "wisdom books" and ancient Jewish philosophy with Torah.

Huppah—in the wedding ceremony, the canopy under which the couple stands, symbolically beginning their life under a common roof.

Kabbalah—tradition; specifically the mystical tradition in Judaism.

Kaddish—call to *sanctification* of God's Name with congregational response, expressing the hope that "His kingdom come"; used in worship and also recited by mourners as evidence of their faith in God; possibly source of Christian "Our Father who are in heaven."

Kahal—congregation; also communal organization of Eastern European Jewry.

Kaplan, Mordecai M.—Jewish theologian, founder of Reconstructionism (born 1881).

Kashrut—kosher laws.

Kavanah—attunement of the heart to God in prayer and Mitzvot.

Kedushah—*sanctification* of God in public worship; "Kadosh, kadosh, kadosh . . . holy, holy, holy is the Lord of Hosts . . . " (Isaiah 6:3).

Ketubah—marriage contract, setting forth the duties of the husband toward his wife.

Ketubim—collected writings; third part of the Tenakh, including Psalms, Job, and so on.

Kibbutz—cooperative settlement in modern Israel, whose settlers hold all property in common.

Kiddush—the *sanctification* of the Sabbath and holy days over a cup of wine; part of the traditional Sabbath and holy day observance.

Kiddush HaShem—*sanctification of God's Name* by the Jews' general conduct in the world at large as they live up to divinely ordained ethics; the term is also used to denote martyrdom in behalf of the Jewish faith.

Kiddushin—the sanctification of married life, namely, the marriage ceremony; a "setting apart."

K'lal Israel—the union of Israel, the Jewish people as a whole; used specifically in terms of religious unity.

Knesset—assembly; also name of the parliament of Israel.

Kol Nidre—declaration opening the service on the eve of Yom Kippur, known for its haunting melody.

Kos—cup, from *kosas,* to measure out; in Kiddush, Habdalah, and the wedding ceremony (during which bride and groom share the cup), it becomes the symbol of the destiny measured out by God for man and woman.

Kosher—all right, fit, proper; designation given to foods and other items signifying that they are usable under Jewish law; the term has entered general American usage standing for right, proper.

Lulab—palm branch, one of the four plants used in worship on Sukkot.

Maariv—evening prayer.

Maccabees—priestly family who led the Jews to independence in the war against the Syrians (167 B.C.E.); its descendants became high priests and kings (see **Hanukkah**).

Magen David—shield of David; six-pointed star; a symbol of Judaism.

Mahzor—prayerbook for the festivals.

Maimonides, Moses—leading medieval Jewish philosopher, theologian, codifier of Jewish law (1135–1204).

Makom—place; a name of God who encompasses every place and all time.

Malakh—angel.

Maror—bitter herbs eaten at the Passover Seder in commemoration of the bitterness of Egyptian slavery.

Masorah—tradition; *Masoretes* are the establishers and preservers of the traditional version of Holy Scriptures.

Matzah—unleavened bread; "the bread of affliction" and of deliverance, eaten at Passover instead of leavened bread.

Mazel tov—expression meaning congratulations, good luck (Mazel means star or constellation; *Mazel tov*: may the constellation be good!).

Megillah—scroll; specifically the Scroll of Esther, read at Purim.

Mendelssohn, Moses—philosopher; "father" of Western-oriented, modern Jewry (1729–1786).

Menorah—candelabrum; seven-branched menorah used in the Temple; the symbol of Judaism and coat of arms of the State of Israel. A nine-branched menorah is used on Hanukkah.

Messiah—the anointed one; the human ruler who is forecast for the end of days to bring peace to humanity and rule over the perfect society.

Mezuzah—a small scroll containing selections of Scripture, including the Shema, placed on the doorposts of Jewish homes.

Midrash—*search* for meaning; homiletic commentary on the Scriptures; also applied to individual exegetic portions.

Mikveh—ritual bath; also used for immersion of converts.

Minhag—custom and practice (plural *minhagim*).

Minhah—afternoon prayer.

Minyan—quorum of ten, needed for public worship.

Mishnah—review; the interpretations of Torah passed along by word of mouth (Oral Torah) and finally codified c. 200 B.C.E. (see **Talmud**).

Mitzvah—commandment (plural *Mitzvot*); Mitzvah is God's command, both religious and ethical; Mitzvah is also the Jew's response to the divine call, by way of action.

Mohel—a pious man who performs the act of circumcision.

Mussaf—additional service on Sabbath and holy days, reflecting the significance of these days and commemorating the sacrificial service at the Temple of old.

Ne'eelah—closing service on Yom Kippur.

Nebee-im—(singular, *Nabee*) prophets; the Books of the Prophets, second part of the Tenakh.

Neo-Orthodoxy—Western-oriented orthodoxy (see **Orthodoxy**).

Niddah—the woman maritally "separated" during the menstrual period.

Olam haba—the world to come (*Olam hazeh:* this world).

Oneg Shabbat—the delight of the Sabbath; also used for communal Sabbath celebrations outside formal worship.

Orthodoxy—traditional form of Judaism, believing in the literal truth of Torah and its absolute historicity, and the binding force of Halakhah as promulgated by ancient and later sages of Torah.

Pale—area in Russia where Jews were permitted to reside during the period of the Russian Empire.

Pentateuch—the Five Books of Moses; first part of the Tenakh.

Pessah (Passover)—festival of spring and rebirth, marking Israel's freedom from Egyptian bondage.

Pharisees—sect of ancient Judaism; heirs and transmitters of the high ethical standards of the prophetic ideals; interpreters and molders of Jewish law (Oral Torah), holding Oral Torah to have been revealed at Sinai together with written Torah; believers in immortality of the soul, freedom of will, divine providence, the existence of angels, and the resurrection of the dead. Frequently misjudged in history, they are acknowledged as the masters of Judaism and revered for their sincerity of heart and soul.

Pilpul—a method of hairsplitting dialectic in the study of Talmud.

Piyutim—liturgical poems.

Proseuche—early term for the synagogue building where religious gatherings were held.

Purim—carnival-like spring feast, commemorating the liberation of Jews from extermination in ancient Persia, as related in the Book of Esther, which is read.

Rabbi—teacher; the ordained spiritual leader of a congregation. Rabbi is a "degree" obtained in America after approximately five years of postgraduate study in a Jewish theological school. Traditional ordination empowers a rabbi to hand down authoritative decisions on religious law, based on Halakhah.

Rashi—foremost commentator on Bible and Talmud (1040–1105).

Reconstructionism—religious movement, founded by Mordecai M. Kaplan; explains Judaism as the creation of the Jewish people—defining it as an evolving religious civilization—and the Jewish people's ultimate concern with ethical nationhood. Reconstructionism utilizes scientific insights as tools for interpreting Judaism and sees in it a way to meet the societal issues of our time. It calls upon the American Jew to live in two civilizations, the American and the Jewish.

Reform—liberal religious movement, based on the scientific study of religion, seeking to make Judaism relevant to modern times. It does not regard Halakhah as divinely grounded and leaves its observance to the conscience of the individual. In recent years, Reform has become increasingly more traditional, emphasizing the spirit of K'lal Israel.

Rosh Hashanah—New Year's Day, an autumn festival; beginning of a ten-day period of penitence.

Sadducees—sect of conservatives in the period of the second Temple, centering around the priesthood (the descendant of Zadok, who anointed Solomon, hence the name *Sadducees*), and concerned with the perpetuation of Temple worship. Antagonists of the Pharisees, the Sadducees denied the validity of Oral Torah, the immortality of soul, resurrection, angels, and divine providence; some became worldly.

Sanhedrin—the Jewish Supreme Court and lawmaking body in the times of the Temple; administrators of the law.

Seder—*order;* the order of the family service at Passover.

Sefardim—Jews whose ancestors lived in Spain; now primarily Jews in Mediterranean countries, who developed their own customs in the course of history. A number of Sefardic Jews live in America and have established congregations.

Sefer Torah—the Scroll of the Torah, containing the Five Books of Moses.

Selihot—prayers of forgiveness, especially those during the penitential period.

Shabuot—Feast of Weeks (seven weeks after Passover), commemorating the giving of the Torah at Mt. Sinai.

Shaddai—name of God, who is with the Jews wherever they are; found on the Mezuzah.

Shaharit—morning prayer.

Shalom—peace; also name of God meaning absolute perfection, peace being *perfection* (root of the word); greeting between the people in the State of Israel.

Shamash—*server,* name for the beadle in the synagogue; also used for the serving candle in the Hanukkah menorah, used to light the others.

Shebarim—a three-times broken sound on the **shofar,** signifying the sobbing of a contrite heart.

Shekhinah—name for God, dwelling within His world, resting in the midst of the people.

Shehitah—slaughter of animals in accordance with Jewish dietary law.

Shema—*Hear,* the first word of the affirmation of faith: "Hear, O Israel, the Lord our God, the Lord is One" (Deuteronomy 6:4–9, and also including Deuteronomy 11:13–21, Numbers 15:37–41), hence standing for the whole affirmation.

Sh'mini Atzeret—eighth day of the Sukkot festival.

Shivah—seven days of mourning after the death of a close relative.

Shoa—Holocaust; Nazi extermination of six million Jews.

Shofar—ram's horn; sounded on Rosh Hashanah, the month preceding it, and at the end of Yom Kippur.

Shohet—man trained in Jewish law who slaughters animals in accordance with ritual requirements.

Shtetl—small, wholly Jewish Eastern European town surrounded by a non-Jewish world; developed its own way of life and and its own culture.

Shul—the school; popular name for synagogue, testifying to its character as a place of instruction.

Shulhan Arukh—"The Well-Prepared Table," written by Joseph Karo and published in 1565; the authoritative code for Orthodox Jewish practice.

Siddur—the prayer book.

Simhat Torah—*Rejoicing in Torah;* final day of the Sukkot festival, when the cycle of the annual Torah reading is completed and the new one begun; celebrated with joyful processions and dance. The day has become a time of public witnessing for Judaism by Russian Jews.

Sukkah—a small hut or booth, covered by branches and leaves, in which the family takes its meals during the **Sukkot** festival.

Sukkot—fall festival of thanksgiving for the blessing of the harvest and protection.

Synagogue—building where the congregation meets for prayer, study, and assembly; formerly used to mean the congregation itself.

Tallit—a four-cornered garment with tassels (*tzitzit*) on it, worn to serve as a constant reminder of the presence of God; traditionally worn by the male members of the congregation during morning worship and by the leader of worship at all services; frequently in the form of a "prayer shawl."

Talmud—"The Compendium of Learning," consisting of *Mishnah* and *Gemara.* Two versions of the Talmud, one in Palestine, the other in Babylonia, completed about 500 C.E. The latter is the basic source for Jewish law and codes.

Tanna (plural, Tannaim)—the teachers who speak in the *Mishnah*.

Tefillah—prayer.

Tefillin—phylacteries; small cubes containing scrolls with several scriptural selections, including the Shema (Exodus 13:1, 11; Deuteronomy 6:4–9, 11:13–21). Scrolls and containers, made of parchment, are worn by men during the morning service on weekdays, placed on the forehead and left arm by means of attached leather bands.

Tehillim—*praises;* Hebrew term for Psalms.

Tekiah—a long-drawn sound on the **shofar,** "awakening the slumbering conscience."

Tenakh—abbreviation for Hebrew Holy Scriptures, arrived at by combining the first letters of the three sections that constitute them: *T*orah, *N*ebee-im, *Kh*etubim.

Terefah—*torn,* referring to animals that are therefore not usable as food; term is generally used for food that is not **kosher.**

Teruah—a whimpering, nine times broken sound on the **shofar;** the weeping of a heart aware of its sinfulness.

Teshuvah—*return* to God; repentance.

Torah—*instruction;* specifically, the divinely revealed instruction of Holy Scriptures; used to designate the Five Books of Moses—Genesis, Exodus, Leviticus, Numbers, and Deuteronomy; the first part of the Tenakh; used in wider connotation as Tenakh as a whole. In a still wider sense, it includes written and Oral Torah, the whole body of authoritative teaching and instruction and its evolving tradition. Also term for the Scroll, from which the scriptural portion is read publicly.

Tosafot—additions, written by Rashi's successors during the twelfth and thirteenth centuries in France, explaining his commentary on the Talmud.

Tzaddik—a righteous person; in Hasidism the master of a Hassidic group.

Tzedakah—righteousness; used as term for charity.

Tzitzit—the tassels on the four-cornered robe, the **Tallit.**

Yahrzeit—anniversary of the death of a family member.

Yamim Noraim—Days of Awe; the period from Rosh Hashanah through Yom Kippur, a time of repentance.

Yeshivah—academy of advanced talmudic studies.

Yetzer—the drive, inclination; Yetzer Ha-Tov: inclination toward good; Yetzer Ha-Ra: drive toward evil.

YHVH—name of God, pronounced *Adonai,* a substitute term for the unfathomable Name.

Yiddish—basically a medieval German, having undergone its own development as the spoken language of Ashkenasic Jewry, including additions from other languages; used by Ashkenasic Jews throughout the world, including America.

Yom Kippur—Day of Atonement.

Zaddik—pronounced *Tzaddik* (see **Tzaddik**).

Zion—hill in Jerusalem, location of David's castle; in a wider sense, Temple, Jerusalem as a whole, or even all the Land.

Zionism—a movement to obtain a Jewish state and life center in Palestine. The founder of political Zionism was Theodor Herzl.

Zohar—medieval mystical book.

INDEX